CRITICAL APPROACHES TO FICTION

Shiv K. Kumar
Keith McKean

ATLANTIC

PUBLISHERS & DISTRIBUTORS (P) LTD

Published by

ATLANTIC

PUBLISHERS & DISTRIBUTORS (P) LTD

7/22, Ansari Road, Darya Ganj,
New Delhi-110002
Phones : +91-11-40775252, 23273880, 23275880, 23280451
Fax : +91-11-23285873
Web : www.atlanticbooks.com
E-mail : orders@atlanticbooks.com

Branch Office
5, Nallathambi Street, Wallajah Road,
Chennai-600002
Phones : +91-44-64611085, 32413319
E-mail : chennai@atlanticbooks.com

Disclaimer

The author and the publisher have taken every effort to the maximum of their
skill, expertise and knowledge to provide correct material in the book. Even
then if some mistakes persist in the content of the book the publisher does not
take responsibility for the same. The publisher shall have no liability to any
person or entity with respect to any loss or damage caused, or alleged to have
been caused directly or indirectly, by the information contained in this book.
Hence, the book should be taken as a general guide only.

The publisher has fully tried to follow the copyright law. However, if any work is
found to be similar, it is unintentional and the same should not be used as
defamatory or to file legal suit against the author/publisher.

If the readers find any mistake we shall be grateful to them to point those to us so
that these can be corrected in the next edition.

All disputes are subject to the jurisdiction of Delhi court only.

Printed in India at Nice Printing Press, A-33/3A, Site-IV,
Industrial Area, Sahibabad, Ghaziabad, U.P.

TO THE CORNELL UNIVERSITY LIBRARIES
THEIR COURTESY MADE OUR WORK POSSIBLE

PREFACE

This collection of modern critical essays on the various aspects of fiction —plot, character, language, theme, setting, and technique—has grown out of our experience teaching English to college students. Most students lack the background and the critical tools necessary to an understanding of fiction. Most instructors try to fill this gap by lecturing or by recommending favorite critical articles. Clearly, this is not enough. Students frequently need more help than we can give them, and much more than they can pick up from reading an occasional outside essay. And it is apparent that teaching the subject matter itself too often precludes teaching the theory that underlies it.

This book is designed to meet this need of the student for an easy acquaintance with critical theory and practice. It places in his hand, for his organized study or casual exploration, twenty-six of the finest essays published in the last fifteen years gathered from over forty leading journals. A volume such as this can find use in several kinds of courses. It should be a boon in any study involving the novel or short story: freshman and sophomore English, introduction to literature, and courses devoted more exclusively to fiction. In addition, it can certainly serve as an ancillary text in creative writing classes and studies in literary criticism.

The essays themselves should appeal to students at all levels. We have made every effort to select intellectually rigorous articles that hit at central problems while avoiding any trace of obscurity or excessive pedantry. The beginning student should find in these pieces an exciting introduction to the world of critical thought; the more advanced student should find here familiar subjects treated in a fresh and subtle way.

Many friends have helped in the preparation of this volume. We are particularly grateful to Jeana Savu Dragash who translated the French passages in Bowling's article "What is the Stream-of-Consciousness Technique?" and to Carolyn Moyer for her help at many points.

Shiv K. Kumar
Keith McKean

CONTENTS

the novel
and the short story
—retrospect and prospect

Saul Bellow believes that the popular argument that the creation
of the novel is a dying art is unduly pessimistic. The finest
modern fiction, he admits, does not give us anything like the
traditional hero, plot, style, or even setting. Despite these signs
of decay, however, he thinks the modern novel can be
rejuvenated if our writers have the imagination and intelligence
to come up with new values—to present a new way of
life. Of course, these fresh ideas about man's condition must
never be didactically presented; rather, the possibilities
must be merely shown in the flesh and blood of
the new fiction.

where do we
go from here:
the future of fiction

SAUL BELLOW

We know that science has a future, we hope that government will
have one. But it is not altogether agreed that the novel has anything but
a past. There are some who say that the great novelists of the twentieth
century—Proust, Joyce, Mann, and Kafka—have created sterile masterpieces, and that with them we have come to the end of the line. No
further progress is possible.

It does sometimes seem that the narrative art itself has dissolved.
The person, the character as we knew him in the plays of Sophocles or
Shakespeare, in Cervantes, Fielding, and Balzac, has gone from us. Instead of a unitary character with his unitary personality, his ambitions, his
passions, his soul, his fate, we find in modern literature an oddly dis-
persed, ragged, mingled, broken, amorphous creature whose outlines are
everywhere, whose being is bathed in mind as the tissues are bathed in
blood, and who is impossible to circumscribe in any scheme of time. A
cubistic, Bergsonian, uncertain, eternal, mortal someone who shuts and
opens like a concertina and makes a strange music. And what has struck

3

artists in this century as the most amusing part of all, is that descriptions of self that still have hold of us are made up of the old unitary foursquare traits noted according to the ancient conventions. What we insist on seeing is not a quaintly organized chaos of instinct and spirit, but what we choose to call "the personality"—a presentably combed and dressed someone who is decent, courageous, handsome, or not so handsome, but strong, or not so strong, but certainly generous, or not so generous, but anyway reliable. So it goes.

Of all modern writers, it is D. H. Lawrence who is most implacably hostile toward this convention of unitary character. For him this character of a civilized man does not really exist. What the modern civilized person calls his personality is to Lawrence figmentary: a product of civilized education, dress, manners, style, and "culture." The head of this modern personality is, he says, a wastepaper basket filled with ready-made notions. Sometimes he compares the civilized conception of character to a millstone—a painted millstone about our necks is the metaphor he makes of it. The real self, unknown, is hidden, a sunken power in us; the true identity lies deep—very deep. But we do not deal much in true identity, goes his argument. The modern character on the street, or in a conventional story or film, is what a sociologist has recently described as the "presentation" self. The attack on this presentation self or persona by modern art is a part of the war that literature, in its concern with the individual, has fought with civilization. The civilized individual is proud of his painted millstone, the burden which he believes gives him distinction. In an artist's eyes his persona is only a rude, impoverished, mass-produced figure brought into being by a civilization in need of a working force, a reservoir of personnel, a docile public that will accept suggestion and control.

The old unitary personality which still appears in popular magazine stories, in conventional best-sellers, in newspaper cartoons, and in the movies, is a figure descended from well-worn patterns, and popular art forms (like the mystery novel or the western) continue to exploit endlessly the badly faded ideas of motives and drama or love and hate. The old figures move ritualistically through the paces, finding, now and then, variations in setting and costume, but they are increasingly remote from real reality. The functions performed by these venerable literary types should be fascinating to the clinical psychologist who may be able to recognize in these stories an obsessional neurosis here, a paranoid fantasy there, or to the sociologist who sees resemblances to the organization of government bureaus or hears echoes of the modern industrial corpora-

4

tions. But the writer brought up in a great literary tradition not only sees these conventional stories as narcotic or brain-washing entertainments, at worst breeding strange vices, at best performing a therapeutic function. He also fears that the narrative art, which we call the novel, may have come to an end, its conception of self exhausted and with this conception our interest in the fate of that self so conceived.

It is because of this that Gertrude Stein tells us in one of her lectures that we cannot read the great novels of the twentieth century, among which she includes her own *The Making of Americans,* for what happens next. And in fact *Ulysses, Remembrance of Things Past, The Magic Mountain,* and *The Making of Americans* do not absorb us in what happens next. They interest us in a scene, in a dialogue, a mood, an insight, in language, in character, in the revelation of a design, but they are not narratives. *Ulysses* avoids anything resembling the customary story. It is in some sense a book about literature, and offers us a history of English prose style and of the novel. It is a museum containing all the quaint armour, halberds, crossbows, and artillery pieces of literature. It exhibits them with a kind of amused irony and parodies and transcends them all. These are the things that once entranced us. Old sublimities, old dodges, old weapons, all useless now; pieces of iron once heroic, lovers' embraces once romantic, all debased by cheap exploitation, all unfit.

Language too is unfit. Erich Heller in a recent book quotes a typical observation by Hofmannsthal on the inadequacy of old forms of expression. Hofmannsthal writes, "Elements once bound together to make a world now present themselves to the poet in monstrous separateness. To speak of them coherently at all would be to speak untruthfully. The commonplace phrases of the daily round of observations seem all of a sudden insoluble riddles. The sheriff is a wicked man, the vicar is a good fellow, our neighbor must be pitied, his sons are wastrels. The baker is to be envied, his daughters are virtuous." In Hofmannsthal's *A Letter* these formulas are presented as "utterly lacking in the quality of truth." He is unable, he explains, "to see what people say and do with the simplifying eye of habit and custom. Everything falls to pieces, the pieces to pieces again, and nothing can be comprehended any more with the help of customary notions."

Character, action, and language then have been put in doubt and the Spanish philosopher Ortega y Gasset, summing up views widely held,

5

says the novel requires a local setting with limited horizons and familiar features, traditions, occupations, classes. But as everyone knows, these old-fashioned local worlds no longer exist. Or perhaps that is inaccurate. They do exist but fail to interest the novelist. They are no longer local societies as we see them in Jane Austen or George Eliot. Our contemporary local societies have been overtaken by the world. The great cities have devoured them and now the universe itself imposes itself upon us, space with its stars comes upon us in our cities. So now we have the universe itself to face, without the comforts of community, without metaphysical certainty, without the power to distinguish the virtuous from the wicked man, surrounded by dubious realities and discovering dubious selves.

Things have collapsed about us, says D. H. Lawrence on the first page of *Lady Chatterley's Lover,* and we must each of us try to put together some sort of life. He offers us a sort of nature mysticism, love but without false romanticism, an acceptance of true desire as the first principle of recovery. Other writers have come forward with aesthetic or political or religious first principles. All the modern novelists worth mentioning aim at a point beyond customary notions, customary dramas, and customary conceptions of character. The old notion of a customary self, of the fate of an all-important Me displeases the best of them. We have lived now through innumerable successes and failures of these old selves. In American literature we have watched their progress and decline in scores of books since the Civil War, from buoyancy to depression. The Lambert Strethers, the Hurstwoods and Cowperwoods, the Gatsbys may still impress or please us as readers, but as writers, no. Their mental range is no longer adequate to these new circumstances. Those characters suit us better who stand outside society and, unlike Gatsby, have no wish to be sentimentally reconciled to it, unlike Dreiser's millionaires have no more desire for its wealth, unlike Strether are not attracted by the power of an old and knowing civilization.

This is why so many of us prefer the American novels of the nineteenth century, whose characters are very nearly removed from the civil state—*Moby Dick* and *Huckleberry Finn.* We feel in our own time that what is called the civilized condition often swings close to what Hobbes calls the state of nature, a condition of warfare, in which the life of the individual is nasty, brutish, dull and short. But we must be careful not to be swept away by the analogy. We have seen to our grief in recent European and especially German history the results of trying to bolt from all civilized and legal tradition. It is in our minds that the natural and the civil, that autarchy and discipline are most explosively mixed.

But for us here in America discipline is represented largely by the enforced repressions. We do not know much of the delights of discipline. Almost nothing of a spiritual, ennobling character is brought into the internal life of a modern American by his social institutions. He must discover it in his own experience, by his own luck as an explorer, or not at all. Society feeds him, clothes him, to an extent protects him, and he is its infant. If he accepts the state of infancy, contentment can be his. But if the idea of higher functions comes to him, he is profoundly unsettled. The hungry world is rushing on all continents toward such a contentment, and with passions and desires, frustrated since primitive times, and with the demand for justice never so loudly expressed. The danger is great that it will be satisfied with the bottles and toys of infancy. But the artist, the philosopher, the priest, the statesman are concerned with the full development of humanity—its manhood, occasionally glimpsed in our history, occasionally felt by individuals.

With all this in mind, people here and there still continue to write the sort of book we call a novel. When I am feeling blue, I can almost persuade myself that the novel, like Indian basketry, or harness-making, is a vestigial art and has no future. But we must be careful about prophecy. Even prophecy based on good historical study is a risky business, and pessimism, no less than optimism, can be made into a racket. All industrial societies have a thing about obsolescence. Classes, nations, races and cultures have in our time been declared obsolete, with results that have made ours one of the most horrible of all centuries. We must, therefore, be careful about deciding that any art is dead.

This is not a decision for a coroner's jury of critics and historians. The fact is that a great many novelists, even those who have concentrated on hate, like Céline, or on despair, like Kafka, have continued to perform a most important function. Their books have attempted, in not a few cases successfully, to create scale, to order experience, to give value, to make perspective and to carry us toward sources of life, toward life-giving things. The true believer in disorder does not like novels. He follows another calling. He is an accident lawyer, or a promoter, not a novelist. It always makes me sit up, therefore, to read yet another scolding of the modern novelist written by highly paid executives of multimillion-dollar magazines. They call upon American writers to represent the country fairly, to affirm its values, to increase its prestige in this dangerous period.

7

Perhaps, though, novelists have a different view of what to affirm. Perhaps they are running their own sort of survey of affirmable things. They may come out against nationalism, or against the dollar, for they are an odd and unreliable lot. I have already indicated that it is the instinct of the novelist, however, to pull toward order. Now this is a pious thing to say, but I do not intend it merely to sound good. It should be understood only as the beginning of another difficulty.

What ideas of order does the novelist have and where does he get them and what good are they in art? I have spoken of Lawrence's belief that we must put together a life for ourselves, singly, in pairs, in groups, out of the wreckage. Shipwreck and solitude are not, in his opinion, unmixed evils. They are also liberating, and if we have the strength to use our freedom we may yet stand in a true relation to nature and to other men. But how are we to reach this end? Lawrence proposes a sort of answer in *Lady Chatterley's Lover,* showing us two people alone together in the midst of a waste. I sometimes feel that *Lady Chatterley's Lover* is a sort of *Robinson Crusoe* for two, exploring man's sexual resources rather than his technical ingenuity. It is every bit as moral a novel as *Crusoe.* Connie and Mellors work at it as hard and as conscientiously as Robinson, and there are as many sermons in the one as in the other. The difference is that Lawrence aimed with all his powers at the writing of this one sort of book. To this end he shaped his life, the testing ground of his ideas. For what is the point of recommending a course of life that one has not tried oneself?

This is one way to assess the careers and achievements of many modern artists. Men like Rimbaud, Strindberg, Lawrence, Malraux, even Tolstoy, can be approached from this direction. They experiment with themselves and in some cases an artistic conclusion can come only out of the experimental results. Lawrence had no material other than what his life, that savage pilgrimage, as he called it, gave him. The ideas he tested, and tested not always by an acceptable standard, were ideas of the vital, the erotic, the instinctive. They involved us in a species of nature-mysticism which gave as a basis for mortality, sexual gratification. But I am not concerned here with all the particulars of Lawrence's thesis. I am interested mainly in the connection between the understanding and the imagination, and the future place of the intelligence in imaginative literature.

At this point in a lecture this is a rather large subject to announce, but what I have in mind is relatively simple. It is necessary to admit, first, that ideas in the novel can be very dull. There is much in modern literature, and the other arts as well, to justify our prejudice against the didactic. Opinion, said Schopenhauer, is not as valid as imagination in a work of art. One can quarrel with an opinion or judgment in a novel, but actions are beyond argument and the imagination simply accepts them. I think that many modern novels, perhaps the majority, are the result of some didactic purpose. The attempt of writers to make perspective, to make scale and to carry us toward the sources of life is, of course, the didactic intention. It involves the novelist in programs, in slogans, in political theories, religious theories, and so on. Many modern novelists seem to say to themselves, "what if," or "suppose that such and such were the case," and the results often show that the book was conceived in thought, in didactic purpose, rather than in the imagination. That is rather normal, given the state of things, the prevalence of the calculating principle- in modern life, the need for conscious rules of procedure, and the generally felt need for answers. Not only books, paintings, and musical compositions, but love affairs, marriages, and even religious convictions often originate in an idea. So that the *idea* of love is more common than love, and the *idea* of belief is more often met with than faith. Some of our most respected novels have a purely mental inspiration. The results are sometimes very pleasing because they can so easily be discussed, but the ideas in them generally have more substance than the characters who hold them.

American literature in the nineteenth century was highly didactic. Emerson, Thoreau, Whitman, and even Melville were didactic writers. They wished to instruct a young and raw nation. American literature in the twentieth century has remained didactic, but it has also been unintellectual. This is not to say that thought is lacking in the twentieth-century American novel, but it exists under strange handicaps and is much disguised. In *A Farewell to Arms* Hemingway makes a list of subjects we must no longer speak about—a catalogue of polluted words, words which have been ruined by the rhetoric of criminal politicians and misleaders. Then Hemingway, and we must respect him for it, attempts to represent these betrayed qualities without using the words themselves. Thus we have courage without the word, honor without the word, and in *The Old Man and the Sea* we are offered a sort of Christian endurance, also without specific terms. Carried to this length, the attempt to represent ideas while sternly forbidding thought begins to look like a curious and highly sophisticated game. It shows a great skepticism of strength of art. It makes

9

it appear as though ideas openly expressed would be too much for art to bear.

We have developed in American fiction a strange combination of extreme naïveté in the characters and of profundity implicit in the writing, in the techniques themselves and in the language, but the language of thought itself is banned, it is considered dangerous and destructive. American writers appear to have a strong loyalty to the people, to the common man; perhaps in some cases the word for this is not loyalty, perhaps it might better be described as *fear*. But a writer should aim to reach all levels of society and as many levels of thought as possible, avoiding democratic prejudice as much as intellectual snobbery. Why should he be ashamed of thinking? I do not claim that all writers can think, or should think. Some are peculiarly inept at ideas and we would harm them by insisting that they philosophize. But the records show that most artists are intellectually active, and it is only now in a world increasingly intellectualized, more and more dominated by the productions of scientific thought, that they seem strangely reluctant to use their brains or to give any sign that they have brains to use.

All through the nineteenth century the conviction increases in novelists as different as Goncharov in Russia and Thomas Hardy in England that thought is linked with passivity and is devitalizing. And in the masterpieces of the twentieth century the thinker usually has a weak grip on life. But by now an alternative, passionate activity without ideas, has also been well explored in novels of adventure, hunting, combat, and eroticism. Meanwhile, miracles, born of thought, have been largely ignored by modern literature. If narration is neglected by novelists like Proust and Joyce, the reasons are that for a time the drama has passed from external action to internal movement. In Proust and Joyce we are enclosed by and held within a single consciousness. In this inner realm the writer's art dominates everything. The drama has left external action because the old ways of describing interests, of describing the fate of the individual, have lost their power. Is the sheriff a good fellow? Is our neighbor to be pitied? Are the baker's daughters virtuous? We see such questions now as belonging to a dead system, mere formulas. It is possible that our hearts would open again to the baker's daughters if we understood them differently.

A clue may be offered by Pascal, who said there are no dull people, only dull points of view. Maybe that is going a little far. (A religious philosophy is bound to maintain that every soul is infinitely precious and, therefore, infinitely interesting.) But it begins perhaps to be evident what my position is. Imagination, binding itself to dull viewpoints, puts an end to stories. The imagination is looking for new ways to express virtue. American society just now is in the grip of certain common falsehoods about virtue—not that anyone really believes them. And these cheerful falsehoods beget their opposites in fiction, a dark literature, a literature of victimization, of old people sitting in ash cans waiting for the breath of life to depart. This is the way things stand; only this remains to be added, that we have barely begun to comprehend what a human being is, and that the baker's daughters may have revelations and miracles to offer to keep fascinated novelists busy until the end of time.

I would like to add this also, in conclusion, about good thought and bad thought in the novel. In a way it doesn't matter what sort of line the novelist is pushing, what he is affirming. If he has nothing to offer but his didactic purpose he is a bad writer. His ideas have ruined him. He could not afford the expense of maintaining them. It is not the didactic purpose itself which is a bad thing, and the modern novelist drawing back from the dangers of didacticism has often become strangely unreal, and the purity of his belief in art for art in some cases has been peculiarly unattractive. Among modern novelists the bravest have taken the risk of teaching and have not been afraid of using the terms of religion, science, philosophy, and politics. Only they have been prepared to admit the strongest possible arguments against their own positions.

Here we see the difference between a didactic novelist like D. H. Lawrence and one like Dostoevski. When he was writing *The Brothers Karamazov* and had just ended the famous conversation between Ivan and Alyosha, in which Ivan, despairing of justice, offers to return his ticket to God, Dostoevski wrote to one of his correspondents that he must now attempt, through Father Zossima, to answer Ivan's arguments. But he has in advance all but devastated his own position. This, I think, is the greatest achievement possible in a novel of ideas. It becomes art when the views most opposite to the author's own are allowed to exist in full strength. Without this a novel of ideas is mere self-indulgence, and didacticism is simply axe-grinding. The opposites must be free to range themselves against each other, and they must be passionately expressed on both sides. It is for this reason that I say it doesn't matter much what the writer's personal position is, what he wishes to affirm. He may affirm principles we all approve of and write very bad novels.

11

The novel, to recover and to flourish, requires new ideas about humankind. These ideas in turn cannot live in themselves. Merely asserted, they show nothing but the good will of the author. They must therefore be discovered and not invented. We must see them in flesh and blood. There would be no point in continuing at all if many writers did not feel the existence of these unrecognized qualities. They are present and they demand release and expression.

M. A. Goldberg distinguishes between (1) the more traditional novel of adventure, like *David Copperfield,* based on a clock or calendar conception of time and stressing external events; and (2) the more modern novel of the individual mind, like *The Catcher in the Rye,* based on a nonlinear conception of time and exploring the multiple layers of human consciousness as they react to outside stimuli. But he sees a rebirth of the novel in a new development: the novel which dwells on the inner life of its chief character in such a way that it has universal application. For example, because it deals with man in general *The Stranger* is a more significant and more philosophical novel than it would have been had it dealt with a particular person.

chronology, character
and the human condition:
a reappraisal
of the modern novel

M. A. GOLDBERG

Crucial to an understanding of the modern novel is a distinction raised in the opening paragraph of J. D. Salinger's *The Catcher in the Rye,* where Holden Caulfield, the 16-year-old narrator, writes:

> . . . The first thing you'll probably want to know is where I was born, and what my lousy childhood was like, and how my parents were occupied and all before they had me, and all that David Copperfield kind of crap, but I don't feel like going into it. . . . I'm not going to tell you my whole goddam autobiography or anything. I'll just tell you about this madman stuff that happened to me around last Christmas. . . .

This distinction between Dickens' "autobiography" and Holden's narrative is a pertinent one, as even the most casual reader of these two texts will recognize.

Typical of nineteenth-century novels, *David Copperfield* was concerned with a series of adventures, structured in chronological or historical order. Dickens was obviously under the assumption that in the unfolding of time or the continuity of days lay the significance of David's life. Actually, the full title of the novel, *The Personal History, Adventures, Experience and Observations of David Copperfield*, points with clarity to this assumption, that the human personality and the varied adventures it undergoes between birth and death are best understood through chronological arrangements. As narrator, David necessarily begins at the beginning with a chapter called "I Am Born." In marked contrast to Salinger's narrator, he announces his concern with clock- and calendar-time at once: "I was born . . . on a Friday, at twelve o'clock at night. It was remarked that the clock began to strike, and I began to cry simultaneously." Thus, having charted the birth, the point of embarkation on his longer journey, the narrator begins to trace the "history" of David Copperfield: his infancy, boyhood, youth, adolescence, young manhood. In rather precise chronological order, Dickens reveals the development of David-the-man from David-the-boy, through a series of determining and determined events. True, Dickens has a notion about the meaning of time, what he himself called his "Carol Philosophy," the belief that evil must succumb before good, that the cunning and crafty (Uriah Heep, Scrooge, the Murdstones) must inevitably yield before the humble and pure of heart. David himself comes to learn this from his own history. This is the significance of his life, the lesson which time reveals to him about the truths of the human condition.

The hero of Salinger's novel has no such notion about what his own history can teach him. To begin with, he disclaims time as an organizing principle. Usual determining factors—where he was born, the nature of his childhood, the occupation of his parents—appear meaningless to Holden Caulfield. At the outset, he insists that this is no "autobiography." Instead, he is limiting himself to "this madman stuff" that happened around Christmas. Apparently the adventures occurring in that one week are offered only because for Holden the ordered events in his life are unimportant; their sequence or chronological arrangement appears to him almost wholly fortuitous. Our final vision of Holden's character is no less clear than our vision of David Copperfield, for those few days are intense and revealing. The reader is allowed to move within Holden, to envision the way in which his past colors his present, in which the past is ever-present within his consciousness. The events of this Christmas week in the life of Holden Caulfield do not lead him to a philosophy. Significantly, they lead him to a psychiatrist's couch. They lead him there, as they would necessarily lead us, when life is lacking in structure or philosophic cohesion. Clearly, the disordered events of that weekend are indicative of the breakdown of the human personality.

Here, I suspect, lies much of a clue to the meaningful distinction between these two kinds of novels. Holden's adventures do not cause the breakdown; they help us, rather, to focus upon it, to understand him and the "phony" world in which he is immersed, a world which for him is lacking in meaning and value. They reveal to us the way in which he himself colors and distorts these events, desperately seeking the values which he can rarely discover.

One could distinguish between these two novels, their grasp of the events and the people who participate in events, by classifying one as a chronological study of life, the other as a study which subordinates chronology as an organizational device—but this is merely symptomatic of a larger complex. Dickens' novel is a book of deeds, of externalized adventures. Salinger's is a novel of the inner consciousness, a mind at work. The first concentrates upon outer events and acts taking place within a phenomenological universe, full of things and persons; it assumes the existence of pattern or purpose. Events are so arranged that significances can be readily deduced from their structure. The second, concentrating upon the internal, recognizes the phenomenological or external as being important only insofar as it lends significance to or is lent significance by the internal. Spatial and temporal connections have obviously been displaced in Salinger's novel by a more fundamental search for axiological connections. Values lie outside the dimensions of time. The concern with inner consciousness, rather than with external phenomena, need not restrict Salinger to clock-time, for within the depths of the unconscious a day can seem a year and ten years ago can seem closer than now, much as for Proust the taste of a *petite madeleine* dipped in tea can cull up associations with a distant past and bring to immediate life the flowers in M. Swann's park, the water-lilies on the Vivonne, the people in his childhood village, the dwellings, the parish church, the whole of Combray and its surroundings.

The significance of this distinction, frequently misinterpreted as a "literary" device, will become increasingly clear in an examination of the background for these two approaches to characterization—the old and the new—and in a recognition of the subtler forces at work within these novels by Dickens and Salinger.

15

Dickens' handling of characterization and events is typical of literary techniques perceptible elsewhere in the century—with Thackeray, Meredith, Trollope, the Brontës, for instance. Yet the roots of all these Victorian novelists can be traced to sixteenth-century Spain, when a new literary form is said to have made its appearance with the publication of *Lazarillo de Tormes*. Before this, narrative fiction, like the romance—*The Cid*, the stories of King Arthur, the tale of Tristan and Iseult—was concerned with medieval attitudes of the aristocracy toward honor, chivalry, loyalty, love. Coincident with the breakdown of the feudal order, *Lazarillo de Tormes* and the picaresque novels which followed in its wake concentrated upon individuals of the lower classes who could find wealth and status through their own wit and cunning. With certain modifications, this is the pattern Cervantes is imitating in *Don Quixote*, which LeSage employs in *Gil Blas*, and which is used by Defoe, Richardson, Fielding, Smollett, Goldsmith. And, of course, Dickens uses this technique in *David Copperfield*. The debt owed to the picaresque tradition is apparent in the very titles of all these novels, for in each case we are offered the "history" or "adventures" of an individual.

Now, all these novels—and a good many more, including many on the best-seller lists today—share one important ingredient: the adventures are arranged as a series of consecutive time units. History assumes a progressive linear form, from which certain principles can be deduced. True, distinctions can be made among the various types of narrative fiction (the epic, the romance, the picaresque tale, the novel of manners, the naturalistic novel), but these distinctions are merely indicative of the varying ways of interpreting events within clock- or calendar-time.

Chronology reveals different truths. In the Arthurian tales, chronology reveals the nobility of the knight, loyalty to the feudal order, the sacredness of courtly love. In medieval lives of saints, the order of happenings might reveal the omnipotence and omnibenevolence of God, the sinfulness of man, possibilities of redemption through Christ. In the picaresque tales, events are arranged to reveal the ridiculousness of the rigid social hierarchy. With the nineteenth-century naturalists, the ordering of adventures within clock-time reveals the operations of scientific determinism, the influence of environment and heredity upon the human condition. The Horatio Alger stories which were quite popular at the beginning of this century arranged events in such a way that the young reader could discern that integrity, perseverance, American "know-how" could lead to wealth, fame, status. This same ordering of events is perceptible in that great work of contemporary "fiction," Norman Vincent Peale's *The Power of Positive Thinking*. The pattern is equally apparent in the typical Hollywood movie, in the soap operas of television, and in the promptings of Madison Avenue.

Occasionally, but rarely, in any historical examination of fiction, exceptions to this pattern can be encountered. Laurence Sterne's *The Life and Opinions of Tristram Shandy* seems to be one such work. From the beginning, Sterne's narrator orders events, not with chronology, but with the association of ideas, as suggested by John Locke's *Essay on Human Understanding* and developed by David Hartley in his *Observations Upon Man*. The novel begins, then, not with Tristram's birth, but with the hour of his conception. Since his father is an orderly as well as an elderly man, he has arranged his existence so that the winding of the clock and the unwinding of his libido coincide with regularity. Tristram's birth, then, is not nearly as important as his mother's association of sexuality with clock-winding. It takes almost the entire book for Tristram to get born, for Sterne's emphasis upon mechanical principles of associational psychology necessarily relegates chronology to an inferior status. Hence, our grasp of Tristram's mother—like our grasp of his father and of Uncle Toby—is not dependent upon what she says or does or how she develops; it is dependent upon the chaotic way she thinks, on what happens internally, the kinds of associations she makes.

Although two centuries have intervened between Sterne and Salinger, *Tristram Shandy* has really much in common with *The Catcher in the Rye* and its disdain of "autobiography," chronologically arranged "adventures." This is not to imply that Sterne's techniques are at one with Salinger's. On the contrary, Sterne's disdain of clock-time and his internalization of character are aimed at satirizing Lockean and Hartleyan psychology and at ridiculing the absurdities of the interior monologue, a device commonly accepted by the twentieth century, but quite alien to the eighteenth-century novel of adventures.

Underlying principles of the novel of adventures become all the more lucid in examining their operation within the nineteenth-century naturalists —with Balzac and Flaubert, de Maupassant and Zola, Hardy and Arnold Bennett (whose principles were still at work in Dreiser and Steinbeck, among others, later in the twentieth century). Implicit, and often explicit, in the writings of the naturalists is a behavioral psychology which is in perfect keeping with the scientific determinism so widely accepted during the last half of the nineteenth century. *Germinal*, for example, is the thirteenth of a series of twenty novels to which Emile Zola devoted nearly twenty-five years of his life. Known briefly as *Les Rougon-Macquart,* the series is appropriately subtitled "The Natural and Social History of a Family During the Second Empire." With the deliberate discipline and objectivity of a scientist, Zola intended to trace the effects of heredity and environment upon the members of this family. Whereas a seventeenth-century Milton is impelled to "assert Eternal Providence,/And justify the ways of God to men," the only function of the artist, according to Zola, is to observe and record. In *Germinal,* the novelist's test tube is Mining Community No. 240 in the north of France, where laborers have inherited attitudes of passive obedience and subordination. At the opening of the experiment, a new chemical is introduced into the test-tube, one Étienne Lantier, a Parisian with an instinct for revolt and insubordination. Zola's assumptions—his artistic principles about the function of the novel; his psychological principles about the function of man; his metaphysical principles about the nature of reality—rest upon the existence of a causally determined universe, subject to the operations of a billiard-ball action. This psychological determinism with Étienne Lantier or his sister Nana, the geological determinism in Charles Lyell, the biological determinism in Darwin and Spencer, the economic determinism in Marx and Engels, are all strikingly analogous. They each involve causally related time-units, arranged to form a linear progression. As a creature of heredity and environment, Étienne Lantier is determined and moved by natural laws which aim at pre-established goals. His varied adventures and involvements —the Tuesday that follows Monday and precedes Wednesday in his life— are understandable only within the larger network visible to the socialist scientist. The reader is asked to understand Étienne's parents and their background. He must know society and politics of Paris during the Second Empire. Above all, he must know the natural laws—economic, biological, social, psychological—at work in the universe. Without this knowledge, he is doomed, like Nana or Étienne, to be moulded and kneaded by these external forces, completely at their mercy.

For all their differences, this school of naturalism reveals a pattern not too remote from that of the middle ages, when the multiplicity of things and the variety of adventures—life and death, fear and hope, body and soul, heaven and hell, good and evil—all were comprehended relative only to Godhead and the Pauline doctrines of original sin and redemption. True, the nineteenth- and twentieth-century naturalists interpreted these events differently. They saw them in relation to natural laws, to scientific determinism, rather than to God. But in both cases what is being examined is the central power at work in the universe, the power which presumably organizes our lives and provides them with significances. In a restricted sense, it is irrelevant whether we call these powers "Zeus," "Jehovah," "Christ," "manna," "morality," "chastity," "love," "environment and heredity," "class-warfare," "scientific determinism." The pattern remains constant. In each case, human life, the people and things and adventures within that life, is viewed as a linear movement proceeding along a sharply defined path. We move through the dark woods, illuminated only by the beckoning star of our destiny. Whether we examine Dante's experience in the Seventh Circle of the Inferno with Ser Brunetto Latini or Étienne Lantier's experience with the Montsou family in Mining Community No. 240, we find ourselves directed by a highly structured series of time-units. A pattern of chronology is revealed. By his structure of events, the artist is displaying the organization of meaningful forces which push, pull, define and determine.

Environment and heredity as conditioning forces are certainly apparent in Defoe's *Moll Flanders*, in Dostoevski's *Brothers Karamazov*, and in William Golding's recent novel, *The Lord of the Flies*. But in none of these cases are they more than incidental in comprehending character or the structure of events. Similarly, we can superimpose upon Salinger's novel a naturalistic ordering, or interpret Holden Caulfield in relation to Dickens' optimistic faith in the mild and meek inheriting the earth—but these equally distort the text. Holden Caulfield must be understood, not as a doer of deeds or a victim of external laws, but as a consciousness structured with multiple layers.

One such layer, for example, involves old Ossenburger, namesake of the Ossenburger Memorial Wing at Penncey. Although the narrator speaks of an "adventure" with Ossenburger, its significance in the chronological sequence is minimal. The "adventure" has occurred long before the Christmas week-end with which the novel opens. It emerges in the third chapter, independent of the flow of time-external, and serves to reveal a layer of Holden's consciousness. Actually, we never know when the actual event with Ossenburger took place within calendar time. We do not know, because for the narrator time is meaningless. Holden is interested only in offering the content of his consciousness, and for him (though perhaps not for us) this has no form. If we are to perceive any continuity, then the consciousness must be peeled, like Ibsen's onion, layer after layer. The particular encounter with Ossenburger is meaningful only in relation to the polarity represented by Holden himself. Necessarily, then, its significance is individual, personal, and highly attenuated. In the flow of external time, in the life of work and days, the encounter with Ossenburger does follow and precede other happenings; but in the flow of inner time, in the consciousness of Holden Caulfield, the incident is never abandoned. It is never lost. Yesterday is everpresent. All his tomorrows are ever-present flickering candles which have lit, do light, and will always light his way to dusty death. Like the drop of rain falling into the middle of a vast ocean, the words and deeds dropped into the puddle of Holden's life never quite sink to the bottom without a flurry of ripples that press onward and forever toward the changing shore.

Of course Salinger is not alone in his emphasis upon the internal and his subordination of the external—with his concern about the novel of the mind, the human consciousness, as opposed to the novel of adventures. For Salinger is attempting to examine reality, to comprehend the meaning of the human personality, in much the same way that is perceptible in Henry James, Virginia Woolf, James Joyce. Gide is preoccupied in the same way in *The Counterfeiters*; Proust, in *The Remembrance of Things Past*; Faulkner, in *The Sound and the Fury* and *As I Lay Dying*. This is a concern apparent in Robert Penn Warren's *All the King's Men*, in William March's *Company K*, in Norman Mailer's *The Naked and the Dead*. Exterior occurrences are offered in all these writers. Events take place within space and time. But the significance of these events, like the significance of the literary techniques involved, is dependent upon a particular consciousness with its own spatial and temporal dimensions. An act, a word, a deed is significant as a leit-motif, a chord struck early in a symphony and struck again and again in increasing intensity during the course of the composition, each time gathering new meaning and new significance from the complexity of sounds and rhythms surrounding it. With Holden Caulfield— as with Mrs. Dalloway or the younger Stephen Dedalus or the narrator in Proust's novels—the position of the act or word within the chronological flow of time can reveal nothing, for inner time is relative. Only within the depths of the subconscious does the particular adventure, which takes place in outer time, assume significance.

The one-after-anotherness of outer time implicit in the novel of adventures has been described as a linear progression, moving along a clearly defined path between birth and death. But with the omnipresence of time in the novel of the inner consciousness, all of one's own time is forever present. Yesterdays are never lost, just as tomorrows are always imbedded in the seeds of today. The outermost limits of clock-time are melted and diffused there, just as the outermost boundaries of people and things vanish, losing their own identity within the relativism of the all-embracing self. In the novel of adventures, individuals are distinct and unique, whether they are David Copperfield or Roderick Random or Gil Blas. But Holden Caulfield is a multilayered composite of everyone and everything with which he has come into contact.

To restrict this unipersonal subjectivism, this relativity of time, to the novel would be much of a distortion. It is basic to the music of Bartok and Hindemith, the paintings of Picasso and Dali, the movies of Ingmar Bergman. In its purest form it is discernible within the psychoanalytic theories of Freud, the philosophy of Bergson, the physics of Einstein. An earlier temptation was to toss off this unipersonal subjectivism as being unreal, to demote it to the realms of the unconscious, to the byways of the fantastic and bizarre. We would identify it with the personal eccentricities of Swift in *Gulliver's Travels,* the prophetic madness of William Blake, the pipe dreams of De Quincey, the childish fancy of Lewis Carroll. Increasingly, however, the modern reader has come to understand this as being more real than the externalities of the novel of adventures, the clock-time of Dickens, the calendar-time of medieval romances, the chronological flow of autobiography.

If we still have reservations about this newer novel of the mind, it is because increasingly it has seemed too limiting, too personal, too highly attenuated. It draws us too much into ourselves for realities, and too much away from the hard core of externals, where things can be weighed, measured and counted. We long for certitudes and concrete ideals which can be shared with others. We crave absolute truths, mathematical symbols that can be marked into the notebooks of our minds in black and white. We want to be able to say to ourselves—but also to others: Here is the secret of existence, where death can have no dominion . . . here is the common wage of our most secret heart . . . we have captured it finally, driven it into a corner . . . we hold it in the palm of our hand, this worm in the apple of knowledge, and now it can be dissected and analyzed. Unfortunately, it is generally ourselves which we have driven into the corner, or held in the palm of a hand, and not some external "it" that can be measured, weighed, and counted. And, when and if we perceive this, we cannot react but with violence and horror. Sometimes, like Holden Caulfield, we too end up on an analyst's couch, after we had thought our future secure through our rising sales of automobiles and encyclopedias, after the gleaming refrigerator in the kitchen has deep-frozen our present, and

21

after the garbage disposal unit has churned away at the more obnoxious parts of our past. Then, we too start examining for perhaps the first time the difference between the external and the internal, the words and deeds as opposed to their meaning and significance. Then, *The Catcher in the Rye* can communicate with clarity and precision.

Classification this far has been restricted to two kinds of novel—the older novel of adventures and the new novel of the mind; the more ancient concern with externality and the contemporary concern with the internal; the clock- and calendar-time of Dickens and the unipersonal subjectivism of time for Salinger and Proust. Another kind of modern narrative can be discerned, however. This is a novel concerned with the human condition. It is involved with the universal, rather than particular events as perceived by the particular consciousness; with human experience, rather than with particular adventures or a particular mind; with the timeless or eternal, rather than the relativity dictated by the restricted universe of self.

Indications of this second conception of modern chronology and character can be detected in Dostoevski and Melville, among others, but not until Kafka and Hesse, Sartre and Mann, Camus and Unamuno is the mutation of the old art form effected. Clearly, the polarity of the persona is much too confining for this group of modern writers; the subjectivism of all experience, too limiting; the Island of the individuated consciousness, too isolated and too rarefied. Though we hold out our hands to the mirror of time, it is never ourselves that we touch, but only a reflection— hard, cold, empty, and shattering. In the point-present, rather, is mirrored all that has been and the potency of all that will be—not just for self, but for man; not man individually, but Mankind, collectively, socially, eternally. We recognize, like Antoine Roquentin in Sartre's *Nausea*, that as men, all alone, suddenly plunged into solitude, run through the streets and pass heavily in front of us, carrying the monstrosities from which they are flee- ing, we must lean against a wall and shout, as they go by: "What is the matter with your science? What have you done with your humanism? Where is your dignity?"

Patterns in Dickens are linear and meliorative, progressing toward some discernible truth. In Proust and Salinger, they are multi-layered, com- plex in their density. But in Kafka and Sartre, they are cyclic, repetitive, and archetypal.

Characters in Salinger and Proust may heed only the ripples circling about the shores of their restricted consciousness, but only by blinding themselves to ripples in adjoining ponds: ponds existent, non-existent, as-yet-to-exist. In Zola, they may seek only the force that drives the rain-drop of an incident into the center of their pond, measuring the distance to shore, the effect of the ripples, the filling of the pond, even while ignoring the significance of rain as an eternal act which men have both welcomed and endured, and will yet endure as long as there are men and rain and human time. But in Sartre, as well as Kafka and Hesse, the pond is viewed as a microcosm of the vast ocean of humanity in which rain is eternally falling.

This distinction between Salinger and Sartre, Proust and Kafka, involves not just two notions about time. It also involves two notions about the nature of reality, the function of art, the significance of the human personality. Psychoanalytic circles would perhaps see these differences articulated most clearly in the comparisons generally drawn between the personal and the transpersonal unconscious. In Proust and Salinger, where time is clearly an individuum, the contents of the unconscious are necessarily limited to infantile tendencies, repressed because of their incompatible character. The drama within each character is continuous during the course of his own experiences, for the present is always colored by the demands of the past. Like the ancient Greek charioteer, the ego struggles to rein and control the conflicting demands from within and without— the latter being the predominant concern for the pre-twentieth-century time dimensions. No wonder, then, that the novelist can take a twenty-four hour session in the life of Stephen Dedalus or Mrs. Dalloway, or the long Christmas week-end of Holden Caulfield, revealing the whole of the life, the entirety of an existence, the organicism of a single being. But for Kafka and Camus, time is a continuum, where struggles and conflicts are transpersonal and primordial, ranging far beyond the life and death of the individual. In the single adventure, the subjective consciousness is always transcended. Far from being restricted to the limiting dimensions of one's being, the adventure is always a scene from a larger drama being enacted in a theatre whose dimensions are more vast than any encompassed by the human eye or brain. It may be, as Jung contends, a psychic residuum of countless experiences of the same kind, inherited from and shared with an ancestry; but it may also be social and political, metaphysical and existential.

Holden Caulfield is only one particular boy, just as David Copperfield is only a particular individual. On the other hand, Kafka's Joseph K., accused of a crime as anonymous as his own "K" and executed like a dog

23

in his anonymity, is all men. Properly, our approach to Holden should be analytic. We must study his particular construction, the development of his individuality, much as with David Copperfield our theological and moral orientation understands his bounded being in relation to a set of determined goals. True, the reader can identify himself with both of these characters, despite their particularity and uniqueness. But identification can only be partial, for always the reader is doomed to be separate and distinct. With Joseph K., where the perspective is necessarily synoptic and symbolic, it is ourselves that we uncover. Kafka's Gregor Samsa, awakening one fine morning to find himself transformed into a gigantic cockroach, is symbolic of all men awakening to the reality of self: bestial, unthinking, dark and impotent. And Camus' Meursault, who comes to recognize that death is the only certitude, is all men opening their hearts to the benign indifference of the universe.

We may tend to see Dostoevski or Melville within this same group of modern novelists concerned with what I have been calling "the human condition." But is not their conception of chronology, like their grasp of characterization, a foreshadowing of Kafka and Camus, much as Sterne foreshadows Proust? Both Dostoevski and Melville, working within the limitations of an antiquated psychology and theology, succeeded—because of their own genius, and despite those limitations—in anticipating what is clearly a twentieth-century phenomenon. The insights of Shakespeare certainly moved him far beyond the limitations of Renaissance psychology and physics—much as the artistry of Dickens who wrote *Bleak House* far transcended that of Dickens who wrote *The Posthumous Papers of the Pickwick Club,* and much as Joyce in *Ulysses* succeeded in moving far beyond *A Portrait of the Artist.*

It has, of late, been frequently suggested that the novel as a literary form came to an end with Henry James. After James, presumably, nothing remained to be done. Quite the contrary, of course, I suggest that drastic changes of form are perceptible within twentieth-century fiction. We are witnessing, not the death of the novel, but rather its mutation and re-birth.

24

PART TWO
plot

Using R. S. Crane's definition of plot as a synthesis of
action, character, and thought, J. Arthur Honeywell
explains how a typical eighteenth-century novel achieves
this synthesis by having a definite beginning and ending;
whereas a typical nineteenth-century novel achieves the same
objective by having a sequential evolution. The contemporary
novel, however, introduces a new concept of plot as a
movement in the reader's mind from appearance to reality.
In his attempt to bring reality closer to fiction, the modern
novelist disregards clock time as a convenient mode of
organizing experience and allows his characters to float freely
along their streams of consciousness. This may explain,
concludes Honeywell, why the seemingly unrelated,
contradictory, and inconsequential elements of experience
acquire a new significance in this form of writing.

plot in the
modern novel

J. ARTHUR HONEYWELL

Perhaps the clearest way to give a general indication of the nature
of plot in the modern novel is to start by discussing briefly the concept
of plot itself. In "The Concept of Plot and the Plot of *Tom Jones*," one of
the few recent attempts to develop the idea of plot as a central critical
concept, R. S. Crane gives a short history of the term and then defines
plot as "the particular temporal synthesis effected by the writer of the
elements of action, character, and thought that constitute the matter of
his invention." [1] This definition can serve as a starting point, since a brief
analysis of the notion of plot as the temporal synthesis of the materials of
the novel will reveal some of the possibilities of plot development and, by
contrast with the other possibilities, how plot operates in many modern
novels.

[1] R. S. Crane, "The Concept of Plot and the Plot of '*Tom Jones*'," in: *Critics
and Criticism* (Chicago: The University of Chicago Press, 1952), p. 620.

If plot is thought of as a temporal synthesis, then obviously it has two central characteristics. First, it operates as an organizing and unifying principle. It provides the synthesis which insures that the materials of a novel are experienced as all cohering into one unified object—the novel itself in its wholeness. Secondly, it operates in time. Since the experience of reading a novel is a temporal process and since the plot is the organization of this temporal process, the plot of a novel inevitably has the quality of developing in time. This raises the question of how temporal syntheses can be achieved.

For any temporal progression to be experienced as a significant and organized whole, three requirements must in some way be met. First, it must have a definite beginning and a definite ending. Otherwise, the progression cannot be distinguished from what went before and what comes after and so cannot be either conceived or experienced as a single thing. Secondly, the progression must somehow be sequential, that is, each event must arise out of preceding events and give rise to succeeding events. If this is not accomplished, then the result is a mixture of progressions rather than a single temporal progression. Thirdly, the events which make up the progression must all be somehow related in the more general sense of all belonging to the same "world" or the same "vision of reality." That is, there must be a general context which encompasses both the beginning and ending and the sequence of events and gives to them their significance. Otherwise there is no possibility of conceiving of or experiencing the events as parts of a coherent whole; they would be merely fortuitous results of random causal interactions having no meaningful interrelations. Although each of these requirements must somehow be met in any novel (or, in special cases where unusual effects are desired, must be deliberately neglected), it is usually the case that novelists place their emphasis on one of the three and subordinate the other two. As a result, it is possible to distinguish three distinct kinds of plot.

Novelists of the eighteenth century tended to construct their plots around definite beginnings and endings. The temporal progression of their novels was a movement from a natural starting point to a definitive ending —an ending of the "happy ever after" variety if the novel had a comic structure. The synthesis was that provided by a single action which moved, usually by way of reversals and discoveries, from a natural beginning point to a natural ending. This is the kind of plot which Aristotle analyzes in the *Poetics* and with which Professor Crane is concerned in his analysis of the plot of *Tom Jones*. One of the problems of constructing a plot of this kind is that of achieving the sense of finality which the ending requires, and eighteenth-century novelists tended to solve this problem with some variation of "poetic justice." The action is brought to a stage in which the good characters, after a period of difficulties, achieve on a permanent basis the conditions which insure their happiness and the bad characters are placed in conditions which insure their suffering. The major distinction which results is that between tragic and comic plots, although many variations of these two modes are possible. When the final and permanent happiness of the central characters is of a worldly sort, as in *Tom Jones* and *Humphry Clinker,* the action forms a comic plot. When the final and permanent happiness of the central character is of an other-worldly variety and is the result of worldly misfortune and death, as in *Clarissa,* the action forms a tragic plot. It follows also that plots of this kind require a certain kind of characterization. Most important, the central agents must be clearly characterized as virtuous, and thus deserving of happiness, or evil, and thus deserving of suffering. Only when this is done can the ending be constructed to provide that sense of justness which makes it definitive and final. Thus Fielding, Richardson, and Smollett all take pains to construct characters who are either virtuous or evil and to make the distinctions clear to their readers.

Early in the nineteenth century, most clearly with the novels of Sir Walter Scott, the fashion began to change. Novelists began to subordinate the problem of beginnings and endings to the problem of constructing a logical sequence of events, a sequence in which no event occurred without a reason or cause. The temporal progression of their novels tended to become a clearly articulated causal sequence from one state of affairs to another—in its more extreme form a "slice of life" in which both beginning and ending were arbitrary. The synthesis was achieved by establishing a single causal sequence in which each event is shown to be an effect of previous causes and the cause of subsequent effects. No longer are endings distinguished by their finality: rather they tend to become open-ended or at least ambiguous in terms of justice. Characteristic endings of this sort are those of *The Red and the Black, Crime and Punishment, Madame Bovary, The Return of the Native,* and the *Ambassadors.* The central problem of constructing plots of this sort is that of achieving the sense of causal or rational sequence which provides the organization of the events, and novelists tended to solve this problem by placing a specific type of character in a specific set of conditions and then letting the logic of the situation work itself out to its rational conclusion. What is important

29

is not the ending but the insight into the operation of the causal laws and influences which condition human affairs. The major distinction which results is that between the realistic novel and the romance. When the set of conditions established is patterned on the details of ordinary life and the characters are presented as being for the most part passively influenced by these conditions, the novel tends toward the realistic or naturalistic mode. When, on the other hand, the set of conditions established includes the supernatural or at least the abnormal and the characters are presented as being active in manipulating or responding to these conditions, then the novel tends toward the mode of romance. The requirements of characterization also change. Central characters no longer have to be clearly virtuous or the reverse, but they do have to have clearly defined motives based on clearly defined passions and modes of behavior. Only with such characters can the causal sequence be made explicit. Characters such as Julian Sorel, Raskolnikov, Emma Bovary, Becky Sharp, Eustacia Vye, and Strether, although none are unambiguously virtuous or evil, are all constructed around passions and rules of action which bring them into conflict with the conditions surrounding them. The causal sequence is such that an ending of the final, "happy ever after" variety is inconceivable for any of the characters mentioned. Even death does not achieve the sense of finality and justness which Richardson manages in *Clarissa*, mainly because the conditions which make the death a logical conclusion are presented as still operating, whereas in *Clarissa* Richardson both eliminates the conditions which cause Clarissa's death and makes it clear that Clarissa achieves the supreme happiness of eternal bliss.

During the first two decades of the present century the fashion in plot development began changing again. Novelists lost interest in constructing logical or rational sequences and turned to the third possibility, that of structuring the events of the novel so as to present a coherent "world" or vision of reality. When the reader starts a novel like *Ulysses*, he is immediately confronted with a great variety of what appear to be incongruous, contradictory, and inconsequential facts. As he reads structural relations begin to emerge which tie the various facts together and give them significance. By the time he has finished, if not the first then the second or third reading, these structural relations are so firmly established that most of the facts have acquired significance and even the incongruities and contradictions can be seen to have meaning, to be a part of the reality of the world of the novel. The temporal progression of plots of this kind can then be described as a movement from appearance—the maze of apparently

unrelated facts—to reality—the structural relations which, when apprehended, give significance and meaning to the facts. The synthesis is that
established by the structural relations which emerge as the novel progresses and which are firmly established as the "reality" of the world of
the novel by the time the novel ends.

An early example of this kind of plot is that of *The Good Soldier* by
Ford Madox Ford. The novel begins with Dowell, the narrator, looking back
at events of his past life which in his naiveté he has totally misunderstood.
He has seen only the appearance of these events and has been blind to
their real significance. The progression of the novel is that of Dowell's
attempt to make sense of these past events. He fits together apparently
unrelated facts, resolves apparent contradictions, gains insight into the
motivation of the people involved, changes his evaluations of people and
events, so that by the end of the novel he has a better insight into the
realities of these past events than any of the other characters involved and
has himself changed from being naive to being realistic. The reader, following Dowell's train of thought throughout the novel, moves in a similar
way from the superficial appearances of the facts to an understanding of
the realities of the situation and so of the real significance of the facts.

It should be stated at once that the fact that modern novelists tend to
share basic assumptions about the construction of plots does not preclude
a great diversity in the application of those assumptions. Like the novelists
of the eighteenth and the nineteenth centuries, they have achieved a wide
variety of plot development within the limits of their shared assumptions.
The central problem of constructing modern plots is that of establishing the
structural relations which give coherence and significance to the at first
apparently unrelated facts and which thus express a specific view of reality. But the patterns which emerge as structures of reality can take many
forms. They can be universal patterns or archetypes which are presented
as structuring the affairs of men at all times and places. Such archetypes
are present in *Ulysses* (as the title itself suggests), *Finnegans Wake*, many
of the novels of Thomas Mann, and other novels based upon mythical patterns. They can be social and institutional patterns which make sense of
otherwise incongruous and inexplicable events. In *Absalom, Absalom!*, for
example, the facts of the Sutpen story become significant and intelligible
only as the social patterns of the South emerge during the course of the
novel. In *The Good Soldier*, it is the sense of the social realities of Edwardian England which emerges as the facts of Dowell's story become intelligible. Or the structure of reality can be found in the subtle nuances and

feelings, often incongruous and without rationale, which pervade even an ordinary mind on an ordinary day. The novels of Virginia Woolf and Nathalie Sarraute explore patterns of this kind. When the mind becomes less ordinary, such nuances become the feeling of nausea in the presence of existence explored by Sartre or the ironies and paradoxes of the life of the imagination explored by Nabokov in *Pale Fire*. The structure of reality, finally, can be found in underlying psychological patterns basic to the nature of men. The novels of D. H. Lawrence explore the degradations and victories of the psyche as it struggles to realize its true nature, while Lawrence Durrell's *Alexandrian Quartet* makes use of the psychological complexities and patterns taken by love in modern society. Even this short list gives some indication of the diversity of structures which can be found to give coherence and significance to the "facts" of the human condition.

Since the time of Aristotle, the concept of plot has been associated with the concepts of discovery and reversal. There are discoveries and reversals in the better modern plots, but their nature is different from those used in the plots of earlier centuries. In eighteenth-century plots, formed as they were around a unified action, the appropriate kind of reversal was a reversal in the line of action from a movement toward one state of fortune to a movement toward another. In *Tom Jones*, for example, near the end of the novel the action seems to be moving unalterably toward Tom's disgrace and death when, as a result of certain discoveries, the line of action reverses itself completely and moves quickly to the highest state of fortune for Tom that he, or the reader, can imagine. The discoveries appropriate to such reversals of fortune consist of such things as the discovery of identity, of character, or of past events. In *Tom Jones* the discovery that Blifil had, in the past, concealed the evidence of Tom's parentage leads to the discovery of Tom's identity. This, in turn, leads to the recognition of Tom's virtuous character. This sequence of discoveries initiates the reversal of the action leading to Tom's final good fortune. Richardson, in *Clarissa*, handles reversals differently, but they are still reversals of the line of action. He constructs his plot around frequent changes of direction as Clarissa, and along with her the reader, given the changing information at her disposal, alternatively sees the action as moving toward good fortune or bad. The resulting constant fluctuation between hope and fear is central to the interest of the reader. The discoveries appropriate to these reversals are those made by Clarissa as she observes the actions and estimates the character of Lovelace and the other agents in a position to help or harm her.

Nineteenth-century plots, formed as they were around a causal sequence resulting from an opposition between the central characters and their surroundings, turned on reversals of intention and moral maxims. Typically the central character starts with one intention and one set of moral maxims, discovers that actions based on them lead to untenable conflicts with his surroundings, and ends by changing his intentions and his maxims. In *Crime and Punishment,* for example, Raskolnikov starts with the intention of improving the condition of men by murdering the old woman and with the utilitarian maxims he associates with such an intention. The act of murder, based on these convictions, leads to conflicts which were unforeseen and which soon become untenable. The reversal is completed in the last chapter where, sent to Siberia after his confession and trial, he is seen in the process of adopting convictions of a religiously humanitarian nature, convictions quite the reverse of those he held at the beginning. The discovery appropriate to such a reversal is generally the discovery of aspects of the surroundings left out of account by the original intention and maxims. In Raskolnikov's case it is the discovery of the religious side of life, in particular the sense of a more than merely utilitarian aspect to justice and mercy, which initiates his confession and subsequent reversal of convictions. In *The Ambassadors* the reversal and discovery take the same general form. Strether has come to Europe with the maxims of capitalistic New England and the intention of bringing Chad home. He gradually discovers aspects of Parisian life, in particular the aesthetic side of human life, which the New England maxims failed to take into account. Finding his original convictions untenable, he reverses his intention—he urges Chad to stay in Paris—and adopts a new maxim—that of gaining nothing for himself at the expense of other people—one he now sees as the reverse of the New England maxims.

Twentieth-century plots are formed around a movement from appearance to reality constituted by the emergence of structural patterns which give coherence and intelligibility to facts previously seen as unrelated and incongruous. These plots turn on reversals of perspective and reversals of valuation. What generally happens is that events and characters seen at one point in the novel in one perspective are seen at a later point in a different and often opposed perspective. The result of the reversal of perspective is often a reversal of valuation. In *The Good Soldier,* for example, Dowell (and the reader) at the beginning see Florence, Leonora, and Edward in the perspective of the superficial social conventions of Edwardian England. Since Edward is seen to have broken the conventions in such a way as to injure the others, he is evaluated as of relatively bad character while the two women are judged to be relatively innocent. By the end of the novel, as a result of the fuller understanding of the facts by Dowell (and the reader), these three characters are seen in another and more adequate perspective, a perspective centering on private virtues and motives rather than public conventions, with the result that Edward is now evaluated as relatively innocent and even virtuous in some ways and the two women are judged to be primarily guilty of the misfortunes which have affected them all. The discovery appropriate to this kind of reversal is the discovery of the realities of the situation. In *The Good Soldier* it is the discovery of the private lives and characters of the agents behind the public facade.

The same general type of reversal and discovery operates in a different manner in a novel like *Ulysses*. In *Ulysses* the title suggests at the beginning the perspective in which to evaluate Bloom; he is to be judged against Ulysses, a traditional hero. Seen in this perspective, Bloom is at first evaluated as a timid, inept, ignorant, vulgar, and overly docile character, lacking all the virtues of a traditional hero like Ulysses. As the reader follows Bloom through his day in Dublin, however, seeing him respond to the various episodes of the day and learning more about his private attitudes and convictions, the perspective and the evaluation tend to change. Judged not against the traditional hero but against the other Dubliners whom he meets during the day as he responds to the challenges of modern urban life, Bloom begins to be seen as something of a hero himself and to share with Ulysses some qualities—qualities such as curiosity, tolerance, a sense of adventure, a regard for wife and children—which many of his compatriots do not possess. He becomes a typical modern anti-hero.

One of the problems presented by a difficult novel like *Ulysses* is that most readers have been unable to perceive the reversal of perspective and evaluation during the first reading, which means they have been unable to follow the plot. Indeed the early critical judgments tended to see only the negative side of Bloom's character, his appearance of lacking all the qualities prominent in the traditional hero. It is only in recent years that critical opinion has recognized in Bloom the modern versions of some of the traditional heroic virtues found in Ulysses.

The concept of the anti-hero suggests some of the problems of characterization in modern novels resulting from the requirements of the new kind of plot. If the movement from appearance to reality is to involve a reversal of perspective and evaluation, then characters must be so constructed as to have two main aspects: a public side, that which is most apparent from the few facts in the reader's possession during the early parts of the novel, and a private side, that which emerges as the reader acquires more insight into the realities of the character and his situation. If the reversal of evaluation is to be pronounced, then the private side must be different from and even opposed to the public side. In terms of the publicly accepted and traditional conventions, Bloom is a nobody; in terms of his private aspirations and convictions, he is something of a modern hero. This doubling of character is itself a source of many of the apparent contradictions and incongruities which occur in modern novels and which have given it a reputation for obscurity.

The character of the anti-hero fits perfectly the requirements of modern plots. The anti-hero is a character who, judged by the publicly recognized conventions and standards of morality and importance and the traditional appearances of heroism, is evaluated as a person of no social importance, as often engaging in morally reprehensible actions, and as lacking all the qualities associated with the heroic. But the anti-hero also has a private side. When, as a result of the reader's insight into the realities of the world of the novel, he is judged in the perspective of more realistically grounded standards of morality and importance and the realities rather than the appearances of heroism, a reversed evaluation is made in which he becomes, in his own way, moral, important, and heroic. This is not to say that all modern novels contain anti-heroes, but this mode of characterization fits the plot requirements so well that it is often used. This is why many modern novels are filled with characters existing on the outskirts of their society, characters who reject positions of social importance, who ignore the precepts of conventional morality, and who scoff at the traditional heroic postures. This also suggests the reason why in many modern novels the characters who hold the conventionally important public positions—the generals, priests, ministers, doctors, psychiatrists, government officials, and in general the leaders of society—often turn out in the end to be despicable characters lacking any true sense of morality and justice, any real importance on the personal or familial level, and any real heroism. In these cases the reversal of evaluation is working in the opposite direction, moving from high to low rather than from low to high.

One of the reasons why many modern novels have been called experimental is because the new type of plot has required innovations in technique. In nineteenth-century novels the reader is introduced immediately to the causal influences operating in the novel, since only then can he follow with understanding the causal sequence as it progresses. This requires narrative methods which follow the causal sequence of the story in its temporal progression. In modern novels, on the other hand, the reader must not be introduced immediately to the causal influences operating in the story, for it is his gradual insight into these influences as they emerge from the welter of facts that constitutes the plot of the novel. The new methods of narration were devised to achieve this gradual emergence of significance.

One procedure often used is the separation of the sequence of the presentation of the story from the story itself and its causal sequences. In *The Good Soldier*, for example, the story told is that of the complex affair involving Dowell, Edward, Florence, Leonora, and Nancy. The presentation of the story, on the other hand, consists of Dowell's attempt to make sense of the affair after the events have occurred. The result is that the causal sequence of the story itself is broken up as Dowell jumps backwards and forwards in time in his attempt to understand the significance of the facts he has to work with. The temporal movement of the presentation of the story follows a line of increasing significance and meaning, not the line of causal influences in the story itself. Such a method of narration is perfectly adapted to plots which move on a line of increasing significance and understanding from appearance to reality. *Absalom, Absalom!* uses similar methods. The Sutpen story is what is presented, but the presentation is done by Quentin and Shreve long after Sutpen has been dead and follows a line of increasing understanding rather than the line of causal influences.

Another procedure is the use of the stream of consciousness technique to record the events in the mind of one or more characters during short periods of time. In *Mrs. Dalloway*, for example, the reader is presented with events in Clarissa Dalloway's consciousness during a single day. The story being presented, however, includes many past events which Mrs. Dalloway remembers during that day. Similar techniques are used in a more complex way in *Ulysses* and *The Sound and the Fury*. The effect of all these techniques is to break up the causal sequence of the story and to allow the facts to emerge in such a way that the reader is involved in a movement of increasing understanding of the realities of the story.

One consequence of modern plots and their techniques is that the reader is involved in the plot to an unusual degree. The reader is presented with what seem to be contradictory and inconsequential facts; there is no narrator who understands the story and who can tell the reader what standards of morality are operating in the novel, what constitutes good or bad fortune for the characters, or what the cause and effect relations are. It is the job of the reader to actively contribute to the plot by seeking for the significant relations between the facts and by grasping the resulting patterns of reality as they emerge from the facts. In particular, he must, on the basis of the evidence he has, work out for himself the moral standards, the sources of happiness and suffering, and the operative causes in the world of each novel.

This analysis of modern plots and their consequences for characterization and methods of narration should explain why many modern novels are difficult to read and present the appearance of obscurity. It is not that modern novelists are interested in difficulty or obscurity for their own sake. It is rather that in order to construct plots which achieve a temporal synthesis by means of a movement from appearance to reality they must start by plunging the reader into the appearances, into the midst of seemingly unrelated, contradictory, incongruous, inconsequential, and even fantastic facts, and let him discover for himself as he reads the structures of reality which gradually emerge, if the reading is successful, to give meaning to the facts and coherence to the novel.

Walter O'Grady asks us to think of the plots of novels as the interaction between two important elements: the exterior situations, incidents, and the interior states of mind, events. Of course, the author must start with what is given, but the essence of plot is change. A plot is not so much a structure, which suggests something static, as it is a process—the continuing interrelatedness of incident and event. For example, O'Grady perceives the flow of a novel like James's *The Ambassadors* as the interaction of external and internal happenings moving forward in time toward a significant change of attitude on the part of Lambert Strether.

on plot in modern fiction: hardy, james, and conrad

WALTER O'GRADY

E. M. Forster distinguishes between story and plot.[1] Story he calls the narrative of events arranged in their time sequence, while plot is likewise a narrative of events, but with the emphasis falling on causality. "The King died and then the Queen died" is a story, but "the King died and then the Queen died of grief" is a plot. The difference is that while each contains two incidents, the second contains the reason for one of the incidents. But Forster does not examine closely enough. "The King died because he was old" is not of the same order as "the Queen died because of grief," nor even of "the litmus paper turned red because the solution was acidic." The difference seems to lie in the fact that the grief of the queen is an internal, non-physical human event. What Forster has given us is one external event causing a change in an internal situation, which internal event causes another external event. Thus what we have in plot is two exterior events, one interior event, an interior situation and change. We may say that this is merely the inter-action of character and plot, yet this phrase has meaning only if the plot is considered as the totality of exter-

[1] E. M. Forster, *Aspects of the Novel* (London: Edward Arnold, 1958), p. 82–83.

nal events. But why should the emotion of love be considered less **an** event than the action of marrying? Why is a new perception not considered as happening to a character in the same way as inheriting a fortune is considered as happening to him? The difference does not lie in the fact that one is an incident and the other a state, for being rich is as much a state as being in love, and inheriting a fortune will no more, or perhaps no less, direct our actions than a new perception or awareness. In the novel there is a given interior situation, and grief or a thunderstorm, love or a car accident operate on this interior situation in the same way. All that we can say now is that some events are external and some are internal. The relationship between them will be examined in more detail later.

If we return to Forster's example of a story, that is "the King died and then the Queen died," we note that this is something more than "the cat died and then the dog died." It is more even than "John died and then Joe died." There are degrees of interest here, with the highest degree appertaining to the first story. This cannot be because of the external events, which are the same. It cannot be because of the interior situation or the interior events, for they are not given. It must therefore reside in the exterior situation. By making the people who died a king and queen, Forster postulates for us a situation which, although exterior, has a direct bearing on the interest of the story. At the beginning of his novel, an author may postulate whatever exterior situation he wishes. There may be war or peace, drought or rain; the characters may be poor or rich, married or single, urban or rural; they may have a physical disability or be involved in any kind of relationship with other characters. For the novelist, all probable situations exist. The exterior situation might be said to stand in the same relationship to the working out of the plot as oxygen to fire. It is necessary for it to exist, but it is used up in that working out. It can never return in exactly the same form.

These two given situations, the interior and the exterior, are the beginning point of any novel. This does not mean that the novel starts with a delineation of them. They may never be made explicit by the novelist, and may only become apparent as the plot works out. The exterior situation may have been created by the interior situation or the character or characters, and conversely, the interior situation may have been created by the exterior situation. It is not the business of the novel to examine this, for we must grant the novelist his given situations. His characters may involve themselves in an external state because of their makeup, as Verloc does in *The Secret Agent*. They may be thrust into some situation merely because of the power of that situation, and through no activity of their own, as Tess Durbeyfield is. Or the exterior situation may exist with its own power, which combines with the interior situation of the character to provide the given situation of the novel, as is the case with Lambert Strether. We should note that the process by which the author arrives at the opening situation does not involve one of these three possibilities to the exclusion of the others. All opening situations result from a combination of these. It is more a question of whether the author puts the emphasis on the characters involving themselves, or on the characters being involved by circumstances. Of the three writers whom we shall consider, Henry James comes closest to striking a balance between the power of the internal situation and the power of the external situation. In all novels, the juxtaposition of these two states is the spark which sets the plot in motion. It might be said that given a certain interior state, and given a certain exterior state, it is impossible that things remain the same; the novel is the working out of the process of change.

When we examined Forster's plot, we noticed that it implied the existence of five things: an external situation, an internal situation, an external event, an internal event, and change. Up to now we have examined the external and internal situations and their relationship. We turn back now to examine the external and internal events and their relationship. An external event we shall call an incident, an internal event we shall call an event.

Both incidents and events are part of what may be called the action of the novel. We have seen earlier that one is not more important or significant than the other, that they are, in fact, of the same order. An incident may be caused by a combination of an event and an exterior situation, or it may happen to a character and be caused by fate or circumstance. What is important to notice is what the incident does. It seems to me that an incident can either reveal character or form it, and that in fact all incidents do both of these in varying degrees. Likewise, an incident may reveal or form a situation. Depending upon the weight which the author puts on the revelatory or formulative aspects of the function, we may call an incident indicative or formative. Thus, when Strether meets Chad and Madame de Vionnet on the river, we have an incident which is caused by chance, which reveals the true situation existing, and which helps to re-form Strether's perceptions and sensibilities. In this case, the weight of the incident is thrown upon the revelation of the situation, and we could call it an indicative incident.

41

What stands out from a consideration of these four aspects of a plot, is the inter-relationship of all of them, the fact that each works upon the other to produce the fifth aspect, change. Here we can see that the concept of structure, indeed the very term structure, is misleading when applied to the novel. Structure implies a static relationship, whereas the novel is concerned with fluid relationships. I do not mean fluid relationships between characters, but between the component parts of the novel. We might more correctly use the concept of molecular structure to indicate this relationship: just as the form of any molecular structure is determined by the rate and direction of flow of the molecules, so the final form or meaning of the novel is determined by the rate and direction of the flow between the interrelated parts of the novel. Plot I take to be this flow. This is only another way of saying that plot is the inter-flow between external situation, internal state, incident, event, and change. It is revealing to examine a novel from the point of view of what force and direction an author gives to his plot. Does the novelist give more weight to the interior state or the exterior situation as the generator of events? Does the flow of events turn back upon itself to modify the external situation, or does it produce some change in the internal situation? Or are the events and incidents indicative rather than formative? According to Robert Liddell, "The process of working out one's conception in fiction is not at all like arranging flowers, putting this here, that there, and giving a pull or a twist to a leaf or a spray in order to make it stand out. It is very much more like giving birth to a baby." [2] I do not know if Mr. Liddell has ever arranged flowers. But this quotation illustrates how difficult it is to talk of the novel without using metaphorical language, and how far many modern critics are stretching for metaphors. It seems to me that we must try to refrain from indulging in comparisons which only apparently clarify, and examine the work as critics. This critical examination of the novel may require an entire new terminology. In defining Henry James's conception of art, R. P. Blackmur writes: "The subject of art was life, or more particularly someone's apprehension of the experience of it, and in striving truly to represent it art removed the waste and muddlement and bewilderment in which it is lived and gave it a lucid, intelligible form." [3] If we stop the flow of the plot of *The Ambassadors* at two or three points in the novel, and determine what direction and weight James is giving to that flow, we may perhaps

[2] Robert Liddell, *A Treatise on the Novel* (London: Jonathan Cape, 1947), pp. 85–86.
[3] Henry James, *The Art of the Novel,* Introduction by Richard P. Blackmur (New York: Charles Scribner's Sons, 1947), p. XV.

perceive something of how his art truly represents his apprehension of life, and of how that *art* becomes part of our experience of life. We are not concerned with judging whether James's apprehension of life is good or bad, valid or invalid. We are concerned solely with the art or craft involved. We can then apply the same method to *Tess of the D'Urbervilles* and *The Secret Agent.*

If a certain exterior situation had not existed, Lambert Strether would never have gone to Paris. Had he not gone to Paris, he would never have changed. But if anyone other than Lambert Strether had gone to Paris, that person would not have changed in the same way, and perhaps would not have changed at all. John Verloc could not react to such a situation, nor could Angel Clare, nor John D'Urberville. This is obvious, but it serves to point up the fact that James gives equal weight to the interior and exterior situation in the production of incidents and events. There is no mechanism in this novel such as we can find in Conrad and to a greater extent in Hardy. Two situations interact to produce a few incidents and a great number of events. The only real incident in the first two books is Strether's meeting with Maria Gostrey, and here James throws the entire weight not on the incident of meeting, but on the events which it triggers in Strether: ". . . and what he finally sat there turning over was the strange logic of his finding himself so free. He felt it in a manner his duty to think out his state, to approve the process, and when he came in fact to trace the steps and add up the items they sufficiently accounted for the sum." [4] The flow here is forward, the incident causes the event, it does not change the situation. It is, moreover, a formative rather than an indicative incident.

In the same way, Strether's first meeting with Chad is an incident which causes an event. Chad has changed, and this change changes Strether: "The phenomenon that had suddenly sat down there with him was a phenomenon of change so complete that his imagination, which had worked so beforehand, felt itself, in the connection, without margin or allowance. It had faced every contingency but that Chad should not *be* Chad, and this was what it now had to face with a mere strained smile and an uncomfortable flush" (pp. 136–137). It is indicative of the direction of this incident that Waymarsh is oblivious of the change: "The social sightlessness of his old friend's survey [of Chad] marked for him afresh, and almost in a humiliating way, the inevitable limits of direct aid from this source" (p. 137). This is an example of an incident being both formative,

[4] Henry James, *The Ambassadors* (New York: Charles Scribner's Sons, 1909), I, 81.

43

or event causing, and indicative. Even Maria Gostrey is not aware of the change in Chad, and because we conceive of her internal situation as being one of perception and awareness, in spite of her ignorance of Chad we might expect her to notice the shock to Strether. Here James obviously directs the incident towards the internal event of Strether's changing awareness. Throughout the novel Strether is learning, or rather, he is being taught, even how to enter a theatre box at ten o'clock at night: "he had on the spot and without the least trouble of intention taught Strether that even in so small a thing as that there were different ways" (p. 140). That everything else in the novel flows into this stream of the events in Strether's mind is indicated by Chad's remark to him, "I haven't put you through much—yet" (p. 154).

A third and revealing incident is the accidental meeting of Strether with the two lovers at the country inn. This is an incident caused by accident or chance. It does not change the original external situation; it merely completes the revelation of that situation to Strether. James does not allow the confrontation to affect either Chad or Madame de Vionnet, beyond a momentary disaccommodation; it does not change their relationship. But the incident does trigger a series of events in Strether until finally it and the original situation become unimportant to him. In Strether's perceptions Madame de Vionnet loses some of her lustre, indeed begins to seem old; Chad begins to seem unworthy of what he has, or at least of the concern which Strether had shown for him. Again James directs the incident towards events in Strether's consciousness; "He was, at that point of vantage, in full possession, to make of it all what he could." [5]

Thus we see that the entire direction of the flow of *The Ambassadors* is inward. The external situation, the internal situation, the incidents are all directed to the internal event. The change in the novel is an internal change, the growing awareness of Strether; it might be said that Strether does not cause incidents which change the situation, but that incidents and situation cause Strether. Perhaps this is what is meant by the novel of "character," but surely such a term destroys the idea of the organic relationships existing in a novel.

When we look at *Tess of the D'Urbervilles* we see that Hardy has the novel moving in a different direction. Here the internal and external situations combine to cause an incident, but this incident turns back upon its direction of flow and modifies the external situation. The incidents in the

[5] Henry James, *The Ambassadors* (New York: Charles Scribner's Sons, 1909), II, 262.

novel are, therefore, formative, but have a different function than those of *The Ambassadors*. Tess is deposited in one situation after another, none of them really of her own choosing, for the most important incidents are accidental.

The death of Prince is one of the generating happenings in the novel; it is an accident arising out of the given situation, and Hardy throws the whole weight of the incident on the sense of the modified situation arising out of the incident. Tess must make the trip with the hives because of the poverty of the family, because of her father's drunkenness and illness, and because of her own pride. The result of the accident is the worsening of this situation: "The haggling business, which had mainly depended on the horse, became disorganized forthwith. Distress, if not penury loomed on the distance." [6] Tess must make the decision to go to the D'Urbervilles, but there is little opportunity to not make it. The situation forces her, and introspection and examination will not change that. Hardy scarcely mentions Tess's mind: "Having at least taken her course, Tess was less restless and abstracted, going about her business with some self assurance in the thought of acquiring another horse for her father by an occupation which would not be onerous. She had hoped to be a teacher at the school, but the fates seemed to decide otherwise" (p. 56). The movement to the D'Urbervilles is a change from one bad situation to a potentially worse one. Her seduction is another accidental incident, from her point of view, which again changes her situation more than it changes her. The internal event is, really, contained in the chapter head, "Maiden No More." Once again the incident is directed to the change in situation and Tess's attempt to come to terms with that situation, and to live some kind of peaceful life within the terms offered by her environment. She suffers, but the internal events are not re-presented as they are in James. She changes internally, but Hardy does not choose to focus on this: "Almost at a leap Tess thus changed from simple girl to complex woman. Symbols of reflectiveness passed into her face, and a note of tragedy at times into her voice. Her eyes grew larger and more eloquent. . . . her soul that of a woman whom the turbulent experiences of the last year or two had quite failed to demoralize" (p. 127).

The actual function of Tess in the novel is to be always looking for a new departure, a way out of the situation in which she finds herself through no fault of her own. Even her final desperate condition, in which

[6] Thomas Hardy, *Tess of the D'Urbervilles* (London: Macmillan and Co. Ltd.), p. 40.

she is living with Alec when Angel Clare returns, is forced upon her by the necessity of looking after her mother and family. The stabbing is a last fierce outcry against being forced into situations, positions into which she did not put herself and over which she has no control.

We might say, then, that if the direction of flow of *The Ambassadors* is forward and inward, the flow of Hardy's novel is outward and backward. The incidents in both are formative, but James directs them ahead to the formation of a new consciousness, while Hardy directs them backward to the modification of an old situation.

In *The Secret Agent* Conrad orders and directs all situations and incidents to one climactic incident, the attempt to blow up the Greenwich Observatory and the consequent destruction of Stevie. The given combination of Verloc's interior situation and the exterior situation in which this has involved him combine to produce the interview with Mr. Vladimir. This interview does not change Verloc's interior state, it does not cause an event, it merely stirs up that state. There is no real change in Verloc, only an increase of anxiety. The exterior situation does not change, it becomes more pressing. This is an example of an incident being directed not towards change, but toward the production of another incident. There is a difference in the nature of incident as used by Conrad and as used by James and Hardy. For the latter two, incident is generally formative as well as indicative. In *The Secret Agent* incident is generally indicative only. In this sense, this novel is the most uncharacteristic of Conrad's work. After the interview with Vladimir, Verloc is still the pragmatic anarchist, the seeker after security and comfort, the good provider. His relationships with his wife, mother-in-law, brother-in-law and fellow anarchists remain on the same uninvolved plane as before. His situation is more precarious but essentially the same; his attitude towards anarchy and government is unchanged. Anarchy is a way of making a living, while government is something that is not thought about.

It is interesting that in all three of our authors accident plays an important part in the working out of the plot. The accident of Stevie stumbling produces the major incident in the novel. In what direction does Conrad point this incident? Verloc remains morally uninvolved and unchanged by it; it was "as much an accident as if he had been run over by a bus while crossing the street." [7] He conceives of himself as not being responsible, of merely trying to do his job and to be a good provider. He cannot understand Winnie's withdrawal from him, and even tries to woo

---

[7] Joseph Conrad, *The Secret Agent* (London: Willam Heinneman, 1921), p. 291.

her when he thinks he has made her see reason. There has been no interior change, no event within the consciousness of Verloc. Nor has Winnie changed, despite Conrad's protestation to the contrary. Her violent reaction against Verloc and the ultimate act of stabbing him are merely the obverse side of the coin of her love for Stevie. This love had previously led her to give up the man she wanted to marry, and now it forces her to commit a deed which will make her give up her life. What has changed is the exterior situation of Verloc, both as an anarchist and in relation to his wife. Whether or not he is caught by the police, he will never again be able to function in the world of Vladimir. Whether or not he knows it, his relationship with his wife has turned to one of hatred. Conrad has directed the given interior situation, the exterior situation, the incidents which their combination produces, to a complete destruction of the exterior situation. In this sense he is closer to Hardy than James, although there is a very great difference in degree of emphasis. The flow of his plot, like Hardy's, is backwards and outwards.

There is no attempt here to judge the relative values of the different kinds of plot. How an author determines the direction and flow of his incidents, what weight he gives to value and situation, will depend on what he is trying to do. In spite of my strictures against metaphor, I have been forced to use one throughout. As in all writing on the novel, this is a dangerous oversimplification. An author may direct his plot towards the internal event, but this does not mean that there is no modification of the external situation. In most novels all things will coexist. It is a question of determining where the main emphasis has been placed, that is, to return to the metaphor, which is the main stream and which are tributaries. What this is, perhaps, is a suggestion of a different way of looking at a novel, a way which will not explain the novel away, but which will help to make it seeable. I do not know if it could be applied to all novels; I doubt it. but at least in the rejection of this concept of plot as the interacting flow, we would be forced to examine the relationships between the parts of the novel, and to determine the kind of change which it conveys.

The modern short story is not formless, episodic, or casual, observes A. L. Bader; on the contrary, it does have a distinct structure, though not one as tightly organized as in the traditional story. In this essay, the author analyzes the ways in which most contemporary short-story writers manipulate their materials into a symbolic design. One of the methods used in the modern short story is that of indirection, suggestion, or implication. Instead of rounding off an action definitively, such writers reveal its meaning through a casual glance, gesture, or remark. In such a form of short story that works through indirection rather than explicit statement, the reader is often invited to supply the missing links himself, as in William March's "A Haircut in Toulouse" or John O'Hara's "Are We Leaving Tomorrow?"

the structure
of the
modern short story

A. L. BADER

Any teacher who has ever confronted a class with representative modern short stories will remember the disappointment, the puzzled "so-what" attitude, of certain members of the group. "Nothing happens in some of these stories," "They just end," or "They're not real stories" are frequent criticisms. An examination of the reviews of the yearly O'Brien anthologies as well as of the collections of leading short-story writers discloses a similar attitude on the part of many professional critics. Sometimes the phrase "Nothing happens" seems to mean that nothing significant happens, but in a great many cases it means that the modern short story is charged with a lack of narrative structure. Readers and critics accustomed to an older type of story are baffled by a newer type. They sense the underlying and unifying design of the one, but they find nothing equivalent to it in the other. Hence they maintain that the modern short

49

story is plotless, static, fragmentary, amorphous—frequently a mere character sketch or vignette, or a mere reporting of a transient moment, or the capturing of a mood or nuance—everything, in fact, except a story.

These charges, it seems to me, are not borne out by an examination of representative modern short stories. In this article I shall compare and analyze a number of stories, old and new, in an endeavor to demonstrate that the modern short story does have structure, that is, a basic design or skeletal framework; that this structure is essentially the same as that of the older story; and that what is frequently taken to be lack of structure is the result of various changes in technique.

The older type of story is the story of traditional plot. By a story of traditional plot I do not necessarily mean what has come to be known as "the plot story," although the latter is one example of the type. I mean any story (1) which derives its structure from plot based on a conflict and issuing in action; (2) whose action is sequential, progressive, that is, offers something for the reader to watch unfold and develop, usually by means of a series of complications, thus evoking suspense; and (3) whose action finally resolves the conflict, thus giving the story "point." The structure of traditional plot stories is essentially dramatic; somewhere near the beginning of the story the reader is given a line of progression to follow—a clear statement of the conflict, or a hint of it, or sometimes merely a sense of mystery, of tension, or a perception that a conflict exists although its nature is not known—and from this point on he follows the action to a crisis and a final resolution. There is a geometrical quality to plot structure of this type; just as a proposition is stated, developed by arguments, and finally proved, so a conflict is stated at the beginning of a story, developed by a series of scenes, and resolved at the end. The test for unity of such a structure is simple: Each scene, incident, and detail of the action not only must bear a direct relation to the conflict and its resolution but must also carry its share of significance at the particular point in the progression that it occupies. Thus the reader's sense of unity, of having watched something develop to the point of completion, is derived from the writer's focusing upon conflict and the eventual resolution of conflict.

Obviously, stories of traditional plot are capable of considerable variation; plot is not necessarily a strait jacket, as in the formula story, and it is only one of the elements of complete short-story form. Hence plot may be the dominant element in a story, or again it may be subordinated to elements such as character, theme, or atmosphere. Conflict may be of two fundamental types: external conflict, in which a character struggles

50

against a tangible obstacle, and internal conflict, or conflict within a character. Also, there are wide differences as to how soon the conflict is made apparent to the reader and how much of it he is allowed to understand early in the story.

Jack London's "Love of Life" is a convenient example of the story in which plot is dominant and external. A prospector in the Far North, deserted by his partner and without food and ammunition, successfully overcomes the threat of death by starvation, exposure, and the attack of wild animals. The conflict here is between man and the forces of nature; it is apparent early in the story, and it is the focus of the reader's attention throughout. The action is progressive or sequential—consisting of a series of incidents, each a minor conflict in itself. The resolution occurs when the man reaches safety, and only when the outcome is no longer in doubt is the story completed. A second example, Sarah Orne Jewett's "A White Heron," shows character dominant over plot. A nine-year-old girl, a lover of nature, is asked by a young ornithologist to reveal the haunts of the white heron in order that he may secure a specimen for his collection, but the girl refuses. The conflict is internal, between the girl's love for the beautiful bird and her desire to make the young man happy and win for her grandmother the reward he offers. The conflict, however, does not make its appearance until the mid-point of the story, since the first half is given over to characterization on which the resolution of the conflict eventually turns. Yet, despite its differences, the story conforms to the same structural pattern of traditional plot that the London story exemplifies. All that is claimed for plot here is that it furnishes the skeletal structure of the older type of story, whether it be a so-called "atmosphere story" like "The Fall of the House of Usher," a psychological story like "Markheim," or a story of theme like "Ethan Brand." [1]

By contrast the modern story frequently seems to be without narrative structure and, as was stated earlier, has been called plotless, fragmentary, and amorphous. Certainly there is evidence to show that the modern writer has attempted to break away from traditional plot. Plot, he feels, is unreal, artificial. Sherwood Anderson's remarks on plot in *A Story-teller's Story* are typical: " 'The Poison Plot' I called it in conversation with my friends as the plot notion did seem to me to poison all story-telling. . . . In the con-

---

[1] The surprise-ending story is only a seeming exception. While it is true that in stories such as Aldrich's "Marjorie Daw" and those of O. Henry the *real* story is hidden until the end, the reader nevertheless follows a conflict in the form of a progression of scenes and incidents, and the surprise ending merely contributes a new understanding to the progression and resolution of the conflict.

struction of these stories there was endless variation but in all of them human beings, the lives of human beings, were altogether disregarded. . . . it was certain there were no plot stories in any life I had known anything about." The same belief in the antipathy between plot and realism is seen in a challenging article by Bonaro Overstreet: "The nineteenth century story teller was a master of plot. The twentieth century fellow, seeing that life was not made up of neatly parcelled collections of incidents, took his rebel stand." [2]

Now, it seems to me that statements such as these are not so much protests against plot as against the misuse of plot. Fundamentally, they are protests against plot based on formulas and their "deceptive sentimentalizing of reality," [3] which the writers find artificial. Yet plot is not necessarily artificial. Conflict, the basis of plot, is the very stuff of life, whether the individual writer tends to see it within the mind or in the external world. The kind of conflict the writer chooses, and the method by which the conflict is developed, may vary, and should vary, from story to story according to the individual aims of the writer; but the resultant plot need not illustrate the platitudes and mechanical patterns of the formula stories. And the fact is that modern stories which presumably satisfy their authors on the score of realism do exhibit the traditional structure of conflict, action, and resolution. The charges of plotlessness, of loose, invertebrate structure, that have been made against the modern story seem to me to be better explained by changes in modern technique.

Chief among these changes are the stricter limitation of subject and the method of indirection. The modern writer's desire for realism causes him to focus upon a limited moment of time or a limited area of action in order that it may be more fully explored and understood. One result is that he frequently finds a story in material which would yield nothing to an earlier writer. Naturally he makes little use of plot complication, because he regards plot complication as artificial, and doubly so if the subject is limited. More important than this limitation of subject, however, is the marked emphasis upon indirection, which seemingly stems as much from the pervasive modern desire for subtlety as from the realistic ideal. To suggest, to hint, to imply, but not to state directly or openly—this is a favored contemporary technique. The method is well described by L. A. G.

[2] Bonaro Overstreet, "Little Story, What Now?" *Saturday Review of Literature,* **XXIV** (November 22, 1941), 4.
[3] Warren Beck, "Art and Formula in the Short Story," *College English,* V (November, 1943), 59. Professor Beck demonstrates convincingly that the formula story is basically the story of sentimental platitude.

Strong: "The modern short story writer is content if, allowing the reader to glance at his characters as through a window, he shows them making a gesture which is typical: that is to say, a gesture which enables the reader's imagination to fill in all that is left unsaid. Instead of giving us a finished action to admire, or pricking the bubble of some problem, he may give us only the key-piece of a mosaic, around which, if sufficiently perceptive, we can see in shadowy outline the completed pattern." [4] In other words, as will be apparent in the following analyses, the reader must supply the missing parts of the traditional plot in many modern stories.

A case in point is William March's "A Haircut in Toulouse" from his collection *Some Like Them Short:*

> A veteran of World War I meets an old war comrade, Bob Decker, at a Legion reunion in France. Decker, grown stout and middle-aged, appears ridiculous in a flamboyant costume of gold-braided, bell-bottomed trousers, white silk blouse, wide crimson sash, and sombrero. He tells his friend a story that he has never told to anyone else. After the war, in Toulouse, he went to a French barber shop where his attempts to explain to the barber that he wanted "clippers on the neck but nothing off the top" were misunderstood; and out of sheer inability to protest further, he submitted to having his hair curled. To his surprise, he liked the result; it "brought out something in me that I didn't even know was there before." But almost immediately he reflected that if he appeared at his barracks with his hair curled, he would never live down the resulting ridicule. He then picked up the clippers and sheared a path through the curls on his head, forcing the barber to complete the job, while inwardly he lamented his lack of freedom to do as he wished.
>
> At the conclusion of this narrative, Decker's wife and twelve-year-old daughter join the friends. After the introductions, Mrs. Decker apologizes for her husband's costume and adds, "All the boys from his Post are dressed just like he is." But the daughter says, "Don't you think Daddy looks *silly* dressed that way?" For a moment "the expression in his eyes must have been the same as it was when he picked up the French barber's clippers; but it passed almost at once and

---

[4] L. A. G. Strong, "The Short Story: Notes at Random," *Lovat Dickson's Magazine,* II (March, 1934), 281–82.

he smiled. . . ." He draws the child to him and says mildly, "Don't you suppose Daddy knows that as well as you do?"

If the synopsis is momentarily puzzling, so is the story, because the method is that of indirection. The writer's aim here is to depict a conflict within a character, to let us see within a man, to catch a glimpse of what is individual in him, even though it is usually hidden from the world. Decker, seemingly a conformist, secretly desires to individualize himself, to play the beau, to flout the conventions in the matter of dress, but he fears public ridicule. Some fifteen years before the time of the story, he yielded to his fear of ridicule when he sheared off his curled hair; and he has continued to yield. Now, because all the members of his post have chosen a flamboyant costume for the reunion, he can appear in a way that delights him, but beneath his gay exterior—and that is the real point of the story—lies the unhappy awareness of his own absurd appearance, and it is brought to a focus by his daughter's remark and his reply: "Don't you suppose Daddy knows that as well as you do?"

Once understood, the story is seen to possess the traditional elements of narrative structure. There is a conflict, the conflict is not immediately apparent to the reader, and it is the chief aim of the writer to make the reader see and understand it in order that he may understand the man Decker. It is made apparent by action, but here the story departs sharply from the traditional technique. There are two seemingly unrelated scenes —one in the barber shop at Toulouse, the other in the hotel lobby when the wife and daughter appear. The seeming lack of relationship is deliberate; the emphasis is not upon the sequence of the scenes, their progression, or what has been called earlier their geometrical quality. Rather it is upon their meaning. The aim of a story of this kind is a perceived relationship. Given, in L. A. G. Strong's language, the parts of a mosaic, the reader must find the pattern. The "key-piece" of the mosaic is the statement: ". . . the expression in his eyes must have been the same as it was when he picked up the French barber's clippers"; and when at the very end of the story Decker says, "Don't you suppose Daddy knows that as well as you do?" the reader's mind should, in a moment of illumination, connect the two statements as well as supply what is omitted. The omissions, of course, are clear statements of what Decker's internal conflict is, and the fact that he has been repeatedly frustrated by convention.

Finally, the story satisfies the third requirement of plot structure in that the action resolves the conflict. Here again the method is indirect; the resolution is by implication. Instead of being taken into Decker's mind by the writer, we are given two objective statements, one about the look in the man's eyes and the other what he says. Having furnished the reader with the requisite hints, the writer stops. The suggestion is that *this time* Decker hoped to satisfy his own desire to dress as he wished as well as to escape ridicule. But his daughter's remark has recalled him unhappily to the reality of a world of conventional judgment, and the immediate conflict is resolved when once more he recognizes frustration. It is, of course, true that the story derives much of its power from its ability to project the reader's imagination beyond the limits of the story, to make him see that Decker's life has included many such experiences and that presumably his frustration will continue to the end of his life. Also it should be observed that in a story of this type the resolution and moment of perception are practically simultaneous and that the emotion is evoked principally at the end when the reader understands the situation.

Such a story, then, may be said to have the traditional elements of structure. Its principle of unity is that of the perceived relationship; each incident contributes to the perception of that relationship, there is an ordered arrangement of the parts, and no one incident can be omitted without destroying the unity and hence the meaning of the whole. Obviously, such a story puts demands upon both writer and reader. The suggestions and implications must be nicely calculated to reveal neither too little nor too much, and the reader must be alert to seize upon what is given and construct from it the desired pattern of meaning.

A second example of the modern type of story is John O'Hara's "Are We Leaving Tomorrow?" from his collection *Files on Parade:*

> A young couple, Mr. and Mrs. Campbell from Montreal, are staying at a resort hotel in the States. They keep a good deal to themselves, although Mrs. Campbell, "a pleasant, friendly little woman," has a nodding acquaintance with some of the other guests. Quite by chance they meet Mr. and Mrs. Loomis in the hotel bar and talk small talk over their drinks. We learn that "Mrs. Campbell was almost gay that afternoon." Mr. Campbell, however, has said nothing.
>
> One evening, after a movie shown by the hotel management, Mr. Loomis insists on buying the Campbells a drink. When he gives his order, Campbell tells the waiter to bring the bottle, and, after a moment's incredulity, Mr. Loomis con-

firms the order. The talk is idle gossip of movie stars, and Campbell, drinking steadily, is curiously aloof; but, as the Loomises feel this and address their remarks to him, he begins to respond in an exaggerated way, nodding before it is time to nod and saying, "Yes, yes, yes," very rapidly. Then he tells a story. "It had in it a priest, female anatomy, improbable situations, a cuckold, unprintable words, and no point." The Loomises, shocked and embarrassed, say "Good night" and leave.

Mrs. Campbell, who has lowered her eyes all during her husband's story, now says, "I wonder if the man is still there at the travel desk. I forgot all about the tickets for tomorrow." Her husband asks, "Tomorrow? Are we leaving tomorrow?" Her answer is "Yes," and she gets up to see about the tickets.

Here again both story and synopsis may offer momentary difficulty. Yet the "key-piece" of the mosaic has been provided by the writer. Linked to a chronic alcoholic who is offensive when drunk, Mrs. Campbell spends her life taking him from one resort to another. What happens in the story, it is suggested, is the repetitive pattern of their lives. Arrived at a new hotel, they at first remain aloof, but after a time Mrs. Campbell's natural friendliness causes her to speak and nod to other guests. Sooner or later, presumably by chance, they are brought into social relationship with others, Mr. Campbell reveals himself for what he is, and his wife feels the necessity of moving on, of "leaving tomorrow."

Aside from the fact that the story is not as compressed in time as March's "A Haircut in Toulouse," it shows generally similar characteristics. First of all, there is conflict in the story—an immediate conflict between Mr. and Mrs. Campbell, but, from a broader point of view, a conflict between Mrs. Campbell's desires for normal social companionship and the social mores which she can never satisfy because of her husband's character. As in the March story, the conflict is not immediately apparent to the reader, although the whole point of the narrative is to make him understand it and, by understanding it, sympathize with Mrs. Campbell. Again, the conflict is revealed through action which is not sequential in the dramatic sense but which has as its aim a perceived relationship. There are four scenes: the opening picture of the Campbells as mere spectators at the hotel; the chance meeting with the Loomises; the second meeting with the Loomises when Campbell tells his story; and the final scene with its moment of illumination when we perceive the entire situation and behind it the pattern of the Campbells' lives. The "key-piece" is Mrs. Campbell's "Yes," to her husband's question, "Tomorrow? Are we leaving tomorrow?" It is at this point that all previous scenes and details, when the requisite omissions are supplied, fall into a pattern of meaning. In this case the principal omissions concern the Campbells' past; the reader must see that what occurs in the story has occurred many times before. Finally, the immediate conflict is resolved when it becomes apparent that Mrs. Campbell has failed once more to achieve her desire; but, as in the March story, the resolution and moment of perception are simultaneous, the emotion is evoked at the end, and the basic conflict is not resolved, since Mrs. Campbell's life will probably continue to be a series of "leaving tomorrow's."

Another way of demonstrating the existence of structure in such a story is to re-form the parts into the conventional dramatic pattern. The story could begin, for example, by showing the Campbells arriving at a new resort. Next we might learn what Mrs. Campbell's problem is, how she longs for social companionship, and how frequently she has tried to make just such a new start as she is making when the story opens. After the first chance meeting with the Loomises, she would build her hopes anew, only to have them dashed by her husband's conduct at the second meeting with the Loomises. The ending would be the same—a reference to tickets and to leaving tomorrow. If the story were written according to the dramatic pattern, the traditional structure of conflict, sequential action, and resolution would stand forth clearly. The reader, knowing the situation early in the story, would follow the action principally to learn the outcome; the question would be: Will Mrs. Campbell succeed or fail? As the story is actually written, however, an understanding of the situation, that is, the conflict, and the outcome or resolution are reached simultaneously. Yet the elements of narrative structure are present, despite the different pattern.

Thus, it seems to me, the modern short story demonstrates its claim to the possession of narrative structure derived from plot. Basically, its structure is not very different from that of the older and more conventional type of story. but its technique is different, and it is this difference in technique that is frequently mistaken for lack of structure by readers and critics.

character

Mary McCarthy argues here that although modern writers have accurately recorded their characters' sensibilities—the "little shimmers of consciousness"—or the world of violent action in a bull ring, they have not given us the kind of real people that live in the works of Tolstoy or Dickens. Even the technique of dramatic monologue as employed in *The Adventures of Augie March, Henderson the Rain King, The Catcher in the Rye,* or *Lolita,* she says, works against the creation of memorable characters. These novels are "impersonations, ventriloquial acts," and the author is only imitating the voice of Augie or Holden, seldom speaking in his own. In brief, the modern novel tends to avoid the common world of real people in order to explore the impressions of what Mary McCarthy calls a "slithery" antihero.

characters in fiction

MARY McCARTHY

In Belgrade, the other day, an interviewer asked me what book I thought best represented the modern American woman. All I could think of to answer was: *Madame Bovary.* It occurred to me afterwards that I might have named *Main Street* or Henry James's *Portrait of a Lady.* What else? I tried to remember women in American books. Hester Prynne, Daisy Miller, Scott Fitzgerald's flappers and Daisy in *The Great Gatsby,* Temple Drake in *Sanctuary,* Dos Passos' career women, Ma Joad in *The Grapes of Wrath.* But since then? It was like leafing through a photograph album and coming, midway, on a sheaf of black, blank pages. Was it possible that for twenty-five years no American woman had had her likeness taken? "Submit a clear recent photo," as they say in job applications. But there was none, strange as it seemed considering the dominant role women are supposed to play in American life.

So I tried the experiment with men. The result was almost the same. Captain Ahab, Christopher Newman in *The American,* Caspar Goodwood, Adam Verver, the wicked Gilbert Osmond, Babbitt, Elmer Gantry, Gatsby, Mac and Charley Anderson in Dos Passos, Jason in *The Sound and the*

Fury, Colonel Sutphen in *Absalom, Absalom,* Flem and Mink Snopes, Studs Lonigan. After that, nothing, no one, except the Catholic priests of J. F. Powers, the bugler Prewitt in *From Here to Eternity,* and Henderson in *Henderson the Rain King.*

Someone might see this as a proof of the conformity of modern American life; there are no people any more, it might be claimed—only human vectors with acceleration and force. But in my experience this is simply not true. There are more people than ever before, at least in the sense of mutations in our national botany, and this is probably due to mobility—cross-fertilization. Take as an example a gangster who was in the slot-machine racket, decided to go straight and became a laundromat king, sent his daughter to Bennington, where she married a poet-in-residence or a professor of modern linguistic philosophy. There are three characters already sketched out in that sentence and all of them brand-new: the father, the daughter, and the son-in-law. Imagine what one of the old writers might have made of the wedding and the reception afterwards at "21." The laundromat king or his equivalent is easy to meet in America; there are hundreds of him. Try teaching in a progressive college and interviewing the students' parents. And do not pretend that the laundromat king has no "inner life"; he is probably a Sunday painter, who has studied with Hans Hofman in Provincetown. What, for that matter, was the inner life of Monsieur Homais in *Madame Bovary*? People speak of the lack of tradition or of manners as having a bad effect on the American novel, but the self-made man is a far richer figure, from the novelist's point of view, than the man of inherited wealth, who is likely to be a mannered shadow.

The relation between parents and children (Turgenev's great theme) has never been so curious as in America now, where primitivism heads into decadence before it has time to turn around. America is full of Bazarovs but only Turgenev has described them. Nobody, so far as I know, has described an "action" painter, yet nearly everyone has met one. Nobody has done justice to the psychoanalyst, yet nearly everyone has gone to one. And what a wealth of material there is in that virgin field, what variety: the orthodox Freudian, the Horneyite, the Reichian, the Sullivanite ("inter-personal relations"), all the different kinds of revisionists, the lay analyst, the specialist in group analysis, the psychiatric social worker. Social workers themselves have become one of the major forces in American life, the real and absolute administrators of the lives of the poor, yet no one since Sinclair Lewis and Dos Passos has dared write of them, unless you count the young author, John Updike, in *The Poorhouse Fair*, who presents a single specimen and lays the story in the future. Imagine what Dickens would have done with this new army of Beadles and the Mrs. Pardiggles behind them or what he would have done with the modern architect as Pecksniff, with the cant formula "Less is more." No serious writer since Dos Passos, so far as I know, has had a go at the government official, and the government official has not only multiplied but changed (like the social worker) since Dos Passos' time, producing many subvarieties. And what about the Foundation executive? Or the "behavioral scientist"? The fact is that the very forces and institutions that are the agents and promoters of conformity in America—bureaucracies public and private and the regimented "schools" and systems of healing and artistic creation—are themselves, through splits and cellular irritation, propagating an array of social types conforming to no previous standard, though when we look for names for them we are driven back, *faute de mieux*, on the old names: Pecksniff, Mrs. Gamp, Bazarov, Mrs. Pardiggle, Babbitt. When Peter Viereck, in a book of non-fiction, wanted to isolate a new kind of conformist intellectual he could think of nothing better to call him than "Babbitt Junior." It is as though a whole "culture" of plants and organisms had sprung into being and there were no scientists or latter-day Adams to name them.

This naming is very important, yet only two names in recent fiction have "stuck": Gully Jimson (Joyce Cary) and Lucky Jim (Kingsley Amis). Some interest in character is still shown by writers in England, perhaps because it is an island and hence more conscious of itself. But even in England the great national portrait gallery that constituted the English novel is short of new acquisitions. The sense of character began to fade with D. H. Lawrence. After *Sons and Lovers*, we do not remember figures in Lawrence's books, except for a few short malicious sketches. There are hardly any people in Virginia Woolf (Mr. Ramsay in *To the Lighthouse* stands out) or in Forster or Elizabeth Bowen or Henry Green; they exist in Ivy Compton-Burnett but tend to blur together like her titles. Waugh has people, and so had Joyce Cary. You find them in the short stories of V. S. Pritchett and in the satires of Angus Wilson. But the last great creator of character in the English novel was Joyce. It is the same on the Continent. After Proust, a veil is drawn. You can speak of someone as a "regular Madame Verdurin" or a "Charlus," but from Gide, Sartre, Camus, no names emerge; the register is closed.

The meaning of this seems plain. The novel and the short story have

63

lost interest in the social. Since the social has certainly not lost interest in itself (look at the popularity of such strange mirror-books as *The Lonely Crowd*, *The Organization Man*, *The Exurbanites*, *The Status Seekers*), what has happened must have occurred inside the novel and the short story— a technical or even technological crisis. An impasse has been reached within the art of fiction as a result of progress and experiment. You find a similar impasse in painting, where the portrait can no longer be painted and not because the artists do not know how to draw or get a likeness; they do. But they can no longer see a likeness as a work of art. In one sense, it is ridiculous to speak of progress in the arts (as though modern art were "better" than Rembrandt or Titian); in another sense, there *is* progress, an internal dynamic such as one finds in the processes of industry or in the biological process of aging. The arts have aged too, and it is impossible for them to "go back," just as it is impossible to recapture the youth or reinstitute a handicraft economy, like the one Ruskin dreamed of. These things are beyond our control and independent of our will. I, for instance, would like, more than anything else, to write like Tolstoy; I imagine that I still see something resembling the world Tolstoy saw. But my pen or my typewriter simply balks; it "sees" differently from me and records what to me, as a person, are distortions and angularities. Anyone who has read my work will be at a loss to find any connection with Tolstoy; to Tolstoy himself both I and my work would be anathema. I myself might reform, but my work never could; it could never "go straight," even if I were much more gifted than I am. Most novelists today, I suspect, would like to "go straight"; we are conscious of being twisted when we write. This is the self-consciousness, the squirming, of the form we work in; we are stuck in the phylogenesis of the novel.

The fictional experiments of the twentieth century went in two directions: sensibility and sensation. To speak very broadly, the experiments in the recording of sensibility were made in England (Virginia Woolf, Katherine Mansfield, Dorothy Richardson, Elizabeth Bowen, Forster), and America was the laboratory of sensation (Hemingway and his imitators, Dos Passos, Farrell). The novel of sensibility was feminine, and the novel of sensation was masculine. In Paris, there was a certain meeting and merging: Gertrude Stein (a robust recorder of the data of sensibility) influenced and encouraged Hemingway; Joyce, who experimented in both directions, influenced nearly everyone. The sensibility tendency today is found chiefly in such minor English writers as Henry Green and William Sansom; in America, it is represented by Katharine Anne Porter, Eudora

Welty, Jean Stafford, and Carson McCullers. The masculine novel of sensation, more admired always in Europe than at home, seems to have arrived at the Beat Generation, via Caldwell, Dashiell Hammett, James M. Cain, Raymond Chandler; its attraction toward violence propelled it naturally toward the crime story. The effect of these two tendencies on the subject matter of the novel was identical. Sensation and sensibility are the poles of each other, and both have the effect of abolishing the social. Sensibility, like violent action, annihilates the sense of character.

Beginning with our own. In violence, we forget who we are, just as we forget who we are when engaged in sheer perception. Immersed in a picture, an effect of light, or a landscape, we forget ourselves; we are "taken out of ourselves"; in the same way, we forget ourselves in the dentist's chair. We are not conscious of our personality. In sensation, we are all more or less alike. Heat, cold, hunger, thirst, pain are experienced by man, not men. And sensibility is only a refinement of sensation; the sense of blue or green made on our retina is more finely discriminated in an art critic than it is in the average man or the color-blind person, but no useful division, humanly speaking, could be made between those, say, who saw turquoise as green and those who saw it as blue. The retina is not the seat of character. Nor are the sexual organs, even though they differ from person to person. Making love, we are all more alike than we are when we are talking or acting. In the climax of the sexual act, moreover, we forget ourselves; that is commonly felt to be one of its recommendations. Sex annihilates identity, and the space given to sex in contemporary novels is an avowal of the absence of character. There are no "people" in *Lady Chatterley's Lover*, unless possibly the husband, who is impotent. To cite the laundromat king again, the moment of orgasm would not be the best moment for the novelist to seize upon to show his salient traits; on the other hand, to show him in an orgone box (i.e., in the frame of an idea) would be a splendid notion. Similarly, the perambulating sensibility of Mrs. Dalloway, her quivering film of perception, cannot fix for us Mrs. Dalloway as a person; she remains a palpitant organ, like the heroine of a pornographic novel. The character I remember best from Virginia Woolf is Mr. Ramsay in *To the Lighthouse*, a man who lacks the fine perceptions of the others; i.e., from the point of view of sensibility he is impotent, without erectile aesthetic tissue.

Sensation and sensibility are at their height in the child; its thin, tender membrane of perception is constantly being stabbed by objects, words, and events that it does not understand. In lieu of understanding, the child "notices." Think of the first sections of *A Portrait of the Artist as a Young Man* and of Aunt Dante's hairbrushes (why was she called Dante?) and the quarrel about Parnell (who was Parnell?) at the Christmas dinner table. Or the beginning of *Dr. Zhivago,* where the child Yury, taken to his mother's funeral, looks out the window at the cabbages, wrinkled and blue with cold, in the winter fields. Yury, being a child, cannot comprehend the important event that has happened to him (death), but his eye takes in the shivering cabbages. Everyone experiences something like this in moments of intense grief or public solemnity, such as funerals; feelings, distracted from their real causes, attach themselves arbitrarily to sights, smells and sounds. But a child passes a good part of his life in this attentive state of detachment.

Now two characteristics of the child are that he cannot act (to any purpose) and he cannot talk (expressively); hence he is outside, dissociated. And it is just this state, of the dissociated outsider, that is at the center of modern literature of sensibility and sensation alike. Camus's *The Stranger* or *The Outsider* begins with the hero's going to his mother's death bed and being unable to summon up the appropriate emotions or phrases.

It is modern but it is not new. The inability to say the appropriate thing or to feel the appropriate thing, combined with a horrible faculty of *noticing,* is an almost clinical trait in the character of Julien Sorel and in most of the Stendhalian heroes. Tolstoy was a master of the tragi-comedy of inappropriate feelings, gestures, and sensations. Take the first chapter of *Anna Karenina,* where Stepan Oblonsky, who has been unfaithful to his wife with the French governess, finds a foolish smile spreading over his features when she taxes him with it—a *smile* of all things. He cannot forgive himself that awful, inadvertent smile (he ascribes it to a "reflex"), which causes her to shut herself up in her room and declare that all is over. Vronsky's toothache, near the end of *Anna Karenina,* as it were dunce-caps the climax; it is the distracted intrusion of the commonplace into a drama of tragic passion. Anna has killed herself, and Vronsky is on the train, going off to the Serbo-Turkish war as an "heroic volunteer" with a squadron equipped at his own expense; his face is drawn with suffering —and with the ache in his big tooth, which makes it almost impossible for him to speak. But "all at once a different pain, not an ache but an inner trouble, that set his whole being in anguish, made him for an instant forget his toothache." He has "suddenly remembered *her,*" as he had last seen her mangled body exposed on a table in the railway shed. And he ceases to feel his toothache and begins to sob. At every station the train is seen off by patriotic society ladies with nosegays for the heroic volunteers, and these flowers, like the toothache, are ridiculous and painful—beside the point.

The point, however, is there, inescapably so (the corpse in the railway shed is more cruelly alive than the toothache), and this is the difference between Tolstoy (Stendhal too) and the fragmented impressionism of twentieth-century literature, where the real world is broken up into disparate painterly images out of focus and therefore hypnotic and trance-like. The world of twentieth-century sensibility, in contrast to that of Tolstoy, is a world in slow motion, a world which, however happy it may seem, is a world of paralyzed grief, in which little irrelevant things, things that do not belong, are noticed or registered on the film of consciousness, exactly as they are at a funeral service or by a bored child in church.

In the modern novel of sensibility the shimmer of consciousness occupies the whole field of vision. Happenings are broken down into tiny discrete sensory impressions, recalling pointillism or the treatment of light in Monet. The novel of sensation is less refined and seemingly more "factual": "It was hot"; " 'Give me a drink,' I said." But these too are the *disjecta membra* of consciousness passing across a primitive perceptual screen. A child cannot talk, and the modern novel of sensation, like that of sensibility, is almost mute; these rolls of film are silent, with occasional terse flashes of dialogue, like subtitles. The only form of action open to a child is to break something or strike someone, its mother or another child; it cannot cause things to happen in the world. This is precisely the situation of the hero of the novel of sensation; violence becomes a substitute for action. In the novel of sensibility, nothing happens; as people complain, there is no plot.

Once these discoveries had been made, however, in the recording of the perceptual field (i.e., of pure subjectivity), the novel could not ignore them; there was no turning back to the objectivity of Tolstoy or the rational demonstrations of Proust. The "objective" novel of Sarraute, Robbe-Grillet, and Butor is simply a factual treatment of the data of consciousness, which are presented like clues in a detective story to the events that the reader guesses are taking place. The very notion of character is ruled out. One way, however, remains open to the novelist who is interested in character (which means in human society)—a curious back door. That is the entry found by Joyce in *Ulysses*, where by a humorous stratagem character is shown, as it were, inside out, from behind the screen of consciousness.

The interior monologue every human being conducts with himself, sotto voce, is used to create a dramatic portrait. There is no question but that Mr. Bloom and Molly are characters, quite as much as the characters of Dickens or any of the old novelists—not mere bundles of vagrant sensory impressions but articulated wholes. Their soliloquies are really half of a dialogue—a continuous argument with society, whose answers or objections can be inferred. Mr. Bloom and Molly are pathetically social, gregarious, worldly, and lonely: misunderstood. This sense of being the victim of a misunderstanding dominates *Finnegans Wake*, where the hero is Everybody—the race itself. Nothing could be more vocal than these books of Joyce: talk, talk, talk. *Finnegans Wake* is a real babel of voices, from the past, from literature, from the house next door and the street; even the river Liffey chatters. We would know Mr. Bloom anywhere by his voice, the inmost Mr. Bloom; the same with Molly. Joyce was a master mimic of the voice of conscience, and Mr. Bloom and Molly are genuine imitations. This blind artist was the great ventriloquist of the novel. A sustained power of mimicry is the secret of all creators of character; Joyce had it while Virginia Woolf, say, did not. That is why Joyce was able to give shape and body—in short, singularity, definition—to the senseless data of consciousness.

The notion that life is senseless, a tale told by an idiot—the undertheme of twentieth-century literature— is affirmed again by Faulkner in *The Sound and the Fury*. Yet here, as in *Ulysses*, characters appear from the mists of their own reveries and sensations: the idiot Benjy, Jason, Dilsey the Negro cook. And a plot, even, is indicated for the reader to piece together from clues dropped here and there: the story of Caddy and the castration of Benjy and Quentin's suicide. The materialization of plot and character prove that there *is* being, after all, beyond the arbitrary flux of existence. Following Joyce and Faulkner, the imitation-from-within became almost standard practice for writers who were impatient with the fragmented impressionist novel and who had assimilated nonetheless some of its techniques. To use the technique of impressionism to create something quite different—a character study—seems the manifest intention of Joyce Cary in *The Horse's Mouth*, where the author, as it were, impersonates the eye of Gulley Jimson, an old reprobate painter down on his luck; the dancing, broken surface is only a means, like the muttering of an inner dialogue, to show the man in action, incessantly painting in his mind's eye as he boozily peregrinates the docks and streets. Something very similar is John Updike's *The Poorhouse Fair*, which is seen through the resentful hyperopic eye of an old man sitting on the porch of a county poorhouse. The sign of this kind of writing, the mark of its affiliation with the pure impressionist or stream-of-consciousness novel, is that when you start the book you do not know where you are. It takes you quite a few pages to get your bearings, just as if you were bumping along inside a sack in some fairy story; then you awake to the fact that the consciousness you have been thrust into is named Benjy and is feeble-minded or is a criminal old painter with a passion for William Blake's poetry or a charity patient whose eyesight, owing to the failing muscles of old age, bends and distorts everything in the immediate foreground and can only focus clearly on what is far off. Once you know where you are, you can relax and study your surroundings, though you must watch out for sudden, disorienting jolts and jerks—an indication that the character is in movement, colliding or interacting with objective reality.

The reader, here, as in *Ulysses*, is restricted to a narrow field of vision or to several narrow fields in succession. Now something comparable happens in recent books that, on the surface, seem to owe very little to the stream-of-consciousness tradition and to take no interest in the mechanics of perception or the field of vision as such. I mean such books as *Augie March, Henderson the Rain King, The Catcher in the Rye, Lolita,* and two of my own novels, *The Groves of Academe* and *A Charmed Life.* These books are impersonations, ventriloquial acts; the author, like some prankster on the telephone, is speaking in an assumed voice—high or deep, hollow or falsetto, but in any case not his own. He is imitating the voice of Augie or of Holden Caulfield and the book is written in Augie's or Holden's "style." The style is the man (or the boy), and the author, pretending to be Augie or Holden or Humbert Humbert, remains "in character" throughout the book, unless he shifts to another style, that is, to another character. These books, in short, are dramatic monologues or series of dramatic monologues. The reader, tuned in, is left in no doubt as to where he is physically, and yet in many of these books he finds himself puzzled by the very vocal consciousness he has entered: is it good or bad, impartial or biased? Can it be trusted as Huck Finn or Marcel or David Copperfield could be trusted? He senses the author, cramped inside the character like a contortionist in a box, and suspects (often rightly) some trick. In short, it is not all straight shooting, as it was with the old novelists.

This is not a defect, yet it points to the defects of the method, which can be summed up as a lack of straightforwardness. There is something burglarious about these silent entries into a private and alien conscious-ness. Or so I feel when I do it myself. It is exhilarating but not altogether honest to make believe I am a devious red-haired man professor with bad breath and bits of toilet paper on his face, to talk under my breath his sibilant, vindictive thought-language and draw his pale lips tightly across my teeth. "So *this* is how the world looks to a man like that!" I can say to myself, awestruck, and so, I expect, John Updike, twenty-five years old, must have felt when he discovered what it felt like to be an old pauper with loosened eye-muscles sitting on a poorhouse porch. But I cannot know, really, what it feels like to be a vindictive man professor, any more than a young man can know what it is to be an old man or Faulkner can know what it is to be a feeble-minded adult who has had his balls cut off. All fictions, of course, are impersonations, but it seems to me somehow less dubious to impersonate the outside of a person, say Mrs. Micawber with her mysterious "I will never leave Mr. Micawber," than to claim to know what it feels like to *be* Mrs. Micawber. These impersonations, more-over, are laborious; to come at a character circuitously, by a tour de force, means spending great and sometimes disproportionate pains on the method of entry. I read somewhere that Salinger spent ten years writing *The Catcher in the Rye*; that was eight years too long. Granted, the book is a feat, but it compels admiration more as a feat than as a novel, like the performance of a one-armed violinist or any other curiosity. This could not be said of *Huckleberry Finn*; Mark Twain's imitation of Huck's language is never, so to speak, the drawing-card. In the cases of Salinger, Updike, myself, one wonders whether the care expended on the mechanics of the imitation, on getting the right detail, vocabulary, and so on, does not con-stitute a kind of advertisement for the author, eliciting such responses as "Think of the work that went into it!" or "Imagine a twenty-five-year-old being able to take off an old man like that!" One is reminded of certain young actors whose trademark is doing character parts, or, vice versa, of certain old actresses whose draw can be summed up in the sentence "You would never guess she was sixty."

Yet you might say that it was a fine thing for a well-paid writer in his twenties to know from the inside what it was like to be an aged charity patient. Very democratic. True, and this is a real incentive for the novelist of the twentieth century. The old authors identified with the hero or the heroine, a sympathetic figure whose dreams and desires resembled the author's own. *"Madame Bovary, c'est moi,"* said Flaubert, and no doubt there was quite a lot of Madame Bovary in him or of him in Madame Bovary. Allowing for the differences of circumstance and intellect, he could have been Emma Bovary; the stretch of imagination to encompass her circumstances and her intellect was a great step, of course, in the democratization of the novel, and the naturalists, English and French, pushed further in this direction, with their studies of servant girls, factory operatives, and of the submerged poor in general. Even James tried it with his poor little anarchist, Hyacinthe Robinson. Yet here, as in Flaubert, there is still the idea of a hero or a heroine—mute inglorious Cinderellas who never went to the ball; what separates the author from the hero or the heroine is fate or social destiny. Their souls are not alien. But for the writer today (the writer who has any interest in character) it has become almost obligatory not merely to traverse social barriers but to invade the privacy of a soul so foreign or so fetal as to seem beyond grasp. Take *Ulysses.* Molly Bloom is not a soulmate of Joyce's or a sister under the skin. She is as far removed from Joyce as you could get and still remain human—the antipodes. Mr. Bloom is closer, but he is not Joyce as he might have been if he were Jewish, an advertising canvasser, and married to Molly. He is an independent, sovereign world to which Joyce has managed to gain access. There is no doctrine of "sympathies" or a-touch-of-nature-makes-the-whole-world-kin underlying *Ulysses.* Or underlying *The Sound and the Fury,* where Faulkner explores the inner life of the mental defective Benjy—his own, you might say, diametrical opposite. Much of modern literature might be defined as the search for one's own diametrical opposite, which is then used as the point-of-view. The parallel would be if Dickens had tried to write *David Copperfield* from within the sensibility of Uriah Heep or *Oliver Twist* through the impressions of Fagin.

Difficulty alone (though it always exercises a charm) does not explain the appeal of such enterprises for modern writers. There is something else—a desire to comprehend, which seems to be growing stronger as the world itself becomes more incomprehensible and dubious. The older writers, when they sought their characters from among the poor and the obscure, assumed that there was a common humanity and were concerned to show this. But it is that very assumption that is being tested, tried out, by the writers of today when they start examining their own opposites. I will give an illustration from my own work to show what I mean, rather than presume to speak for others.

When I first had the idea of the book called *The Groves of Academe,* it presented itself as a plot with a single character at the center. An unsavory but intelligent professor who teaches modern literature in an experimental college is told that his contract will not be renewed for reasons not specified but because in fact he is a trouble-maker; whereupon, he proceeds to demonstrate his ability to make trouble by launching a demagogic campaign for reappointment, claiming that he is being dismissed for having been a Communist and parading himself as the victim of a witch-hunt. This claim is totally false, but it is successful, for he has gauged very well the atmosphere of a liberal college during the period of anti-Communist hysteria that reached a climax in Senator McCarthy. No one in that liberal college stops to inquire whether he has really been a Communist because everyone is too preoccupied with defending his right to have been one and still remain a teacher; even the college president, knowing (who better?) that politics has nothing to do with the professor's being dropped from the faculty, yields as a professional liberal to this blackmail. Now the normal way of telling this story would be from the outside or from the point of view of one of the professor's sympathizers. But I found I had no interest in telling it that way; to me, the interest lay in trying to see it from the professor's point of view and mouthing it in the cliches and the hissing jargon of his vocabulary. That is, I wanted to know just how it felt to be raging inside the skin of a Henry Mulcahy and to learn how, among other things, he arrived at a sense of self-justification and triumphant injury that allowed him, as though he had been issued a license, to use any means to promote his personal cause, how he manipulated and combined an awareness of his own undesirability with the modern myth of the superior man hated and envied by mediocrity. To do this, naturally, I had to use every bit of Mulcahy there was in me, and there was not very much: I am not a paranoid, nor a liar, nor consumed with hatred, nor a man, for that matter. But this very fact was the stimulus. If I could understand Mulcahy, if I could make myself *be* Mulcahy, it would get me closer to the mystery, say, of Hitler and of all the baleful demagogic figures of modern society whom I could not imagine being. There was no thought of *"Tout comprendre, c'est pardonner"* or of offering a master-key to public events like *Darkness at Noon*. What I was after was something much more simple, naive, and childlike: the satisfaction of the curiosity we all feel when we read in the paper of some crime we cannot imagine committing, like the case of the man who insured his mother-in-law at the airport and then planted a bomb in the plane she was taking. Certain crimes, certain characters, in their impudence or awfulness, have the power of making us feel *bornés*, and in a sense I wanted to tiptoe into the interior of Mulcahy like a peasant coming into a palace. The question was the same as between the peasant and the king: did we belong to the same species or not? The book is not an answer, but an experiment, an assaying.

There is an element of the private game, even of the private joke, in this kind of writing—a secret and comic relation between the author and his character. An arcane laughter, too infernal for the reader to hear, quietly shakes such books; the points, the palpable hits (inspired turns of phrase, *trouvailles* of vocabulary) may altogether escape the reader's notice. Indeed, it sometimes happens that the reader is quite unaware of what the author is doing and complains that the style is full of cliches, when that, precisely, is the point. Or the glee of the hidden author may produce uncanny noises, such as the giggle or whinny overheard sometimes in *Lolita* testifying to who-knows-what indecorous relations between the author and Humbert Humbert. Joyce salted his work with private jokes, hints, and references that no one but he could be expected to enjoy, yet with Joyce it added to the savor. Lesser writers (or at least I) find themselves constrained by the naturalistic requirements of the method, the duty to keep a straight face, stay in character, speak in an assumed voice, hollow or falsetto, as though in a game that has gone on too long and that no one knows how to stop. There are moments when one would like to drop the pretense of being Mulcahy and go on with the business of the novel.

To return to the question of character. What do we mean when we say there are "real people" in a book? If you examine the works of Jane Austen, who, everyone agrees, was a creator of characters, you will find that the "real people" in her books are not so often the heroes and heroines as the minor characters: Lady Catherine de Bourgh and Mr. Collins, Mr. and Mrs. Bennet, Lady Bertram, poor Miss Bates, Emma's friend Harriet, the timorous and valetudinarian Mr. Woodhouse. These beings are much more thoroughly and wonderfully themselves than the heroes and heroines are able to be; the reason for this is, I think, that they are comic.

Or turn to *Ulysses*. Who would deny that Stephen Dedalus, a straight character, seems less "real" than Mr. Bloom and Molly, less "real" than his father, Mr. Dedalus? In what does this "reality" consist? In the incorrigibility and changelessness of the figure. Villains may reform, heroes and heroines may learn their lesson, like Emma or Elizabeth or Mr. Darcy, or grow into the author, like Stephen Dedalus and David Copperfield, but a Lady Catherine de Bourgh or a Molly Bloom or a Mr. Dedalus, regardless of resolutions, cannot reform or change, cannot be other than they are.

73

Falstaff is a species of eternity; that is why the Hostess's description of his death is so poignantly sad, far sadder than the pretty death of Ophelia, for Falstaff, according to the laws of creation, should not die. This was Queen Elizabeth's opinion too when she demanded his resurrection and Shakespeare obliged with *The Merry Wives of Windsor*. "Mortal men, mortal men," Falstaff sighs speciously, but he himself is an immortal, an everlasting, like Mr. and Mrs. Micawber who, when last heard of, were still going strong in Australia. The same with Mrs. Gamp, Pecksniff, Stepan Oblonsky, Monsieur Homais, Stepan Trofimovitch, old Karamazov. Real characterization, I think, is seldom accomplished outside of comedy or without the fixative of comedy: the stubborn pride of Mr. Darcy, the prejudice of Elizabeth, the headstrongness of Emma. A comic character, contrary to accepted belief, is likely to be more complicated and enigmatic than a hero or a heroine, fuller of surprises and turnabouts; Mr. Micawber, for instance, can find the most unexpected ways of being himself; so can Mr. Woodhouse or the Master of the Marshalsea. It is a sort of resourcefulness.

What we recognize as reality in these figures is their implacable resistance to change; they are what perdures or remains—the monoliths or plinths of the world. Pierre in *War and Peace* seems more real than Levin, his opposite number in *Anna Karenina*. This is because Pierre is fat—fat and awkward and wears a funny-looking green civilian hat at the Battle of Borodino, like a sign of his irreducible innocent stoutness. Thanks to a streak of cruelty or sarcastic sharpness in Tolstoy, most of his heroes and heroines are not spared a satirical glance that picks out their weak points: Vronsky's bald spot, Prince Andrei's small white hands, the heavy step of the Princess Marya. They live as characters because Tolstoy is always conscious of their limitations, just as he is with his comic figures; he does not forget that Anna is a society woman and Vronsky a smart cavalry officer—types that in real life he disapproved of and even detested.

The comic element is the incorrigible element in every human being; the capacity to learn, from experience or instruction, is what is forbidden to all comic creations and to what is comic in you and me. This capacity to learn is the prerogative of the hero or the heroine: Prince Hal as opposed to Falstaff. The principle of growth in human beings is as real, of course (though possibly not so common) as the principle of eternity or inertia represented by the comic; it is the subjective as opposed to the objective. When we identify ourselves with the hero of a story, we are following him with all our hopes, i.e., with our subjective conviction of human freedom; on the comic characters we look with despair, in which, though, there is a queer kind of admiration—we really, I believe, admire the comic characters *more* than we do the hero or the heroine, because of their obstinate power to do-it-again, combined with a total lack of self-consciousness or shame. But it is the hero or the heroine whose fate we feel suspense for, whom we blush for when they make a mistake; we put ourselves in their place from the very first pages, from the minute we make their acquaintance. We do not have to *know* the hero or the heroine to be on their side; not even a name is necessary. We are pulling for them if they are called "K." or "he." This mechanism of identification with the hero is very odd and seems to rest, almost, on *lack* of knowledge. If a book or story begins, "He took the train that night," we are surer that "he" is the hero (i.e., our temporary double) than if it begins, "Richard Cole took the five forty-five Thursday night." Or "Count Karenin seated himself in a first-class carriage on the Moscow-Petersburg express." We would wait to hear more about this "Richard Cole" or "Count Karenin" before depositing our sympathies with him. This throws an interesting light on the question of character.

In the modern novel, characteristically, there is little suspense. No one reads *Ulysses* or *Finnegans Wake* or *The Sound and the Fury* or *Mrs. Dalloway* for the sake of the story, to find out what is going to happen to the hero or the heroine. The chief plot interest in these books is to try to find out what happened before the book started: what was in that letter the chicken scratched up? what had Earwicker done in Phoenix Park? why does Benjy get so excited every time he is taken near the golf course? what is biting Stephen ("agenbite of inwit")? who, really, has been Clarissa Dalloway? The absence of suspense means that the cord of identification between the reader and the hero has been deliberately cut. Or put it a different way: the reader, as I have said, wakes up in a foreign consciousness, a bundle of impressions, not knowing where he is. The first reaction is a mild panic, an attack of claustrophobia; far from the reader's identifying, say, with Stephen at the outset of *Ulysses*, his whole wish is to fight his way out of Stephen into the open world, in order to discover where Stephen is and what is going on. And even when these fears have been quieted (Stephen is in a tower; he lives with Buck Mulligan, a medical student; his mother has just died), new fears surge up and always of a locative character, so that the reader is put in the position of a perpetual outsider, hearing what Stephen hears, seeing what Stephen sees but failing to get the drift often, asking bewildered questions: "Where am I?" "Who is talking?" "What's up?" An anxiety about location (the prime clinical symptom in the reader of the modern novel) precludes interest in direction; in any case, the end is foreordained: nothing can happen to Stephen but to become Joyce. Stephen is neither subject nor object, neither hero nor comedian, but the bombarded center of a perceptual all-out attack; in this sense, *Ulysses* is a scientific study in the logistics of personality. And in science the only hero can be the scientist; the rest is data. The difference can be felt by a comparison with Proust. Proust's Marcel is still a hero, followed by the reader with suspense, to learn what will happen with his grandmother, what will happen with Gilberte, what will happen with Albertine—something more *can* happen to him than to become Proust. Marcel is a pure subject, despite the attention he pays to studying and analyzing his reactions; if the book is, in part, a reconstruction of anterior events, it is Marcel himself, not just the reader, who is trying to find out what actually took place before the book started, and this quest for certainty is itself a hero's goal.

In the old novels, there was a continual fluctuating play between the hero and the "characters," that is, between the world as we feel it to be subjectively and the world as we know it as observers. As subjects, we all live in suspense, from day to day, from hour to hour; in other words, we are the hero of our own story. We cannot believe that it is finished, that we are "finished," even though we may say so; we expect another chapter, another installment, tomorrow or next week. In moments of despair, we look on ourselves leadenly as objects; we see ourselves, our lives, as someone else might see them and may even be driven to kill ourselves if the separation, the "knowledge," seems sufficiently final. Our view of others, on the contrary, cannot but be objective and therefore tinged with a sad sense of comedy. Others are to us like the "characters" of fiction, eternal and incorrigible; the surprises they give us turn out in the end to have been predictable—unexpected variations on the theme of being—themselves, of the *principio individuationis.* But it is just this principle that we cannot see in ourselves. What is happening in modern literature is a peculiar reversal of roles: we try to show the object as subject and the subject as object. That is, can I be inside Professor Mulcahy and outside me? The answer is I cannot; no one can. There can only be one subject, ourselves, one hero or heroine. The existentialist paradox—that we are subjects for ourselves and objects for others—cannot be resolved by technical virtuosity. The best efforts, far from mastering the conundrum, merely result in the creation of characters—Benjy, Jason, Molly, Mr. Bloom, and so on—who are more or less "successful" in exactly the old sense, more or less "realized," concrete, objectively existent. Choirs of such characters make up the modern novel. What has been lost, however, in the continuing experiment is the power of the author to speak in his own voice or through the undisguised voice of an alter ego, the hero, at once a known and an unknown, a bearer of human freedom. It would seem, moreover, that there was a kind of symbiosis between the hero and the "characters," that you could not have the one without the others or the others without the one. The loss of the hero upset a balance of nature in the novel, and the languishing of the "characters" followed. Certainly the common world that lies between the contemporary reader and the contemporary author remains unexplored, almost undescribed, just as queer and empty a place as Dickens' world would be if he had spent eight years recording the impressions of Fagin or the sensory data received by Uriah Heep in the slithery course of a morning's walk.

Marvin Mudrick dwells on the distinction between history and fiction throughout his discussion because he uses it repeatedly to show how fiction is more philosophical than a verifiable record of the past. At the center of his argument is the assertion that the development of character, revealed by event and, in turn, influenced by event, is a most significant feature of the novel. In fact, a long narrative is as rich and resonant in complexity as the characters whose natures it depicts. Thus our greatest novelists, like Dostoevski in *The Brothers Karamazov,* can create a whole community of complex individuals who give us better insight into human weakness and strength than the real figures of recorded history.

character and event
in fiction

MARVIN MUDRICK

Here is a definition, from Webster's New Collegiate Dictionary, of the word "fiction": "1. A feigning or imagining; as, by a *fiction* of the mind. 2. That which is feigned or imagined; esp., a feigned or invented story. 3. Fictitious literature; specif., novels. 4. *Law.* An assumption of a possible thing as a fact irrespective of the question of its truth."

Or we may begin by considering what fiction is not. It is not, for instance, biography, which in its legitimate procedures we can safely say has nothing to do with feigning or imagining, or with the assumption of possible things as facts irrespective of the question of their truth. When somebody exclaims, looking up starry-eyed from a book on the life of somebody else, "It reads just like a novel!" his enthusiasm is the index of a hardened incapacity to take either mode seriously. The first criterion of biography is truth, and at the first sign of untruth—whether its cause seems to be the biographer's dishonesty, or his insistence upon fitting things in with Procrustean neatness ("just like a novel"), or his plain ineptitude at recognizing and arranging facts—at that sign the document before us ceases to be biography.

Moreover, what a man actually said and did—so seldom verifiable by the reader, so perishable in the oblivions of history—has a special preciousness that, ready as we are, to concede everything to fiction, we tend to undervalue. The biographer or historian who lies, to the extent to which he lies, casts doubt on the possibility of ever retrieving the sense of how it was to be alive—how life uniquely and quotidianly went—in any of the innumerable personal and communal pasts of mankind. Parson Weems invented an anecdote about a future General and President who said, "I cannot tell a lie"; and when the American boy discovered that the anecdote was itself a lie, he grew up to be the elder Henry Ford, who said, inventing modern America, "History is bunk."

What about the great biographies, however—those that we consider, in their scope and proportions and justness of illustrative detail, not only true annals of a life and time but works of art? How nearly is their greatness related to their truth? Suppose a scholar were to discover and demonstrate that Boswell's Dr. Johnson never existed, that his books were written by a committee consisting of Sir Joshua Reynolds, Edmund Burke, and Oliver Goldsmith, and that Boswell's biography is a stupendous hoax of the sort that a number of literary amateurs think they have exploded regarding the Stratford actor William Shakespeare. Or even that, though Dr. Johnson did live and was quite capable of such actions and assertions as Boswell attributed to him, Boswell's Dr. Johnson is in fact the ingenious and plausible hallucination of an uncannily imitative and spectacularly unscrupulous young coxcomb (as in any case Boswell was) who chose to lie his way to immortality. Certainly, *The Life of Johnson* would become a literary curiosity, neither truth nor fiction, rather like Macaulay's History; its interest for us would be inward toward the motives and aberrations of the author, not outward toward the actions and assertions that would—if the account were truthful—throw generous light upon the man and the time they pretend to represent.

Nor do we need to invent such a case. Ford Madox Ford was one of the most intelligent and gifted men of letters during the past century: he was a great editor, a sympathetic friend to most of the first-rate poets and novelists of his time, and a distinguished and prolific writer on a variety of subjects in a variety of genres. His numerous autobiographical pieces include fascinating and characteristic anecdotes about writers he did in point of fact know well: James, Conrad, Lawrence, Pound, and many others. Only, it is clear—from much other evidence and testimony—that probably most and possibly all of the anecdotes he tells are false, that at almost every moment he is arousing and baffling our expectation of truth, that not merely what he reports James or Lawrence to have said and done on particular occasions, but the alleged occasions themselves, are the product of his fertile and imaginative incapacity to recall and represent anything that actually happened. (Dr. Johnson—as recorded by Boswell! —has a definitive opinion on this sort of incapacity. "Talking of an acquaintance of ours, whose narratives, which abounded in curious and interesting topics, were unhappily found to be very fabulous; I mentioned Lord Mansfield's having said to me, 'Suppose we believe one *half* of what he tells.' JOHNSON. 'Ay; but we don't know *which* half to believe. By his lying we lose not only our reverence for him, but all comfort in his conversation.' BOSWELL. 'May we not take it as amusing fiction?' JOHNSON. 'Sir, the misfortune is, that you will insensibly believe as much of it as you incline to believe.' " Which is exactly what happens with fanciers of James or Conrad or Lawrence or Pound, who skim through Ford's pages looking for anecdotes they incline to believe.) Now it is noteworthy that, though Ford was also a novelist, this incapacity to tell the truth did not conversely amount to a talent for fiction; quite the contrary: the characters and events in his carefully constructed and beautifully written novels seem at length, not distinct substantial creations, but muffled cries for help, troubled pre-figurings of some truth he is trying to tell only about himself. The compulsion to lie derives, obviously enough, from an obsession with unpalatable truth; and, though both phenomena may properly engage the student of literary pathology, neither is related to the talent for biography or the talent for fiction.

Fiction is not truth; nor is it falsehood; nor is the talent for fiction a talent, as Plato suggested, for lying. "It is not the function of the poet," says Aristotle (and the word "poet" we may replace for our purpose, as Aristotle's description warrants, by the cumbersome but more general term "writer of fiction")—"It is not the function of the poet to relate what has happened, but what may happen . . . according to the law of probability or necessity. The poet and the historian differ not by writing in verse or in prose. . . . The true difference is that the latter relates what has happened, the former what may happen. Poetry, therefore, is a more philosophical and a higher thing than history: for poetry tends to express the universal, history the particular." And Aristotle is plainly staking off the province of what since his time has come to require a more inclusive name than "poetry" when he remarks that "the poet or 'maker' should be the maker of plots rather than of verses; since he is a poet because he imitates, and what he imitates are actions. And even if he chances to take an historical subject, he is none the less a poet; for there is no reason why some events that have actually happened should not conform to the law of the probable and possible, and in virtue of that quality in them he is their poet or maker."

So we may, on the authority of Aristotle, begin to supersede our sketchy and cautious dictionary definition by a fuller and more adventurous working definition. Fiction, for Aristotle, is the representation in language of an action which, whether or not it has actually happened, achieves its meaning and magnitude not (as an action in history or biography must do) by conforming to accomplished fact, by arousing and satisfying our expectation of truth, but by conforming to the law of probability or necessity. Fiction may be in prose or in verse, it may be comic or tragic, it may be narrative or dramatic or expository, it may be long or short; but it does not represent character or virtue or wisdom or any other quality directly—what it represents is any probable or necessary sequence of events that start from and arrive at: what it represents is a complete and self-sufficient action.

Now this definition, if we provisionally accept it, gives us our theoretical base of operations. Not only does it establish as generally, and perhaps as uncontroversially, as possible what fiction is, but it offers autonomy to each of the modes of fiction, and it does not exalt one mode above any other. As soon as the critic assumes that fiction is a direct representation of character, of qualities and virtues, then that mode of fiction which seems to him to represent most directly and most economically truth and justice, goodness and wisdom, will tend to crowd out all the others. The naive critic may prefer the drama or even the cinema, because in these modes he is confronted by "real persons," the very embodiments of qualities. And there are such brilliant exclusivist heresies as that of Yvor Winters, who has ended by refusing serious consideration to all modes of fiction except the short expository poem.

Perhaps the major difference between fiction in prose (short stories, novellas, novels) and fiction in verse (every genre of verse from the lyric to the epic) is that whereas in verse fiction the emphasis is strongly on the language that defines the action, in prose fiction the emphasis is quite as strongly on the action that defines the characters. In prose fiction the unit is not, as in poetry, the word, but the event—a fact that helps to explain why prose fiction so remarkably survives the sea-change of language even in bad translations (for evidence, look up some of the nineteenth-century English translations of Turgenev and Dostoevski still embalmed in Everyman's Library), and why almost no poetry, even narrative poetry, survives translation at all (look up any English translation of Pushkin's narrative poem *Eugene Onegin*, and then any translation of his novel *The Captain's Daughter*; or glance at any English "modernization" of that most novelistic of supreme poets, Chaucer). Fiction—as, having reached the point of distinguishing it from poetry, and by right of common usage, we may abbreviate the term "prose fiction"—fiction, like poetry and Mr. Eliot's Sweeney, "gotta use words" to talk to us; the words are the only visible structure of the fictional event, the event comes to us only through the words that constitute it, and doubtless the more precise the language —other things being equal—the more fictionally effective the event. Yet great fiction can survive, not only translation, but a measurable proportion of bad and dull writing in the original. One of the reasons for this fact —an embarrassing fact for admirers of fiction—is, of course, mere length: short stories are longer than lyrics, most novels are longer than dramas or epics; and just as an epic can have dullnesses (even Homer nods) that would sink a lyric, so a work of fiction of the mere physical bulk of *The Brothers Karamazov* has room for patches of bad writing that no epic could survive. A more fundamental reason, however, may be discoverable in the major difference—the difference in emphasis—between fiction and poetry.

In the beginning of poetry is the word; in the beginning of fiction is the event (and this hypothesis seems to be borne out empirically for working poets and novelists, as well as theoretically for critics). The word is particular and special; the event is less particular, at least to the degree to which it seems conceivable in different ways, susceptible to a variety of verbal formulations. Yet the formal and repetitive regularities of meter tend to generalize the event, as prose tends to fragment and particularize it. So that we may try to state the relation between language (a meaningful sequence of words) and action (a complete, causally linked sequence of events), in poetry and in fiction both, as a balance of opposing impulses. The action which metrical language defines is likely to be typical, general, thematically summarizable by aphorism and metaphor; the words of a poem must therefore be precise and special enough to establish, nevertheless, the individual force, the poignant singularity, of the action (as in two very dissimilar poems with very similar actions—Herrick's "To Corinna, Going A-Maying," and Marvell's "To His Coy Mistress"). On the other hand, the action which prose defines is likely to be a sequence of highly detailed and circumstantial events; the words of a work of fiction need, therefore, not be so precise and special (if indeed they give the impression of being *too* precise, too "poetic," they will overload and damage the particularity of the events); and the thematic quality of fiction, the sense of its general application to human affairs, comes, more indirectly, from the gradual accumulation of its particular events into a nexus of characters and human relationships—a "world." The poet moves, by way of meter, from the particularity of his words to the typicality and general applicability of his action. The writer of fiction moves, by way of prose, from words which must at least give the impression of not arrogating all right of precision to themselves, through the precise particularity of his events, to the typicality and general applicability of the world of characters and relationships into which his events ultimately cohere. One can make up lists of exceptions: Chaucer and Shakespeare, to mention only English poets; but this is only to say that the very greatest poets combine the virtues of poetry and fiction (nor do they manage to combine these virtues by writing short expository poems). It remains safe to say that the virtues of poetry are not necessarily the virtues of fiction.

Moreover, though both poetry and fiction "move," the fact that the unit of fiction is the event indicates that movement is a prime determinant in the nature of fiction. We may define a fictional event as the representation in language of any psychic or psychophysical phenomenon which is observed as a process rather than as an entity. To start with event, as the writer of fiction does, is to accept the obligation to observe as processes even those phenomena we ordinarily observe as entities: *i.e.*, persons and things. It is in the nature of fiction, then, to emphasize change and development: not, as in philosophy, in terms of principle; nor, as in poetry, through the ideogrammic summations of aphorism and metaphor; but change and development caught continuously in the act. It follows that ideally, in fiction, characters and events are indistinguishable; that characters observed as entities or as principles or as ideograms impede the fictional action; that events do not illustrate character, they are the media in which processes are observed in the act of individuating those continuously changing phenomena we call persons and things. All of which is not to say that characters may not be abstractly considered, or that they may not in some special ways transcend the events that constitute them.

Yet fictional events are combinations of words; and the dependence of fiction on language remains so slippery and equivocal an issue as to exasperate poets and those critics who are committed to poetry. The lightning of fiction seems to strike between events and characters, and the fact that it must be conducted through an atmosphere of language will not soothe the partisans of poetry. Not that they do not have their favorite novelists. They do; and the novelists are those who are claimed to be capable of handling language with extraordinary precision, subtlety, economy, virtuosity, mastery—what you will by way of compliment. One name that turns up often is Conrad (who also is capable of handling language, now and then, as a *bad* poet handles it). But the name that recurs like incense and prayer is Henry James.

The arguments about James continue, and on neither side do they appear conclusive. It is (to use an uncritical word) suspicious that his most eminent and most nearly convincing admirers are those men of letters— critics and poets—who make clear that their first devotion is to poetry, and that they extend this devotion to James because they find him the novelist who writes almost as precisely, with almost as subtle a sense of the circumscriptive and evocative power of words and phrases, as the best poets. It is equally suspicious that much of the depreciation of James speaks with the voice of offended philistinism: a voice which insists that James is a snob, that he writes only about rich and idle people, that he does not know what "real life" is like, that his style begins in effeteness and ends in obscurantism, that to take pleasure in James is to retreat into the hermitage of mere art.

Still, without settling the place of James, a few additional remarks about his work may be pertinent to the notions of fiction being advanced here. The partisans of poetry, it will be assumed, agree that subtlety of language is no end in itself; that language is significantly subtle in proportion as it makes persuasive and valuable connections and discriminations between human phenomena; that the action which the language purports to represent must in fact be adequately represented, and of sufficient magnitude to be worth representing.

The Portrait of a Lady is usually regarded as one of James's best novels; by those admirers of James who dislike his last phase (Dr. Leavis, for one), it is often regarded as his masterpiece. The action of the novel is characteristically Jamesian, and in its outline certainly of sufficient dignity and magnitude: the awakening of a charming and ingenuous American girl to saddened self-knowledge, to a kind of unpracticeable wisdom, by her giving herself in marriage to that immemorial American dream of corruption, the worldly European (or Europeanized) fortune-hunter. The novel is written with all the affectionate evocation of locale, and of the varied de-

85

tails of cultivated human behavior, that James excels at; it savors its enormous length, proceeding with a majestic deliberateness of documentation in an intelligent and lucid prose that has none of the involutions and frequent archnesses of James's late manner; it is, as James himself declared, his first conscious and planned effort—and, it is fair to add, an heroic effort—to write a great novel.

Yet consider what James does at the very heart of his action, the awakening itself. One huge section of the novel concludes as the heroine, still all unknowing, marries the fortune-hunter. The next section opens several years later, and shortly we discover that the heroine now knows all. Do we wish to learn *how* she has come to know all, how her feelings of innocent idolatry were gradually worn away by evidence too compelling to ignore? Do we perhaps even believe that it is almost by definition the novelist's talent to show such events in the act of occurring? It is not that James has altogether forgotten his responsibility: soon after, he devotes a passage to the heroine's thoughts, in which we are offered some elaborately developed metaphors—a distant figure at an unreachable window, a serpent in a bank of flowers—to make up for the missing events. But the procedures of poetry will not necessarily work for fiction. And we are led, by this evasion of responsibility, to reëxamine the characters who come to us by way of these metaphors, as well as by way of the events that have preceded: a type of heroine, a type of blackguard, a type of gentle hero, a type of soiled woman—all of them unfolding their not very complicated natures, at enormous length, in conversation and conduct the high-minded subtlety of whose language often implies distinctions of a subtlety to be found nowhere in the text, and is liable to suggest an enervated triviality of human resources.

There are, of course, easier targets in James than *The Portrait of a Lady*. One might illustrate some of the curious uses of James's high-minded uneventful subtlety: to inflate simple antitheses that would be better reduced to aphorisms (as in "The Real Thing"); to divert our attention from the mere stupidity of a protagonist who, for the purposes of the story, must be seen as intelligent but obsessively insensitive (as in *The Beast in the Jungle*; to elevate beyond criticism the hysterical melodrama of cynical thrillers (like *The Turn of the Screw*) or of pretentious thrillers (like *The Jolly Corner*); to diffuse that reverent adolescent haze of words which James finds the ideal medium for his ideal women (as in *The Wings of the Dove*); to project that sort of pervasive and directionless irony which suggests less a capacity for discrimination than an incapacity for decision, or which may even suggest a meretricious Empsonian toying with language for the sake of implying any meaning the reader would like (a fault that is perhaps inherent in James's late manner). So that when fiction seems by its language to aspire to the precision of poetry, it may only be endeavoring to conceal the absence or the failure of its own proper powers.

The unit of fiction is the event. Dickens is a considerably less fastidious writer than James; but he is a better novelist because of his mastery of event, of movement and process. Jane Austen is quite as fastidious a writer as James, and the fastidiousness of her language is always in the service of her mastery of event. Moreover, although the unit of fiction is the event, although no writer can create memorable fiction who does not have the talent for conveying in language an immediate sense of the detail, the amplitude, the vividness, and the importance of specific human events, it is equally axiomatic that the fictional event does not terminate in itself, that its aim is to ascertain the shape and meaning of those individual lives, and of their relations with one another, that are created by, and with steadily increasing salience figure in, and may therefore ultimately be said to constitute, the total action. The distinctive talent of the writer of fiction is to make events; the mark of his maturity is to offer, by way of events, a community of individual lives in the act of defining themselves.

One of the recurring anxieties of literary critics concerns the way in which a character in drama or fiction may be said to exist. The "purist" argument—in the ascendancy nowadays among critics—points out that characters do not exist at all except insofar as they are a part of the images and events which bear and move them, that any effort to extract them from their context and to discuss them as if they are real human beings is a sentimental misunderstanding of the nature of literature. The "realistic" argument—on the defensive nowadays—insists that characters acquire, in the course of an action, a kind of independence from the events in which they live, and that they can be usefully discussed at some distance from their context. The purists have trouble with Chaucer, Shakespeare, and the great novelists, many of whose characters manifest an individual vitality which, though it incontestably springs from nowhere but dramatic or fictional events, seems so extravagantly in excess of any specifiable dramatic or fictional function as to invite further inquiry. The realists have trouble with almost all dramatists except Shakespeare, and with the writers of allegory, whose characters manifest only as much individual vitality as is necessary to suggest and to discharge their function in the events that beget and contain them. For our purpose, however, it is most

87

notable that the purists—who are, of course, the partisans of poetry— have special trouble with characters in fiction.

The fictional character is a fairly recent invention of Christian Europe. Whether people were—or are—ever as complicatedly distinguishable from one another as the great nineteenth-century novelists would have us believe, the requirement and acceptance of such complicated uniqueness in the literary representations of human beings is almost as recent as the novel itself. No doubt it has something to do with the Renaissance, or with that still earlier turning—as in Dante and Chaucer—from the vision of man as a community of souls bent on salvation, to the more prosaic (and therefore more novelistic) fascination with the details and diversity of man's conduct on earth; a turning that Erich Auerbach (in *Mimesis*) has described as it paradoxically occurs in Dante, in the very poem that is the enduring monument of the Christian view of man:

> In our passage two of the damned are introduced in the elevated style. Their earthly character is preserved in full force in their places in the beyond. Farinata is as great and proud as ever, and Cavalcante loves the light of the world and his son Guido not less, but in his despair still more passionately, than he did on earth. So God had willed; and so these things stand in the figural realism of Christian tradition. Yet never before has this realism been carried so far; never before —scarcely even in antiquity—has so much art and so much expressive power been employed to produce an almost painfully immediate impression of the earthly reality of human beings. It was precisely the Christian idea of the indestructibility of the entire human individual which made this possible for Dante. And it was precisely by producing this effect with such power and so much realism that he opened the way for that aspiration toward autonomy which possesses all earthly existence. In the very heart of the other world, he created a world of earthly beings and passions so powerful that it breaks bounds and proclaims its independence.

And one can observe this same process, the dissociation of the individual life from the divine scheme that has hitherto been regarded as containing and expressing it wholly, at a later and more acute stage in Chaucer and Shakespeare. Still, for the purposes of literary representation, the norm of humanity remained emblematic and typical man: Chaucer's contemporaries were Gower and Langland; Shakespeare's were Marlowe and Jonson. It is as if the individualizing power in Dante that Auerbach describes—the power to compel us to take a human being as valuable and interesting beyond his collective and what Auerbach calls his "figural" value—was given only to the supreme Christian poets; until, in eighteenth-century Europe, the emergence of industrialism and the general breakdown of the sacramental view of life made the dissociation virtually complete, and opened the sources of individual conduct to general scrutiny. Prose narrative is as old as Europe; but, with several astounding exceptions (the most astounding, *The Tale of Genji,* having been written in eleventh-century Japan), the novel, that vehicle for the minute and leisurely inspection of human events and individual motives, begins in eighteenth-century Europe.

It is not surprising that in its early exuberance the novel discovered not merely the individual but the freakish, the source of whose conduct is so disablingly individual, so stamped into the very physique, as to preclude choice or even consciousness. Three of the four major eighteenth-century English novelists are caricaturists; indeed, from this standpoint, Dickens himself is perhaps the best and certainly the most fertile eighteenth-century novelist, whose proper effect—an inexhaustibly self-generating sequence of grotesque events and characters—is occasionally spoiled by a Victorian infusion of melodrama and pietistic sentimentality. By the nineteenth century, however, except for Dickens, the first exuberance was played out, and had been succeeded by an interest in the representation of individual lives the sources of whose conduct suggest, more or less forcefully, personal consciousness and at least the possibility of personal choice and change. The eighteenth-century novel is characteristically episodic and optimistic; it travels and discloses, rather than develops. But Fielding's eighteenth-century definition of the novel as "a comic epic poem in prose" becomes within a century prodigiously inadequate; for if choice is possible, tragedy is possible; and the novels of Stendhal and Flaubert, of Tolstoy and Dostoievsky and Turgenev and Goncharov and Gogol, of Jane Austen and George Eliot (not to mention the *Clarissa Harlowe* of Fielding's great hostile contemporary, Richardson), are by Fielding's definition not novels at all.

In nineteenth-century fiction, the image of the individual personality emerges for the first time as an identifying feature of a literary genre. This point would be more obvious in English literature if it were not for such stunning anachronisms as Chaucer and Shakespeare; but they can also help us to make the point. The image of Chaucer's Pandarus or Pardoner, of Shakespeare's Iago or Falstaff, enforces such an impression of complex and unexhausted vitality, of other choices which might have been made and of other powers which might have been exercised, that the image survives the events whose effect and fulfillment it is.

The now universally scorned nineteenth-century commentators on Shakespeare discussed Shakespeare's characters as if they had had an historical existence independent of their dramatic function. Today we know that fictional or dramatic characters are only more or less efficient patterns of words subordinate to larger patterns; but it remains a fact that legends can gather round Hamlet as they gather round historical figures, and that a Volpone or a Piers Plowman or a Tamburlaine repels curiosity except in the work in which he assumes his own more specialized kind of vigorous life. In respect of their personages, Chaucer and Shakespeare and great fiction bear an immediate resemblance to history, to the recorded and recoverable past: the Antony we extrapolate from various historical accounts (as well as from two of Shakespeare's plays!) and the Antony of Shakespeare share a bounty of individual vitality that lifts them dolphin-like out of the element they live in; on the other hand, Shakespeare's Antony and Marlowe's Tamburlaine (for the comparison with Dryden's Antony would be too easy) are related only through the imposingly fulfilled function of each as the hero of a drama; and between Marlowe's thundering verse-reciter and the historical and legendary conqueror, there is almost no resemblance beyond the name. Fiction is more philosophical than history, says Aristotle; but it can also *be* history. Hamlet, or Raskolnikov, or Anna Karenina is, finally, not only a character in a play or a novel, but a datum of the past, a fact of history, an exemplar of the transcendence of the individual personality as well as of its immersion in events; a human resource like the great men of the past; history's double face of avoidable experience. "Those who cannot remember history," said Santayana, "are condemned to repeat it"; and the statement might be made about those who are indifferent to the human resources of fiction.

Yet, in the work of fiction, a character lives in and is an aspect of events; and events have their own internal cause, duration, magnitude, and consequence. The events of a work of fiction may be linear and unresonant: simply and clearly motivated, of sufficient duration and magnitude to gratify expectation and sustain interest, with clear and simple consequences. Pushkin's *The Captain's Daughter*, a novel written by a poet, is an instance: its characters are only perfectly adequate to its events, and its events are chosen and ordered with a precision and inevitability analogous to the precision and inevitability with which words are chosen and ordered in a poem. Narrative—which is the action of a work of fiction considered exclusively as a sequence of events—is complex and resonant in direct proportion to the complexity of the individual lives whose natures it suggests. The writer may, then, choose, as Pushkin does, to articulate an action that in the linearity of its movement scarcely requires characters at all. In a novel-length narrative, such a choice is both rare and difficult: narrative that proceeds beyond a certain length begins to suggest, or ultimately begins to require, characters of some depth and salience (even *The Captain's Daughter* is barely long enough to be called a novel). Narratives of short-story or novella length, on the other hand, are likely to approach the conditions of poetry for the reason of length alone: the shorter the work of fiction, the more likely are its characters to be simply functions and typical manifestations of a precise and inevitable sequence of events (as the aphorisms of a poem develop, explicitly or implicitly, out of a precise and inevitable sequence of words). In a few short works of fiction, the precision and inevitability of the events, and the typicality of the characters, enact an intense and grandly single-minded vision of man's destiny on earth: of which two great instances are Tolstoy's *The Death of Ivan Ilyich* and Melville's *Billy Budd*, perhaps the two greatest short works of fiction ever written.

Such short fiction, however, is still rarer than novels like *The Captain's Daughter*. Most great fiction generates interest through those of its events which establish a community of complex individual lives; through the events which dramatize the collisions between these lives, it achieves intensity. There are no Emma Bovarys or Elizabeth Bennets in short fiction: to establish a community in which such characters can be conceived to exist requires the time and space, and the uncertainty, of a novel. The partisans of poetry point out, quite correctly, that novels have nothing like the inevitability of poems: "Anything can happen in a novel." Character, in fiction as in life, is fate, but it is also potentiality. Elizabeth Bennet would not be so memorable a character if she did not appear capable of many things she does not in fact do, or if she did not do some things that appear not quite consistent yet somehow are acceptable and enlightening. Characters are consistent: they live through an ordered sequence of events; they have motives, and their conduct has consequences. But the great fictional character also appears as a kind of primal energy, a pretext and a vindication for startling and enlightening events, which themselves are not necessarily "lifelike" or "probable" or even "possible" but which realize human potentiality. Consistency sometimes expresses only the incapacity of the novelist to create such an impression of primal energy. Even Dostoevski, in *The Idiot*, weakens our impression of Nastasya Filippovna by making too direct and simple a connection between her earlier mistreatment by Totsky and her present suicidal capriciousness —a quality in beautiful women which, as Dostoevski shows elsewhere, solicits and will endure no single explanation, indeed no explanation at all if the character radiates the energy and pathos of the damned and illuminates, as Nastasya Filippovna does, all the characters fatally drawn to her.

To associate Emma Bovary and Elizabeth Bennet and Nastasya Filippovna is also to suggest a distinction within the genre of the novel itself. Both *Madame Bovary* and *Pride and Prejudice* are novels about a society. The former sardonically questions the basis of its society, the latter is genteelly mocking; but the assumption in both is that society determines and encloses the lives of its members, so that the happy ending of *Pride and Prejudice* is acceptance by a society, and the unhappy ending of *Madame Bovary* destruction by one. Nastasya Filippovna and Prince Myshkin, on the other hand, though they too exist in a recognizable society, more crucially exist in an arena of contending cosmic forces, as the figures of an epic do. *The Idiot* will have to be classified, then, under the apparently unavoidable hybrid term, "epic novel."

Ezra Pound defines an epic as "a poem containing history." We have already spoken of history in its sense of the recorded and recoverable past. If now we take it, as Pound does, in its other and more comprehensive sense of the total simultaneity of possible events, an epic novel is a novel containing history—a novel, that is, in which the characters not only function in the action but recapitulate the history of man in the cosmos. Lawrence's *The Rainbow* is a novel with history: its action not only engages and defines a community of individual lives, but measures the energy of these lives against the cyclical succession of the generations of man on earth. *War and Peace* is a perhaps too obvious instance: it has hundreds of pages of heavily interpreted history-textbook documentation, it represents a struggle of cosmic opposites under the image of a great war between two contending peoples; but much of its documentation, and most of its interpretation, are ill-tempered patriotic journalism somewhat disguised by occasional magnificent descriptive passages; and the ill-prepared, uneasy domestic epilogue allows one to suspect that Tolstoy would have liked, but was too intelligent, to accept imbecile domesticity as the merited goal of a cosmic hero's life. *The Brothers Karamazov* is a more useful instance. "The Legend of the Grand Inquisitor" recapitulates the history of Christianity in parable as Ivan and Alyosha and Father Zossima recapitulate it in life; opposing moral forces of cosmic magnitude rend the spirit of each of the major characters and make judgments and decisions, for the characters and the reader alike, terrifyingly difficult and absolutely essential. Fiction becomes history as it differentiates itself into persons, and as it synthesizes itself into a vision: Ivan Karamazov is history as a datum of the recoverable past; *The Brothers Karamazov* is history as a moment of full human consciousness. It may be unnecessary to add that epic novels are very long, and that no ordinary happy or unhappy ending under social auspices will do. An epic novel may end—all passion spent—in the exhausted but superearthly serenity of Alyosha Karamazov; or—as *The Idiot* ends—in tragedy; or—as *The Rainbow* ends—in the promise of a new cycle of history.

The epic novel is an effort to reachieve the sacramental view of life without evading or surrendering the modern secular fact of the complex personality. Society recedes, and the characters in an epic novel are accountable only to God and to the fullness of human experience (a formulation that brings to mind such bogus contemporary efforts as Camus's solemnly diagrammed allegories and Graham Greene's shrewdly calculated melodramas). In *The Idiot*, the action is of Scriptural boldness: Prince Myshkin, a Christ figure in appearance and in fact, is permitted by reason of his apparent innocuousness to penetrate a society whose ruling passions are greed and lust; and by his impossible example of Christian charity and his never quite understood exhortations to love, releases these passions from the meanness of their social confinement and allows them grandly to shatter two families, to drive a man to murder, to confirm one woman in a despair that leads her to choose a sacrificial death, to exasperate another woman into a sacrificial marriage, and to send the Prince back to the asylum from which he first came. The Prince practices Christian love and, since he is impotent in the secular society that can see divine love only under the image of sexual love, betrays two women who expect him to be not only God but man; he suffers from epilepsy, the sacred disease that gives him his shining instant of total understanding just before he collapses into the pit of the unconscious forces which he seems to have been pledged to reconcile and overcome; his strong and discriminating compassion for all who think they need him embitters and alienates each one, who will accept only all the Prince's compassion; he is an idiot, since only a person of inadequate wits can ignore the conventions and mean appetites of a secular society, in order to perceive those human abysses which no society can acknowledge, and for which no redeemer is in this latter age likely to be forthcoming.

In such a novel, in which human potentiality is simultaneously baffled and liberated, limiting notions of character and event will no longer serve. Each of the characters (except Myshkin) is a complex personality firmly committed to his society, and each (except, perhaps, the rather too conventional villain, Totsky) is a primal energy capable of as many incarnations as crisis exacts. Each of the events shows distinct and opposing personalities in collision, and each releases unsuspected energies that transcend personality. Even ordinary chronology will not serve: in the first twelve chronological hours of the novel, the number of crucial events and of the characters which they introduce and develop suggest a lifetime of experience, but with such an effect of prophetic intensity as not to violate or even to rouse our sense of chronological probability. Time is transcended because Myshkin is God in human events, creator and specific suffering personality, a thorn in the side of the commonplace human beings whom he transfigures and damns before they expel him back into the pure darkness of idiocy, of unmanifested personality. *The Idiot* is a supreme instance of history, of the simultaneous manifestation of a cosmos of human resources, which Myshkin evokes in order, compassionately and unintentionally, to destroy them. Characters and events become one: personality is the sum of human resources, which manifest themselves as the sum of human events; and the tremendous action which releases and vindicates these events is nothing less than the creation and destruction of the moral universe.

Fiction, seeking words only just precise enough, begins with the single contrived event. In its successful instances, it gives the ancient and always renewable pleasure of circumstantial and articulated narrative. In its great instances, it accumulates into images of persons more particular and more complete, more prodigal of energy and more indicative of human possibility, more instructively responsive to one another in a living society, than the figures of recorded history. In its supreme instances, it accomplishes a vision of history more comprehensive than recorded history, and realizing that apocalypse of man's place in the cosmos which is the substance of wisdom, and which philosophy—the love of wisdom—delights in contemplating.

Too many students of literature, urged on by their teachers, look at short stories to find some facet of the author's philosophy —the theme. This undiscriminating search for moral significance may leave the impression that stories are merely arbitrarily related bits and pieces of episode, description, and dialogue. In order to see the aesthetic whole, the essential unity of the various aspects of short fiction, Theodore A. Stroud advises that one try to discover the overall pattern which will explain why a story starts where it does, why it includes what it does, and why it ends where it does. Using such classic examples as Katherine Mansfield's "Miss Brill," William Faulkner's "Delta Autumn," and Ernest Hemingway's "The Short Happy Life of Francis Macomber," Stroud shows how one may find the unity in a story as a change in the chief character or characters. The character may, for instance, alter his attitude toward himself or toward others; he may proceed from ignorance to knowledge; or he may seemingly guide events only to do something which leads to his own destruction. There are, of course, stories which occasion a change in the reader, not the characters, or theme stories, but the most useful guide for unifying modern short stories is to discover an important change in character.

a critical approach
to the short story

THEODORE A. STROUD

Viewed in any reasonable perspective, all approaches to literature result in oversimplification, in that they fix upon one aspect as the most rewarding to explore. There are several questions which imaginative works seem almost inevitably to evoke; yet the very act of phrasing the questions exalts one critical position and places the others at a disadvantage. Furthermore, the critical approach that each teacher prefers is largely determined by accidents of personality or training. However disturbing this conclusion may be, it is almost forced upon us as our views are challenged on every side by colleagues whose intelligence and powers of discrimination we respect.

Unfortunately, whenever we seek to make students conscious of a variety of critical approaches, more difficulties emerge. Not only do we feel pressed for time, but we lack assurance of what would constitute a sampling of other approaches. If we persist, we tend to leave students convinced of the sterility of other views, since the insights worthy of a critical position come only to its enthusiastic practitioners.

Some of these problems, at least, can be solved if teachers can exchange interpretations of frequently reprinted stories in a form that can be used for class discussion, together with an explanation of the principles being applied. This study is a contribution to that goal. It is directed toward answering *one* of the basic critical questions about fiction—namely, what approach will most adequately explain why the author begins where he does, includes what he does, and ends as he does? I am convinced that most stories have a pattern, which, once formulated, permits us to appreciate how the parts fit into one whole. Such an inquiry seems logically prior to, and hardly less important than, any of the other basic issues. But my conclusions are tenable only if others find the analyses illuminating and the distinctions applicable to other stories.

At the present time "plot" has become a pejorative term, reserved for stories intended to evoke a simple kind of suspense. Prestige attaches instead to the stories which have a "theme," preferably discernible as a system of symbols and not as an explicit moral. Writers are viewed as determining what to include or exclude with the incalculable intuition of a somnambulist; all rational concern with unity and plot is dismissed as likely to mislead the readers. How did such a climate of opinion ever develop? Let us digress momentarily to speculate about the reasons.

Although the tale had been a prominent oral genre for centuries, it was only in the eighteenth century that an expanding audience gave its written form any real impetus. But what the period gave with one hand it took away with the other, for narrative literature (even the novel) steadily lost in prestige. The semantic parallel of this shift was that the word "poet," which had previously signified the writers of narratives (especially tragedy and epic), came to refer primarily to lyricists. The new genre recouped its fortunes, however, with the theory and practice of E. A. Poe, who promoted the idea of selecting episodes and words which contributed to a single mood and thus permitted the short story to compete with the Victorian lyric.

In a few generations the lyric began to emphasize images and symbols, and many short-story writers came to feel that Poe's influence was stifling the genre. Coincidentally several Russian writers were brilliantly illustrating the potentialities of the "primitive" folk tale, with its apparent looseness. Instead of returning to the nature of the narrative and reconsidering the implications of its form, the leaders of the revolt more or less consciously sought to prove that the short story could excel the lyric "at its own game"—namely, in organizing symbols to produce "pure poetry'" (the modern equivalent of Longinian sublimity). One can hardly censure them for seeking to usurp the throne of the lyric poet. But there is reason to suppose that the effort was rather sporadic, that most writers were at the same time conscious of the potentialities of narratives. Has this desire to excel the lyric poet resulted in stories without self-justifying parts? If so, the tendency is encouraged by critics who view the episodes of a "serious" story as little more than pretexts for distributing and even obscuring, a set of symbols. In another vein, Malraux insists that modern writers no longer consider the work as an object but rather as a "stake" signalizing the fact that some restless genius has explored a new area of the human mind.

In the face of such critical opinions, anyone should hesitate to generalize about the kinds of unity he expects to find in modern stories. Instead he may treat stories, lyrics, and plays indifferently as reflecting certain universal traits of language used for emotive purposes. Or he may focus on the "strategies" of the writers or on the system of impulses directing their choice of materials, as Kenneth Burke chooses to do. But Burke also observes that a work of art "survives as an objective structure, capable of being examined in itself"; and this line of inquiry is the one we have chosen to pursue. Variations in audience reaction and possible shifts in the intention of the writer seriously complicate any effort to treat the work as an artificial object. But the effort seems worth while if we can avoid the necessity, on the one hand, of lumping together such disparate genres that statements about their structure must be disappointingly vague and, on the other, of building hypotheses about the author's impulses upon our inferences about the work.

Obviously, what the reader sees first about a work is its words and then the minor organizing principles of syntax, of logical discourse, and of narrative episodes. Ultimately, he discerns its principle of organization, not in a relatively few half-concealed symbols scattered throughout the episodes, but in the power the total story has to affect its readers' feelings, not accidentally, but as human beings who share part of the author's culture. A story inevitably impresses different readers in diverse ways; it occasionally stirs up obsessions which paralyze the critical faculties. If not, we can distinguish between our accidental reactions to a story (Isn't this character like my mother? That incident reminds me of my neighbors! Such filthy language!) and the reactions which the writer had a right to expect (What is that character *really* like? What will happen to him next? How ironical to have that happen to him right now!). By further minimizing reactions to single episodes or minor characters in a story, we come to recognize the power of the story as a whole, as a mingling of some degree of anxiety and relief, pathos and frustration, amusement and self-satisfaction, or other compatible reactions. Perhaps the most striking reassurance that we have validly formulated the emotional impact of the story is the accompanying glimpse of its unity and completeness.

From this analysis of our impression, which may be viewed as the end of the story, should evolve a way of correlating the means, that is, the successive units of narration, dialogue, description, or commentary which combine to impart that unique pleasure. Primarily, the concern is with discerning the pattern in the work, why apparently irrelevant episodes are included, or some events expanded and others telescoped, rather than with an estimate of its excellence. But there is no escaping the implication that the pleasure natural to fictitious narratives somehow depends upon a feeling of completeness. If so, a story that defies analysis as a whole is artistically defective—whatever the merits of its various parts.

Many present-day stories seem disconnected or chaotic, but we need only to penetrate beneath the surface or the mode of presentation to recognize integrating principles. The occasional story which seeks to reflect the chaos of our times by means of utter irrelevancies has chosen a plausible, but probably a self-defeating, artistic principle.

In most of the stories today, as in previous centuries, the completeness results from the units or episodes in a story being combined to make credible a "change" in one of the characters. And all the episodes in such stories, upon consideration, appear to bear upon this change, either as weakening or as strengthening his resistance to becoming a person perceptibly different from what he was in the beginning. The changes may be roughly characterized as taking place either in the character's moral traits (the psychologists might call them "behavior patterns") or in his attitude toward himself or others. In previous centuries a third change, in the fortune or estate of the person, was rather commonly employed to interlink the events, but today such stories are largely limited to pulp magazines. This is not to imply that the central characters in serious stories today never face disaster, but the concern is ordinarily not with their ultimate prosperity or prestige but with what effect the threat will have on their personalities. Only rarely are adventure stories conceived in a form sufficiently complex to deserve analysis. Exceptions include such well-known stories as Crane's "The Open Boat" and Jack London's "To Build a Fire."

The other types of change present a bewildering picture, with all their overlapping and combination. Obviously, some change in attitude must accompany any moral variation; sometimes changes in sentiment have moral consequences, such as the change from antipathy to affection in conventional love stories. Some of the changes which serve to configure the incidents in a story may seem far less significant than the one from dislike to love, at least when they are viewed as phenomena in real life. But fiction has the power, as it constructs a microcosm in which the characters live and of which they form the ingredients, to endow with significance what would otherwise be trivial changes. If readers often fail to see this aspect of stories, it may be because their interests and training have led them to look elsewhere. Some idea of the pattern thus described may be gathered from the following analysis of Katherine Mansfield's very brief story, "Miss Brill."

At the beginning, Miss Brill is mildly happy because she is able to compensate for her lack of companionship by her faculty for personifying a fur neckpiece and her ability to participate vicariously in the activities of strangers she observes. Superficially, the story is merely one of her visits to the park on Sunday afternoons, except that she is disturbed by a fortuitous insult. Yet almost from the first, the details (composed of her observations except for one almost imperceptible action on her part) have an order about them which grows believably out of her imaginative reactions. We are permitted to witness how, with subtle logic, her sensations begin to coalesce in a new impression of her surroundings: the band performing showily under the influence of a larger audience (the opening of the season), her regular seat on a bench (reserved), her skill at converting random conversations into drama, and her unsatisfied craving to participate. Having thus revealed the traits underlying her behavior, her impressions evolve at an even faster pace: the spectacular nature of the kaleidoscopic crowds (a sharp contrast to the regular audience), the scenery viewed as a stage drop, the pantomimic interplay of the strollers (each with its appropriate musical theme).

Born of this flux is her notion that the park is a stage, and, instantaneously, that she and the "regular audience" are part of the performance. In her imagination, details facilely slide into place to carry out the analogy, and happiness overwhelms her in the impression of "belongingness." But a necessary concomitant is pride, betraying her into a momentary but positive commitment of vital significance. For this woman—expert at "listening as though she didn't listen"—is now so self-confident, so blissful in her delusion that her lonely monotony is dramatically purposeful, so pleased that a hero and heroine had materialized to confirm her interpretation of the scene, that she "prepared to listen" with a "trembling smile."

The crushing rebuff she receives is evidently accidental, but the minute episodes somehow appear to be sequential or related as cause and effect. Her every perception contributes to her emotional state and in some fashion promises her happiness, yet makes probable her final misery. It would be difficult to find a better illustration of how a writer should seek to make the episodes of his stories come about unexpectedly, and yet in retrospect seem probable.

Our initial awareness of Miss Brill's precarious balance between sadness and happiness prepares us for the concatenation of events which destroys that balance and permits the pitiful irony of the variant of "Pride goeth before a fall." Thus, at the end, even inanimate objects have the power to make her unhappy; she has been permanently relegated to the "dark little rooms or even—cupboards."

Are the critics who view this story as a "portrait in miniature" giving us any clue to its real nature? No matter how often they speak of it as a masterpiece, I maintain that they are not. If the story were longer, the critics would probably have assumed that it is organized by a "theme." For there is a tendency today among critics and teachers to find "themes" everywhere and, thereby, to credit the author with a desire to inculcate some form of morality. A typical example is the recent analysis of Hemingway's "The Short, Happy Life of Francis Macomber" as having for its theme "the final victory of Man over Death" (West and Stallman's *The Art of Modern Fiction*, pp. 260 ff.). The theme is said to be "adequately embodied in the action . . . and properly intensified by the other elements." But this view distracts us from the actual way in which the details of the story interlock to change a personality. Macomber's act of cowardice has consequences which evoke his inner resources to triumph over those who feel superior and thus ironically to bring about his death. But what he really triumphs over is his fear, not death; nor is death the cause of his victory, even though the particular form death takes here makes it a consequence of his victory, a confirmation, and a source of irrevocability. Other forms of death might be plausible—for example, at the claws of a wounded animal—but could never give a pattern to the events.

Before we consider the small fraction of stories that are actually organized as arguments, however, let us continue the analysis of what it means for a story to be organized around a change.

It must be recognized that several characters in a story may change incidentally, but ordinarily only one changes as a *result* of a concatenation of stimuli which constitute the parts of the story. Sometimes two characters are related as undergoing reciprocal changes; so that, for instance, the happiness of one requires misery for the other. Sometimes even more: Gorki's "Twenty-six and One" is a rare example of a story in which a large group is treated as a single personality undergoing a change. But further distinctions and qualifications are necessary if the reader is to identify the various pleasures such stories may afford. For, ordinarily, recognizing that a change is critical is tantamount to discovering the "plot." Only then do we rationally comprehend the emotions vaguely produced as we read the story for the first time.

One distinction concerns the possible variations in our attitude toward the central character. As soon as the other characters in a work establish the mores of his world, we tend to wish him good or bad fortune in varying degrees. Our urge to mete out punishment may be fervent, as toward Midge in Lardner's "The Champion," who victimizes defenseless and innocent people. An almost equally vicious character, such as Farrington in Joyce's "Counterparts," may excite relatively little fervor if his associates seem only slightly less vicious. The deserts of some characters are neatly balanced, or our good wishes are called for merely by their helplessness or immaturity. Ordinarily, our attitude is determined by what the character wants for others, viewed in the context of how others treat him.

In order to obtain the pleasure intended by a story, we must judge by similar signs how much weight to give the events which appear to the recipient as distressing or satisfying, insulting or complimentary. In farces, death is amusing; in some stories a look of contempt may cause permanent damage. Also we must infer his responsibility for what he does and undergoes, the amount of ignorance involved in his actions, from the quality of the little world he inhabits—not from real life analogues, unless the words so direct us. An instance in point is the occasional criticism of

Lardner's "Haircut" because the mentally deficient Paul is incapable of planning a successful murder. He is part of a world, however, in which cruel practical jokes seem inextricably connected with, if not exactly the product of, stupidity. How appropriate it is, then, that the weakest member of that society should somehow perpetrate the grimmest practical joke of all!

Another distinction in the character of "change" stories evolves from the relation between the central character and the events. At one extreme the central character is active, in that he primarily determines what is to happen next and seems to control even the accidents. In such stories the opening establishes the hero's goal and hints at some alternatives. And in his surge toward a goal, the central figure will either guide his fortunes safely through a crisis or shape the events ironically to bring about his misery or destruction. Such a quasi-tragic figure is Kendall (in Lardner's "Haircut"), who is responsible for the episodes which constitute his revenge and thus for inciting his own murder. Moreover, he is in the ironical position of having contributed greatly to the popular feeling in the town that Paul cannot be held mentally responsible for the deed. The barber thus comes to be the perfect narrator: he exhibits the kind of thinking that would have made it futile for Doc Stair to report the shooting as murder.

One further brief example: Once Davidson (in Maugham's "Rain") is conscious of Sadie's profession, he unmistakably shapes the events to his will. His self-destruction is ironically due to the fact that he eliminates from the prostitute all signs of sex (that is, the trappings and gestures against which a Puritan upbringing would condition him) and thus makes it credible for him to succumb to his sexual urges—at the very moment when he feels he has succeeded in eliminating a symbol of evil. Here again we may observe the appropriateness of McPhail as narrator, for in the first half of the story he establishes enough moral authority and objectivity to outweigh the powerful religious symbols cloaking Davidson's personality. That function accomplished, he lets Davidson take the stage as a tragic protagonist.

Incidentally, our comments on these two stories have for the first time raised questions about the function of narrators. If in this study no systematic distinction is made between the change being represented and the technique of representing it, the assumption is that one cannot discern the nature of a particular plot without partly accounting for the method of presentation. In fact, the validity of a hypothesis about the plot can often be tested by its implications for the choice of narrator or point of view.

In contrast to these "active" heroes, a far more popular type of short story is built around a passive character, to whom all the episodes *appear* as accidents. Here the events can no longer be linked as cause and effect; instead, they seem to be introduced to disturb the emotional balance of the central character and thus to facilitate a certain kind of change in him. In such stories the "hero" moves from ignorance to knowledge about himself or others, even though what he comes to "know" may be manifestly false. Since initially he has no goal, except some vague desire to be happy or secure, he obviously will not determine what is to happen next or do anything more than react to the situations as they arise. It is no accident that many such stories center around children or adolescents, for their receptive passivity is both credible and dramatic.

In analyzing such stories, we need to recognize the interplay of means and ends. The traits of the central figures serve as a means to make the "change" probable, but the "change" is a means to the total effect. The minor characters are means either to show the major figure for what he really is or to strip him of his defenses against the "change." Images, figures, symbols, may reflect what the character is becoming, or they may be that which he comes to know. Thus, for example, when the boy in Wallace Stegner's "Butcher Bird" is driven to see that the shrike symbolized all that disturbed him in his father, his attitude toward his father correspondingly changes from respect to loathing. His mother and the other characters serve to produce a susceptibility to the symbol. Again, in Robert Penn Warren's "Christmas Gift," it is irrelevant to ask whether the storekeeper is the kind of person who would give the boy candy (although the action should not violate our impression of the storekeeper). It is appropriate if it somehow has an emotional impact on the boy and contributes to his climactic change of attitude, implied by his action of giving candy to the doctor.

Kenneth Burke holds that whenever a story is essentially tragic, destiny seems to "bring about a representative kind of accident which belongs with the agent's particular kind of character." But why, it seems pertinent to ask, cannot incidents seem to "belong" in any story? Observe, for example, the opening of Steinbeck's "The Leader of the People": the hero is a self-centered boy, vaguely rebelling against authority and intensely bored with his surroundings. Isn't there something peculiarly appropriate about the accidental arrival of his grandfather, who exemplifies romance to the boy and boredom to his parents? My contention is that pattern is aesthetically preferable to random order and is ordinarily discernible in stories which we hear praised as having a character who "burst the bonds" of the plot. Furthermore, if irony is characteristic of the most satisfying patterns, it may be evoked by arranging the events so that one or more of them appear to reinforce the character's original state of mind, only later to undermine it. An apparent compliment, for instance, may seem to strengthen a hero's confidence in himself, only to have him recognize it later as hypocritical when his self-respect is in the balance.

This view may be further tested and illustrated by an analysis of William Faulkner's "Delta Autumn." Readers of the story tend to stress Roth's love affair or its racial implications and to view McCaslin as a mouthpiece for the author's views. But only when we recognize him as the passive central character on whom the events converge will the story cease to be a series of passages having merely symbolic or dramatic merit.

For the story to achieve its proper effect, we must first know what is to be changed. Thus the opening events lead us to credit McCaslin with such impressive virtues as integrity, patriotism, humanity, and prudence—all revealed in the context of a traditional hunting trip. At first puzzled by the way his grandnephew is being taunted, McCaslin is further upset by having Roth challenge him as once Socrates was challenged by Thrasymachus: "It's only because folks happen to be watching him that a man behaves at all." In his eloquent rejoinder, McCaslin momentarily becomes a surrogate for the Creator, full of compassion for erring men. His conception of a God of hunters forces grudging admiration even from his associates.

Later he lies in bed recalling how at the beginning of adolescence he was consecrated to this God in a quasi-religious ceremony and how later he rejected a family inheritance as a protest against the sins of his society. Gradually the years have freed him from that bitterness and from physical passion as well; and now he achieves an Olympian detachment in his reflections on "this puny evanescent clutter of human sojourn."

But of such thoughts is fashioned the sin of pride. The term "hubris" might be preferable, for the attitude springs from real virtues. His feeling of righteous indignation toward Roth for his affair with a Negro woman deserves our approbation. But a few hours later when she mysteriously arrives, the feeling betrays him into assuming that she is a culprit bound over to his judgment. It makes him incapable of realizing that, symbolically, she is a doe come voluntarily to participate in a perverted version of his own "religious ceremony": there can be no other plausible explanation if she scorns the money and has no delusions about Roth's marrying her. She admits her guilt readily, then regains the initiative by charging

McCaslin with having caused Roth's moral degeneration. A moment later McCaslin is catapulted by his horror of miscegenation into senile bitterness, into the gift-bribe of the hunting horn, and into advice worthy of Roth himself. Momentarily, at least, his belief in the inherent dignity of the Negro is undermined by his passion. At this point here triumph is complete, and she expresses it magnificently: "Old man, have you lived so long and forgotten so much that you don't even remember anything you ever knew or felt or even heard about love?" The irony is that he *had* known the night before when he was speaking to the hunters: ". . . at that instant the two of them [man and woman] together were God."

How much he suffers for having denied love and thus having betrayed his deepest religious convictions is revealed by indirection in the final paragraphs. Twice we have phrases suggesting a kind of death (with "grieving rain" outside) and reminding us of Roth's insult: "Where have you been all the time you were dead?" But the most significant inferences about his mood of self-hatred are to be drawn from the italicized jeremiad. The passage restates a topic frequently in his thoughts the day before, but now he pronounces judgment with such intensity as to imply that he includes himself in the total depravity of what God created. Thus, at the end, when the hunters are hurrying to conceal Roth's latest crime of doe-killing, we are hardly surprised to see McCaslin recognize this symbolic confirmation but remain inert. Literally and symbolically, he has made his last hunting trip.

One final illustration of a "change" story deserves inclusion because it exhibits how neatly one symbol may give the episodes of a story almost an organic synthesis. In Dorothy Parker's "Big Blonde," a widely reprinted story, the author makes no pretense to subtlety in establishing the character of Hazel as vain, subnormal, and craving social approval. Even the events are blurred in telling to resemble their impress on her mind. But one incident is significantly not blurred: ". . . a big, scarred horse pulling a rickety express wagon crashed to his knees before her. The driver swore and screamed and lashed the beast insanely, bringing the whip back over his shoulder for every blow, while the horse struggled to get a footing on the slippery asphalt. A group gathered and watched with interest." Even with her imperfect grasp of reality, she dimly realizes that the incident is symbolic. And with the failure of her suicide attempt, the realization of her true status becomes complete: she at last identifies herself with "a long parade of weary horses and shivering beggars, and all beaten, driven, stumbling things." To anyone interested in part-whole relationships, the

105

lashing she witnesses is far more than a figurative hint of the narrator's attitude toward Hazel: one has merely to conjure up the implications of this symbol to grasp the unity of the parts, their mutual appropriateness. If she is equivalent to a draft horse, then this is the story of her becoming immeasurably weary as her vitality wanes, flinching at the very thought of pressing her feet against the ground. In this same context, all the men are drivers, their identity of no consequence. Even the physician is identified as a driver by his initial appearance on the scene with a mistress. And he is to be identified with the driver lashing the fallen horse to its feet when he "plunged his thumbs into the lidded pits above her eyeballs, and threw his weight upon them." The parallelism of the climax is inescapable: the driver deprives Hazel of her only means of escape.

Many short stories, however, are not organized around a change. We are justified in stressing this pattern chiefly because a search for it will often disclose an alternative one. Of the various possibilities, one might think first of stories in which the events almost cry out for a change in the central character, but none occurs; for example, Stevenson's "A Lodging for the Night" or Silone's "Mr. Aristotle." Another group would include stories which are hybrids, part essay, part fiction. An example is Proust's "Filial Sentiments of a Parricide," in which the narrator is stimulated by the ironic juxtaposition of a letter and a news story to speculate about the disturbing paradoxes encompassed by a human soul.

In still another type of story one character is central, but the change is in the reader, not the character. For the reader is confronted with the puzzling inconsistency in the traits of the character or is somehow induced to conjecture about the motives underlying his behavior. The narrator may carry the reader along with him from ignorance to knowledge, or he may merely collect the data from which the reader infers an answer. In either instance, we can establish this movement as a pattern only when it accounts for all the episodes and even for the choice of the narrator. Thus in Chekhov's "The Darling," a vegetative woman is oddly charming and self-sacrificing. At the very end she suddenly comes into focus as a psychological vampire because of the boy's complaint in his dream: "I'll give it to you. Get away. Quit your scrapping." Here alone can we find the explanation of Chekhov's selection of data: loss of a father, death of two husbands, departure of a lover, and acquisition of a "son." (Note how Chekhov almost systematically canvasses the possibilities of her relations to males.)

Somewhat comparable in form is Eudora Welty's story, "A Worn Path." From almost the beginning we become curious about the "long way" which this ancient Negro woman feels impelled to travel. At every turn we catch glimpses of her poetic hallucinations, her hypnotic determination, and her instinctive benignity and shrewdness, sharpened rather than blurred by her senility. The trip becomes a mysterious pilgrimage, and the traits of her personality will not fall into place until we learn her motive for this oft repeated trip. Out of his simple cynicism, the hunter who rescues her offers us a false but plausible lead: she "wouldn't miss going to town to see Santa Claus." This conjecture seems confirmed by her efforts to pocket the nickel he drops, so that only the fantastic quality that her consciousness imparts to the scenes keeps his remark from poisoning our anticipation. She arrives, and we are still kept in suspense by her senility. As she receives the medicine for her grandson, she acts to recall our suspicion of her cupidity. Then the suspicion is ironically reversed. The pattern of her personality revealed and even confirmed by her selfless use of the money, we rest content in our admiration, buoyed up by echoes of legendary quests—even the Holy Grail.

In a different category are the "theme" stories, the ones we can validly describe as being patterned in a certain way because of the author's desire to enrich our moral perceptiveness. Sometimes (but not nearly so often as many readers suppose) a set of symbols does actually body forth a moral concept. They may give the story an allegorical cast, as in Katherine Anne Porter's "Flowering Judas," in which the report of a nightmare reveals to us, if not to the heroine, how her rejection of *all* forms of love is a betrayal of the life-principle itself. (Note again the apparent exhaustion of the possibilities; this feature frequently appears in stories *not* patterned by a "change.") A vaguely comparable use of dreams occurs in Italo Svevo's "The Sparrows": in his waking hours the hero writes an apologia for his pointless existence in fables about sparrows but only in his sleep mourns his sparrow-like frustrations.

It is very natural and even profitable to extract some more or less explicit comment on human nature from a story and assume that the story exists for the sake of the comment. The result is often unfortunate, however, in that (1) the story is left a pastiche of arbitrarily connected parts, and (2) the writer is shown to lack ingenuity, for almost anyone could invent a situation which would more adequately support the thesis. How can a writer hope to convince us, for instance, that all men have their price unless his exhibit is a man shown as unlikely to accept a bribe?

And in a longer story this writer might well pretend to exhaust the possibilities: several persons of widely differing ages or estates must yield to bribery before the story "proves" its thesis. An effective illustration of how all men (represented by four men of varied professions), when Western civilization has blown itself up, will miss the culture unutterably more than the comforts is found in Van Tilburg Clark's "The Portable Phonograph." Similarly, in Peter Taylor's "Their Losses," three elderly southern women are introduced as representatives of a vanishing social class. The initial parallelism of their circumstances at first seems too pat, but it soon becomes appropriate for these three people, whose diverse ways of life are converging on extinction, to be traveling to or from a funeral. The friction generated by their being thrown together, as their train travels through scenes equally symptomatic of a decaying era, leads them to reveal their otherwise suppressed despair.

Categories other than the ones described are to be found, as well as various hybrids. But by means of these schematic distinctions, it should be possible to discern the unique pattern which accounts for the details of a story. Perhaps the teacher should again be cautioned about his concern with the moral intention of an author. The dogmatist judges all stories according to his own standard and tends to read a moral into any story he likes. Other teachers fall quite plausibly into the position that *any* moral concept will serve as the basis for good stories, so long as it convinces the reader of its sincerity. The writer's capacity to produce memorable characters and events depends, they imply, on the sincerity of his belief in a theme. Since men may dedicate their lives to a cause, however, and still not promote it by stories that "ring true," this view ends by substituting one mystery (What are valid signs of sincerity?) for another (Why is the work satisfying?).

Once the teacher can resist looking at the parts of a story as signs of the author's philosophy, or even of his sincerity, he must still develop a capacity for dismissing his personal concept of reality—that is, if he is to discern a pattern (or any defections from it). The world of the story may be ruled by sex—or be completely devoid of the sex drive. Neither frame of reference seems realistic, but either may become artistically necessary to the structure and its end product. Actually, if we may return to the opening distinction, it may be naïve to believe that people change or, on the other hand, to suppose that they have enough stability in their traits to make a change significant. The signs of change in flesh-and-blood persons are so fallible that any view whatever can be documented. In a world of fiction, however, the audience approaches the ideal status of knowing the truth about (1) the character's initial behavior pattern, with special attention to areas under fire; (2) his reaction to significant stimuli and their cumulative effect; and (3) any variations in his personality. That this information is often suspensefully delayed or gradually revealed is granted, but the complete story, with relatively few exceptions, permits trustworthy inferences on all these points.

Yet here is no intention of suggesting that readers should ignore questions of verisimilitude, morality, or any other issue which will enrich their social impulses or increase their understanding of human motives. My only contention is that, *whenever* the inquiry turns to part-whole relationships in stories, other issues are both irrelevant and misleading; for a simultaneous concern with structure *and* values will continue the impression that many serious stories are composed of arbitrarily related episodes, highly uneven in dramatic worth and symbolic significance.

language

Wendell V. Harris defends the traditional style (or "the assured style," as he calls it,) as a medium of communication that subscribes to the ideals of lucidity, conciseness, and urbanity. He then discusses three main factors responsible for the abandonment of the "assured style" in the fiction of James Joyce, Virginia Woolf, Samuel Beckett, William Faulkner, Henry Green, and others: first, the failure of the contemporary novelist to discover a standpoint from which life could be contemplated in any wholeness; second, the continuing shift toward the private and highly eccentric outlook of certain novelists (e.g., the stream-of-consciousness novelists); and third, the emergence of a new concept of realism that stresses the importance of the dark and depressing aspects of life (e.g., George Moore's *Esther Waters* and Thomas Hardy's *Tess of the d'Urbervilles* and *Jude the Obscure*). These factors, Harris concludes, have led to unprecedented ambiguity and obscurity in modern fiction.

style and the twentieth-century novel

WENDELL V. HARRIS

One of the most intriguing literary successes in recent years is that of Vladimir Nabokov's *Lolita*. Achieving far more than the comparatively brief period of popular currency which clever advertising men seem to be able to guarantee for almost any novel, especially one which has such obvious elements of naughtiness and sensation, *Lolita* was discussed not only in homes where shelves are burdened by the flashy covers of book-of-the-month club choices but in college classrooms, not only by the sensation-seeker and omnivorous novel reader but by the intelligent and well-read. However, the enthusiasm of the more judicious readers was generally qualified and the praise of the reviews ambivalent. The usual pattern was to record enjoyment of the novel while at the same time hedging by deprecating the perverse subject matter, or a thinness of substance, or perhaps Nabokov's apparent lack of seriousness.

A few critics went rather far afield in their attempts to account for what seemed to them the brilliance of the novel. In *Lolita*, says Leslie Fiedler, "Richardson, Mrs. Stowe, and Henry James are all controverted, all customary symbols for the encounter of innocence and experience stood on their heads." Further, the novel "is the final blasphemy against the mythical innocence of the woman and the child. . . ."[1] But most of the published evaluations contrive finally to point to the same general area as the source of its merit: its undeniably brilliant style. For, after all, *Lolita* represents perhaps the most cleverly written trash of the twentieth century—its trashiness deriving not from its detailing of perverse sexual desires, but from its complete lack of significance beyond the pleasures offered by its narrative style. There is much that is overwritten, as in the section describing the murder of Quilty, and the constant dependence on sexual metaphors, though perhaps at times justified by the kind of mind Humbert manifestly possesses, is often an indulgence either in sensationalism or puerility. Nevertheless, as a whole, the style established in the remarkable first paragraph is kept up fairly well throughout the book, and raised to a splendid level in the long central section describing roadside America. One can look back at almost any random paragraph, and the ease, fluency, and humorous aptness of the narrative will almost always be found appealing, rarely becoming either flat or distractingly overwrought. Consider for instance the paragraph which opens Chapter VIII:

> Although I told myself I was looking merely for a soothing presence, a glorified *pot-au-feu*, an animated merkin, what really attracted me to Valeria was the imitation she gave of a little girl. She gave it not because she had divined something about me; it was just her style—and I fell for it. Actually, she was at least in her late twenties (I never established her exact age for even her passport lied) and had mislaid her virginity under circumstances that changed with her reminiscent moods. I, on my part, was as naïve as only a pervert can be. She looked fluffy and frolicsome, dressed *à la gamine*, showed a generous amount of smooth leg, knew how to stress the white of a bare instep by the black of a velvet slipper, and pouted,

[1] *Love and Death in the American Novel* (New York: Criterion, 1960), pp. 327–328.

and dimpled, and romped, and dirndled, and shook her short curly blond hair in the cutest and tritest fashion imaginable.[2]

I cite the stylistic felicity of *Lolita* not because the novel's merits have been insufficiently recognized (on the whole they have been vastly exaggerated) but because its reception raises a much more important question than the determination of that novel's ultimate value—the question of what has happened to style in the twentieth-century novel that the appearance of a work whose merit is simply that it is well written should attract so much attention. One must at this point make clear what is meant by "style," make clear that the word is being used here to refer simply to the felicity of an author's choice and arrangement of words, and that the underlying assumption is that there is a delight produced by the apt phrasing of a thing which exists separately from, although of course it helps present, the significance of the thing told or described.

It hardly need be said that there exists no agreement on this or any other description of style. One common view is expressed by George Saintsbury: "Style is the choice and arrangement of language with only a subordinate regard to the meaning to be conveyed."[3] But an equally common view is that represented by John Middleton Murry's "Style is a quality of language which communicates precisely emotion or thoughts, or a system of emotion or thoughts, peculiar to the author."[4] The emphasis of the former is on our sense that the successful stylist has added an additional source of pleasure to his writing; the latter equates style with the exact communication of the author's thoughts and emotions. My own view allows us to have it both ways, arguing that when truly exact communication is achieved, when the phrasing is not merely adequate but perfectly adapted to the exact shade of meaning, enjoyment of the miracle constitutes a bonus, an additional delight.

Now clearly there are in one sense as many styles as writers, and in another perhaps only two—good and bad. It all depends on how many pigeonholes one wishes to number. This understood, one may point out that different as were the styles of the great nineteenth-century English novelists, part of the "superadded delight" in almost every case was the success with which those writers succeeded in conveying that they understood the world about which they were writing. Thus the greater portion

[2] New York: G. P. Putnam's Sons, 1958, pp. 27–28.
[3] *The Collected Essays and Papers of George Saintsbury, 1875–1920,* Vol. III (London: J. M. Dent and Sons, 1923), p. 64.
[4] *The Problem of Style* (London: Oxford University Press, 1922), p. 71.

of the important novels of the nineteenth century might very well be described as having been written in an "assured" style.

When one casts about for an example of such a style, the temptation is to cite the obvious, to choose from among Dickens' inimitably vivid character sketches (of Mrs. Gradgrind, the Reverend Chadband, or Mr. Dick, for instance) or James's careful dissections of a state of mind (one of the paragraphs delineating the exact shade of Strether's ambivalence would do nicely) of Thackeray's sweeping sketches (on how to live on nothing a year perhaps) or one of those balanced paragraphs of Jane Austen in which, as John Middleton Murry points out, "two quite different birds of aberration are beautifully dropped" [5] as clean satiric hits are scored on both sides of a social situation. But all such examples present us quite as much with the unique genius of a writer as with sheer stylistic mastery. For that, I should like to cite an example from one of Trollope's minor novels which, while it perhaps has a Trollopean ring, is nevertheless exemplary of the combined clarity, economy, and control we expect from the best nineteenth-century fiction.

> Sir Harry Hotspur of Humblethwaite was a mighty person in Cumberland, and one who well understood of what nature were the duties, and of what sort the magnificence, which his position as a great English commoner required of him. He had twenty thousand a year derived from land. His forefathers had owned the same property in Cumberland for nearly four centuries, and an estate nearly as large in Durham for more than a century and a half. He had married an earl's daughter, and had always lived among men and women not only of high rank, but also of high character. He had kept race-horses when he was young, as noblemen and gentlemen then did keep them, with no view to profit, calculating fairly their cost as a part of his annual outlay, and thinking that it was the proper thing to do for the improvement of horses and for the amusement of the people. He had been in Parliament, but had made no figure there, and had given it up. He still kept his house in Bruton Street, and always spent a month or two in London. But the life that he led was led at Humblethwaite, and there he was a great man, with a great domain around him,—with many tenants, with a world of dependants among whom he

spent his wealth freely, saving little, but lavishing nothing that was not his own to lavish,—understanding that his enjoyment was to come from the comfort of others, for whose welfare, as he understood it, the good things of this world had been bestowed upon him.[6]

There is a delight to be felt in the mastery with which Trollope draws the character of one who has inherited along with his property and position the feudal virtues appropriate to his station. The reader is given to know almost simultaneously that Sir Harry's talents and understanding are limited, but that his employment of those talents, and the benevolent cast of his understanding, are praiseworthy. The combined limitation and rectitude of mind of a man who keeps race-horses "thinking that it was the proper thing to do for the improvement of horses and for the amusement of the people" is perfectly established in the fourth sentence, a sentence which despite its simplicity repays further analysis. Part of its effect would disappear were the word "fairly" to be removed, as would much of the accuracy of the delineation of the mind of the country squire were the closing phrases to be tampered with: horses may be, are to be, improved, but the people may, seemingly at best, only be amused. One notes with appreciation also the contrasting connotations of the two uses of the verb "to understand" in the last sentence—the honorific in "understanding that his enjoyment was to come from the comfort of others," and the lightly pejorative comment on the capacities of Sir Harry's mind conveyed in "for whose welfare, as he understood it, the good things of this world had been bestowed upon him."

The reasons for the abandonment of the assured style are three. Perhaps the most important was the failure of individual novelists to attain to the larger vision (or if that seems to be putting it rather stuffily, the failure to discover a standpoint from which life could be contemplated in any wholeness, the failure to make the phenomena they observed wholly explicable to themselves). It is in this sense that "the style is the man" has its clearest meaning: the assured, confident, incisive style is the work of a man whose mind has attained those qualities for itself. Where these are absent, the hieratic quality disappears, to be replaced by tentativeness, frivolity, perversity, or, at best, undistinguished competence.

The second major cause of the deterioration of the assured style has

[6] *Sir Harry Hotspur of Humblethwaite* (London: Oxford University Press, 1928), pp. 1–2.

been the continuing shift toward the expression not of the vision which, properly developed, will be accessible and assented to by all (the writer as spokesman for mankind), but of the private, highly particularized and increasingly more eccentric outlook of an individual. The novel has therefore tended more and more to record the uncertain, limited, and at least partially erratic viewpoint of a "character" rather than the mature survey of a thoughtful and intelligent author. This contemporary interest in the point of view of the individual ego has been of course partially responsible for the increased use of first-person and especially stream-of-consciousness narration. However, although one must bear in mind that the style of first-person narrative is only indirectly that of the author inasmuch as it is a means of characterizing the narrator, one may still legitimately protest that placing the story in the mouth of a character does not relieve the author of his stylistic responsibility. If because of structural advantages he chose a narrator whose manner of telling the story does not in some manner add delight, he does so at the peril of limiting his readers to the connoisseurs of sophisticated form. Indeed, that the academically approved contemporary novelists are not relished by the vast public commanded in their own time by a Dickens or a Trollope is not unrelated to the irritating style of most current narration, whether in first or third person.

The third contributing cause was the rather curious interpretation of what constitutes truly serious literature which began to become noticeable at the end of the nineteenth century. Despite the opposition of Robert Louis Stevenson and others, the identification of serious intention with "unvarnished" realism and the further identification of "realism" with the exploration of the darker side of life can be seen growing from the time of Moore's *Esther Waters* and Hardy's *Tess* and *Jude*. The realists of the 1890s were attempting three things: the extension of the range of subject matter permissible in fiction, the avoidance of ingenious and complex plots, and the right to dwell on the tragedy and sorrow in the world.[7] None of these intentions is incompatible with a carefully wrought style, and I am aware of no realists who explicitly prescribed the use of pedestrian prose. Nevertheless, it cannot be denied that since about 1900, those fictionists who have devoted themselves to serious analyses of man's state and to pointing out man's errors and follies have tended to employ an undistinguished style, leaving to those who wrote lighter literature the cultivation of the fortunate turn of phrase. Thus it is that the delights of

---

[7] I have developed this point further in *English Fiction in Transition,* V:5 (1962), 1–12.

pure style are to be found in the twentieth century in such writers as Beerbohm, Thurber, De Vries, and Kingsley Amis. *Lolita*, we may notice, is also, despite its mordant satire on aspects of American life eminently deserving of censure, essentially a nonserious book. Devoted to setting before us the view of life of a sexual, moral, and cultural deviate, and most successful in the long section detailing the course of Humbert and Lolita's flight, with all the possibilities of social satire this opens up, it depends heavily on the picaresque tradition and is in essence a contribution to the ever-popular genre of rogue literature. Those who see it as a serious moral or philosophical denunciation are, I'm afraid, quite as naïve as those who believed Defoe's protestations of the moral intentions of *Moll Flanders*.

As the assured style disintegrated, a major problem for the serious twentieth-century novelist became finding the means of stylistically representing the complexities and dubieties which now seem to preclude any pretense to assurance. Unfortunately, despite the praise which has been accorded many a twentieth-century stylistic experiment, the problem remains largely unsolved, and writers, readers, and critics have in many cases been satisfied with what can only be described as so many substitutes for style.

One of these substitutes is an obvious and insistent preciousness, particularly observable among the women novelists, which all too often seems to strive to create the effect of narration by a person of unusual, not to say eerie, sensibilities. Take for example the opening sentence of Elizabeth Bowen's *The Last September*: "About six o'clock the sound of a motor, collected out of the wide country and narrowed under the trees of the avenue, brought the household out in excitement on to the steps." [8] Now the purpose of good descriptive style would seem to be either to make the thing described more vivid or to sum up, in evocative phrasing, aspects of a thing which the reader will recognize perhaps consciously for the first time, and rejoice to find so neatly captured. The passage above does neither—the word "collected" being particularly annoying since it suggests an agent who has done the "collecting," though manifestly none is present here. The word distracts from both the vividness (since the idea it conveys is extraneous), and from the recollection of how a motor actually sounds in a confined space. Little more functional is the description of the summons to dinner: "Strokes of the gong, brass bubbles, came

[8] London: Jonathan Cape, 1949, p. 13. For ease in documentation and to indicate the frequency in individual works of what I have called "substitutes for style," I have limited my examples to relatively few authors and works.

bouncing up from the hall," or that of the sound of Mr. Montmorency settling back in his chair: "Creaks ran through the wicker, discussing him,
then all was quiet." [9] Pleasant enough conceits perhaps, but do they not
suggest an overly strenuous attempt at striking description? The strain
which Miss Bowen puts on her metaphors and similes is at times more
than they can bear. "Gerald's straight, round writing had, to her imagination, a queer totter, like someone running for life in tight shoes." "He
watched her hand, on a tree-trunk, pick like a bird at the scaly bark." [10]
Were these similes charged with a larger, perhaps a symbolic significance,
they would be more readily explicable, though probably not even then
justified. But it is only by placing tremendous demands on one's ingenuity
that one can draw out (or is it "read in") an explanation of how the first
comparison explicates Gerald's personality or the second furthers our
understanding of Lois.

The same sense of exaggeration is to be deplored in a good many of
Virginia Woolf's figures of speech. Typical is the description from *To the
Lighthouse* of Lily Briscoe's reaction to a conversation with Mr. Bankes.
"Suddenly, as if the movement of his hand had released it, the load of her
accumulated impressions of him tilted up, and down poured in a ponderous avalanche all she felt about him. That was one sensation. Then up
rose in a fume the essence of his being. That was another." [11] Nothing in
the novel, in Lily's subsequent or previous actions, in any way explains this
feeling; neither does the feeling explain any of Lily's actions or seem of
much ultimate influence on her. Altogether, the figure is simply too highly
wrought for the sequence it describes. A few pages later occurs another
figure of the same sort describing Mrs. Ramsay's reaction to the knowledge that her Swiss maid's father is dying in Switzerland. "Scolding and
demonstrating (how to make a bed, how to open a window, with hands
that shut and spread like a Frenchwoman's) all had folded itself quietly
about her, when the girl spoke, as, after a flight through the sunshine the
wings of a bird fold themselves quietly and the blue of its plumage
changes from bright steel to soft purple." [12] The situation is not commensurate with the intensity of the simile; moreover, the simile evades rather
than clarifies the real sequence of thought and emotion Mrs. Ramsay is to
be presumed to be experiencing. The same disparity manifests itself at
times in Woolf's tendency to employ figures not merely exaggerated but

[9] *Ibid.*, pp. 31 and 44.
[10] *Ibid.*, pp. 223 and 261.
[11] New York: Harcourt, Brace & Co., 1927, p. 39.
[12] *Ibid.*, p. 45.

incongruous. A single example, again from *To the Lighthouse*, will suffice. Lily Briscoe's insight into Tansley's vanity is figured as the ability to see "as in an X-ray photograph, the ribs and thigh bones of the young man's desire to impress himself, lying dark in the mist of his flesh—that thin mist which convention had laid over his burning desire to break into the conversation." [13] No doubt any critic of ingenuity can explicate the passage, finding all sorts of significance in the metaphor, but nevertheless, does one in soberer moments really wish to defend the comparison?

One wishes not to be misunderstood; the criticism here is not intended to be ill-natured nor is it intended as an attack on Mrs. Woolf's work as a whole. There is a great deal to admire both in her analysis of life and development of a technique through which to present that analysis, but there remains the anomaly of a writer who could produce the superb effect of the second section of *To the Lighthouse* allowing herself elsewhere in the same novel such annoying stylistic devices.

Although the English writers in general provide the more extreme examples of pseudo-style, Eudora Welty represents the same trend in American fiction. She depends heavily on the grotesque figure of speech for her effects—figures which perhaps sort well with the grotesque characters she prefers to portray, but do nothing to assuage the vague feeling of talent gone mad which one occasionally experiences reading her stories. "Now the intense light like a tweezers picked out her clumsy, small figure. . . ." "There was effort even in the way he was looking, as if he could throw his sight out like a rope." "If desperation were only a country, it would be at the bottom of the well." "Two greyhounds in plaid blankets, like dangerously ecstatic old ladies hoping no one would see them, rushed into, out of, then past the corridor door. . . ." "The lady, having seated herself, smoothed down the raincoat with rattles like the reckless slamming of bureau drawers. . . ." [14]

But it is not only the feminine writers who betray what is ultimately either an innocence of or contempt for style. One of the most irritating of the better male novelists in this regard is Lawrence Durrell, who is capable of producing really fine prose as in the passage from *Justine* describing the midnight departure of Melissa from Alexandria. But Durrell commits in the same volume the most irritating offenses against style; even in the

---

[13] *Ibid.*, p. 137.
[14] *A Curtain of Green* (New York: Doubleday, Doran & Co., 1941), pp. 207 and 240; *The Wide Net* (New York: Harcourt, Brace & Co., 1943), p. 191; *The Bride of the Innisfallen* (New York: Harcourt, Brace & Co., 1955), pp. 56 and 51.

passage describing the farewell to Melissa one is annoyingly prevented from indulging in complete admiration by the final clause of the last sentence which unconvincingly compares the train to liquid pouring down the tunnel. One of the worst passages occurs early in the novel just as the reader is beginning to be fully entrapped by the atmosphere Durrell is weaving. Justine has brought Darley home for the first time and as they enter the house begins to call to Nessim. "We went from room to room, fracturing the silences. He answered at last from the great studio on the roof and racing to him like a gun-dog she metaphorically dropped me at his feet and stood back, wagging her tail. She had achieved me." [15] Whatever the temptation, here are a metaphor and a simile Durrell should have resisted strenuously. The relation between Justine and Nessim is hardly that of bird-dog and master; that between Justine and Darley even less that between bird-dog and prey; least of all is the atmosphere with which Durrell elsewhere seeks to envelop Justine enhanced by the ascription of canine attributes.

Henry Green is also frequently guilty of the overly ingenious and unfunctional figure of speech—I think little needs to be added to the bare citation of two passages from *Caught*. The first is a description of a mother-daughter relationship in terms of a botanical image. "For she mourned the fruit of her own body, what had, so to say, been grafted on her by Howells, but which in the fullness of time, when ripe, had dropped away alive, with a live life of its own she did not comprehend, to be grafted by a stranger with this helpless bundle. . . ." The second is a description of a Negro singer. "As she stood there, gently telling them in music, reflecting aloud, wondering in her low, rich voice, the spot light spread a story over her body and dazzled her cheeks to bend and blend to a fabulous matching of the mood in which she told them, as she pretended to remember the south. . . . The music floated her, the beat was even more of all she had to say, the colour became a part, alive and deep, making what they told each other, with her but in silence, simply repeatedly plain, the truth, over and over again." [16] This is not style but verbal license, appropriate perhaps to the attainment of the final step of the mystic vision but not to the performance of a blues singer, however inspired.

Another refuge, so obvious as to require no more than mention, is a penchant for symbolic or at least unnecessarily elaborate structural form.

[15] New York: E. P. Dutton & Co., 1960, p. 32.
[16] *Caught* (London: Hogarth Press, 1943), pp. 81 and 111.

We need not pause here over the cyclic process by which the recognition of the value of symbolism and careful patterning in fiction brought into being a generation of critics who elevated that value into a primary desideratum and thus called forth a generation of writers happy to oblige them by including increasingly complex matrices of symbolism in their work. That the existence of recognizable symbolic elements and structural complexities does not in itself guarantee the value of a work has become, I think, increasingly obvious, but I should like to point out a few examples of particularly meretricious structure.

We may return to Miss Bowen's *The Last September* for obvious examples of precious patterning. Most noticeable are the chapter headings: "The *Arrival* of Mr. and Mrs. Montmorency," "The *Visit* of Miss Norton," "The *Departure* of Gerald" (italics mine). Arrival-Visit-Departure: clever, but, despite the sort of point which the professional explicator is enabled to make concerning the book's undeniable chronicling of the arrival and departure of a season, or a young man, or a girl's love, or a "last September," essentially meaningless. Similarly precious is the link between the penultimate paragraph and the opening one: the first beginning with the sound of an arriving automobile, the final but one closing on the receding sound of the destroyers' automobile. Further, to balance the "collecting" of the earlier car's sound, the "sound of the last car widened." Again clever, painstaking, and a good example of the kind of thing pointed out to admiring undergraduates as evidence of the subtle sophistication of contemporary fiction, but not in this case adding to the significance of the work in which it appears.

Equally annoying are the thin threads of symbolic allusion it has become customary to weave through the twentieth-century novel. A good example is Forster's over-use of the metaphor which provides the title to *A Room With a View*. The comparison of those whose lives open onto a view with those who exist closed in by four walls is in itself effective, but the figure becomes very much attenuated in being employed in the title, the first major incident, and at least two later crucial discussions. One has the uneasy feeling that Forster has tried to eke a novel out of a metaphor and a veil of sensibility—the novel lacks the solidity which can be given by what the nineteenth century knew as style.

Henry Green is particularly susceptible to this kind of thing. In *Back*, Green allows himself a series of completely adventitious comparisons between his hero's uneasy consciousness of being unfaithful to a woman's memory and Peter's three denials of Christ. To be sure that the allusion is not missed, Green invests it with a pretentious phraseology at the first occurrence: "So Charley bowed his head, and felt, somehow, as if this was the first time that he had denied her by forgetting, denied one whom, he knew for sure, he was to deny again, then once more yet, yes thrice." [17] The word "denies" is both ostentatious and irrelevant applied to the gradual weakening of Charley's memory of the now deceased wife of another man.

Another direction in which the fictionists of the twentieth century have fled precipitately away from the strongly evocative and happily apt style of the past—one which felt no shame in dealing in that which "oft was thought, but ne'er so well express'd"—is toward the eccentrically enigmatic and obscure, toward the expression which hints at a chain of thought or relationship unfortunately inaccessible to the reader. It is unfair to attack such passages out of context, where their meaning and relevance are necessarily even more cryptic, but I have attempted to avoid all misrepresentation in the following examples.

On the ninth page of Green's *Caught*, Richard Roe's day in the country with his son Christopher is being described.

> They threw wet sticks to see who could send these amongst the deer that moved off faster than they came up, merging ahead until these heraldic cattle were a part of the mist, unidentifiable in the rain. Christopher was light-hearted. His father had regrets. He wished it had all been less, as a man can search to find he knows not what behind a netted brilliant skin, the eyes of a veiled face, as he can also go with his young son parted from him by the years that are between, from her by the web of love and death, or from remembered country by the weather, in the sadness of not finding. [18]

Individual phrases here are of course susceptible of any number of interpretations—so many in fact that the central meaning of the passage, whatever it is other than the expression of vague regret, disappears into the mist of phrases. Note especially the pronoun "it" in "He wished it had all been less. . . ." Of course we are here again at one of those passages which any critic with a pretense to competence can at need annotate. The "it" may mean the day, or a feeling of portent, or the difference between the father's feelings and those of the son. Any of these, and myriad

[17] London: Hogarth Press, 1946, p. 93.
[18] *Caught,* p. 9.

others, can be defended in notes, explications, commentaries. Yet the fact remains that there is no undeniable referent for "it," and the reader will be well advised not to succumb to undue modesty and assume that failure to understand such a passage is evidence of a deficiency in one's sensibilities.

Halfway through the first section of *To the Lighthouse* as the girls Minta and Nancy walk to the cliff at the edge of the sea, we are provided with another of these apparently subtle and pregnant passages:

> What was it she wanted, Nancy asked herself. There was something, of course, that people wanted; for when Minta took her hand and held it, Nancy, reluctantly, saw the whole world spread out beneath her, as if it were Constantinople seen through a mist, and then, however heavy-eyed one might be, one must needs ask, "Is that Santa Sofia?" "Is that the Golden Horn?" So Nancy asked, when Minta took her hand. "What is it that she wants? It is that?" And what was that? [19]

Well! this would seem to be quite a profound revelation engendered by holding hands with someone of the same sex in whom one is no more interested than Nancy in Minta—if it could just be discovered what the nature of that revelation is intended to be. "And what was that?" indeed.

Eudora Welty, almost all of whose stories flirt with the realms of fantasy, has developed her propensity for the obscure phrase so completely that she manages often enough to puzzle a reader by the existence of a single word in an otherwise lucid sentence. For instance, the thoughts of the traveling salesman of "Death of a Traveling Salesman" are thus described: "But he had never seen this hill or this petering-out path before— or that cloud, he thought shyly, looking up and then down quickly. . . ." [20] Why a man in Bowman's state should regard a cloud "shyly" remains a mystery.

Finally, there is irony in the fact that the writers of the twentieth century to whom the admiring critic is most likely to give the name of stylists are for the most part those who have gone furthest in developing a manner of writing obscure, ambiguous, and demanding; in especial Joyce among the English writers, Faulkner among the American. The laborious ingenuity which produces such prose is far removed from the sense of

[19] *To the Lighthouse,* p. 112.
[20] *A Curtain of Green,* p. 233.

fortunate effortlessness concealing all labor of the writing table which was formerly the goal of the prose stylist. Once again, perhaps, it is advisable to put the present criticism in as accurate a perspective as possible. No lover of twentieth-century fiction could wish Joyce's *Ulysses* and *Finnegans Wake* or Faulkner's *The Sound and the Fury* unwritten—just as no thoughtful critic of the novel could expect or wish anything approximating them to be written in the future. They are brilliant works; each is also a brilliant *cul de sac*. None of the three can be regarded as opening new territory for the novel; on the contrary each simply claimed for itself a region at one of the furthest boundaries of the novel as it then existed and continues to exist. No further homesteads in those demesnes would have a *raison d'être*.

There is another point about which we should be clear: the difficulty and complexity of these novels are not such as are simply engendered by novelty. Critics have pointed out that nothing of Joyce or Faulkner seems as difficult today as it once did—to which the reply is that having been provided with sufficient keys, guides, commentaries, and explications, we are all able, by assiduous application, to see the central themes and significances of these works and the means by which these are wrought. But they are not fundamentally like those many works of the past which, seemingly immensely difficult at the time of publication, proved upon one's becoming habituated to their novelties quite as readily intelligible as the literature to which one had been previously accustomed. Does anyone foresee the day when a reader armed only with intelligence and culture can come to these novels and without external aid see clearly either the larger patterns or the smaller ingenuities?

Having made these points, we may return to the paradox that the quality of style should, with the strange exception of Hemingway, seem to reside almost wholly with the masters of a complexly baffling prose medium, and that there should be almost no candidates for the title of stylist who depend essentially on the qualities of lucidity, conciseness, and urbanity. Bearing this in mind one may counsel restraint and temperance in the awarding of palms. Fascinating, significant and worthy of study as Joyce's later works are, when an astute critic such as Dorothy Van Ghent comments at the end of her discussion of *Portrait of the Artist* that Joyce/Dedalus is going forward in search of the final epiphany which will reveal " 'everything and everywhere' as one and harmonious and meaningful" [21] one may demur that, granted this is the goal, the harmony and meaning achieved in *Ulysses* and *Finnegans Wake* are finally arbitrarily imposed and purely schematic—the great revelation must yet be awaited. Even had

[21] *The English Novel* (New York: Holt, Rinehart & Winston, 1953), p. 276.

Joyce given us a work which could simultaneously mean all things, it would vouchsafe merely a sweeping vision of that matrix of confusion to which we wish to bring unity, harmony, and meaning.

Samuel Beckett, in many ways Joyce's heir, seems to have, intuitively at least, grasped just this point, for in Beckett we have arrived at the far side of the attempt to incorporate "everything and everywhere" into a structure of meaning and find ourselves wandering in the limbo of poly-faceted unmeaning. It is hard to imagine a more terrifying statement of this situation than in Beckett's most famous work, for that which Godot withholds finally is not his presence but *the explanation*; until his arrival all conjecture must be inconclusive, all speculation incredibly meaning-less—and Godot does not come. Two denials coalesce in *Waiting for Godot*: the use of language will not in itself guarantee that any meaning is conveyed, and there will be no explanation-bearer. And it is, of course, Beckett's decision to limit himself to the portrayal of meaningless action in a meaningless world which makes possible the somewhat specious fascinations of his prose style. Consider for instance the following quota-tion from that diary of a dying, largely senile old man, the contents of which wholly make up *Malone Dies*:

> Or it is perhaps an evening in autumn and these leaves whirl-ing in the air, whence it is impossible to say, for here there are no trees, are perhaps no longer the first of the year, barely green, but old leaves that have known the long joys of sum-mer and now are good for nothing but to lie rotting in a heap, now that men and beasts have no more need of shade, on the contrary, nor birds of nests to lay and hatch out in, and trees must blacken even where no heart beats, though it appears that some stay green forever, for some obscure reason. And it is no doubt all the same to Macmann whether it is spring or whether it is autumn, unless he prefers summer to winter or inversely, which is improbable.[22]

Such a style would be intolerable if representing a clearly auctorial point of view, or even that of ordinary first-person narrative. As the product of the meanderings of mind of an old man for whom all meaning except private associations has largely disappeared and to whom the world has narrowed to the unintelligible series of events at Saint John of God's, how-ever, the reader is willing to accept and enjoy the linguistic ingenuity with

[22] New York: Grove Press, 1956, p. 58.

127

which Beckett combines slang, pedestrian statement, inflated rhetoric, parody, and occasional poetry. Nor have the fantastical and solipsistically eccentric characters who inhabit the comic world portrayed in *Murphy* any such claim to realism that we are troubled about the verisimilitude or even finally the meaning of their speech. The radical irresponsibility of Beckett's characters, symbolized most clearly perhaps by Murphy's yearning to enter the world of the certifiedly insane, absolves them from the responsible use of language, while the absurdity of their actions licenses the excesses of the narrator of those actions.

One finds even in enthusiastic critics at least partial support for the belief that what is most admired in Beckett is, after all, simply verbal dexterity divorced from meaning. Ruby Cohn's elaborate examination of his work in the 1959 number of *Perspective* devoted to Beckett concludes: "Some of civilization's most precious music is no more than that—improvisation upon a theme—and even if that theme is nothing, the improvisation may be, has been masterly." And in the same issue Samuel I. Mintz closes his even more ingenious and philosophically sophisticated analysis with the following reflection: "In *Murphy* we are treated to a rigorous and illuminating exploration of the Self, refracted through the medium of Cartesian ideas, in an energetic prose style that is ironical in tone and very witty. If all this leads to silence, it is the most eloquent way of getting there."

"If that theme is nothing"! "If all this leads to silence"! There is an undeniable fascination in a paradoxical employment of language which denies meaning to itself, but there is a danger in such tactics that is ultimately more than literary, for it constitutes a metaphysical denial of the adequacy of language for the reduction to order of man's experiences. Yet this ordering is, finally, the goal of literature, of all great literature, and though it is possible to say that Beckett's style exactly communicates the chaos he wishes to project, one is entitled to reverse the equation and point out that Beckett's work conveys with exactness nothing beyond an enveloping sense of the crumbling of all stable reference points. If language is ultimately the basic tool which man has at his disposal for the ordering of human experience, it must remain the great triumph of language, and ultimately of style, to be able to reduce incident, character, and detail to their proper and fitting places in the provisional order it creates. The means of achieving that triumph amid the ruins of all the earlier intellectual structures from which man derived direction and assurance is, for the twentieth-century novelist, still to seek. In the meantime, the Nabokovs reign.

128

Language, according to Richard M. Eastman, is one of the most potent instruments in the hands of a novelist. In the first part of this essay he analyzes, giving examples from Ernest Hemingway, Herman Melville, George Eliot, and others, the various elements of style in fiction: diction, sentence structures, syntax, and sound patterns. In the course of his analysis, he shows how a novelist may achieve certain effects by using specific or general words, formal or informal diction, simple or complex sentence structures. Highly coherent sentence structures, according to the author, are used by such traditional novelists as Henry Fielding or Samuel Johnson; whereas contemporary novelists like Virginia Woolf and William Faulkner have attempted to create the effect of stylistic fluidity by eliminating the organizing apparatus of punctuation and connectives. Style, argues Eastman, is cognitive, being a mode of creating and schematizing reality. It reflects a novelist's vision of life and is therefore fundamental to the craft of fiction.

style

RICHARD M. EASTMAN

Of all the novelist's instruments, language itself exerts the most pervasive control. Moreover, style offers its own pleasure and instruction. Every reader knows the immediate delights which rise sentence by sentence from the writing of a great talent who can make almost every statement the occasion of wit, of expressive grace, of deepening perspective.

Yet no agreement has been reached as to a method of measuring style objectively so as at the same time to show its artistic force. The following pages will put forward, with some attempt at system, the concepts most commonly applied to literary language, together with illustrations of the kind of pragmatic insight which can be reached with them.

Since words are the building material of style, one may begin with diction. An elementary distinction between *specific* words and *general* words appears in the following parallel versions, one of which comes from Hemingway's *The Sun Also Rises*:

A	B
Bill and I got down and went into the posada. There was a low, dark room with saddles and harness, and hayforks made of white wood, and clusters of canvas rope-soled shoes and hams and slabs of bacon and white garlics and long sausages hanging from the roof.	We got down and went into the inn. There was a room filled with stable gear, shoes, and preserved foods.

Version B is of course the general one; and it seems pallid beside Hemingway's original. Hemingway implicitly wishes to *make present* a scene from the Spanish countryside; hence he specifies "posada" instead of the generic term "inn"; he inventories the contents of the room so as to fill the reader's imagined picture.

Much the same function is served by *concrete* diction, which shares with specific diction its particularity of reference but specializes in details of sight, hearing, smell, taste, and the like, which address the bodily senses. Thus:

> Coming to the edge of the wood, they saw the sky in front, like mother-of-pearl, and the earth growing dark. Somewhere on the outermost branches of the pine-wood the honeysuckle was streaming scent. (D. H. Lawrence, *Sons and Lovers*)

Here the immediacy of the scene is developed by the colors of sky and earth, the scent of honeysuckle; they invite the reader not only to believe the scene but to partake of it as if physically there.

General diction, however unsuited to such ends, does have its own functions, which are to summarize, to abstract, to abridge. This passage from Hardy's *Tess of the d'Urbervilles* maintains general diction in order to convey the philosophical orientation of his heroine:

> Upon her sensations the whole world depended to Tess; through her existence all her fellow-creatures existed, to her. The universe itself only came into being for Tess on the particular day in the particular year in which she was born.

To specify Tess's actual birth-date, the names of her "fellow-creatures," and the geographical bounds of her "world" would destroy the metaphysical concern of the passage.

Diction may also be described by its *formality* or its *informality*, as it draws on the special vocabularies and usages of relaxed conversation, slang, dialect, or, on the other hand, of serious public communication. Huck Finn writes in the idiom of an untaught Missouri boy (the distinctly informal expressions are italicized):

> *Well, I went fooling along* in the deep woods till I judged
> I *warn't* far from the foot of the island. I *had* my gun *along* but
> I *hadn't shot nothing*. . . .

Mark Twain might have chosen the stately vein common in nineteenth-century authors:

> I continued my explorations through the virgin timber until,
> in my estimation, I was approaching the foot of the island.
> Although I had brought my fowling piece, so far I had caught
> sight of no game.

But the impact of a barefoot boy confiding in the reader would utterly vanish.

Formal diction has several important subcategories, denoted by the terms *technical, foreign, allusive,* and *learned*. At one point in *Moby-Dick* Melville discusses whales in the language of geology (the technical expressions are italicized):

> . . . All the *Fossil Whales* hitherto discovered belong to *the Tertiary period,* which is the last preceding *the superficial formations*. And though none of them precisely answer to any known *species* of the present time, they are yet sufficiently akin to them in general respects, to justify their taking *rank* as *Cetacean fossils*.

The whale, treated by Melville at almost every level of vocabulary, drawing upon special fields of knowledge from theology to geology, gradually acquires an enormous plane of reference, suited to its function as a large allegorical symbol.

Within a few pages of *Barchester Towers*, Trollope, in describing the expatriate Stanhope family, employs several foreign expressions to convey an appropriately exotic effect:

The *far niente* of her Italian life had entered into her very soul, and brought her to regard a state of inactivity as the only earthly good. . . . Her copious rich brown hair was worn in Grecian *bandeaux* round her head. . . . He had none of the *mauvaise honte* of an Englishman.

Allusive diction is illustrated by Hardy, who magnifies the personal drama of a country girl by associating it with the recorded wisdom of great Western writers:

"By experience," says Roger Ascham, "we find out a short way by a long wandering." Not seldom that long wandering unfits us for further travel. . . . Tess Durbeyfield's experience was of this incapacitating kind. . . . She—and how many more—might have ironically said to God with Saint Augustine, "Thou hast counselled a better course than Thou hast permitted."

Learned diction is exemplified by the reply of the scholar Edward Casaubon to his wife's eager questions during a wedding tour of Rome in George Eliot's *Middlemarch*:

"But do you care about [the Raphael frescoes]?" was always Dorothea's question.

"They are, I believe, highly esteemed. Some of them represent the fable of Cupid and Psyche, which is probably the romantic invention of a literary period, and cannot, I think, be reckoned as a genuine mythical product. . . . [Raphael] is the painter who has been held to combine the most complete grace of form with sublimity of expression. Such at least I have gathered to be the opinion of the conoscenti."

Casaubon's diction helps to show up his character, through the irony of his absolute but unconscious failure to give the *personal* reaction which his wife longs for. Instead, he fobs off on her the stock judgments of the art historians, being careful to inject such qualifiers ("I believe," "I have gathered") and such impersonal verb construction ("has been held") as to relieve himself of all responsibility for any personal involvement with Raphael whatever.

Language may also be described as either *literal* or *figurative*, according to the presence of metaphor and analogy. Conrad sets forth a moment in a terrible storm:

A big, foaming sea came out of the mist; it made for the ship, roaring wildly, and in its rush it looked as mischievous and discomposing as a madman with an axe. (*The Nigger of the "Narcissus"*)

The sentence opens literally, recounting the objective event, the advancing sea wave; then the madman metaphor both amplifies the violence of the wave and conveys the subjective panic of the sailors watching it. Thus figurative language can intensify immediacy; it can suggest emotional coloring. It can also express judgment, as in this bit of irony from *The Egoist*:

The great meeting of Sir Willoughby Patterne and Miss Middleton had taken place at Cherriton Grange, the seat of a county grandee, where this young lady of eighteen was first seen rising above the horizon. She had money and health and beauty, the triune of perfect starriness, which makes all men astronomers.

Drawing upon the scientific and religious overtones of star watching to describe the blunter masculine motivations, Meredith obtains a cynical contrast appropriate to a satire of manners. Finally, where figurative language is used pervasively (as in *Moby-Dick*), the reader comes to take all literal events as emblematic of general truths lying behind. A highly metaphoric style is the natural medium of allegory.

A first-rate novelist uses language which is inherently fresh; yet he may employ triteness for realism or irony. Sinclair Lewis has George Babbitt express himself in an arid rush of hackneyed good-fellowship:

"I was saying to my son just the other night—it's a fellow's duty to share *the good things of this world* with his neighbors, and *it gets my goat* when a fellow *gets stuck on himself* and *goes around tooting his horn* merely because he's charitable."
(*Babbitt*)

These clichés (the worst are italicized) have the authentic dullness of a complacent businessman, which is all the more oppressive because of the unconscious irony in which Babbitt trumpets his modest charity to a helpless stranger whom he has just given a lift in his car.

In sentence structure a different range of effects is to be found. The mere length of an author's sentences may give a characteristic feel to his

133

writing, as in Hemingway's clipped lines or the massive periods of Henry James. In Crane's *The Red Badge of Courage*, short sentences help to establish the urgent, fragmented reactions of a man confused in combat:

> The youth was not conscious that he was erect upon his feet. He did not know the direction of the ground. Indeed, once he even lost the habit of balance and fell heavily. He was up again immediately. One thought went through the chaos of his brain at the time. He wondered if he had fallen because he had been shot. But the suspicion flew away at once. He did not think more of it.

Later, as the youth gains assurance, the sentences lengthen; they attain a momentum and rhythm appropriate to sustained action:

> When the enemy seemed falling back before him and his fellows, he went instantly forward, like a dog who, seeing his foes lagging, turns and insists upon being pursued. And when he was compelled to retire again, he did it slowly, sullenly, taking steps of wrathful despair.

In pattern, sentences may be restricted to simple, direct-line structures: that is, subject-verb-complement, with few modifiers and only the simplest coordination. Or they may extend to highly complex units in which the information is organized into main, secondary, and tertiary structures, as in this example from Fielding's *Tom Jones* (the subordinated material is italicized):

> The person *principally assistant on this occasion, indeed the only one who did any service, or seemed likely to do any,* was the landlady: she cut off some of her hair, and applied it to the wound to stop the blood; she fell to chafing the youth's temples with her hand; and *having expressed great contempt for her husband's prescription of beer,* she despatched one of her maids to her own closet for a bottle of brandy, *of which, as soon as it was brought, she prevailed on Jones, who was just returned to his senses, to drink a very large and plentiful draught.*

To see what Fielding has done, one might recast the passage using only the simplest and most direct constructions (seven sentences for Fielding's one):

> The landlady was the only person to help. She cut off some of her hair and applied it to the wound to stop the blood. Then she fell to chafing the youth's temples. Her husband suggested beer, but she refused contemptuously. Instead, she sent one of her maids to her own closet for a bottle of brandy. Jones now returned to his senses. She persuaded him to drink a very large and plentiful draught.

This second version is efficient; it is easy to read; but its plain structures imply that the vision of the writer is very similar to that of the excited people he describes. Fielding's original opens with a climactic series of modifiers which identify the efficient landlady in utter contrast to the paralyzed crowd. Without pausing to begin a new sentence, Fielding then reports her actions directly and energetically. Her contempt for her husband is thrust into the middle of her busyness—a delightful commentary on the landlady's capacity to remain vain and rude throughout a Samaritan's errand. Jones' revival breaks into the sentence to synchronize perfectly with the landlady's magnificent efficacy. Fielding has not merely narrated a line of action; he has highlighted character, and he has maintained comic contrast, using every turn of syntax to refine his effect. The implicit vision is urbane, and in this urbanity—the product of style—lies the pleasure of the crude scene.

Highly coherent sentence structure is generally a mark of the older novelists, who often achieved a formal grace (as did Fielding and Austen), sometimes severe in its symmetry as in Johnson's *Rasselas*. This excerpt is spaced so as to stress the syntactical pattern:

> [The prince remarked]
> that if it was possible to be easy in decline and weakness,
>   it was likely that the days of vigour and alacrity
>   might be happy;
>   that the noon of life might be bright,
> if the evening could be calm.

Johnson's symmetery could be schematized thus:

> If A then
>   B;
>   B′
> if A′.

Since *Rasselas* is essentially a reflective essay on the nature of happiness, such calmly balanced structure seems appropriate both in tone and in its precise accommodation of Johnson's logic.

So smoothly does complex syntax do its work of assigning emphatic ideas to main structure and lesser ideas to minor structure, that the reader often takes the subordination for granted, as in the sentence:

> To earn my way through college, I robbed several banks.

Here the abnormal action—robbing banks—takes the main clause in accordance with the reader's customary expectations. But the subordination might be turned upside down:

> While robbing banks, I was able to take several college courses.

When the abnormal action is thus relegated to an incidental phrase, it takes on a shocking casualness. Such inversions of subordination allow the novelist to imply unusual valuations of experience, for either comic or serious effect. The device has seldom been used more tellingly than in Virginia Woolf's *To the Lighthouse*:

> [Mr. Ramsay, stumbling along a passage one dark night, stretched his arms out, but Mrs. Ramsay having died rather suddenly the night before, his arms, though stretched out, remained empty.]

Not only does the death of the main character fail to receive so much as one sentence to itself, but it appears in a participial phrase in a sentence already downgraded by bracketing. Since one theme of Mrs. Woolf's novel is the transcending of death, the eccentric subordination of the idea of death relates directly to her total concern.

Certain novelists have experimented much further toward the subversion of conventional syntax, using the effects of apparent incoherence:

> I hit him my open hand beat the impulse to shut it to his face his hand moved as fast as mine the cigarette went over the rail I swung with the other hand he caught it too before the cigarette reached the water he held both my wrists in the same hand his other hand flicked to his armpit under his coat behind him the sun slanted and a bird singing somewhere beyond the sun we looked at one another while the bird singing. he turned my hands loose. (*The Sound and the Fury*)

Faulkner eliminates the organizing apparatus of punctuation and connectives so that all actions and sensations come in a flat rush which seems true to the impotent fury of a youth trying to assault a stronger man.

Sound patterns make up. another group of stylistic effects at sentence level. The implicit rhythms established by short and by long sentences have been mentioned. *Rhythmic repetition of structure* is illustrated by Dickens, for whom it was a favorite device (the format is here adapted to the effect):

> Fog everywhere.
> Fog up the river,
>> where it flows among green aits and meadows;
> fog down the river,
>> where it rolls defiled among
>>> the tiers of shipping, and
>>>> the waterside pollutions of a great (and dirty) city.
> Fog on the Essex marshes,
> fog on the Kentish heights.
> Fog creeping. . . . (*Bleak House*)

Alliteration, or the repeated use of selected vowel or consonant sounds within a brief space, appears in this passage from Dos Passos' *Manhattan Transfer* (sample alliterations are typographically marked):

The Fog swirLed and FLiCKered with CoLors in ConFetti

about him. Then the trumpet FeeLing ebbed and he was

FaLLing through a black manhole. He STood STockSTill. A

policeman's BallBearing eyes searched his face as he paSSED,

a STout Blue column waving a nightSTick.

Sound patterns have several uses. They may be used onomatopoetically, to imitate the sound of the thing described. Rhythms in particular may speed or retard the forward movement of narration. All sound patterns work as organizing devices which bind together and stress the passages where they appear.

Although the analysis of style quite properly attends to such individ-

137

ual effects as so far described—and can hardly illuminate a novelist's skill without demonstrating his brushwork at selected points of the whole canvas—a full consideration of style must attempt to generalize the novelist's manner. From a page-by-page exposure to the language of a given novel, the reader will become aware, for example, of what may be called the narrator's *degree of presence*. The writing may seem so objective that the narrator seems barely on hand at all, except as an impersonal observer:

> On an evening in the latter part of May a middle-aged man was walking homeward from Shaston to the village of Marlott, in the adjoining Vale of Blakemore or Blackmoor. The pair of legs that carried him were rickety, and there was a bias in his gait that inclined him somewhat to the left of a straight line. (Thomas Hardy, *Tess of the d'Urbervilles*)

Or the narrator may join the reader as a flesh-and-blood companion who vivaciously reacts to his own story:

> When don't ladies weep? At what occasion of joy, sorrow, or other business of life? . . . About a question of marriage I have seen women who hate each other kiss and cry together quite fondly. How much more do they feel when they love! . . . Let us respect Amelia and her mamma whispering and whimpering and laughing and crying in the parlour and the twilight. (William Thackeray, *Vanity Fair*)

In between the dispassionate recorder and the engaged participant, another narrator may pose as a detached spectator drily commenting to the reader as from the next theater seat (the undertone remarks are placed in brackets):

> "Unhand it, sir!" said Mrs. Proudie. [From what scrap of dramatic poetry she had extracted the word cannot be said; but it must have rested on her memory, and now seemed opportunely dignified for the occasion.] (Anthony Trollope, *Barchester Towers*)

The narrator may also speak at a given *level of artificiality*, just as a man may appear to his friends in shorts, in business suit, in masquerade, in dinner jacket. Besides the common stances of colloquial spontaneity and literate formality, Western literature has developed certain traditional modes of address, each with its set conventions. Here Fielding adopts the lofty, ornate metaphors of epic poetry to obtain comic incongruity in describing an assault upon his hero's chastity:

> As when a hungry tigress, who long has traversed the woods in fruitless search, sees within the reach of her claws a lamb, she prepares to leap on her prey; or as a voracious pike, of immense size, surveys through the liquid element a roach or gudgeon, which cannot escape her jaws, opens them wide to swallow the little fish; so did Mrs. Slipslop prepare to lay her violent amorous hands on the poor Joseph. . . . (*Joseph Andrews*)

The stern prophetic majesty of biblical exhortation runs through the following passage of *Moby-Dick*, in which the narrator addresses the mast-watch who has been lulled into a narcotic oblivion:

> There is no life in thee, now, except that rocking life imparted by a gently rolling ship; by her, borrowed from the sea; by the sea, from the inscrutable tides of God. But while this sleep, this dream is on ye, move your foot or hand an inch; slip your hold at all; and your identity comes back in horror. . . . Heed it well, ye Pantheists!

Hawthorne takes the theatrical stance of melodrama to heighten the climactic moments of *The House of the Seven Gables*:

> At last, finding no other pretext for deferring the torture that she was to inflict on Clifford, . . . —dreading, also, to hear the stern voice of Judge Pyncheon from below stairs, chiding her delay,—she crept slowly, a pale, grief-stricken figure, a dismal shape of woman, with almost torpid limbs, slowly to her brother's door, and knocked!
> There was no answer!

To ennoble the sad yearnings of the heroine of *Sister Carrie*, Theodore Dreiser occasionally soars (or sinks) into the gorgeous strains of older sentimental poetry:

> Oh, Carrie, Carrie! Oh, blind strivings of the human heart! Onward, onward, it saith, and where beauty leads, there it follows. Whether it be the tinkle of a lone sheep bell o'er some quiet landscape, or the glimmer of beauty in sylvan places, or

the show of soul in some passing eye, the heart knows and makes answer, following.

From such matters the reader begins to infer a personality implicit in the narrator's language: a "character" with its own moral stature and its own emotions. Trollope describes the heroine of *Barchester Towers* in her maternal privacy:

> A regular service of baby worship was going on. Mary Bold was sitting on a low easy chair, with the boy in her lap, and Eleanor was kneeling before the object of her idolatry. As she tried to cover up the little fellow's face with her long, glossy, dark brown locks, and permitted him to pull them hither and thither, as he would, she looked very beautiful in spite of the widow's cap which she still wore. There was a quiet, enduring, grateful sweetness about her face. . . .

That the narrator dotes on the scene is clear from the good-humored exaggeration, "a regular service of baby worship," supported by such an endearment as "the little fellow." The narrator's description of Eleanor's beauty expresses his frank admiration for a wholesome unassuming woman. It is just this congenial common sense which sets the basic tone of *Barchester Towers,* directing the reader's sympathies to the people of simple heart and his tolerant amusement to the hypocrites and self-seekers.

Quite a different temperament pervades Dickens' description of Coke-town in *Hard Times*:

> You saw nothing in Coketown but what was severely workful. If the members of a religious persuasion built a chapel there—as the members of eighteen religious persuasions had done—they made it a pious workhouse of red brick, with sometimes (but this is only in highly ornamental examples) a bell in a birdcage on the top of it. . . . All the public inscriptions in the town were painted alike, in severe characters of black and white. The jail might have been the infirmary, the infirmary might have been the jail. . . . Fact, fact, fact, everywhere in the material aspect of the town; fact, fact, fact, everywhere in the immaterial.

The narrator's dry indignation at an inhumanly utilitarian culture is conveyed by the bitter juxtaposition of religion and ugliness ("pious workhouse"), by the extremity of statement ("You saw *nothing*," "*All* the public inscriptions"), by the hammering "fact, fact" of the final lines. In other novels Dickens could assume geniality, high spirits, tenderness; but the narrator of *Hard Times* is a grim prosecutor pressing an indictment home to the jury of his readers.

Style as just considered may be an index either of the narrator's personality or of individual characters whose speech and thought the novelist may stylize to reveal distinctive qualities of temperament. At a final level, style is *cognitive*—it is a way of organizing and creating reality; it reflects and extends the basic vision of life contained by the novel; thus it can be examined as evidence of the novelist's own values. The necessary stylistic analysis may well touch on nearly every concept mentioned. In Dos Passos' *Manhattan Transfer*, for example, the protagonist Jimmy Herf stops on a New York sidewalk, tired and perplexed (the passage is divided to show its stylistic phases):

> For a moment not knowing which way to go, he stands back against the wall with his hands in his pockets, watching people elbow their way through the perpetually revolving doors;
>
> softcheeked girls chewing gum, hatchetfaced girls with bangs, creamfaced boys his own age, young toughs with their hats on one side, sweatyfaced messengers,
>
> crisscross glances, sauntering hips, red jowls masticating cigars, sallow concave faces, flat bodies of young men and women, paunched bodies of elderly men,
>
> all elbowing, shoving, shuffling, fed in two endless tapes through the revolving doors out into Broadway, in off Broadway.

The present tense ("he stands") conveys the immediacy of metropolitan life, unpatterned by any retrospection. Once Jimmy Herf's mental and physical orientation is indicated, the passage becomes a flowing catalog of Herf's sights. Syntactically this material is hardly organized except as an atomistic plurality of phrases, as if to correspond with the weary confusion of Herf's consciousness. Yet his sensations do move through a significant progression, as can be observed in the diction. First Herf sees New York people grouped as classes: "softcheeked girls," "young toughs," etc. Then the human image refracts into drab anatomical fragments:

"sauntering hips," "red jowls," etc. Finally the body fragments dissolve into motions—elbowing, shuffling—which stream out into the final metaphor of two ceaseless tapes feeding in and out, out and in. This is Herf's vision—and since Herf's testimony is certified in many ways by the author —it is the vision of *Manhattan Transfer*: of a metropolis which dehumanizes its population, of an ant-hill culture without soil.

Two mealtimes in fiction will demonstrate the diversity of vision which style helps to make possible. Jake Barnes, the narrator of Hemingway's *The Sun Also Rises*, tells of a suppertime in Spain:

> The girl brought in a big bowl of hot vegetable soup and the wine. We had fried trout afterward and some sort of stew and a big bowl full of wild strawberries. We did not lose money on the wine, and the girl was shy but nice about bringing it. The old woman looked in once and counted the empty bottles.

Samuel Johnson describes the feeding of Prince Rasselas and his party:

> They thanked him, and entering, were pleased with the neatness and regularity of the place. The hermit set flesh and wine before them, though he fed only upon fruits and water. His discourse was cheerful without levity, and pious without enthusiasm. (*Rasselas*)

What can be inferred from these two accounts, so much alike in scale and menu? Evidently the Hemingway account comes from a narrator who prizes the elemental pleasures of eating and drinking. Dishes are enumerated with naive comprehensiveness, and with stress on quantity (big bowl of soup, big bowl of strawberries, many bottles). Other matters are restricted to the occupational routine which a diner at an inn would casually note while eating: the waitress, the price, the old woman keeping track. The syntax is artlessly simple: not a single subordinate clause, not a single inversion or interruption of normal sentence order. The implicit vision is that of the physical life untroubled, for the moment, by interpersonal tensions or by the ordering of values.

In *Rasselas*, by contrast, food is a mere incidental, summed up in one sentence with four general nouns ("flesh and wine," "fruits and water"); yet the author does distinguish between the visitors' fare and that of the hermit, seeing in it a clue to the hermit's outlook. The same curiosity directs his description of the setting (its "neatness and regularity") and the conversation. The diction also expresses an interest in generalizing, rather than any fascination with sensory surface. Although the sentence structure seems plain, it does organize the events into logical classes, one sentence each being devoted to entering, eating, listening. The balancing of the phrases "cheerful without levity" and "pious without enthusiasm" conveys a systematic assessment of the hermit's temperate qualities. Altogether the implicit vision is that of a reflective and curious common sense.

These illustrations by no means exhaust the stylistic observations which are possible in inferring a novelist's value patterns. Such limits can be set only by the reader's powers of describing language, his sensitivity to logical arrangements, and his philosophical breadth.

In this essay Jaroslav Hornát defines style not as a purely grammatical category, but as a linguistic means of embodying the author's intentions. Basing her analysis on the syntactic characteristics of the prose style of each period, she traces the development of style in fiction from the age of Shakespeare to the present day. If the sixteenth- and seventeenth-century style was marked by rhetoric and use of long sentence periods (as in Thomas Deloney's *The Pleasant History of Jack of Newbury* and Jonathan Swift's *Gulliver's Travels*), the eighteenth-century style emerged as a more pliant and natural form of communication. The nineteenth century marks a step forward in molding a style that is colloquial, unvarnished, direct, and more functional in its semantic contents. This progression toward fluidity and indeterminateness in style achieves its culmination in the novels of William Faulkner and Ernest Hemingway.

some remarks on
fiction style,
old and new

JAROSLAV HORNÁT

It is not the purpose of this study to cover the vast field of differences between the older and modern modes of fiction style. What we intend to do within the limited scope of our discussion is to point out—by way of a few selected examples—some syntactic features characteristic of various historical stages in the development of style in fiction written in English. These features, observed in the chronological order of the material under examination and conceived from one general aspect, will appear as a continuous changing tendency in the gradual evolution of prose style in fiction. As a starting-point, the prose style of the 16th century, the Shakespearian period, is considered and then some instances of the 18th, 19th, and 20th century stylistic patterns to complete the picture.

"Style," which is a difficult word to define, will not be considered here as a purely grammatical category, but as a linguistic means of expressing (or verbally materializing) the author's creative intentions. In such an approach, the subjective element cannot be entirely suppressed or eliminated from our conception of "style," and the authors' specific qualities in individual cases will be recognized as a more or less important agent. On the whole, however, we believe that conclusions of a general nature, obtained by such textual analyses and their mutual comparison, may be useful in illustrating the dependence of artistic realization (or verbal materialization) of a sentence or paragraph in fiction on some historically conditioned "rules" of stylistic expression.

In Tudor and Elizabethan times, when fiction in England begins to develop rather considerably—next to poetry and drama—as the third literary genre, prose style may be generally described as one with strong elements of rhetoric, indulging in long sentence periods, adorned with various rhetorical figures or *schemata*. Rhetoric at the time was closely associated with logic (both subjects were taught, hand in hand, in English universities and schools). This close connection of logic and rhetoric constituted an important moment that asserted itself as a formative principle in the process of realizing a literary utterance. the basic unit of which, in a work of fiction, is in a narrower sense the sentence and in a broader sense a paragraph or even more extensive stylistic patterns. With the 16th and 17th century authors, the logical process formed designs (or schemes) that precisely governed the sentence construction. Not only in the sense that one item followed another in linear succession, that any statement had to ensue in logical consequence from the preceding statement; but also in the sense that all the logical windings—explanatory parentheses and digressions—had to be duly expressed through grammatical means as well: an exact stratification of co-ordinate and subordinate relations in a syntactical arrangement, corresponding to the same values in logical arrangement, was obligatory.

An example will elucidate the point. It is the beginning of *The Pleasant History of Jack of Newbery* by Thomas Deloney (1597):

> In the daies of King *Henrie* the eight, that most noble
> and victorious Prince, in the beginning of his reigne, *Iohn
> Winchcomb*, a broad cloth Weauer, dwelt in *Newberie*, a towne
> in *Barkshire*: who for that he was a man of a merry disposition,
> & honest conuersation, was wondrous wel-beloued of Rich

and Poore, specially, because in euery place where hee came, hee would spend his money with the best, and was not at any time found a churle of his purse. Wherefore being so good a companion, hee was called of old and younge *Iacke* of *Newberie*: a man so generally well knowne in all his countrey for his good fellowship, that hee could goe in no place but he found acquaintance; by means whereof, *Iacke* could no sooner get a Crowne, but straight hee found meanes to spend it: yet had hee euer this care, that hee would alwaies keepe himselfe in comely and decent apparell: neyther at any time would hee bee ouercome in drinke, but so discreetly behaue himselfe with honest mirth, and pleasant conceits, that he was euery Gentlemans companion.[1]

The logical subject of the utterance (the basis of the statement or the theme about which the affirmation is made) [2a] is throughout the whole paragraph Jack of Newbery, and all the nuclei of the string of statements (or the rhemes, i.e. all that is affirmed about the logical subject of the utterance) [2b] refer to him as the given theme. We come to know when and where he lived, what he was, what his character and his walk of life were like. And all this in one logical (and syntactical) sequence. One can easily perceive that a modern writer would convey the whole body of information, contained in our quotation, in a stylistically quite different way. But any disturbance of this logical (and syntactical) sequence by dividing the compound sentences into shorter simple sentences, by substituting co-ordinate relations for subordinate ones, would more or less deform one of the substantial specific features of Deloney's stylistic pattern which ranks him among his contemporaries and makes him—regardless of other linguistic and non-linguistic qualities—one of the typical representatives of Elizabethan fiction.

Let us now, after this example from roughly 1600, proceed further and see how an analogous case is solved by an 18th century writer. The following is the opening paragraph from Swift's *Gulliver's Travels* (1726):

My father had a small estate in *Nottinghamshire*; I was the third of five sons. He sent me to *Emanuel-College* in *Cambridge*, at fourteen years old, where I resided three years, and

[1] *The Works of Thomas Deloney*, ed. F. O. Mann, Oxford 1912, p. 3.
[2ab] These are Vilém Mathesius' concepts and terms; see his *Obsahový rozbor současné angličtiny na základě obecně lingvistickém*, ed. Josef Vachek, Praha 1961, pp. 91ff., and p. 234, section B, II, of J. Vachek's English summary.

applied myself close to my studies: but the charge of maintaining me (although I had a very scanty allowance) being too
great for a narrow fortune; I was bound apprentice to Mr.
James Bates, an eminent surgeon in *London,* with whom I continued four years; and my father now and then sending me
small sums of money, I laid them out in learning navigation,
and other parts of the mathematics, useful to those who intend
to travel, as I always believed it would be some time or other
my fortune to do. When I left Mr. *Bates,* I went down to my
father; where, by the assistance of him and my uncle *John,*
and some other relations, I got forty pounds, and a promise
of thirty pounds a year to maintain me at *Leyden:* there *I*
studied physic two years and seven months, knowing it would
be useful in long voyages.[3]

A comparison of the two texts reveals that they have very much
in common. As to the logical subject of the utterance, the latter passage
is again, in essence, a monothematic one: we are offered some introduc-
tory information about Gulliver, narrator of the story. Here, too, the author's
logical process makes a route similar to that of Deloney's, each subsequent member in the series of observations relating to the main theme is
logically attached to, or results from, the previous one. The stylistic expression, however, is more natural than it was in the case of Deloney. This is
made possible, in Swift, by alternating two grammatical subjects: one of
them being Gulliver, the other Gulliver's father. The correspondence between the two planes, logical and syntactical, is loosened, some relations
of the rhemes to the logical subject that are semantically subordinate are
transferred to the level of grammatical co-ordinateness, and the entire
body of information which in Deloney is, in fact, presented at a stretch in
two long compound sentences (viz. the many grammatical words: *"who for
that* he was," *"wherefore,"* "by means *whereof,"* joining the whole logical
sequence together linguistically) falls apart into a series of relatively
shorter and syntactically more or less independent sentences. Yet this
loosening of the older strict correlation between logic and syntax is only
a partial one and from this point of view Swift's stylistic expression (we
refer to the passage cited above) marks a transitional step towards a more
pliant and variable interplay of the two spheres.

Apart from this "enumerative type" of utterance, based on a linear

---

[3] Jonathan Swift, *Gulliver's Travels,* VEB Deutscher Verlag der Wissenschaften,
Berlin 1955, p. 45.

148

sequence of its component members, another stylistic pattern illustrative of the "older" kind of prose style may be demonstrated, in which the correlation between logic and syntax is clearly reflected in an exemplary form. This time, our sample has been chosen from Fielding's *Joseph Andrews* (1742):

> By those high people, therefore, whom I have described, I mean a set of wretches, who, while they are a disgrace to their ancestors, whose honours and fortunes they inherit (or perhaps a greater to their mother, for such degeneracy is scarse credible), have the insolence to treat those with disregard who are at least equal to the founders of their own spendor. It is, I fancy, impossible to conceive a spectacle more worthy of our indignation, than that of a fellow, who is not only a blot in the escutcheon of a great family, but a scandal to the human species, maintaining a supercilious behaviour to men who are an honour to their nature and a disgrace to their fortune.[4]

The thematic kernel of this rather complicated passage is the censure of persons who look down upon those in an "inferior" position. In terms of style, the thought is expressed by way of a comparison, the key words being the pairs of concepts: *disgrace* plus *scandal* and *honour* versus *disgrace*, placed in contrasting parallels. It is not the artistic appeal here that matters, but the logical argument based on an antithesis, conditioning the stylistic construction of the whole paragraph.

This "argumentative type" of utterance where compound sentences are unfolded round certain key semantic kernels indicates the close affinity in stylistic technique of the 18th century authors with that of the Elizabethan prose writers. The latter, especially the work of the euphuists, offer much evidence of the same method. A nice analogy is to be found in Shakespeare's *Hamlet*:

> *Ophelia.* Could beauty, my lord, have better commerce than with honesty?
> *Hamlet.* Ay, truly; for the power of beauty will sooner transform honesty from what it is to a bawd than the force of honesty can translate beauty into his likeness: this was sometime a paradox, but now the time gives it proof.[5]

[4] Henry Fielding, *Joseph Andrews,* Everyman's Library, 1912, p. 201.
[5] *Hamlet,* III, 1.

Hamlet's play on the words *beauty* and *honesty* is made conspicuous by grammatical parallelisms and the alliterative quality of the prefixes in the verbs *transform* and *translate*. The emphasis, again, (if we consider the utterance as an independent unit, devoid of connotations implied by its broader context) is on the "aesthetic" felicity of the argument due both to its logical "wittiness" and "appropriate" wording. The core of meaning in both passages, Fielding's and Shakespeare's respectively, is the evidence in favour of a "philosophical" thesis: (1) conceited people, though well-born, are sometimes a disgrace to their fathers and mothers, while honest people, though of a humble origin, are an honour to their nature and a disgrace to their step-motherly fortune; (2) beauty and honesty do not go together. These propositions constitute the basic themes of the passages, which are thus again of a monothematic nature.

Doubtless, a more detailed examination of further materials from the same point of view would yield the rather commonplace inference that the current prose style of the 18th century is in many respects dependent on the older stylistic tradition, at least as far as descriptive and discursive passages are concerned. It is less rhetorical, less ornamental, and therefore more functional as to its semantic contents; the structure of sentences and clauses, however, is accommodated to similar logical designs. Substantial progress, compared with earlier stylistic practice, is evident especially in direct speech. An unprecedented number of "colloquial" phrases and idioms is to be found and the dialogues become more natural. Highly typical, nevertheless, of the 18th century, is the monothematic quality of compound sentences and paragraphs referred to in our comments on the texts so far cited.

In this connection, e.g., the question of creating atmosphere in a work of fiction—the atmosphere of place, time, and situation—is interesting. The Elizabethan authors are rarely concerned with creating the atmosphere of place or time. What we mostly meet with in their works, is the atmosphere of situation which implicitly follows from the description of the action. The novelists of the 18th century know how to prepare an atmosphere of situation, which marks a notable step forward. Yet they can very seldom rouse the acute inner tension between the atmosphere of situation and the action proceeding against its background that not merely contemporary authors but also the 19th century novelists are able to evoke. Here is an example from Dickens' *David Copperfield* (1849–50):

> As my mother stooped down on the threshold to take me
> in her arms and kiss me, the gentleman said I was a more

highly privileged little fellow than a monarch—or something like that; for my later understanding comes, I am sensible, to my aid here.

"What does that mean?" I asked him, over her shoulder.

He patted me on the head; but somehow, I didn't like him or his deep voice, and I was jealous that his hand should touch my mother's in touching me—which it did. I put it away as well as I could.

"Oh, Davy!" remonstrated my mother.

"Dear boy!" said the gentleman. "I cannot wonder at his devotion!" [6]

When depicting this scene, Dickens relied on what he had already made clear, or indicated, earlier in the narrative. After David's inquiries (addressed to Peggotty) about widowed people's possibilities of remarrying, after Peggotty's "little indecision," her evasive answer and "queer" looks, the reader is led to divine what David's lot most probably will be and his sympathies for the hero, in spite of the latter's apparent "uncivility" will not only continue, rather increased than abated, but he is also prompted to share David's repulsion for his future step-father, irrespective of Mr. Murdstone's kind treatment (at the moment) of the boy. Thus an important atmosphere of situation originates over which, maybe, the reader lives more intensively (as he can understand the hero's experience from a more general and, perhaps, more mature perspective) than the child whose hatred of Murdstone, here, is only impulsive. It is not necessary to put all in *verbis expressis*. An abbreviated, short-cut delineation may be used, with blank spaces left for the reader's fancy to fill in within the limits rather suggested than defined by the description. In contrast with the foregoing examples, the considerable stylistic variety of the utterance is remarkable, with the corresponding division of sentences into shorter sections and the alternation of the descriptive parts with curt direct speeches. Logical links may be relaxed, as the inner coherence of the scene is sufficiently secured by the uniform atmosphere of situation. The aesthetic appeal is shifted from the rational level to the emotional level, with the result resembling the effect of poetry, not of the "verbal" but imaginative kind. It is the artistic image that is relevant here, not the literal meaning of the description.

Stylistically, such imaginative values cannot be enlivened by sticking strictly, in the process of verbal materialization, to the "logical" patterns

[6] Charles Dickens, *David Copperfield,* Thomas Nelson and Sons, London, Edinburgh, Dublin and New York, n. d., p. 19.

of utterances, since logical sequences of strings of statements or group-
ings of the rhemes round some logical kernels rather demand descriptions
and affirmations of a monothematic quality. However, in a delineation
where any kind of atmosphere becomes a concomitant agent, such stylistic
methods must be found unsuitable and even unfeasible.

An examination along these lines of the quotation from *David Copperfield* will illustrate the point. With respect to the broader context, the scene
is, of course, focused on David as the hero of the novel. Yet the intended
effect, based on the first "collision" between the boy and his step-father
to be, requires the introduction and interplay of three characters of equivalent importance in the given situation, namely of David, his mother, and
Mr. Murdstone: each of them plays his role, the actions or speeches of
each represent themes in themselves, and only the sum or combination
of all these various themes makes up a literary unit or entity able to convey the integral meaning intended. Three logical subjects enter into the
framework of this artistic image; the passage is no longer monothematic,
but a polythematic one. Here we have already realized one of the potentialities of modern prose.

The last quotation was introduced to show how the question of evoking the atmosphere of situation may be solved in a work of fiction along
with the stylistic consequences. This kind of atmosphere generally appeared in connection with the development of plots (descriptions of the
action or the dialogues between or among the acting characters), in the
works of "older" writers usually as a secondary attribute. The creation
of the atmosphere of time and setting, however, was a different case. As
has already been said, it occurred rather rarely in the Elizabethan novels,
but could be found even there, e.g. in Thomas Lodge or Robert Greene,
especially in their later stories. With the 18th century novelists, the description of milieu and time-frames are already quite common phenomena.
Nevertheless, what we usually do not come across up to modern times,
is the parallel creation of these kinds of atmosphere with the development of the action. If an "older" author wanted to evoke, e.g., the mood
of a lovely morning, he would stop the flow of the action for a time, insert
the desirable or needful passage and then return to the place where he
had left the description of the action, or resume, after this parenthesis or
digression, the task of the narrator of the plot. See, for instance, the following passage from *Joseph Andrews*:

> . . . As soon as the wench had informed him [the surgeon] at
> his window that it was a poor foot-passenger who had been

stripped of all he had, and almost murdered, he chid her for disturbing him so early, slipped off his clothes again, and very quietly returned to bed and to sleep.

Aurora now began to shew her blooming cheeks over the hills, whilst ten millions of feathered songsters, in jocund chorus, repeated odes a thousand times sweeter than those of our laureat, and sung both the day and the song; when the master of the inn, Mr. Tow-wouse, arose, and learning from his maid an account of the robbery, and the situation of his poor naked guest, he shook his head, and cried, "good-lack-a-day!" . . .[7]

It seems, therefore, that this parallel presence of the atmosphere of setting or time on the one hand, and the development of action or plot on the other hand, or the interaction of the two planes, is a significant feature of modern prose. To illustrate this as briefly as possible, the following short example from Hemingway's *The Old Man and the Sea* (1952) has been selected:

The sun rose thinly from the sea and the old man could see the other boats, low on the water and well in toward the shore, spread out across the current. Then the sun was brighter and the glare came on the water and then, as it rose clear, the flat sea sent it back at his eyes so that it hurt sharply and he rowed without looking into it.[8]

There are two parallel lines of happenings centred round two basic themes: the sun and the old man. The sentences "The sun rose thinly from the sea" and "the sun was brighter and the glare came on the water" evoke a graphic vision of a natural phenomenon, independent of the old man; yet at the same time the hero's situation is projected against the background of this setting. A third theme, the water surface, cleverly introduced in the first compound sentence, functions as a connecting link between the two parallel lines of happenings, in the second compound sentence: "the glare came on the water and . . . the flat sea sent it back at his eyes . . ." What is important, giving a vivid imaginative quality to the treatment of the action, is that the author does not reduce his interest to a mere statement when and where this or that happened or was happen-

[7] *Joseph Andrews,* p. 45.
[8] Ernest Hemingway, *The Old Man and the Sea,* Moscow 1963, p. 37.

153

ing, but creates the atmosphere of time and setting parallel with the gradual progress of his central plot.

An author of the "older school" would undoubtedly deal with the same or similar situation in a different way. Moreover, he would probably disagree with this mode of stylistic expression, because it violates that monothematic principle he had become accustomed to and which enabled him to link all the constituents of the utterance by means of "proper" correspondence in the spheres of logical and syntactical arrangement. Cf. the following example:

> The sun had been now risen some hours, *when* Joseph, finding his leg surprisingly recovered, proposed to walk forwards . . . (our italics).[9]

There are not two independent themes, the sun and Joseph, in this utterance, but a basic one (Joseph as the logical subject) and a subsidiary one (the sun), defining the time of the hero's proposal, but not evoking the picture of a natural phenomenon or scenery upon which the reader's imagination may delay for a second (cf. the quotation from Hemingway) as a statement in its own right and charged with a full artistic (not only informative) function. In fact, Fielding's utterance here is a monothematic one.

In modern prose the alternation of several equivalent themes (logical subjects) or the accumulation of a practically unlimited number of equivalent themes (logical subjects) is not only possible but is preferred. Such accumulative stylistic patterns are characteristic of William Faulkner's prose:

> It was after sunset. Upon the mirror-smooth water even the little foul skiffs—the weathered and stinking dories and dinghies of oyster- and shrimp-men—had a deptheless and fairylight quality as they scattered like butterflies or moths before a mechanical reaper, just ahead of the trim, low, martial-coloured police-launch, on to which at the moment the photographer saw being transferred from one of the skiffs two people whom he recognized as being the dead pilot's wife and child. Among them the dredge looked like something antediluvian crawled for the first time into light, roused but not alarmed by the object or creature out of the world of light

---

[9] *Joseph Andrews*, p. 167.

and air which had plunged without warning into the watery fastness where it had been asleep. "Jesus," the photographer said. "Why wasn't I standing right here: Hagood would have had to raise me then. Jesus God," he said in a hoarse tone of hushed and unbelieving amazement, "how's it now for being a poor bastard that never even learned to roller-skate?" The reporter looked at him, for the first time. The reporter's face was perfectly calm; he looked down at the photographer, turning carefully as though he were made of glass and knew it, blinking a little, and spoke in a peaceful dreamy voice such as might be heard where a child is sick—not sick for a day or even two days, but for so long that even wasting anxiety has become mere surface habit: "She told me to go away. I mean, to go clean away, like to another town." [10]

Compared with Hemingway's favourite stylistic patterns, Faulkner's reveal a marked difference: the polythematic quality remains, but whereas the economic, curt manner of expression which makes Hemingway adjust the ratio of co-ordinate and subordinate elements plainly in favour of the former, and thus reduce to the minimum or eliminate the logical links (i.e., in linguistic terms, the grammatical words joining the utterance syntactically together) that are concomitant attributes of subordinateness, Faulkner's patterns, encompassing vast areas of observations, do not eliminate them but assimilate within the system of his polythematic style.

To sum up, from the viewpoint of the functional perspective, taking into account the semantic and syntactic planes of literary utterances and their mutual relations, four model stylistic patterns can be set up: (1) monothematic with logical links; (2) monothematic without logical links; (3) polythematic with logical links; and (4) polythematic without logical links. From the analyses on the basis of these criteria of some literary texts, the following conclusions might be, let us say "hypothetically," inferred. While the presence or absence of logical links is only a relative indicator of styles "traditional" and "modern" (though their reduction in more advanced stages in the development of fiction style is clearly visible) we may say that it is the tendency to pass from the monothematic to the polythematic in stylistic patterns that marks a relevant criterion for distinguishing between what we have called in the title of this paper, with a certain licence, "old" and "new" fiction styles. To define more accurately,

---

[10] William Faulkner, *Pylon* (1933[1]), The Albatros, Hamburg–Paris–Bologna, 1935, p. 184.

when and where this tendency has originated, what new combinations or variants of stylistic expression (the model patterns will, of course, hardly occur with uniform consistency in pure, unmixed forms) have been made possible by its appearance, and what specific shapes its application may assume in particular literary works, would be a task for a much more detailed and systematic study.

theme

How does a novelist work a moral change in his reader's reactions? Derwent May answers by suggesting that a reader, through close identification with a character or scene, is quickened into sharp awareness of the moral consequences of his own actions. A creative novelist, as distinct from a "moral" novelist, does not draw upon any preconceived notions of morality to impose upon the reader but prefers rather to stimulate certain desirable moral responses through symbolic action. He simply suggests, "Don't you feel a *need* to be like this and a horror of being like that?" (for example, D. H. Lawrence, Henry James, Joseph Conrad, and James Joyce).
In the second part of the essay, the author asks a related question. What kind of moral criticism can be brought to bear upon a novel? Here again he suggests a basic distinction between the novelist who invites his reader to participate in a situation, or share the feelings of a character, and the moralist who may complain that the novelist has *left out* certain essential facts about the people involved so that the situation revealed to us may please us; whereas if its full consequences were displayed, it would dismay us (as in D. H. Lawrence's *The Border Line* or *The Plumed Serpent*).
According to Derwent May, the novelist is obviously giving us only an impressionistic rendering of a symbolic situation, not a definitive moral commentary on it.

the novelist as moralist and the moralist as critic

DERWENT MAY

In what sense, if any, is the serious novelist a moralist? What have his activities in common with that other indefatigable preoccupation of men—the labelling of courses of action as "right" or "wrong"? As a question about the "poet," it is one of the oldest literary questions; as a question about the novelist it goes back to the first appearance of the novel. But about the answer, common agreement has probably diminished rather than increased. In this article I want to indicate what I think is the *kind* of interest that some greater English novelists have had in leading their readers to take up distinctively moral attitudes; and also to say something briefly about the possibility of criticism of the novel from a moral standpoint.

There is one point on which agreement may perhaps be assumed as a preliminary clearing away. This is that in no novel that we can now take seriously does the author ask us to accept on his word the explicit assertion that a character is "good" or "bad." Dickens may describe Nicholas Nickleby's father as a "worthy gentleman," but since he tells us virtually nothing about him, this is scarcely to be taken as a recommendation of his ways—it is a mere shorthand indication that he had the characteristics that people conventionally consider worthy. And I shall assume that we are prepared to make such a transcription—into purely non-moral descriptive terms—for all such examples of moral comment not backed up by demonstration, in those novelists we continue to consider important.

In fact—and this is the first important point—our readiness to do this is not just an *incidental* characteristic of novels we praise—it is a corollary to a major reason why we praise them. It means that, for the most part, the novelist has given us all the necessary facts, using his art there, and left the act of applying moral labels, if it is a relevant act at all, to us. And this is what we feel that the novelist must do. The novelist's own view that an act of judgment on his characters is permissible, may sometimes be found more openly expressed in his prefaces. But observations in prefaces to the effect that a character is "noble" or "base" (examples from Henry James) must likewise be set aside in our consideration of what the novelist actually *does* for us; here he is merely allowing himself the privilege of a reader, a privilege that he would not claim in his purely professional rôle.

All this does not mean, however, that in his own way a novelist may not be interested in working a development in his reader's moral attitudes. "Working a development" rather than simply "proposing a change" —this distinction is crucial to what I want to argue, as will be seen. I do not think that the novelist is in a position to venture into the field where the question at issue is the moral rightness or wrongness inherent in solitary deeds that affect no one else—if such deeds exist, and if questions in that field have any meaning at all. But in so far as "moral" may be taken to mean "regarding the rightness or wrongness of actions in which one or more persons (or gods or animals whose feelings we imagine we can share) are affected by one or more other persons," I think that the novelist may not only be "interested in morality" but act indeed as a powerful moral influence. And basically there are, I think, two truly moral responses that the novelists I have in mind are concerned with getting from their readers—namely, "A shouldn't do this to B" (or "A should do this for B"), leading to "I shouldn't do that to X" (or "I should do that for X"). What is classic and unique to the art of the novel is its power to create these attitudes in its readers; and to create them with their full consent.

A certain type of novel, normally (and significantly) *dismissed* as a "moral" story, deserves that peremptory treatment and that somewhat paradoxical stigma—just because it does not in fact tend towards creating either of these attitudes in its readers, for all its moral claims. This is the "moral" novel that tries to seduce or frighten us into ways that the author thinks desirable for us or the world or him, by telling a story in which the "wrong" by his lights all come to a sorry end and the "good" conclude in prosperity. If we draw a parallel between ourselves and the characters, as we are supposed to do, the attitude of mind we are likely to find ourselves in will not be either of the moral ones referred to above but the unmistakably amoral one, "I had better not do anything like that or I shall pay for it." Not of course that this is the reason we reject that kind of novel—we do that because the novel outrages our knowledge of the way things actually do happen in life. The assault on us may be more subtle, however, as it often is in Dickens, where we commonly see men punished by their own feelings of guilt. This, if convincing, may make a good or great work of art (it is after all, in essence, the story of Lady Macbeth), but it will still not be a moral novel in the sense described above, as will be seen in a minute. Dickens, however, tips many of his stories over into the "grisly warning" category simply by pressing these lashes of the conscience on us a little too anxiously. John Carker in *Dombey and Son*, and Carton in *A Tale of Two Cities* are instances. Of Carker, who has committed some minor dishonesty in youth and never forgotten it, we read, "He was not old but his head was white; his body was bent or bowed as if by the weight of some great trouble; and there were deep lines in his melancholy face. The fire of his eyes, the expression of his features, the very voice in which he spake, were all subdued, as if the spirit within him lay in ashes." Sydney Carton, guilty of youthful debauchery and "accidia," it is true, but still an amiable and remarkably able young man, is driven

161

to a welcome self-sacrifice in order to appease his fearful sense of sin and failure. Both suffer excessively in their consciences for their comparatively minor defaults: a man *may* suffer like this, we feel, but Dickens presents it to us as a normal thing that everyone else around takes for granted too, sighing but comprehending. Carker's sister, for all her loving sympathy, rubs it in most terribly. (It is not immediately relevant to discuss here the compulsion that led Dickens to revert again and again to this warning.)

The reference to Lady Macbeth indicates, however, that this kind of story brings us to the frontier of a major literary tradition, that numbers amongst its products some of the greatest English novels—yet a tradition that is still not to be claimed as a moral tradition in the sense that it is concerned with awaking or confirming either of the two moral attitudes already described. This, in brief, is the tradition that asks the question, "What are a man's needs unto himself?" The English novel is haunted with this question, and it receives there no unsubtle answer. Nor is the tradition a purely literary one, of course—it feeds on the questions men ask themselves in life at least as urgently as they ask themselves moral questions. In fact it is a question that all novels must in some degree concern themselves with—unless there is at least one figure in a novel with whose "needs unto himself" we can feel in active sympathy, the book is likely to be no more than a farce or a tirade.

But the tradition I speak of here is the one that does not simply include in its stories one or more characters whose quest for satisfaction we can find acceptable, but takes a hero and makes his obscure or insistent needs the major question of the book. That these needs and satisfactions may in some sense or other be social ones, and moral ones, does not alter the emphasis in this tradition on the satisfaction, or lack of it, that the hero experiences in the way he handles his relationship with the creation about him. *Lord Jim* is perhaps one of the purest examples of what I mean. It scarcely offers a moral comment on Jim's preoccupations —that is to say, the influence of his acts on other people is hardly pointed at all. The novel simply traces his responses to the situations he finds himself in, their consequences in his own life, and the way they lead to his death; turning, then, to us it says: "So it was." (I say "simply"—I mean "simply" from a moral point of view, not from an artistic or psychological one.) We may be made more sharply aware of a similar compulsion to observe the dictates of honour in our own lives, a need perhaps less clearly formulated before Conrad gave us its image in *Lord Jim*; we may see more sharply than before the tragic possibilities of observing such a compulsion in ourselves; at the least, if we do not feel strongly either of those things, we may understand the actions of other men like Jim more clearly; the gain in any case is real, in the first two cases it may be tremendous, but we can scarcely say that a moral change has been worked in us. Even if these newly-sharpened perceptions of ours, and the more confident choices they lead to, have desirable consequences in other people's lives, still the other people are only incidental beneficiaries of our clearer pursuit of our own needs.

In some form or other the claims of "honour"—of the need for action appropriate to a man's sense of his dignity—dominate the greater part of Conrad's work, besides much of Henry James's, D. H. Lawrence's, Virginia Woolf's, Joyce Cary's and Graham Greene's. Of course the differences are considerable; as between James and Lawrence, for instance, it is often all the difference between a portrait of failure in the satisfaction of one complex human need and a portrait of success in the satisfaction of quite another. Kate in *The Wings of a Dove* would be very puzzled, one imagines, by Kate in *The Plumed Serpent*—although she might learn something from her. But in either case, the appeal to us from them is an appeal to consider our own true needs. That Kate Croy's plan makes a victim of Milly Theale is not so important to Henry James, or even to Milly, as it is to Kate herself: she is the tragic heroine, and it is her failure that matters, as the warning.

Lawrence enthusiasts (his biographer H. T. Moore is a typical example) often speak with a note of unmistakably moral contempt of characters such as Jimmy in *Jimmy and the Desperate Woman*. But they really do their author a disservice in introducing moral considerations where he so deliberately—defiantly, in fact—excludes them. Lawrence doesn't judge his characters by the question, "Do they do things for other people that they should, or things to other people that they shouldn't?" He appeals to his readers, "Don't you feel a need to be like this? and a horror of being like that? Don't you feel that this is the proper life for you?" His work is filled with a clear dislike for certain kinds of people, but they are not condemned on what may reasonably be called moral grounds—they simply differ from what he personally would like to be, or more often endanger or prevent his sympathetic characters becoming what they want to be. In so far as Lawrence's books lead us to criticise people, it is along the lines, "They mustn't do that to me!"—a legitimate rebel cry, but not strictly a moral attitude.

163

We come finally to those novels which, as I have suggested in the beginning, work a genuine moral influence: genuinely, that is to say, leading us through "A shouldn't do this to B" (or its obverse) to "I shouldn't do that to X" (or its obverse).

It would be absurd to suggest that the influence of novels is likely to play a major part in forming the moral character of anyone. How far any given book has a decisive effect on the people who read it is a question for psychologist and sociologist to answer, but its impact is likely to be negligible compared with the influence of home, school, etc.—the whole social environment starting from long before the day when the child reads his first word. However, I think it is not unreasonable to argue, from one's common experience, that in some measure one is affected by what one reads; what follows assumes a certain kind of reader of whom that is true, and beyond that leans on the qualifications made above.

The real moral force of the novel seems in fact to me to depend on the existence in its readers of two very elementary responses normal to man—the response of gratitude to those who do something for us that pleases us, and of repulsion from those who hurt us. Such responses are no doubt the first springs of morality throughout life—we love and praise the loving, and hate and condemn the unkind. This is still an elementary morality that need not involve self-examination or self-criticism at all. The latter is something we learn, no doubt, in innumerable ways. But the novel may lead us to such self-awareness in an absolutely unique way; and this its remarkable moral power. The power is brought into action when, as readers, we are not only led to identify ourselves with and share the feelings of the person who is capable of being pleased or hurt, but also led simultaneously to identify ourselves with the person whose activities may gratify or harm the former. In our identification with the latter person, we are brought face to face with the consequences of our actions in a sharper way than we ever can be in life—because we ourselves, in our identification with the first person, are as wholly the victim or dependent as we are the doer of good or harm. The simple gratitude or repulsion we feel in the one identification is wholly directed towards—*ourselves* in the other identification.

Examples are naturally legion. In *Great Expectations* we share in imagination Joe Gargery's affection and concern for Pip; at the same time, following Pip's career with a similar sympathetic interest, we are brought irresistibly to the notion, "Pip should not behave like this to Joe," and thus "In similar circumstances I should not behave like this either"—

164

because we "are" Joe as well, and feel his distress as though it were our own and Pip our tormentor. The complementary moral conviction, "A should do this for B," might be illustrated by the relationship of Isabel and Pansy in James's *Portrait of a Lady*. Standing back from the novel, we may feel that Isabel's decision to return to her husband at the end of the book stems from a number of motives, not all of them connected with Pansy. (She is pursuing a "need unto herself.") But the Isabel-Pansy relationship as described by James has its moral force for us in the way I have been describing. Feeling for ourselves how much Pansy's happiness is in Isabel's gift, and hers alone, we share too, in a unique way, the compulsion on Isabel (with whose happiness we are nevertheless equally concerned) to return for Pansy's sake. And "Isabel should do this for Pansy" leads to "I should do this for someone in a position like Pansy's."

What kind of moral criticism can be brought against a novel? Here I only want to make one more point, but if it is true, as I think, it is an interesting one—namely, that the "moral" critic of the novel finds himself doing precisely one of the things that the pure "literary" critic does.

The good novel cannot fail to please the moralist. For what does it do but show unfalteringly the consequences of men's actions, and invite us with unique persuasiveness to share the feelings of all who are involved? Where the moralist may have grounds for complaint is where his own knowledge and imagination tell him that the novelist has *left out* essential facts about the people involved in the events described—with the result that an action shown to us may please us, whereas if its full consequences were displayed, it would dismay. This is the kind of criticism that may sometimes be brought, in particular, against those novels that are mainly concerned with the needs of the hero. One could quote quite a number of examples from D. H. Lawrence. In that very brilliant story, *The Border Line*, for instance, Lawrence is preoccupied with the claims of his heroine; he is indifferent to the consequences to her husband, of her final decision to desert him. It is impossible for him to ignore her husband's feelings completely (this is where novel and story as *forms* exert their admirable pressure), and indeed he needs to show us something of them in order to show his indifference to them; but he treats them curtly, and it is the reader's own moral imagination that insists that more emphasis must be placed on them if justice to the full human reality of the situation is to be done. There is the same curtness in the description of the feelings of the men executed by order of Don Carlos in *The Plumed Serpent*—

a very painful passage for the reader with his own imagination. Lawrence himself, one senses, felt this and fought for his creed of the moment against his deeper impulses there—a fight in which someone like himself in particular was bound to admit defeat eventually (as he seems to have done a year or so later, when he declared that "the leader ideal is a dead ideal").

Another writer against whom the moral critic can find something interesting and relevant to say is Hardy. Hardy's overriding theme is pity for man in the hopelessness of his fate. And when his characters act in ways that hurt other people, it is at times almost comic to watch Hardy so straining his account of the deed as to make it appear that the actor is at that moment not to be held responsible for his acts. In *The Mayor of Casterbridge*, for example, the machinery of excuse comes into play again and again: Henchard is drunk when he sells his wife, out of temper when he dismisses Farfrae, and in the classic passage where Henchard does not admit to Mary-Jane's father that she is still at Casterbridge: "Then Henchard, scarcely believing the evidence of his senses, rose from his seat, amazed at what he had done. It had been the impulse of a moment." This is not to deny Hardy's brilliance, nor the power and beauty of his compassion, but it is a perfect example of the place where moral critic and pure literary critic can chime in together with an objection to a distortion on the canvas at a crucial point.

Of course, the needs of two human beings often conflict in such a way that it is possible for us to share wholly and equally, in imagination, both needs; and then we are silenced as moralists. Words like "A should do this for B" simply do not rise to our lips. So the novel that portrays such a situation in full candour and delicacy stands outside the sphere of moral influence, and outside the province of moral criticism. *Lord Jim* perhaps does this at its conclusion. Jim, like Hamlet, has a cruelty inseparable from his appeal to us. His sensitivity to Brown's shrewd questioning about his own honour leads him to risk the loss of his friends' lives by letting Brown go; while his determination not to run away from the consequences to himself of this act allows him to die and leave his wife hopelessly alone. But we share the compelling need of Jim to act as he does, and we cannot condemn. All we can ask is a question like

> Did he who made the lamb make thee?

And it is a question to which the moralist, like Blake, has no answer.

Gustav E. Mueller argues that since the American novel in the twentieth century is contemporary with European phenomenology and existentialism, it is essentially concerned with the nature of reality. The writer today is preoccupied with the problems of moral freedom and individual responsibility. If reality is coextensive with finite existence and if there is no possibility of transcendence, the novelist will inevitably develop an attitude of pessimism and negation toward life. It is this mood of nihilism that pervades most of the American novels of our time. Because the writer poses and tries to answer some of these metaphysical questions, this kind of novel strikes the reader as being palpably philosophical in conception and structure.

philosophy in the twentieth-century american novel

GUSTAV E. MUELLER

"The motion of the wasted world accelerates just before the final precipice."

William Faulkner, from *As I Lay Dying*

The 20th-Century American novel is very impressive, both in its tens of thousands of pages, in its stylistic quality, and in its social contents. It is a tremendously serious search for essential values in life. This search for values, the critique of their failures and their mutual limitations is traditionally known by the name of philosophy. There is more significant philosophy in the American novel than there is in the output of our philosophy departments.

American literature is contemporary with European phenomenology and existentialism. *Phenomenology* has broken with the 19th-century preoccupation with scientific method; insists on original visions of many essential structures from many points of view; and correlates the subjects viewing their world, and the worlds viewed as they become evident to the viewer's vision. *Existentialism* discovers the existing I-am in his solitary responsibility, undisguised by social conventions and no longer supported by abstract generalities or certainties. It is the tragic sense of life, as Unamuno calls it, to discover your authentic existence in the shattering of all that seemed to be reliable before. Every finite existence in the world is doomed to fall, to disintegrate, to die, and to be forgotten. If, then, reality is identified with finite existences, if there is no genuine transcendence of any kind, then the result is a bitter and pointless rebellion—"no exit." Finitism is nihilism. It prevails in 20th-century American literature.

This bitter gloominess is relieved by superb artistic craftsmanship. For example: Hemingway's *For Whom the Bell Tolls* has a perfect dramatic structure of suspense and tragic resolution as well as a phenomenological language, grasping the clear essence of each situation. Scott Fitzgerald's *The Great Gatsby* is like a subtle scale, balancing two equally dubitable forms of wealth—one of a ruthless businessman with rhetorical pretense of culture, and one of an infantile bootlegger "king"—between them the emptiness of a wasteland of futility and the sordidness of poverty—all contemplated in fairness by the narrator, who is the tip of the scale. William Faulkner pours out, in an unending stream of creative imagination, myths and symbols of his own making so that his Yoknapatawpha County becomes more plausible than any geographical South; the power of his creative fertility is so great that it obliterates the sad story of a progressive degradation of a society which at the same time clings to a guilty and dead past. In his *The Sound and the Fury*, different personal and temporal perspectives gradually elucidate a complex situation spanning thirty years. Dos Passos' *USA* is like a modern symphony changing voices, keys, and harmonies—with stories, subjective reactions, newsreels, and biographical gems of significant contemporaries; it reflects the vastness of these United States—a vastness which becomes a void in which all individuals get lost. They casually and occasionally cross each others' paths without knowing each other; only the reader knows how little they know one another, as in a vacuum in which particles hit each other. None of his numerous characters is interesting in and for himself; there are no selves. What is interesting is only what happens to them—and what happens is plenty.

All these authors are exploring shocking aspects of human existence with a supreme artistic cunning and courage—making use both of Marxist economic and psycho-analytic probing beneath ideological superstructures. Sometimes we seem to come closer to animal than to human psychology; for example, in Philip Wylie's *Generation of Vipers* or *Opus 21*, and intentionally in Aldous Huxley's *Ape and Essence*. But the great novelists achieve, as all great artists achieve, a felt vision of life so encompassing and moving, that the great aesthetic love for men triumphs through all their tears and sneers.

This reminds me of a story by Herman Hesse. Faust wants to be entertained and Mephisto lets him listen to the 20th century. How nice to know, Faust exclaims, that there is music even in hell.

The freedom of mind, which is practiced by these authors and is acquired by the reader, is in itself a great philosophical achievement. This freedom must not be confused with democracy; many Americans say "democracy" when they mean freedom. Our sacred American Constitution, guaranteeing freedom and the moral-legal equality of individuals in spite of their obvious natural-social inequalities, is not the result of any "people's rule," but the work of a choice group of aristocratic intellectuals, steeped in philosophy. I do not say American or European philosophy, because philosophy tolerates no such adjectives. Democracy at best tolerates freedom, but if freedom is in the way of the many, or majority sentiments, it is doomed.

Let us first look at the intellectual-academic climate. A professor in an American college can hardly gain much joy or comfort out of such books as Thorstein Veblen's *Higher Education in America*, Upton Sinclair's *Goosestep*, Albert J. Nock's *Theory of Education in the United States*, the description of "student" life in Thomas Wolfe's *Look Homeward Angel*, Sinclair Lewis' *Arrowsmith*, or Willa Cather's *The Professor's House*. The university is presented as the imitation of a factory, "run" by business men like a business; rewarding dullness, docility and conformity; punishing brilliance, boldness, critical thinking, or originality. As to "student" life, here is a description from Upton Sinclair's *Goosestep*:

> We know the ideal American college student. He comes from our best families, his figure is tall and straight, and his features regular and blank. . . . He is thoroughly skilled, however, in every form of play, and has been raised in a system of conventions which constitute "good manners." He comes to college to spend the four pleasantest years of his life in the company of his social equals. His father and big brothers before him have belonged to the right clubs, and are promi-

nent in the alumni association.

There is only one thing wrong with this four years of paradise, and that is a lot of fool pedants and bookworms, who
think they have something to do with running the college, and
worry a fellow to death. . . . The young gentleman in college
regards these pedants as his natural enemies, and the outwit-
ting of them is one of his entertainments.[1]

This anti-intellectual tradition which dominates and corrupts our so-
called higher education is seen as a vulgar *pragmatism*. (I do not mean
William James!) It subordinates truth to practice, reason to practical whims
and exigencies. It denies and hates truth and the cultivation of it, which
should be the center of learning. This sort of pragmatism cannot assume
leadership in human culture. Santayana's novel *The Last Puritan* put it
this way:

. . . that they *hate* to *think*! They are too busy, too tired; or if
they half form an opinion in spite of themselves, they won't
take the trouble to express it accurately, or to defend it. They
laugh at what people *think*, even at what they think themselves, and respect only what people *do*. Yes, my dear, and
beneath that horrid cynical scepticism, there is something
deeper still. They are *afraid of the truth!* [2]

And Albert J. Nock:

A few months ago, an Italian nobleman, one of the most
accomplished men of Europe, told me he had a curious experience in our country. He wondered whether I had made anything like the same observation, and if so, how I accounted
for it. He said he had been in America several times, and had
met some very well educated men, as an Italian would understand the term; but they were all in the neighborhood of sixty
years old. Under that age, he said, he had happened on no
one who impressed him as at all well-educated. I told him that
he had been observing the remnants of a pre-revolutionary
product, and coming from a country that had . . . Mussolini,
he should easily understand what that meant; that our educa-

---

[1] Upton Sinclair, *Goosestep,* 2nd ed. (published by the author, 1923), p. 356.
[2] George Santayana, *The Last Puritan* (New York: Charles Scribner's Sons,
1936), p. 105.

tional system had been thoroughly reorganized, both in spirit and in structure, about thirty-five years ago, and that his well-educated men of sixty or so were merely hold-overs from what we now put down, by general consent, as the times of igno-rance—hold-overs from pre-fascist days, if I might borrow the comparison. 'But,' I went on, 'our younger men are really very keen; they are men of parts, and our schools and uni-versities really do an immense deal for them. Just try to come round of them about the merits of a bond issue or a motor car, the fine points of commercial ice-caking or retail shoe merchandising, or the problem of waste motion involved in brick-laying or in washing dishes for a hotel, and you are sure to find that they will give a first-rate account of them-selves and they reflect credit on an educational system that turned them out.' My friend looked at me a moment in a vacant sort of way, and presently said that proficiency in those pursuits was not precisely what he had in mind when he spoke of education. 'Just so,' I replied, 'but it is very much what we have in mind. We are all for being practical in education.' [3]

This critique of vulgar pragmatism as corrupting the academic situa-tion illustrates the general problem which consists in this: *These writers revolt against all the major and official American traditions,* of which "prag-matism" is one. But they see this revolt as a hopeless fight; they are swimming "upstream," as Ludwig Lewisohn entitles one of his books. The books become more bitter and joyless, as we move from the "social gos-pel" of John Dewey and the 1910 reform novels, through the gay satire of Sinclair Lewis and H. L. Mencken in the twenties to the utterly disillu-sioned forties. An occasional humor, especially in William Faulkner, is pathetic and grotesque. Many express their protests by voluntary exile, such as Henry Adams, Henry James, T. S. Eliot, Gertrude Stein, Ernest Hemingway, Edith Wharton, and George Santayana. Thomas Wolfe died from exhaustion at the age of 39. He describes his process of alienation in *You Can't Go Home Again,* showing how a greedy, ugly, corrupt busi-ness community violently reacts to the literary mirror held up against it. This society does not respect art, doesn't even know what art is, and does not expect its artists to mature. Many give up, discouraged; others fizzle

[3] Albert J. Nock, *Theory of Education in the USA,* Humanist Publication No. 13 (Chicago: Henry Regnery Co., 1949), p. 66.

out, or sell out.

Besides "pragmatism," there are four main American traditions which are criticized: first, "Christianity"; second, "capitalism"; third, egalitarian democracy; fourth, the transcendentalism and idealism of Freedom and Reason from Emerson to Charles Peirce and Josiah Royce.

1. Christianity is mostly conspicuous by its absence. In all the books I have read, there is not a single major figure to whom it means anything, with the exception of Santayana's *The Last Puritan*. But this Catholic convert is nevertheless bracketed by the author, who says that "religion is a poetry which is believed to be real . . . some good sound tough illusion to buoy him up."

If it is treated at all, it is something which one has been exposed to as a child, and which one is shedding without loss, as in Dos Passos' *USA*. In Dreiser's *American Tragedy*, it appears as a shabby, sweetish, thoughtless, hypocritical, and inconsequential sectarianism.

J. D. Salinger's *The Catcher in the Rye* catches another well-known American caricature of Christianity. We all know the essentially vulgar, vociferous, back-slapping salesman, who confuses his beaming personality with Christian "service." Salinger describes such an undertaker who speaks in the college chapels to the boys. He tells them to do successful business together with Jesus and to be a regular guy as Jesus was. He insists that they should not be afraid to ask Jesus anything at any time, even while driving. He, for one, is not afraid to ask Him to send him fifty more stiffs. His "message" is greeted with the Bronx cheer.

In Sinclair Lewis' *Babbitt* and *Elmer Gantry*, there are satires on slick, comfortable, and flowery bourgeois ministers or ridiculous big-scale revivalists combining biblical-Paulinian orthodoxy with emotional mass-appeal and with money-making; Sinclair Lewis' "Billy Monday"! I illustrate the flowery kind with a passage from Santayana's *The Last Puritan*:

> The music was classical and soothing, the service High Church Unitarian, with nothing in it either to discourage a believer or to annoy an unbeliever. What did doctrines matter? The lessons were chosen for their magical archaic English and were mouthed in a tone of emotional mystery and unction . . . would praise the virtues and flatter the vanity of the congregation, only slightly heightening the picture by contrast with the sad vices and errors of former times or of other nations. . . . An Easter sermon on the Resurrection might prudently avoid

172

all mention of Christ. . . . Instead the preacher might blandly describe the resurrection of nature in the spring, the resurrection of science in the modern world, and the resurrection of heroic freedom in the American character.[4]

But the American 20th-century novel is not only post-Christian, but also, for the most part, non-religious, *if* religion is defined as the response of faith to an absolute Beyond revealing itself as the transcendent ground of all finitudes. One of the few exceptions I have found is the following quotation from William Faulkner's *The Bear*:

> Because He told in the Book how He created the earth, made it and looked at it and said it was all right, and then He made man. He made the earth first and peopled it with dumb creatures, and then He created man to be His overseer on the earth and to hold suzerainty over the earth and the animals on it in His name, not to hold for himself and his descendants inviolable title forever, generation after generation, to the oblongs and squares of the earth, but to hold the earth mutual and intact in the communal anonymity of brotherhood, and all the fee He asked was pity and humility and sufferance, and endurance and the sweat of his face for bread.[5]

Faulkner's Negroes and poor whites, of course, always talk in Christian language, and in *The Sound and the Fury*, there is a rollicking Negro revival sermon.

As to Judaism, Faulkner says: The Jew is "forever alien: and unblessed: a pariah about the face of the Western earth which twenty centuries later was still taking revenge on him for the fairy tale with which he had conquered it." [6]

2. The illusion that the whole economic life of a nation is there for the sake of an unlimited and unscrupulous profit-making,[7] leading to the concentration of more and more economic power in fewer and fewer "interlocking-directorates," to quote Upton Sinclair, is of course a very prominent problem in many of these novelists. Joseph Hergesheimer completely accepts wealth as the standard of human excellence; it provides a plush,

[4] Santayana, *op. cit.*, p. 19.
[5] William Faulkner, "The Bear" from *Go Down Moses*, 2nd ed. (New York: Random House, 1942), p. 257.
[6] *Ibid.*, p. 291.
[7] Cf. my *Dialectic* (New York, 1953), p. 125.

luscious background for blasé, exotic luxury; yet even he, in *Cytherea,* his best book comes close to self-irony. His hero destroys the reality of his family life by his perverse love for an exotic doll. But most authors are dazzled by Marxism and therefore fail to understand that capitalism is not simply identical with the "profit-motive," "the almighty dollar." Dos Passos, Steinbeck, Upton Sinclair, Faulkner, and Hemingway are unanimous in this anti-profit protest. Sinclair's *Jungle* is an unsurpassable record of exploitation of the workers as well as the consumer, for the sake of a brutal inhuman profiteering. Steinbeck's *Grapes of Wrath* is the major reaction against the capitalistic depression of the 1930's, but his "Joads" are so unconscious of what has hit them that they can only think of taking to the road to "go West" as their ancestors had done. Jack London's numerous best-sellers most prominently symbolize this confused escapism mixed with equally confused rebellion: *The Call of the Wild,* one of London's best, is a significant title. His escapades blend infantile regression with disgust at a mechanized social routine; Nietzsche's "blond beasts" and "supermen" (taken literally), cohabit with Darwin's "animal ancestors" and beget the idolized "proletarian" of Marxism. Also torn between acceptance and revolt are writers like Theodore Dreiser who detests the ugliness of poverty and is both fascinated and frustrated by millionaires who are no less vulgar than his plain folks. Edith Wharton's millionaires on Fifth Avenue, in *Age of Innocence,* are pictured satirically as helpless victims of their own business system, which has caught them in the meshes of its competitive so-called economic laws. As soon as one member loses his wealth, all human contact immediately snaps; he is as good as dead.

Sinclair Lewis, who dedicated his *Babbitt* to Edith Wharton, continues in a similar satirical vein; what makes *Babbitt* so wonderfully funny is that this hollow, go-getting business booster believes that he is the paragon of a human culture and the peak of "Progress." That he is, nevertheless, not too sure of that, and of himself, makes him hysterically afraid of any critical thinking, which might remind him of reality. One illustration of this anti-capitalistic writing is a passage from Sinclair's *Jungle* which should suffice:

> The pace they set here, it was one that called for every faculty of a man—from the instant the first steer fell till the sounding of the noon whistle, and again from half-past twelve till heaven only knew what hour in the late afternoon or evening, there was never one instant's rest for a man, for his

hand or his eye or his brain . . . every man lived in terror of losing his job, if another made a better record than he. So from top to bottom the place was simply a seething cauldron of jealousies and hatreds . . . other men, who worked in tank-rooms full of steam, and in some of which there were open vats near the level of the floor, their peculiar trouble was that they fell into the vats; and when they were fished out, there was never enough of them left to be worth exhibiting—some-times they would be overlooked for days, till all but the bones of them had gone out to the world as Durham's Pure Leaf Lard! [8]

3. The socialistic belief, best represented by Upton Sinclair and James Farrell, reached its peak before the First World War, under the leadership of Eugene Debs. The war broke it—the major theme in Dos Passos; it flared up again in the early "red 30's" as a reaction to the de-pression. It seemed that all would be well if one would only expropriate the "tycoons" and turn the economic production and distribution over to the State and to the common man.

This blended with the old American tradition of an egalitarian democ-racy, idealizing equal conditions of prosperity for everybody, and an equal education for all, over-riding Jefferson's humanistic ideal of the same educational opportunities for different needs and values.

This blend, however, of the old American egalitarianism of the frontier with the rootless and mechanized new masses of industrial cities, held together only by external mass organizations, became problematic; the Hitler-Stalin pact of two egalitarian and totalitarian regimes became a symbol and was the breaker of this socialistic-egalitarianism.

But the common man had lost his halo already before this symbolic consummation. William Faulkner says of his *Percy Grimm*, that he had here created a Nazi before Hitler did. The conservative idea that there is a stratification of values and talents reappeared in protest against an un-differentiated, classless society, particularly in the literary criticism of the *New Humanism*. In literature, probably the best illustration would be the novels of Willa Cather, who mourns the loss of cultural integrity in the new society of cheap egalitarianism and commercialism. The Roman church with its hierarchy becomes her poetic symbol for our lost spiritual tradition in *Death Comes to the Archbishop*.

[8] Sinclair, *Jungle* (published by the author, 1920), p. 117.

The distrust of egalitarian democracy reaches back and destroys the legend of an ideal, paradisaical, good old hometown. Not only Lewis' *Main Street* but, more effectively, Sherwood Anderson's *Winesburg, Ohio* reveal a place full of inarticulate, feeble-minded individuals, whose daydreams are caricatures of themselves; there is no genuine communication between them. I think that Anderson is more effective, because the all too obvious satirical intent of Lewis is absent.

Egalitarian democracy developing into an industrial mass-civilization invented the standardized American city without architecture, sculpture, or style; one just as mechanical, sordid, and boring as every other; all full of plain, ugly, or dishonestly imitative churches of around two hundred anti-intellectual Christian sects. Babbitt, of course, gets a kick out of this interchangeable hometown:

> But when I get that lonely spell, I simply seek the best hotel, no matter in what town I be—St. Paul, Toledo, or K. C., in Washington, Schenectady, in Louisville or Albany. And at that inn it hits my dome that I again am right at home. If I should stand a lengthy spell in front of that first-class hotel, that to the drummers loves to cater, across from some big film theayter; if I should look around and buzz, and wonder in what town I was, I swear that I could never tell! For all the crowd would be so swell, in just the same fine sort of jeans they wear at home, and all the queens with spiffy bonnets on their beans, and all the fellows standing round a-talkin' always, I'll be bound, the same good jolly kind of guff, 'bout autos, politics and stuff and baseball players of renown that Nice Guys talk in my home town!
>
> Then when I entered that hotel, I'd look around and say "Well, well:" For there would be the same news-stand, same magazines and candies grand, same smokes of famous standard brand, I'd find at home, I'll tell! And when I saw the jolly bunch come waltzing in for eats at lunch, and squaring up in natty duds to platters large of French Fried spuds, why then I'd stand right up and bawl, "I've never left my home at all!" And all replete I'd sit me down beside some guy in derby brown upon a lobby chair of plush, and murmur to him in a rush, "Hello, Bill, tell me, good old scout, how is your stock a-holdin' out?" Then we'd be off, two solid pals, a-chatterin'

like giddy gals of flivvers, weather, home, and wives, lodge-
brothers then for all our lives! So when Sam Satan makes you
blue, good friend, that's what I'd up and do, for in these States
where 'er you roam, you never leave your home sweet home.[9]

There is nothing funny in William Faulkner's *Pylon* or *Death Drag*; the
rootless, mechanized robots of industrialism are portrayed in their sordid
brutality and ugliness.

4. The idealism of moral freedom and rational responsibility, believing in the dignity and worth of the individual and his cooperative society,
is a dominant American tradition from Emerson to William Torrey Harris,
Charles Peirce, Royce, and Whitehead. In literature its classical representative at the turn of the century is Henry James. Most of his characters are
free agents. They are noble and good at heart; even his most naive and
crude Americans, like his Texan in Paris in *The American* or his *Daisy
Miller*. His style is always highly cultured, smooth, subtle; in retrospect it
now seems academic and intellectual.

In the 20th-century novel, this humanistic idealism becomes a beautiful but unrealistic dream. Everywhere, in Dreiser, Lewis, Wharton, Steinbeck, Hemingway, Dos Passos, and Faulkner, man is a captive of social
circumstances, a victim of an impersonal mechanical system, a patient of
neurotic fixations, driven violently by animal instincts, and smothered by
a guilty past; ideals which their elders lived by are debunked; what seemed
reliable in a respectable tradition is breaking down and is degraded into
empty slogans and high sounding ideology. This victimization of man is
particularly shown in the many poignant and pungent descriptions of
American soldiers in the two world wars; I only mention Faulkner's *Soldiers'
Pay*, Hemingway's *Farewell to Arms* and *The Sun Also Rises*, Norman Mailer's *The Naked and the Dead*, and Thomas Wolfe's *You Can't Go Home
Again*. A good summary of this is Dos Passos' satire on the unknown
soldier in *USA*:

> In the tarpaper morgue at Chalons-sur-Marne in the reek
> of chloride of lime and the dead, they picked out the pine box
> that held all that was left of
>   enie menie minie moe plenty other pine boxes stacked
> up there containing what they'd scraped up of Richard Roe
>   and other person or persons unknown. Only one can go.

[9] Sinclair Lewis, *Babbitt* (New York: Harcourt, Brace and Co., 1922), p. 185.

How did they pick John Doe?

Make sure he ain't a dinge, boys, make sure he ain't a guinea or a kike,

how can you tell a guy's a hundredpercent when all you've got's a gunnysack full of bones, bronze buttons stamped with the screaming eagle and a pair of roll puttees?

. . . and the gagging chloride and the puky dirtstench of the yearold dead . . .

The day withal was too meaningful and tragic for applause. Silence, tears, songs and prayer, muffled drums and soft music were the instrumentalities today of national approbation.[10]

Faulkner's man, in addition to the skepticism and despair engendered by wars, is hopelessly entangled in the guilt of slavery and in unresolvable racial antagonisms from which he cannot extricate himself:

"Took in what?" he said, "Took in washing?" He sprang, still seated even, flinging himself backward onto one arm, awry-haired, glaring . . . the pale lips, the skin pallid and dead-looking yet not ill, the dark and tragic and foreknowing eyes. Maybe in a thousand or two thousand years in America, he thought. But not now! Not now! He cried, not loud, in a voice of amazement, pity, and outrage: "You're a nigger!" . . . Go back north. Marry: a man in your own race. That's the only salvation for you—for a while yet, maybe a long while yet. We will have to wait. Marry a black man. You are young, handsome, almost white; you could find a black man who would see in you what it was you saw in him, who would ask nothing of you and expect less and get even still less than that, if it's revenge you want . . . where cotton is planted and grows man-tall in the very cracks of the sidewalks, and usury and mortgage and bankruptcy and measureless wealth, Chinese and African and Aryan and Jew, all breed and spawn together until no man has time to say which one is which nor cares! . . . No wonder the ruined woods I used to know don't cry for retribution! he thought: The people who have destroyed it will accomplish its revenge. . . .[11]

---

[10] John Dos Passos, *USA* (Boston: Houghton Mifflin Co., 1930), p. 468.

[11] Faulkner, "Autumn Delta" from *Go Down Moses*, 3rd ed. (New York: Random House, 1942), pp. 360–361.

Philosophy is as dialectical as life itself: we have to face our negations. Every critique implies standards of value. Social protests from drifters and drunkards are merely sad and sentimental. But life seen as chaos is saved by virtue of the cosmos, the ideal integrity which lies in the ideal form of a genuine work of art. The movement of critical reason is the battle of life itself. Reason is both essential and existential.

Hemingway moves from disintegration and impotence in *The Sun Also Rises* to a heroic stoicism in his later work. In the beautiful prose-poem, *The Old Man and the Sea,* man, alone and on his own, faces impossible situations of pain and suffering with an absolute courage and integrity. I call it stoic because there is no hope of success or redemption in this heroic endurance of life.

Thomas Wolfe, in his last work, *You Can't Go Home Again,* reaches a profound philosophical understanding of three equally sustaining world-views. One is the *aesthetic* world-view which empowers man to transform the meaningless experience into a meaningful spectacle. In this Wolfe affirms the value of his own artistic existence in the teeth of his adverse experience. Secondly, he understands that the *moral* task to improve life and diminish its suffering is a perennial problem on many levels, vital as well as spiritual. The problem is not invalidated by the failure of societies or individuals to solve it. Thirdly, he balances this moral world-view against the aesthetic within a philosophical contemplation in which the tensions of the aesthetic versus the practical life of man are seen in an eternal order. On this basis, his editor, Ferguson, enjoys the absence of achievements without over-rating this temporal importance. There is a philosophical serenity in this last Wolfe, which over-arches his pains.

The last chapter of *Look Homeward Angel* is the most condensed statement of Wolfe's metaphysics. Eugene Gant, the autobiographical hero of the novel, meets his brother Ben at midnight, standing on the front porch of their father's sculpture shop—although Ben has just died and been buried. In their conversation, experience of externals is derealized, object-thinking is bracketed, to use Husserl's expression. Reality, metaphysical ground is reached and discovered in the soul, which is the subject of the earthly substance, universal and individual, essential and existential, One in the Many; moving, changing--eternally so—the dialectical core, model of, and ingress to all reality:

> And in his vision he saw the fabulous lost cities, buried
> in the drifted silt of the earth. . . . He saw the billion living of

the earth, the thousand billion dead: seas were withered, deserts flooded, mountains drowned; and gods and demons. . . . But, amid the fumbling march of races to extinction, the giant rhythms of the earth remained. . . . His brain was sick with the million books, his eyes with the million pictures, his body sickened on a hundred princely wines.

And rising from his vision, he cried: "I am not there among the cities. . . ."

Then, from the edges of moon-bright silence, Ben replied: "Fool, why do you look in the streets?"

Then Eugene said: "I have eaten and drunk the earth, I have been lost and beaten, and I will go no more."

"Fool," said Ben, "What do you want to find?"

"Myself, and an end to hunger, and the happy land," he answered. . . .

Then, as he thought, Ben said: "There is no happy land. There is no end to hunger. . . ."

"Then I of yours the seeming, Ben? Your flesh is dead and buried in these hills: my unimprisoned soul haunts through the million streets of life, living its spectral nightmare of hunger and desire. Where Ben? Where is the world?"

"Nowhere," Ben said. "*You* are the world. . . ." [12]

In conclusion, we turn from philosophy *in*, to the philosophy *of* 20th-century American literature. This conclusion is hard and unpalatable, but inescapable: What does it all mean? We begin to understand that we must live together with what we call evil; that evil *becomes* evil in opposition against what is held to be good; or, evil is the inevitable other side of the moral medal.

A formal and undialectical ethics used to have valid norms and ideals; what did not live up to its standards was ignored, suppressed, or spuriously inhibited; evil and inferior tendencies were punished, eradicated, or "kept in their place." They were irrational, and the irrational was outlawed or taboo. There were periods, now felt by us as dishonest, when this negative ethics, very sure of itself, seemed to "work."

But, in this century, the irrational emerges defiantly and demonstrates, in individual neuroses and in collective regressions, that the prohibitive

[12] Thomas Wolfe, *Look Homeward Angel* (New York: Charles Scribner's Sons, 1929), p. 624.

ideals of the undialectical ethics are powerless to dam the irrational inundations of the individual and historical scene. Individuals are driven to isolation and desperation; masses become atavistic or primitive and are no longer able to follow critical, discriminating leaders.

If the irrational is not recognized as the nocturnal or subconscious natural root of human existence, it will take its revenge on those who ignore or suppress it. Irrationalism triumphs in collective acts of aggression, destruction, resentment, scape-goating projections of its own blind fury on symbolic victims. Dialectical ethics, therefore, must assimilate and recognize in a total view of reality the power of the irrational pole. This remains evil and self-destructive, but the self learns to live with it.

The animal, subconscious, and inhibited impulses in human nature are limiting the enlightened, cultural, conscious, and regulating functions of the soul. Our writers do their utmost to describe the dark brother in ourselves and make him see himself in their mirror. In seeing himself in their mirror he is tamed.

The same metaphysical revolution can be literally "illustrated" in 20th-century painting. The idyllic "nature" of conventions is gone. The new vision of reality, aided by microscopic discoveries of strange substructures and telescopic disclosures of an astronomic chaos (no "twinkling, twinkling little stars"), is embodied in painting without conventional objects, without subjective perspectives (the pride of the Italian Renaissance), and without guided directions.

A philosophy true to this situation can be neither a monism nor a dualism. A monism of the irrational is impossible, because irrational rebellions pre-suppose rational-moral standards, protesting against which the irrational *becomes* irrational. A pan-irrationalism or vitalism would have to claim that its vision is true, but a true understanding of the irrational is never irrational. A monism of the rational-moral ideal, on the other hand, is illusory, a fool's paradise—"all is well and good"—for which one may piously vote, but which one can never demonstrate. The claim that all is rational paradoxically ends in suppressing all critical reason or thought.

Dualism divides reality into light versus dark, good versus evil, rational versus irrational, hoping to conquer the negative side by the positive side in the end. This tragic struggle is real and good in itself. It always modifies itself, it is always different in different individual situations, but it always remains the same struggle. This ethical reality must be respected; ethics cannot impose its demands on reality—it is an empty utopianism to demand how we should be in a year or in a thousand years. Such illusions are, for example, "to make the world safe for democracy," or "to make this the war to end all wars," or "white supremacy," etc. Every demand creates its own opposition, casts its own shadow; it is this total situation which we must accept, not one of its poles.

Adequate to the situation is the old and ever-new Socratic-Platonic or Hegelian dialectic, which accepts reality as the indivisible and concrete unity of opposites. The negative is no less real than the positive pole, and neither the polarities nor their unity can be abrogated. This dialectic is the essential existence of man. Reality is disclosed and accepted in it. Man, then, has the never-ending and ever-present task to discover his limitations, to explore the uncertain, and to cope with the threatening irrationality of his true situation.

There has been considerable confusion, says Mordecai Marcus, about just what constitutes an initiation story, and this anarchy, in turn, has led to misreading of the stories themselves. If we have a more comprehensive definition of the initiation story, one which allows for various stages of growth and does not always insist on profound meanings, we shall avoid some of the misunderstanding which reigns. In order to clarify the situation, Marcus suggests first that ritual is not necessarily a feature of such stories. He says, moreover, that an initiation story is one which gives us a young protagonist who experiences a significant change of knowledge about himself (or the world) or an actual change in character. In some stories the young person may achieve both new knowledge and a significant change in character. As a further aid to understanding, Marcus advances a threefold division of initiation stories based on stages of maturity. First, there is the tentative initiation, as in Ernest Hemingway's "The Killers," in which Nick is brought to the threshold of maturity; second, there is the uncompleted initiation, as in Katherine Mansfield's "The Garden Party," in which Laura experiences death but is left uncertain; and finally there is the decisive initiation, as in William Faulkner's "The Bear," in which Ike moves firmly into moral adulthood.

what is an
initiation story?

MORDECAI MARCUS

Much recent criticism, apparently beginning with Brooks and Warren's comments on Hemingway's "The Killers" and Anderson's "I Want to Know Why" in *Understanding Fiction* (1943), has used the term "initiation" to describe a theme and a type of story. Ray B. West's history of *The Short Story in America, 1900–1950* (1952) uses the term for one of two major types of short story. Several short story textbooks and textbook manuals employ the term, and other criticism applies it to novels.

The prevalence of inadequate criticism employing the concept of initiation suggests that the term requires clarification. I propose to examine the origins and definitions of this concept, to test it through application to a variety of stories, and to suggest its usefulness and its limitations. For the sake of convenience, I will—with the exception of a few short novels—confine my discussion to short stories.

The name and analytic concept of the initiation story derive basically from anthropology. The most important rites of most primitive cultures center around the passage from childhood or adolescence to maturity and full membership in adult society. Anthropologists call these rites initiation or puberty ceremonies. These ceremonies involve physical torture, cutting of various parts of the body, abstension from and ritualistic use of food, isolation, and indoctrination in secret tribal beliefs. According to most anthropologists the purpose of these rites is to test the endurance of the novice, to assure his loyalty to the tribe, and to maintain the power of the adult community. But a few anthropologists believe that they stem from a psychological compulsion to propitiate the adult community or supernatural powers.

Certain "literary anthropologists" propose a concept of initiation apparently based on the idea of propitiating the adult or supernatural world. For example, Joseph Campbell's *The Hero with a Thousand Faces* (1949) describes initiation as a stage in all human life. He derives his description of initiation from the experience of the typical mythical hero as he seeks adjustment and union with the forces of existence, such as the tempting woman and the threatening father. Other writers have analyzed similar initiation rituals in medieval literature.

A brief description of the ways in which fiction can embody ritual will help to show the relationship between these anthropological ideas and the initiation story, and will also be helpful in analyzing certain initiation stories. Ritual is difficult to define and to apprehend because most human behavior follows prescribed patterns unreflectively. Everyday patterns of behavior are recognized as ritualistic only when they are so exaggerated or deliberate as to appear out of the ordinary. Therefore, the formalized behavior of so-called civilized people will appear ritualistic in fiction chiefly under two circumstances: when it involves a response to an unusually trying situation in which a person falls back on socially formalized behavior, or when an individual pattern of behavior results from powerful psychological compulsion. Ritual may appear in fiction in two more guises: through the portrayal of the formalized behavior of primitives or folkpeople and through symbols which suggest mythological parallels in people or action. Certain psychologists and anthropologists, particularly the disciples of Jung, tend to see a basic unity in all these manifestations of ritual, but it is safe to ignore without refuting this questionable doctrine, for it would not seriously alter most of my analysis.

The anthropologist's ideas about initiation would suggest that an initiation story shows adult society deliberately testing and indoctrinating the young, or shows the young compelled in a relatively universal manner to enact certain experiences in order to achieve maturity. But only a very small proportion of works called initiation stories, or meeting the definitions for them, show adults testing or teaching the young. Ritual does occur in some initiation stories, but it is more often of individual than of social origin. Education is always important in an initiation story, but it is usually a direct result of experience rather than of indoctrination. One concludes that the initiation story has only a tangential relationship to the anthropologist's idea of initiation.

The various critical definitions of the initiation story fall into two groups. The first group describes initiation as a passage of the young from ignorance about the external world to some vital knowledge. The second describes initiation as an important self-discovery and a resulting adjustment to life or society. But definitions within these two categories vary considerably.

According to Adrian H. Jaffe and Virgil Scott initiation occurs when "a character, in the course of the story, learns something that he did not know before, and . . . what he learns is already known to, and shared by, the larger group of the world." [1] Several critics, including Brooks and Warren (p. 344), and West (p. 75), explicitly define initiation as a discovery of evil. Brooks and Warren also state that the protagonist seeks to come to terms with his discovery, and West suggests that in learning to live with his knowledge the protagonist begins to achieve self-understanding.

The remarks of Brooks and Warren, and West, about achieving adjustment and self-understanding give their theories continuity with those which make self-understanding central to the initiation story. Curiously balanced between the two classes of definition is Leslie Fiedler's belief that "An initiation is a fall through knowledge to maturity; behind it there persists the myth of the Garden of Eden, the assumption that to know

[1] *Studies in the Short Story* (New York, 1949), p. 155.

good and evil is to be done with the joy of innocence and to take on the burdens of work and childbearing and death." [2] Less ambiguous concepts of initiation as self-discovery are presented in two discussions of stories by Conrad. Carl Benson believes that *The Shadow Line* presents initiation as "the passage from egocentric youth to human solidarity." [3] Albert J. Guerard finds initiation in *Heart of Darkness* and "The Secret Sharer" to be "progress through temporary reversion and achieved self-knowledge, the theme of man's exploratory descent into the primitive sources of being," but Guerard believes that this knowledge of evil makes us capable of good. [4]

Three of the critics cited insist or imply that initiation stories contain ritual but they offer no distinctions between kinds of ritual. Jaffe and Scott compare initiation plots to fraternity initiation ceremonies. West suggests that Hemingway is always ritualistic (p. 93), and refers to the "ritual of initiation" in "The Killers" and in Faulkner's "That Evening Sun" (p. 99). (The Faulkner story, I believe, does not present initiation.) Guerard's insistence on psychological compulsion and on the appropriateness of bloodshed in "a true initiation story" suggests that he may consider ritual vital to the form. [5]

A synthesis of these ideas will provide a working definition. An initiation story may be said to show its young protagonist a significant change of knowledge about the world or himself, or a change of character, or of both, and this change must point or lead him towards an adult world. It may or may not contain some form of ritual, but it should give some evidence that the change is at least likely to have permanent effects.

Initiation stories obviously center on a variety of experiences and the initiations vary in effect. It will be useful, therefore, to divide initiations into types according to their power and effect. First, some initiations lead only to the threshold of maturity and understanding but do not definitely cross it. Such stories emphasize the shocking effect of experience, and their protagonists tend to be distinctly young. Second, some initiations take their protagonists across a threshold of maturity and understanding but leave them enmeshed in a struggle for certainty. These initiations sometimes involve self-discovery. Third, the most decisive initiations carry their protagonists firmly into maturity and understanding, or at least show them decisively embarked toward maturity. These initiations usually center

---

[2] "From Redemption to Initiation," *New Leader,* 41 (May 26, 1958), 22.
[3] "Conrad's Two Stories of Initiation," *PMLA,* LXIX (1954), 49–50.
[4] Introduction, *Heart of Darkness* (New York, Signet edition, 1950), p. 14.
[5] *Conrad the Novelist* (Cambridge, Mass., 1958), p. 40n.

on self-discovery. For convenience, I will call these types tentative, un-completed, and decisive initiations.

Stories of tentative initiation typically show shocking experiences which leave their protagonists distraught. Since such experiences do not always lead towards maturity, one may demand evidence of permanent effect on the protagonist before ascribing initiation to a story. Stories of very young children offer the greatest problem here. In Chekov's "A Trifle from Life," Katherine Mansfield's "Sun and Moon," and Katherine Anne Porter's "The Circus," young children experience disillusionment in the trustworthiness of an adult, in the permanence of a delightful and pictur-esque event, and in the joyfulness and sincerity of a circus performance. In each story, a child is violently distressed, while the surrounding adults remain uncomprehending or unsympathetic. Only Miss Porter's story sug-gests that the disillusioning experience will have long-range effects, and since the suggestion is that they will be damaging, her story raises the possibility that the maturation process in all initiation stories should be further classified according to the proportion of or balance between emo-tional damage and growth which they show.

Despite one's hesitation to find initiation in these three stories, they are not far removed in theme and structure from many works which critics have called typical initiation stories—for example, several much discussed stories by Hemingway. Among these stories is "Indian Camp," in which Nick Adams watches his father perform a Caesarian operation on an Indian woman and then sees that the woman's husband has killed himself to avoid witnessing her suffering. The story emphasizes Nick's discovery of death, but its conclusion asserts that Nick could not believe he would ever die. If Nick's discovery is to have permanent effects, one must assume that the story's conclusion describes a protective rationalization which cannot last. If this is true, then the story shows an approach to and a temporary withdrawal from mature realization.

Other stories by Hemingway show longer-lasting struggles at thresh-olds of maturity. "My Old Man" shows its protagonist learning that his father was a cheat despised by various people, and he is left struggling for an adjustment to this bitter knowledge. Hemingway's two stories of adolescent discovery of violence, "The Killers" and "The Battler," are perhaps more problematic than "Indian Camp" and "My Old Man." In "The Killers" Nick Adams is confronted with brutal and somewhat imper-sonal violence in the actions of the gangsters, and with despairing passiv-ity in the behavior of the prizefighter Andreson. Various details suggest that Nick has never before witnessed such behavior. The end of the story shows Nick struggling for adjustment to his new knowledge, and contrasts his sensitivity to evil and despair with the insensitivity of Sam and George.

This story marks a tentative initiation into maturity, but analysis of its initiation theme has led to irresponsible interpretations. Brooks and Warren propose that Nick experiences "the discovery of evil" (p. 322), but this phrase makes Nick's experience uniquely symbolic of evil in general, which is more weight than the story can carry. Jaffe and Scott, probably building on Brooks and Warren's interpretation, find the story showing "a person who suddenly discovers the basic nature of existence," and claim that it is "about the meaning of life and man's place in the universe" (pp. 209–210). These interpretations are a far cry from the rather elementary experience of Nick Adams in "The Killers."

Quite possibly the idea that an initiation must be profound and universal has misled these critics. Jaffe and Scott's insistence that initiation is always "into the larger group of the world" may also mislead them, for Hemingway's heroes are always initiated into a select group. Hemingway's "The Battler" records comparable encounters by Nick Adams, but this time he discovers treachery and uncertainty as well as violence. If the experience in "The Killers" is to be called *the* initiation into the meaning of existence, one might as well propose the same interpretation for "The Battler"; but again the idea appears irresponsible. Ray West's idea that "The Killers" is an initiation ritual finds little support in the story, for its only ritual element appears to be the operation of the narrow social codes of the gangsters and the prizefighter.

Disillusion, uncertainty, and violence also create the tentative initiation of Jody Tiflin in Steinbeck's three-part story "The Red Pony," yet the emphasis in this story is markedly different from that in Hemingway's two stories. Jody's farm life bristles with evidence of the uncertainty of life and the dependence of life on death, but only a series of incidents which involve him deeply begin to bring these truths home to Jody. Steinbeck does not show Jody's final realization, but Jody's feelings after he has seen Billy Buck's struggle to bring the colt to birth suggest that Jody will remember his initiating experiences. "The Red Pony" contains occasional suggestions of ritual (chiefly through parallels to primitive rites) in its emphasis on the slaughter of farm animals, and (in the form of individual compulsion) in Jody's constant attention to his pony and to the pregnant mare. In this story Steinbeck's view of the cycle of life is somewhat sacramental. Faulkner's view of nature in "The Old People" is distinctly sacramental. In this story, Ike McCaslin is ritualistically initiated into a communion with nature by Sam Fathers, the old Indian-Negro (the rites derive from a primitive culture), after which Ike sees a vision of the buck he has slain. Sam's instructions and Ike's own vision teach him to respect the sacredness of nature. Faulkner's story places less emphasis than does Steinbeck's on the pervasiveness of death, but it does stress the interdependence of life and death. Both of these stories present tentative initiations, for they give only slight evidence that their protagonists are achieving maturity.

Although stories involving some self-discovery usually move beyond tentative and towards uncompleted initiation, self-discovery may be slight enough or sufficiently compounded with other feelings so that it does not lead beyond the tentative. For example, the protagonist of Joyce's "Araby" is disillusioned about the bazaar he longed to visit, and at the same time gains an insight into his own vanity. Perhaps because we see in him litle struggle for adjustment, the shame which Joyce's protagonist suffers nay seem less of a step towards maturity than the shock which Nick Adams experiences in "The Killers" and "The Battler." Another story which combines some self-discovery with tentative initiation is Dorothy Canfield Fisher's "Sunset at Sixteen," a story about a young girl whose first romantic yearnings and disappointments make her realize that she must experience years of struggle and pain to win through to the final peace of maturity.

The dividing line between tentative and uncompleted initiation is, of course, inpossible to establish precisely. Initiation into knowledge of sex and into sexual desire might easily fit all three categories of initiation stories, but in two well known stories such experience illustrates uncompleted initiation. In Anderson's "I Want to Know Why" a boy recognizes moral conplexity in the lives of two men whose sexual behavior contrasts with their other actions and reveals a combination of good and evil. Although Anderson's protagonist remains profoundly puzzled, the depth of his concern makes it likely that he will continue to strive for understanding. More complex is the uncompleted initiation in Alberto Moravia's short novel *Agostino*, which portrays a boy of thirteen first learning about the nature of sexual relations, then tortured by his relationship to his young and beauiful widowed mother, and finally unable to gain admittance to a brothel, where he had hoped to destroy his oedipal vision of his mother. Agostino's desperation and seething conflicts perhaps give more assurance that he will struggle towards maturity than does the dilemma of Anderson's protagonist.

Another harsh self-discovery accompanying a discovery about human life occurs in Lionel Trilling's "The Other Margaret." As this highly complex story concludes, a thirteen year old girl is forced to recognize that another person, and presumably all men, are responsible for their moral lives no matter what extenuating circumstances exist. From this insight she immediately moves to recognition of her own responsibility. Although the story ends with the girl weeping uncontrollably, the force with which she makes her discovery, its profoundly personal nature, as well as the girl's intelligence and sensitivity, strongly suggest that her discovery will have permanent effects. The smashing of the clay lamb, which object the protagonist's father identifies with her, is certainly symbolic and may introduce a ritualistic element through association with primitive rtes, but ritual, I believe, is not essential to the story.

Self-discovery may be a more gentle correlate of discoveries about human life, as in stories of uncompleted initiation by Jessamyn West and Katherine Mansfield. Miss West's "Sixteen" (the final story in *Cress Delahanty*) portrays a self-centered girl who reluctantly goes home from college to be present at her aged grandfather's death. Details throughout the story suggest that Cress is scornful of the sensibilities of the old, of other people in general, and proud of the rare flowering of her own sensibilities. As her dying grandfather speaks to her of his love for the flower she wears and compares her to his dead wife, Cress realizes that his humanity is like hers, and so she discovers that she has been falsely separating herself from others. The story ends on a note of communion between he dying man and the girl, suggesting that she will change.

A parallel but more complex initiation occurs in Miss Mansfield's "The Garden Party," in which the adolescent protagonist, Laura, is intensely concerned with her relationships to everyone she deals with. Her self-centeredness, unlike Cress Delahanty's, is patronizing, and she is concerned to do what appears right. As the story concludes, Laura discovers the reality and the mystery of death, which discovery seems to ease the burden of living and yet demand that life be understood. Although her problems are not solved, the conclusion suggests that she is in a better position to find life's realities. Laura's almost compulsive concern with the dead man is perhaps psychologically ritualistic, and—as Daniel A. Weiss has observed [6]—her descent to the cottage of the dead man paral-

[6] "Crashing the Garden Party," *Modern Fiction Studies,* IV (1958–59), 363–364.

lels Proserpine's descent to the dead. But these ritual elements are slight. A somewhat comparable theme is presented in Katherine Anne Porter's "A Grave." This story at first portrays a girl of nine who confronts the mystery of birth and death as she bends over the open body of a pregnant dead rabbit. But it is twenty years later that the meaning of this experience crystallizes for her. Rather than portraying an actual initiation, this story shows a mature person remembering from her years of immaturity a symbol for more recent knowledge. But its revelation that growth has occurred strongly parallels the initiation theme. Robert Penn Warren's "Blackberry Winter," which Ray B. West analyzes intensively as an initiation story (pp. 77–80), slightly resembles "A Grave." Warren presents a series of potentially disillusioning experiences which a nine year old boy experiences on one day. At the story's end, flashing ahead thirty-five years to the present, the first-person protagonist implies that the experiences of that day prefigured all of his subsequent life. Unlike Miss Porter's story, however, Warren's gives no indication of how or when the early experience was recognized as a prototype of the later, and the result is a feeling of melodramatic cheating in the conclusion. West's detailed analysis of the story mistakenly insists that the nine year old boy understands the meaning of his experience.

Although these stories by Miss Porter and by Warren make a special use of the initiation theme, they stand at the borderline between stories of uncompleted and decisive initiation. As one might expect, some stories of sexual initiation are likely to stand at a similar crossroads, for initial sexual intercourse is in one sense always decisive but also points toward character development. Hemingway's somewhat cynical story "Up in Michigan" portrays the simple disillusionment of a girl who is half-willingly raped by a man whom she has admired from a distance, but the story stops rather abruptly after her sexual initiation. Far more complex is Colette's short novel *Le Blé en Herbe* (translated as *The Ripening*). In this story, sixteen year old Phillipe spends an idyllic and yet often bitter summer at the sea-shore in the company of a fifteen year old girl, Vinca. Both children are pained by the uncertainties of growing up, but before the summer is over Phillipe has had an extended sexual initiation with a sensual woman of thirty, and then one brief and somewhat unsatisfactory intercourse with Vinca. Although Phillipe develops no sense of sexual guilt from his major experience, its undecided effect on his future, and his great passivity and uncertainty, leave him still bitter and unhappy.

191

Two symbolic details help communicate these feelings and add touches of ritual to the story through association with myth or primitive rite. When Phillipe's lover first invites him into her house, she presses on him a glass of very cold orangeade, and Phillipe repeatedly thinks of the bitterness of the drink as he struggles with his feelings about the woman. When Phillipe returns to the woman's house he tosses a bunch of thistle-flowers into her garden and accidentally wounds her face. Summoning him into the garden, she presses a drop of blood onto his hand. The next time Phillipe returns, their sexual affair begins. Both ritualistic details symbolize his partially disillusioning experience.

Moravia's short novel *Luca*, which portrays a more profound and decisive initiation than Colette's, employs a sexual initiation to create its denouement. *Luca* is pervasively ritualistic, often combining psychological compulsion and mythical parallels. The story traces out the struggles of a fifteen year old boy who feels progressively alienated from his mother and father, his school, and his once precious pursuits. He compulsively rejects all contacts because of their hypocrisy and impurity, and proceeds to cut himself off from life. Ritualistically he gives away his most valued possessions, rejects gestures of friendship, and imagines himself passively dead. In a ritualistic game of hide and seek in the dark (an exaggerated version of the cultural ritual of the beckoning but elusive woman), he grows interested in a woman, but she dies before he can keep an appointment with her. Finally, after long illness and delirium, he is initiated into sex by a much older woman, whom he perceives as an earth goddess; and feeling at last in vital contact with all of life, he moves decisively towards mature acceptance.

A fusion of psychological accuracy and familiar archetypes is also conspicuous in Conrad's "The Secret Sharer." Albert J. Guerard finds in this story the archetype of the mythical night journey, which represents a descent into the unconscious.[7] "The Secret Sharer" unquestionably shows psychological ritual: its protagonist must exert himself to an extreme to conceal his double, and he acts in a trance-like manner. Most striking is his compulsion to drive his ship as close to the land as possible, presumably so that he may show Leggatt his gratitude for the experience of self-discovery. How far he has gone beyond the discovery of courage and endurance amidst loneliness remains problematic, but the final sentences of the story reveal that he has achieved a decisive initiation. Numerous psychologists and mythographers have attested to the universality of the myth of the exploratory night journey.

[7] *Conrad the Novelist*, p. 26.

Clearly formalized primitive ritual occurs in two well known stories which portray decisive initiations: Steinbeck's "Flight" and Faulkner's "The Bear." Pepé, the Mexican boy in "Flight," is suddenly projected into manhood when he must bear the consequences of having killed a man over a point of honor. From the story's opening Pepé's behavior shows rituals of his culture: he practices knife throwing, yearns for manhood, dons his father's garments. Perhaps more ritualistic is his flight from the avenging pursuers. The act itself, with foreknowledge that he is probably doomed, is ritualistic, as are his preparations, his course through the mountains, and his final deliberate confrontation of death after his case is hopeless.

The primitivistic ritual in Faulkner's "The Bear" is identical with the ritual in "The Old People," of which story it is a sequel. Sam Fathers marks the forehead of Ike McCaslin with the blood of his first slain deer, thereby bringing Ike into communion with the wilderness and nature. This incident is less detailed in "The Bear" than in "The Old People," but its meanings are much more deeply explored in additional incidents. Other ritualistic details in the story include Ike's abandonment of his watch, gun, and compass before he can get his first glimpse of the bear, Old Ben, and Sam Fathers' patient training of the dog Lion, who is to bring down Old Ben. Both incidents combine psychological compulsion and the sense of a half-intuited myth, the feeling that nature demands a certain rite. More distinctly psychological are the ritualistic intensity with which Ike pores over his grandfather's ledgers in pursuit of evidence of iniquity, and Ike's decision to renounce the land he has inherited from that grandfather and to adopt the Christ-like trade of a carpenter. All of these rituals are part of a decisive initiation: Ike's establishing a correct understanding of what it means to own the land and of how men may redeem their right to own the land. Faulkner's primitive and psychological rituals in this story are always convincing.

Ritualistic elements lend much coherence and power to these stories of decisive initiation, but ritual is not necessary in such a story. F. Scott Fitzgerald's "The Freshest Boy" describes a decisive point in the life of Basil Lee, which turns him away from egoism and snobbery towards self-discovery and social acceptance. Unfortunately, the turning point in the story—Basil's observation of a major frustration in the life of a football hero—is sentimental, as are some of the accompanying details. Fitzgerald's inability to create a vivid event to change his protagonist makes the story unlike most initiation stories, but Basil's final and decisive turn toward maturity is convincing.

The greater prevalence of ritual in stories of decisive rather than tentative or uncompleted initiation is striking, but it is not too difficult to explain. The full initiations which these stories present usually grow out of strong desires for self-discovery rather than from accidents. Use of psychological compulsion and struggle makes it easy for the writer to incorporate primitive or mythological ritual material when it is available. Primitivistic ritual is perhaps too rare in fiction to be generalized about, but it seems chiefly to accompany decisive initiation. Ritual elements are absent from or unimportant in most stories of tentative and uncompleted initiation, and they are not a definite requirement for decisive initiation.

If such stories as several by Hemingway, Anderson, Trilling, and Miss Porter are to remain in the canon of initiation stories—where they have been placed by various critics—a comprehensive definition like the one I have suggested must be adopted. This definition has the virtues of separating stages of initiation and of avoiding insistence on universal and profound meanings. Furthermore, not only should the critic show caution in ascribing ritual to a story, but he should analyze its type and its precise manifestation. These virtues, in turn, may assist careful analysis of meaning and construction. This definition, of course, has the defect of being so broad that almost any story of developing awareness or character can fit it. However, it is possible to exclude stories of simple recognitions about people and perhaps most stories about adults.

The alternative to my broad three-part definition is the close restriction of initiation to what I have called decisive initiation. Such a definition would insist on a clear-cut entrance into the adult world. Ritual would not be a central requirement for the form, but it would be a distinct likelihood. (Some critics, of course, might wish to limit initiation to stories containing ritual.) This definition might reduce the possibility of over-interpretation of stories such as "The Killers" and "Blackberry Winter," but sensibility will always remain more important than critical terms.

We see, then, that a certain anarchy has unnecessarily prevailed in the idea of the initiation story. Its relationships to anthropological ideas, even those of the "literary" anthropologist, are somewhat tenuous, and its use of archetypes and rituals is exaggerated. As is the case with many literary ideas, its central danger lies in its insistence on phenomena where they simply do not exist—in relying on a concept as a matter of faith. If one believes that initiation stories must present ritual, he may find ritual in "Indian Camp" or "The Circus," where they do not exist (except in the manner in which all human behavior is ritualistic). Leslie Fiedler's insistence that initiation is basically a discovery of guilt is an equally mistaken matter of faith. Many of the initiation stories I have discussed lack ritual and guilt.

Clearly defined and applied with sensibility and without fanaticism, the concept of the initiation story may assist thorough understanding of many works of fiction. But without these virtues, it may well serve only as another tool for reductive or misleading interpretation.

PART SIX
setting

Most contemporary fiction, particularly the stream-of-consciousness novel, observes Giorgio Melchiori, is preoccupied with the new concept of time which singles out some particular instant of illumination as the pivotal center of an entire narrative. Such a moment of acute awareness appears as "epiphany" in James Joyce's *Stephen Hero* ("a sudden spiritual manifestation") or as "moments of being" in the novels of Virginia Woolf. This moment of vision does not submit itself to the conventional notion of the clock as an organizing medium since, like T. S. Eliot's "moment in the rose garden," it embodies life in its fullest range—present, past, and future. An attempt to communicate such moments of heightened perception has led many contemporary novelists to unprecedented experimentation with language (James Joyce's *Finnegans Wake,* for example). Without understanding the moment as a time unit, concludes Melchiori, the reader is likely to miss much of the basic significance in contemporary fiction.

the moment as
a time-unit
in fiction

GIORGIO MELCHIORI

The presence of the past is one of the fundamental motifs of Eliot's poetry—or rather Eliot's achievement is the *full* realization and expression of this presence, the consciousness of which is detectable in the work of writers of all times. Even before writing the *Waste Land* and *Gerontion* Eliot had stated: [1]

> Tradition . . . involves, in the first place, the historical sense, which we may call nearly indispensable to anyone who would

[1] "Tradition and the Individual Talent," *Selected Essays,* 1932, p. 14.

continue to be a poet after his twenty-fifth year; and the historical sense involves a perception not only of the pastness
of the past, but of its presence . . . This historical sense,
which is a sense of the timeless as well as of the temporal
together, is what makes a writer traditional. And it is at the
same time what makes a writer most acutely conscious of his
place in time, of his own contemporaneity.

But in Eliot's later poetry alongside this awareness of the past there
is a growing insistence on the expression of the moment when this awareness is realized. Recent studies in his imagery have pointed out the importance of the "moment in the rose-garden," which, with its symbolical
and religious overtones, recurs again and again in his later poetry. In an
admirable essay [2] Mr. Leonard Unger has retraced the origins and the
reassembling into a recurrent cluster of the images which form the rose-
garden symbol, and has identified it with the "still point of the turning
world": a timeless moment of illumination, a meeting of time and eternity.[3]
The religious significance given to this moment can easily be gathered
from the VII Chorus of *The Rock* (1934), which is based on the first chapter of Genesis.[4]

Then came, at a predetermined moment, a moment in time
    and of time,
A moment not out of time, but in time, in what we call history;
    transecting, bisecting the world of time, a moment in time
    but not like a moment of time,
A moment in time but time was made through that moment:
    for without the meaning there is not time, and that moment
    of time gave the meaning.

Apart from the religious meaning attached to it, the moment in the
rose-garden seems to be the recollection of an extremely intense personal experience of the poet. I think that no clearer demonstration could
be found of an "objective correlative," which Eliot defined as "a set of
objects, a situation, a chain of events which shall be the formula of that
particular emotion." The set of images which consistently cluster round

[2] "T. S. Eliot and the Rose Garden," T. S. Eliot: *A Selected Critique,* ed. L.
Unger, New York, 1948, pp. 374ff.
[3] See too Louis L. Martz, "The Wheel and the Point," *A Selected Critique,* pp.
444ff.
[4] *Collected Poems 1909–35*, 1936, p. 173.

the rose-garden theme is Eliot's objective correlative of the particular emotion provoked by the realization of the complexity and depth of life contained in the space of a single moment. The contributory images have been slowly gathering from the time of "Prufrock" to the *Quartets,* while the realization was growing clearer—and its importance asserted itself so much that the rose-garden cluster became finally the central theme of Eliot's poetry. One quotation from the *Quartets* will be sufficient: [5]

> To be conscious is to be in time
> But only in time can the moment in the rose-garden,
> The moment in the arbour where the rain beat,
> The moment in the draughty church at smokefall
> Be remembered; involved with past and future.
> Only through time time is conquered.

This idea of the moment as a fundamental unit containing life at its fullest, present, past and future, is a corollary to Eliot's earlier conception of the presence of the past. On the other hand, he was neither the only writer nor the first to conceive this idea. We may think, in the first place, of Proust. An experience like the famous one of the *madeleine* happens in a moment. It is, as in Eliot, an instant of extremely acute awareness which recalls into the reality of the present a whole world of the author's past. A momentary flash like this sent Proust *à la recherche du temps perdu.*

Proust and Eliot cannot very well ‚be compared. In Eliot there has always been a deep sense of history, while in Proust the personal, subjective angle prevailed—not that he lacked historical sense: but that the sense of his own individuality was stronger. Proust in fact could project only himself into the past; his moment of revelation is a revelation of himself, of the world of his own feelings and experiences. Eliot instead has a way of trying to efface himself, and the moment of revelation therefore is the revelation of historical and universal values. This universal view is at the root of a philosophical attitude, but the very unaccountability of the moment of revelation suggests a religious interpretation. The historical conscience of Eliot makes it easier for him to pass on to the religious plane.

But what I intend to discuss is this new conception of time which originated in the heightened awareness of the intensity of the moment and of the momentary experience. The acute preoccupation of modern writers with time is now an acknowledged fact, and even a commonplace

[5] *Four Quartets,* 1944, p. 10.

of critical jargon. This has induced several authors who had only a dim apprehension of its real significance, to take advantage of the great general interest aroused in time and memory, and to play successful tricks with them. J. B. Priestley's time plays (in which he takes advantage of recent psychological theories on the subject) are an example of the cleverest form this tendency assumes; works like Hilton's *Lost Horizon* or Nathan's *Portrait of Jenny* show how its magical suggestions can be commercialized. The extremely wide use of the flashback technique in films and even in plays, like Arthur Miller's pretentious *Death of a Salesman,* is significant too. But this is by the way.

The first English novelists to confront the problem with a full consciousness of what they were doing were James Joyce and Virginia Woolf. As early as 1905 Joyce had built up his theory of the epiphanies [6] which he expounded in the first draft of *The Portrait of the Artist as a Young Man* (now published under the title *Stephen Hero* [7]):

> By an epiphany he meant a sudden spiritual manifestation, whether in the vulgarity of speech or of gesture or in a memorable phase of the mind itself. He believed that it was for the man of letters to record these epiphanies with extreme care, seeing that they themselves are the most delicate and evanescent of moments. He told Cranly that the clock of the Ballast Office was capable of an epiphany . . .
>
> —Yes, said Stephen. I will pass it time after time, allude to it, refer to it, catch a glimpse of it. It is only an item in the catalogue of Dublin's street furniture. Then all at once I see it and I know at once what it is: epiphany.—
>
> —What?—
>
> —Imagine my glimpses at the clock as the gropings of a spiritual eye which seeks to adjust its vision to an exact focus. The moment the focus is reached the object is epiphanized . . .

Stephen goes on expounding at some length Aquinas' theory of Beauty, with its three qualities: integrity, symmetry and radiance. Having dealt with the first two, Stephen proceeds:

---

[6] For all this part I am very much indebted to Theodore Spencer's introduction to *Stephen Hero* (1944, p. 13–14) and to Irene Hendry, "Joyce's Epiphanies," *James Joyce: Two Decades of Criticism,* ed. S. Givens, New York, 1949, pp. 27–46.

[7] *Stephen Hero,* edition quoted, pp. 188–90.

—Now for the third quality. For a long time I couldn't make out what Aquinas meant . . . but I have solved it. *Claritas* is *quidditas*. After the analysis which discovers the second quality the mind makes the only logically possible synthesis and discovers the third quality. This is the moment which I call epiphany. First we recognize that the object is *one* integral thing, then we recognize that it is an organized composite structure, a *thing* in fact: finally, when the relation of the parts is exquisite, when the parts are adjusted to the special point, we recognize that it is *that* thing which it is. Its soul, its whatness, leaps to us from the vestment of its appearance. The soul of the commonest object, the structure of which is so adjusted, seems to us radiant. The object achieves its epiphany—

In spite of the fact that the whole of this passage was rejected in the final version of the *Portrait,* there is no doubt that the revolution Joyce effected in the form of the novel owes much to the idea here expressed. The epiphanies, these sudden perceptions, in the space of a moment, of the total meaning and character of a scene, of a person, of a phrase, can be expressed only in a language which will extract the full meaning of each word with all its implications, a language where the intensity of the experience is matched by the verbal intensity. In *Ulysses* Joyce refers again to his epiphanies, and speaks with good-humoured detachment of Stephen's youthful ideal: [8]

Books you were going to write with letters for titles. Have you read his F? O yes, but I prefer Q. Yes but W is wonderful. O yes, W. Remember your epiphanies on green oval leaves, deeply deep, copies to be sent if you died to all great libraries of the world, including Alexandria?

The one-letter titles are in my opinion a further proof of the need Joyce felt for concentration, to reach the maximum intensity in the minimum space of time. But in *Ulysses* what in fact he tried to do was to extend through the length of a whole day the state of epiphany. The revolution in the novel brought about by the stream of consciousness technique —the attempt to follow moment by moment the mental processes in one or more characters—is due mainly to the fact that this technique intro-

Bodley Head edition, 1937, p. 37.

203

duces a new conception of time. Even at its most developed stage, even with Henry James, the psychological novel was dealing with a sequence of external events which, although brought about by very subtle reactions of the characters, and often very subtly analysed, still respected the calendar and the clock. Instead, in books like those of Joyce or Virginia Woolf there are events, but they are important only in so much as they are thought of at a certain moment; what matters is the feeling or thought of the moment, not what is happening.

Virginia Woolf's works are a series of attempts to fix exactly what she called the "moments of being" in the "incessant shower of innumerable atoms" which is life. Her aim and her struggle are summarized by Lily Briscoe in the last sentences of *To the Lighthouse* (1927):

> She looked at the steps; they were empty; she looked at her canvas; it was blurred. With a sudden intensity, as if she saw it clear for a second, she drew a line there, in the centre. It was done; it was finished. Yes, she thought, laying down her brush in extreme fatigue, I have had my vision.

We can compare this late restatement of aim and achievement with the well-known earlier theoretical affirmation: [9]

> Examine for a moment an ordinary mind on an ordinary day. The mind receives a myriad impressions—trivial, fantastic, evanescent, or engraved with the sharpness of steel. From all sides they come, an incessant shower of innumerable atoms; and as they fall, as they shape themselves into the life of Monday or Tuesday, the accent falls differently from of old; the moment of importance comes not here but there; so that, if a writer were a free man and not a slave, . . . there would be no plot, no comedy, no tragedy, no love interest or catastrophe in the accepted style . . . Life is not a series of gig lamps symmetrically arranged; life is a luminous halo, a semi-transparent envelope surrounding us from the beginning of consciousness to the end. Is it not the task of the novelist to convey this varying, this unknown and uncircumscribed spirit, whatever aberration and complexity it may display, with as little mixture of the alien and external as pos-

[9] "Modern Fiction," written April 1919, printed in *The Common Reader*, First Series, 1925, p. 189.

sible? We are not merely for courage and sincerity; we are suggesting that the proper stuff of fiction is a little other than custom would have us believe it.

Compared with this, the passage from *To the Lighthouse* reveals a new awareness of the effort implied in fixing the "moment of importance." Virginia Woolf seems to feel how shattering is the impact of a moment in which the whole of life at its most intense is enclosed. The "extreme fatigue" of Lily Briscoe is the fatigue of Virginia Woolf in trying to render in words the moment of vision. She realizes that everything must be contained in the minimum time unit, but becomes increasingly aware of the impossibility of sustaining the tension. Ten years after *To the Lighthouse*, in the last chapter of *The Years*, she writes:

> There must be another life, here and now, she repeated. This is too short, too broken . . . She hollowed her hands in her lap . . . She held her hands hollowed; she felt that she wanted to enclose the present moment; to make it stay; to fill it fuller and fuller, with the past, the present and the future, until it shone, whole, bright, deep with understanding.
> "Edward," she began, trying to attract his attention. But he was not listening to her . . . It's useless, she thought, opening her hands. It must drop. It must fall. And then? she thought.

Virginia Woolf's novels are a series of efforts to express and hold the moment of vision. She felt this effort as a necessity, or as a mission. But she felt as well, more and more, that the moment, as soon as expressed, would drop, would fall. The variety of techniques she used—so that each of her novels was greeted upon its publication with the adjective "experimental"—witnesses to her endless search for the novel-form which would substitute the single time unit of the fleeting instant for the restful time sequence of days, months and years. She tried to follow Joyce, selecting an ordinary day rich in intense moments of vision (*Mrs. Dalloway*); she bridged together two extended moments years apart (*To the Lighthouse*); she looked for some sort of relaxation in *Orlando*, playing with moments of history; she thought that the right momentary intensity could perhaps be reached through a consistent use of the stream of consciousness technique (*The Waves*); she singled out a whole series of moments over a distance of years (*The Years*); she hoped to sustain the necessary intensity by making the action last only a few hours and mixing together the temporal and the timeless through the performance of a pageant (*Between the Acts*). But the perpetual changes in technique are evidence of the fact that, perfect as each single book might be, the final novel-form to take the place of the traditional one was never found. As she says in the passage quoted from *The Years*, the momentary vision cannot be sustained for long: "It must drop. It must fall. And then?" This question is a question posed also to the modern writer of fiction who will (or, as it seems, must) adopt as his time unit the single instant of utter awareness.

The fact is that the consciousness of the intensity of what happens in the moment requires a tension in the writing which becomes unbearable to both reader and writer when sustained for any length of time. At its most successful the result is a *tour de force*. Joyce, to sustain it in *Ulysses*, had to employ a whole immense symbolic structure. Actually I think that the more and more frequent recourse of modern writers to ancient myths (as the French dramatists' remodelling of the stories of Orpheus or Antigone, Eliot himself basing his plays on the *Oresteia or Alcestis* [10]) is due not only to the wish to give a new version of the fundamental human situations, or to the pleasure taken in brilliant intellectual *divertissements*, but also to their need of a solid framework, strong enough to support such tension in writing.

After *Ulysses*, Joyce, who had always taken a great interest in the form of words, tried to reach a maximum of intensity by increasing to the utmost limits the pregnancy of the words used. He felt that the momentary impressions we receive are so extremely complex and compressed, that although the complexity could only be expressed in many words, the compression required few. In this way he bred and compounded new words to form the unrecognizable language of *Finnegans Wake*; in it the concentration of meaning is reached at the expense of clarity, and at the same time the book, by taking the form of a dream, assumes the right of expanding the moment indefinitely. The solution found seems to evade the problem which still confronts the modern writer who wants to introduce the new time unit into the narrative tradition.

I am speaking particularly of the prose writers, because poetry, as a matter of fact, has always dealt with profound momentary intuitions. To take a random example, Thomas Hardy collected part of his poems under the title *Moments of Vision*. Of course, the fact that this has now been realized by the novelist, that the new time-unit has come as the most revolutionary discovery of the century in the field of prose literature,

[10] T. S. Eliot, *Poetry and Drama*, Cambridge (Mass.), 1951, pp. 38–9.

has given the poets as well a new insight into their own work. As we have seen, to Eliot the realization of the supreme importance of the world contained in a moment gave a sense of such intensity of feeling that it could be equated only with religious experience. On the other hand the quality of poetic intuition has given prose that lyrical pace which is so evident in Virginia Woolf and James Joyce; it has stressed the already existing tendency towards coalescence of the two literary mediums. In fact, prose and poetry have never been closer to each other, even in their rhythms, diction and technical devices.

But, as I said, for the novelist the problem remains: when the time unit is reduced to Eliot's moment in time and timeless, Joyce's epiphany or Virginia Woolf's moment of being, there is not much scope for development of plot and action. It is impossible to build up a narrative in the tradition even of the most penetrating psychological novel. Psychology has in fact spent itself. The psychological analysis has moved from the character to the moment of being. It is no longer a question of individual psychology, but of the analysis of the interplay of persons and things and atmosphere within a moment, as apprehended by one individual mind— the author's—in a phase of heightened perception. So the characters become mere projections of the author, as for instance can be clearly seen in *The Waves,* where all six characters are different aspects of Virginia Woolf which she had tried to separate.

We may say that if *Ulysses* is indeed the novel to end all novels, this is not because of its extravagance in technique, but because it was the first novel in which the consciousness of the new temporal perspective appeared. The technical experiments of Joyce and Virginia Woolf, which at first dazzled their readers, had the effect of diverting attention from the fundamental fact that these experiments were the result of the new conception of time, and that they posed the still open problem of the treatment of this new element in fiction.

No wonder that critics complain that today there is no generation of novelists comparable with those writing in the 'twenties.[11] It is very nearly impossible for a sensitive author to ignore the impact of this transference into the writing of prose of a temporal conception which had been limited for centuries to lyrical poetry; or to ignore the unbearable tension which it calls for in his writing. Even a good critic like Mr. Philip Toynbee seems to be paralysed by it when attempting the novel form. In his *Tea with Mrs.*

[11] See for instance Philip Toynbee, "The Decline and Future of the English Novel," *Penguin New Writing,* no. 23 (1945), pp. 127ff.

Goodman (1947) he boldly faces the problem of expressing a variety of individual reactions to each single moment of time; but the strain that this imposes on the form of the novel is such that the experiment can hardly be called successful. Contemporary novelists, then, work under very difficult conditions. Some of them have preferred to concentrate merely on the stylistic and technical side of their art. Others have tried to devise new narrative forms or to compromise with past ones. This indeed is what the most gifted contemporary prose writers are successfully doing.

Take, for instance, William Sansom. Sansom concentrates his attention on a single fragment of action and fixes it permanently as a timeless experience, emphasizing especially the visual side of it rather than the spiritual implications as Virginia Woolf tried to do. Sansom's by now famous sketch *The Wall* [12] is typical: it is a four-page description of the second during which the façade of a burning building collapses. The story has a tremendous impact; an impact which is increased several-fold by the absolute respect for the minimum time unit. Or let us take a longer story, "Through the Quinquina Glass." [13] There, a whole story is told as if perceived by sudden intuition during a magical suspension of the ordinary time sequence:

> Through the quinquina glass the scene was sunless. The life had left it . . . Something unearthly had happened. I had lowered the glass—yet the scene retained its lurid quality . . . The green gloom persisted . . . This story was coming to my lips with a peculiar fluency . . . I was curiously sure of my words. The dull light of the quinquina glass alone illuminated the scene. The air was breathless.

A story with a fairly normal plot is given in this way a quality of timelessness, of a momentary intuition, acquiring a new and extraordinary intensity. But when the same plot is extended by the same author to ordinary novel length, though the writing is constantly highly-strung, the intensity is necessarily weakened. That is why the impact of *The Body*, Sansom's novel which re-utilizes the plot of the earlier short story, is much weaker: the story is no longer seen through the magic glass of an altered temporal perspective.

Other examples of this timeless quality can be found in the novels of

[12] In *Fireman Flower*, 1944, pp. 108–11.
[13] *Fireman Flower*, pp. 8–9.

Henry Green; in most of them a normal time sequence is eluded by isolating the characters in what have been called "emotional Black Holes of Calcutta," [14] a fog-bound railway hotel (*Party Going*—1939), a castle in Ireland during the war (*Loving*—1945)—places temporarily isolated from the rest of the world, where the normal limits of space and time are abolished by their own narrowness. In his last books the temporal definitions are still vaguer: *Concluding* (1948), and *Nothing* (1950), are set in a near future, by no means Utopian, but rather projecting outside time a present realistically described. Though in Green's case the extratemporal quality of the novels is closer to Kafka's than Virginia Woolf's, there is in him that extreme attention to the stylistic and technical side of writing which is at the same time an approach to poetical diction and a way of adding to the intensity of expression.

The sense of a different temporal perspective has engendered a tendency to adopt an altered physical one as well. Characters and backgrounds are frequently seen from what appears to be a distorted angle. Joyce Cary's *The Horse's Mouth* (1944) is a case in point. The long novel is told by a Blakian artist, and his way of looking at things is obviously highly personal; this produces an alteration of the normal perspective in which facts, things and people are seen, with the result of giving a vision of the world from a new angle, an angle which—one cannot help feeling— is deliberately wrong. As startlingly unreal is the picture given in a book like Graham Greene's *Brighton Rock* (1938), a novel which at first sight seems modelled on obvious tough realistic schemes: but it is just the contrast between this sordid realism and the complex, subtle and abnormal psychology of the characters and their interactions that produces the impression of an alteration in the balance of normal life. I believe that it is not mere chance that the director Carol Reed, in making films out of Greene's scripts (*The Fallen Idol*, *The Third Man*), nearly always holds the camera at a slant: the slanting images grow naturally out of Greene's descriptions of persons and places that, for all their humanity and reality, undergo some sort of deforming violence, acting on the inner nature of men and making things, seen through their eyes, look different.

We can go back to Sansom for a final example: the physical slant given to the hero of his *Equilibriad* (1948) is the externalization of the change in the inner vision of the writer. The title of the book seems particularly well chosen, since it conveys one of the impressions left on the readers by so much of the best contemporary prose. There is about it a

14 Henry Reed, *The Novel since 1939*, 1946, p. 29.

feeling of perpetual tension and alertness, even of fear. The authors are indeed afraid lest their works should lose that stylistic balance which is made the more essential when the world they represent, the physical and the psychical world and the world of time, seems to have lost its equilibrium.

This necessary caution may at times induce too much self-consciousness in the writers and hamper their freedom of expression—it may cause preciosity, but it leads as well to new achievements. It cannot be said that novel-writing is declining as a creative form of expression: it has undergone and is undergoing a process of readjustment. For the time being we can only assess which stage of this process each individual writer has reached.

The technique of background description, particularly description of landscape, has often been ignored by critics of the theory of the novel, observes D. S. Bland. According to him, landscape description in most novels, aside from localizing a scene or situation, projects through a skillful selection of color and detail the mood of a character. Casaubon in George Eliot's *Middlemarch*, for instance, is revealed through the autumnal background; like the November morning, he too is gray and dry. In fact, landscape description, as a part of the general background description, often acquires a symbolical significance which brings the reader closer to the central meaning of a story.

endangering the reader's neck: background description in the novel

D. S. BLAND

We want, I think, very much a Discourse on Description, carried through all the Species of Writing. To show us from what Objects, and how, to draw the finest Circumstances—Thomas Purney, Preface to *Pastorals* (1717)

In spite of the establishment of the novel in a dominant position by the middle of the nineteenth century, it is only in the last fifty years that there has been any really profitable discussion of its nature and processes. Even so, one aspect of the novelist's art, the role and technique of background description, has been somewhat neglected. Book after book can be read, broadcast after broadcast can be listened to, without the subject ever coming up. The moral purpose of the novelist, the nature of the hero, the novel as epic or symbol or what you will, these topics are discussed with unfailing regularity. But the critic who does more than make a conventional nod in the direction of Egdon Heath or the environs of Wuthering Heights is hardly ever to be encountered.

One reason for this neglect is that description—of a sort—is so easy to do, and so frequently done for its own sake, without relevance to the totality of the novel, that the critic avoids so obvious a field for adverse comment. Relevance, in fact, is the key, as Elizabeth Bowen has pointed out in her "Notes on Writing a Novel": "Scene is only justified in the novel where it can be shown, or at least felt, to act upon action or character. In fact, where it has dramatic use." [1] It is this use of relevant, dramatic description that I proposed to examine, though within the limits of this article I can do no more than sketch out the sort of approach I consider desirable.[2] It is easy and tempting to regard descriptive passages in a novel as having little or no relation to problems of plot and character, particularly if these passages strike us as being no more than examples of "fine" writing. But we are learning to pay the same attention to "the words on the page" in a novel as in poetry and drama, and I believe that this attention, directed towards passages of background description, will show that not all of them are as irrelevant as we are sometimes led to believe.

At the same time, we have to recognize that, in its early days at least, the novel owed a great deal to the practice of the landscape painters in the matter of natural description. This relationship between the two arts has introduced a complication into our response to description in the novel which may lie behind the quite sharp division between those who enjoy description and those who find it irrelevant. The history of landscape painting shows that it succeeds in establishing itself as a fully independent genre, unrelated, in the hands of a Constable or a Cézanne, to story-telling or moral issues. When we encounter its equivalent in a novel, then, we tend, according to our temperament, either to welcome it for its own sake, finding in it those emotional satisfactions we find in painting, or to dismiss it because (such is our experience of landscape painting) it seems to have little or nothing to do with the things that the novel ought to be doing.

Because of this complication, therefore, I shall confine my examination entirely to landscape description. But before turning to the influence

---

[1] Elizabeth Bowen, *Collected Impressions* (London, 1950), p. 254.
[2] These limits compel me to confine my attention to English examples. Any extended survey would have to take account, for example, of the carpentry of Balzac's theatre-workshop, the panoramic range of Tolstoy, the *genius loci* of Henry James, and the subjective intensity of Proust.

of landscape painting on the novel I must draw attention to one recent book, Mr. Robert Liddell's *Treatise on the Novel,* which does indeed broach the subject of description, but only to dismiss it as a side issue.

> The aesthetics of descriptive writing have not yet received sufficient attention—it is commonly held in too great esteem, particularly when it occurs in works of fiction. Painting or music that has a strong literary element is now severely criticised. It is time for an attack to be made upon the pictorial element in literature. Mr. Richards, in *Practical Criticism,* has done much to teach us not to look for "pictures" in Poetry— nevertheless, the Novel is still in need of a purge.[3]

Mr. Liddell makes a relevant point when he says that descriptive writing is generally too much esteemed by the reader. It is this esteem which once exalted Mary Webb and which can still miss the true nature of Conrad's achievement. Nevertheless, background description is there in the novel, and has been from the very beginning of its development, and must be taken into account in any comprehensive account of its nature and achievements. I do not wish to suggest that there is anything to be gained by rhapsodising over the "beauties" of a description, particularly when the passage can be detached from the novel without doing much damage to its fabric. But equally, I think, Mr. Liddell is wrong to go so far to the other extreme and ask for nothing more than the sign-posting we get in Elizabethan stage-directions: "a street in London," "another part of the forest"—a map-reference sufficient to enable us to orientate ourselves, but no more. He argues as follows: "Too many stage-directions are boring and confusing if we read a play; if we see them carried out on the stage, the result is a fussy and undignified ritualism. They are worst of all in a novel."[4]

This view can be countered immediately. In his recent study, *The Rise of the Novel,* Professor Ian Watt has shown that one of the distinguishing characteristics of the novel is that it gives its personages "a local habitation and a name." Robinson Crusoe, Pamela Andrews, Tom Jones, these normal forms are distinct from the single names of older heroes and heroines, Macbeth, Portia, and from the type-names of allegory, such as Mr. Badman. The novelist's characters are contemporary figures, moving in a solid world of everyday life. In the more timeless

---

[3] Robert Liddell, *A Treatise on the Novel* (London, 1947), p. 110.
[4] Liddell, p. 112.

worlds of tragic or comic drama it does not matter that the characters are not so localised. Very often, in fact, they cannot be. In *A Midsummer-Night's Dream* we are told that the wood is near Athens, but it turns out to be peopled with very English artisans and fairies. But even if there were not this point to be made about the localisation of characters in a novel, Mr. Liddell could still be criticised for equating too rigidly the stage-direction and the novel's descriptive passages. Properly used, the latter are rather to be equated with the dramatically presented descriptions that we get from the *characters* in a drama. While many of these arise from the nature of the Elizabethan stage and are merely utilitarian, others of them have a deeper significance. Thus, when Duncan and Banquo describe Macbeth's castle, they are certainly letting us know where we are supposed to be; but phrases like "a pleasant seat" and "the air is delicate" have a dramatic irony that lifts the description beyond utility.

As I have indicated, the approach I propose to make towards an examination of the place of description in the novel involves some consideration of landscape painting as an independent genre. The situation is similar to that obtaining in the realm of descriptive poetry. That is, the work of the painter comes first and educates the eyes of the writer.[5]

Professor Watt's point about the localisation of the setting in the pioneer English novels is perfectly valid; but description is put to other uses than this, and it is with the development of these uses that I am concerned. Localisation is a practical matter of placing the characters in an environment within which they can act out their stories. It is equivalent of both the dramatically presented description and the stage scenery of the drama. Thus the interest attaching to Crusoe's island is that of seeing what he can make of it. It is far from being a romantic Treasure Island or Blue Lagoon. In Pamela's case we must be made aware that Mr. B's house has closets to which she can retire to write her letters or avoid a rape. And in *Joseph Andrews* and *Tom Jones* a distinction must be made between a good inn and a bad one, between Allworthy's orderly house and Squire Western's free-and-easy one. The nearest we come in Fielding's work to a piece of natural description for its own sake is a short passage in *Joseph Andrews*.

> Adams continued his subject till they came to one of the
> beautifullest spots of ground in the universe. It was a kind of
> natural amphitheatre, formed by the winding of a small rivu-

⁵ See, for example, Jean H. Hagstrum, *The Sister Arts: The Tradition of Literary Pictorialism and English Poetry from Dryden to Gray* (Princeton, 1958).

let, which was planted with thick woods, and the trees rose gradually above each other by the natural ascent of the ground they stood on; which ascent as they hid with their boughs, they seemed to have been disposed by the design of the most skilful planter. The soil was spread with a verdure which no paint could imitate; and the whole place might have raised romantic ideas in elder minds than those of Joseph and Fanny, without the assistance of love (Bk. III, Chap. V).

But even this, as we shall see, is not "pure" description, though it will appear to be alongside the picture we are given in *Tom Jones* of Allworthy's house and estate, which is much more in line with eighteenth-century taste in landscape description:

It stood on the south-east side of a hill, but nearer the bottom than the top of it, so as to be sheltered from the north-east by a grove of old oaks which rose above it in a gradual ascent of near half a mile, and yet high enough to enjoy a most charming prospect of the vale beneath.

In the midst of the grove was a fine lawn, sloping down towards the house, near the summit of which rose a plentiful spring, gushing out of a rock covered with firs, and forming a constant cascade of about thirty feet, not carried down a regular flight of steps, but tumbling in a natural fall over the broken and mossy stones until it came to the bottom of the rock, then running off in a pebbly channel, that with many lesser falls winded along, till it fell into a lake at the foot of the hill, about a quarter of a mile below the house on the south side, and which was seen from every room in the front. Out of this lake, which filled the center of a beautiful plain, embellished with groups of beeches and elms, and fed with sheep, issued a river, that for several miles was seen to meander through an amazing variety of meadows and woods till it emptied itself into the sea, with a large arm of which, and an island beyond it, the prospect was closed.

On the right of this valley opened another of less extent, adorned with several villages, and terminated by one of the towers of an old ruined abby, grown over with ivy, and part of the front, which remained still entire.

The left-hand side presented the view of a very fine park,

composed of very unequal ground, and agreeably varied with
all the diversity that hills, lawns, wood, and water, laid out
with admirable taste, but owing less to art than to nature,
could give. Beyond this, the country gradually rose into a
ridge of wild mountains, the tops of which were above the
clouds (Bk. I, Chap. IV).

The significance of the chapter-heading here should not be overlooked: "The reader's neck brought into danger by a description." Here
Fielding is apparently warning us to expect something unusual, but what
in fact he offers us is something to which no good Augustan would take
exception. Allworthy's estate displays the expected taste of an eighteenth-
century landowner who has accepted the changes in landscape gardening brought about by the influence of painters such as Poussin and Claude.
What Fielding gives us is not a piece of natural description for its own
sake (this *would* have brought the reader's neck into danger in the middle
of the century) but the panorama of a situation in which nature is so
manipulated as to form a setting for man.[6] We are here at a transitional
stage between the complete formality of the continental garden of the
seventeenth century, and the appreciation of *natural* nature that is to be
a characteristic of the Romantic movement. It is on the principles of this
transitional stage that Pope laid out his five-acre plot at Twickenham, and
the river that meanders through Allworthy's estate is at one with Hogarth's
"line of beauty," the serpentine line that has given its name to the ornamental water in Hyde Park. How transitional the situation was can be seen
by comparing the close of the passage from *Tom Jones* with the paragraph
from *Joseph Andrews*. In the latter the trees are approved of because "they
seemed to have been disposed by the design of the most skilful planter,"
whereas in *Tom Jones* the left-hand scene pleases because it owes *less*
to art than to nature.

Fielding's object in going into such detail should now be obvious. By
this means he both places Allworthy on the social map and displays his
character, that of a quiet-living man of taste, in contrast to Squire Western,
of whose estate we get no such picture. In *Joseph Andrews* the description
is used for another purpose. The charm of the natural amphitheatre chimes

---

[6] Mr. Christopher Hussey has suggested that "the man-made humanised landscape" of the eighteenth century is "England's greatest contribution to the visual arts of the world." See his introduction to Margaret Jourdain, *The Work of
William Kent* (London, 1948), p. 15. His introduction to the companion volume, Dorothy Stroud, *Capability Brown* (London, 1950, rev. 1957), should also
be consulted. The two together form an excellent analysis of the aesthetics of
landscape gardening.

in with and underlines the romantic mood of the lovers, and this, the use of "mood" landscape, is the next stage in the development of description in the novel. In each case, however, the reader is being invited to partici- pate by being reminded of visual experiences with which Fielding sup- poses him to be familiar, experiences derived from his acquaintance with neo-classical landscape painting and the garden-design based on it.

Both Poussin and Claude had painted "mood" landscapes; in Claude's case, a mood of calm contemplation of an idealised Nature. In the hands of Salvator Rosa the mood becomes wildly picturesque, inducing feelings of awe and terror. From looking at pictures of this sort it is only a step to seeking for passages in literature in which the thrill can be experienced. This demand was met by the writers of the novel of terror, and the extent to which they relied on what had been done by the landscape painters is indicated by the following passage from *The Mysteries of Udolpho* in which Mrs. Radcliffe gives the game away completely:

> The scene of barrenness was here and there interrupted by the spreading branches of the larch and cedar, which threw their gloom over the cliff, or athwart the torrent that rolled in the vale. No living creature appeared—except the lizard scrambling among the rocks, and often hanging upon points so dangerous that fancy shrunk from the view of them. This was such a scene as Salvator would have chosen, had he then existed, for his canvass. St. Aubert, impressed by the romantic character of the place, almost expected to see banditti start from behind some projecting rock, and he kept his hand upon the arms with which he always travelled (Chap. III).

There is no question that Salvator Rosa would have painted such a scene. He *had* painted it, not once but many times, and without his example Mrs. Radcliffe might have written very differently. Here we have something that is characteristic of the very essence of *Udolpho*. Even Mr. Liddell would hardly claim that the novel would still be what it is if such passages were reduced to mere stage-directions.

Another characteristic passage is to be found in the prototype of the novel of terror, *The Castle of Otranto*:

> Theodore at length determined to repair to the forest that Matilda had pointed out to him. Arriving there, he sought the gloomiest shades, as best suited to the pleasing melancholy that reigned in his mind. In this mood he roved insensibly to

the caves which had formerly served as a retreat to hermits, and were now reported round the country to be haunted by evil spirits.

In *Joseph Andrews* "one of the beautifullest spots of ground in the universe" happens to accord with the mood of Fanny and Joseph. But Horace Walpole's Theodore actually seeks a setting for his melancholy, and this deliberate association of mood and situation with setting remains a staple feature of fictional description thereafter. This is particularly the case in the nineteenth century. In Disraeli's *Henrietta Temple* (close of Book III) and in Wilkie Collins' *The Woman in White* (first narrative, section XV). for example, the settings are in perfect accord with the emotional crises of the story. In better novels this manipulation rises to the level of symbol, as in the use made of the chestnut tree in *Jane Eyre*. Under it, on a balmy evening, Jane and Rochester become engaged. During the night that follows, it is blasted in a storm. At an earlier period in our literature this would have been an omen merely. Here it is both omen and symbol. The hitherto solid growth is split into two halves. Nor did this use of the device die out with the passing of the Victorian novel. It has been used quite recently by L. P. Hartley in the symbolic deadly-nightshade plant in *The Go-Between*.

In Walpole and Mrs. Radcliffe the situation is, of course, deliberately rigged, and it was therefore easy for Jane Austen to poke fun at the practice in *Northanger Abbey*, particularly as her own tendency in landscape description (as in other aspects of her work) is to look back to a central eighteenth-century position. Now Jane Austen is a writer whom Mr. Liddell especially admires for her restraint in landscape description, so it is worth while pausing to examine her practice in some detail.

We may take as typical of her normal practice the following passage from *Emma*:

> Their road to this detached cottage was down Vicarage Lane, a lane leading at right angles from the broad though irregular main street of the place; and, as may be inferred, containing the blessed abode of Mr. Elton. A few inferior dwellings were first to be passed, and then, about a quarter of a mile down the lane, rose the vicarage; an old and not very good house, almost as close to the road as it could be (Vol. I, Chap. X).[7]

---

[7] My quotations are taken from the standard Oxford edition, edited by R. W. Chapman.

Here every word is utilitarian, with the exception of the ironically used "blessed," and the passage adequately meets Mr. Liddell's call for description that is no more than a map-reference.

But Jane Austen does not always work at this level of utility. Some of her descriptions can be very subtle indeed, and careful reading is required to pierce the surface of restraint. Of this subtlety the following passage will serve as an example:

> It was hot; and after walking some time over the gardens in a scattered, dispersed way, scarcely any three together, they insensibly followed one another to the delicious shade of a broad short avenue of limes, which stretching beyond the garden at an equal distance from the river, seemed the finish of the pleasure grounds. It led to nothing; nothing but a view at the end over a low stone wall with high pillars, which seemed intended, in their erection, to give the appearance of an approach to the house, which had never been there. Disputable, however, as might be the taste of such a termination, it was in itself a charming walk, and the view which closed it extremely pretty. The considerable slope, at nearly the foot of which the Abbey stood, gradually acquired a steeper form beyond its grounds; and at half a mile distant was a bank of considerable abruptness and grandeur, well clothed with wood; and at the bottom of this bank, favourably placed and sheltered, rose the Abbey-Mill Farm, with meadows in front, and the river making a close and handsome curve around it.
>
> It was a sweet view—sweet to the eye and the mind. English verdure, English culture, English comfort, seen under a sun bright, without being oppressive (*Emma*, Vol. III, Chap. VI).

The close of this passage certainly puts the manipulation of Walpole and Mrs. Radcliffe in its place. But though the whole scene has much in common with Fielding (Mr. Allworthy would have felt quite at home here), there is something more to it.[8] The description is divided equally between the Abbey grounds and the Abbey-Mill Farm. Now the latter, of course, is where Robert Martin lives, the farmer whose interest in Harriet Smith has been thwarted by Emma. This description, said Mr. Wilson, helps to "point up" Emma's mistaken and snobbish view of him. In her eyes he is only a

---

[8] In what follows here I am indebted to some points made by Mr. Edmund Wilson in a talk on the B.B.C. a few years ago.

common farmer, unfit to be the husband of a Woodhouse protegée. But through the eyes of Jane Austen herself we are able, in this description, to see Martin at his proper level, the respectable level of the successful yeoman farmer, a rank which Jane Austen herself by no means despised. It is the view of the farm which is sweet and English, and the air of restraint in the closing sentence, though owing something to an eighteenth-century dislike of "enthusiasm," is also appropriate for placing Martin in the social order. Were he a degree lower, he would be indifferent to appearances. A degree higher, and he too would have gone in for "improvements," and would then have run the risk of producing the effect of pretentiousness which *is* criticised in the description of the Abbey estate of Mr. Knightley. This use of the description is of greater importance than the impression which a first or superficial reading of the last sentence will arouse—the impression of a prim withdrawal from the temptations of natural description.

This is not to deny that Jane Austen *is* chary of description. Her attitude in this matter is bound up with her criticism of the "improvements" of the Abbey estate, a criticism which has parallels elsewhere in her work. Thus, the panorama of Bath is humorously dismissed in *Northanger Abbey* for its failure to conform to the picturesque standards of landscape beauty; an element of Marianne's "sensibility" is a belief in those standards; and in *Mansfield Park* considerable areas of the dialogue are given over to discussing improvements. There is no doubt where Jane Austen stands in this matter. It is on the side of restraint; understandably so, when a lack of restraint which had its origin in the same fashionable taste for the picturesque could lead to the over-emphasis of Mrs. Radcliffe's descriptive passages.

It is sometimes claimed that Jane Austen let herself go beyond her normal limits in her treatment of Fanny Price's Portsmouth environment in *Mansfield Park*. Here, indeed, she goes into far more detail than she usually permits herself. But it is not detail in isolation. Cramped living rooms, deficiency of manners, lack of privacy and paucity of books, all the details are intermingled in a picture which is meant to provide a counterbalance to Mansfield Park. Only once in this part of the novel does Jane Austen seem to depart from this strict obedience to the needs of relevance:

> The day was uncommonly lovely. It was really March, but it
> was April in its mild air, brisk soft wind, and bright sun, occa-

sionally clouded for a minute; and everything looked so beautiful under the influence of such a sky, the effect of the shadows pursuing each other, on the ships at Spithead and the island beyond, with the ever-varying hues of the sea now at high water, dancing in its glee and dashing against the ramparts with so fine a sound, produced altogether such a combination of charms for Fanny, as made her gradually almost careless of the circumstances under which she felt them (Vol. III, Chap. XI).

At first it seems that Jane Austen has for once looked at a scene with a painter's eye rather than a novelist's. Even here, however, we are carefully brought back to situation. When our first surprise is over, the passage begins to look something like the Radcliffian concordance of place and mood. What more can Fanny want than a fine day, her family in their Sunday best, and her arm in Henry Crawford's? But the circumstances of which she is almost careless are not of a piece with this idyllic situation:

Nay, had she been without his arm, she would have soon known that she needed it, for she wanted strength for a two hour's saunter of this kind, coming as it generally did upon a week's previous inactivity. Fanny was beginning to feel the effect of being debarred from her usual, regular exercise; she had lost ground as to health since her being in Portsmouth, and but for Mr. Crawford and the beauty of the weather, would soon have been knocked up now.

Above all, Crawford is not Edmund, even though he is improving upon acquaintance. And so it finally appears that description here is not being used to enhance situation, as in Mrs. Radcliffe, but to act as a foil to it, and to that end some expansiveness of detail is necessary.

What Jane Austen withdraws from, then, is the artificiality of the *Udolpho* use of description. She does not withdraw from description which is organic, description which reveals character, mood and situation. Sir Walter Scott had no such scruples. Like Mrs. Radcliffe (from whom he probably learned) he will use a dramatic setting if it suits his purpose, and he is as aware as she is of the influence on vision of the work of the picturesque painters:

If India be the land of magic ... this is the country of romance. The scenery is such as nature brings together in her sublimest

221

moods; sounding cataracts—hills which rear their scatheu heads to the sky—lakes that, winding up the shadowy valleys, lead at every turn to yet more romantic recesses—rocks which catch the clouds of heaven. All the wildness of Salvator here, and there the fairy scenes of Claude (*Guy Mannering*, Chap. XVII).

But in his best work he goes further than Mrs. Radcliffe in that he does not invent such settings, or take them at second-hand from paintings. He uses what is actually present. This comes out clearly in the description of Jeanie Deans' moonlight meeting with the mysterious Wilson, in *The Heart of Midlothian* (Chap. XV):

It was situated in the depth of the valley behind Salisbury Crags, which has for a background the north-western shoulder of the mountain called Arthur's Seat, on whose descent still remain the ruins of what was once a chapel or hermitage, dedicated to Saint Anthony the Eremite. A better site for such a building could hardly have been selected; for the chapel, situated among the rude and pathless cliffs, lies in a desert, even in the immediate vicinity of a rich, populous, and tumultuous capital: and the hum of the city might mingle with the orisons of the recluses, conveying as little of worldly interest as if it had been the roar of the distant ocean. Beneath the steep ascent on which these ruins are still visible, was, and perhaps is still pointed out, the place where the wretch Nicol Muschat, who has been already mentioned in these pages, had closed a long scene of cruelty towards his unfortunate wife, by murdering her, with circumstances of uncommon barbarity. The execration in which the man's crime was held extended itself to the place where it was perpetrated, which was marked by a small cairn, or heap of stones, composed of those which each chance passenger had thrown there in testimony of abhorrence, and on the principle, it would seem, of the ancient British malediction, "May you have a cairn for your burial-place!"

As our heroine approached this ominous and unhallowed spot, she paused and looked to the moon, now rising broad on the north-west, and shedding a more distinct light than it had afforded during her walk thither. Eyeing the planet for a moment, she then slowly and fearfully turned her head towards the cairn, from which it was at first averted. She was at first disappointed. Nothing was visible beside the little pile of stones, which shone grey in the moonlight. A multitude of confused suggestions rushed on her mind. Had her correspondent deceived her, and broken his appointment?—was he too tardy at the appointment he had made?—or had some strange turn of fate prevented him from appearing as he proposed?—or, if he were an unearthly being, as her secret apprehensions suggested, was it his object merely to delude her with false hopes, and put her to unnecessary toil and terror, according to the nature, as she had heard, of those wandering demons?—or did he propose to blast her with the sudden horrors of his presence when she had come close to the place of rendezvous? These anxious reflections did not prevent her approaching to the cairn with a pace that, though slow, was determined.

The language is that of Mrs. Radcliffe—"ominous and unhallowed," "sudden horrors"—but the details of the setting are not fictional, and the occasion of the meeting at such a place and hour is not merely designed to make the reader's flesh creep (though such a motive is of course involved) but is a logical outcome of the situation in which Wilson is placed. Some manipulation of mood and circumstance there certainly is, but there is no law which says that a creative artist shall not manipulate his material. The most we can do is to condemn him if he fails to bring it off, and Scott can successfully plead "not guilty" on this occasion, as on many others.

A subsequent writer who does not always get away with it is Dickens. Much of his description is utilitarian scene-setting, as it is in the work of his eighteenth-century masters, and here his selection of what is relevant and characteristic is usually under control. But he is also one of the first English novelists (if not the first) to raise description to a symbolic level, and when he does so he runs much greater risks. The opening of *Bleak House* is justly famous for its transition from the actual level of a London "pea-souper" to the symbolic fog at the heart of the High Court of Chancery. By contrast, the attempt to make the rain and floods in this novel symbolise the desolation of Lady Deadlock must be adjudged a failure. As a piece of pure description the passage is well enough done:

The waters are out in Lincolnshire. An arch of the bridge in the park has been sapped and sopped away. The adjacent low-lying ground, for half a mile in breadth, is a stagnant river, with melancholy trees for islands in it, and a surface punctured all over, all day long, with falling rain. . . . The weather, for many a day and night, has been so wet that the trees seem wet through, and the soft loppings and prunings of the workman's axe can make no crash or crackle as they fall. The deer, looking soaked, leave quagmires, where they pass. The shot of a rifle loses its sharpness in the moist air, and its smoke moves in a tardy little cloud towards the green rise, coppice-topped, that makes a background for the falling rain.

I agree with Mr. Liddell's view of this passage. What spoils its adequacy as symbol is not the quality of the description itself, but the situation, the melodramatic situation, which it is intended to emphasize.

No particular principle lay behind my original choice of examples to illustrate this article, beyond that of relevance, but it so happens that a pattern of ebb and flow in the effectiveness of these passages does emerge. We began with the utilitarian description required by the novel to localise its characters and their actions to a degree not met with in the older narrative or dramatic forms. The next stage was to place the character in his social setting, as well as within a geographical one, and then followed the manipulation of landscape in the novel of terror to suit the emotions and situations of the characters. This may not seem very effective to us, and the fashion for the novel of terror among the educated classes did not last very long. One would hesitate to attribute its decline to *Northanger Abbey* alone; but Jane Austen does come out strongly against it, and returns to description used as a means of social placing. Scott, however, continues to use atmospheric description (though he does so more naturally than Mrs. Radcliffe) because the nature of his work requires it. Finally, description rises to the level of symbolism in Dickens.

In my next example, the current changes once more. No one could be more utilitarian than Trollope, no one less likely to be suspected of rigging the description to suit a mood or to fashion a symbol. His general level of achievement can be illustrated by the account of Hiram's Hospital in the first chapter of *The Warden*:

Hiram's Hospital, as the retreat is called, is a picturesque building enough, and shows the correct taste with which the ecclesiastical architects of those days were imbued. It stands on the banks of the little river, which flows nearly round the cathedral close, being on the side furthest from the town. The London road crosses the river by a pretty one-arched bridge, and, looking from this bridge, the stranger will see the windows of the old men's rooms, each pair of windows separated by a small buttress. A broad gravel walk runs between the building and the river, which is always trim and cared for; and at the end of the walk, under the parapet of the approach to the bridge, is a large and well-worn seat, on which, in mild weather, three or four of Hiram's bedesmen are sure to be seen seated. Beyond this row of buttresses, and further from the bridge, and also further from the water which here suddenly bends, are the pretty oriel windows of Mr. Harding's house, and his well-mown lawn. The entrance to the hospital is from the London road, and is made through a ponderous gateway under a heavy stone arch, unnecessary, one would suppose, at any time, for the protection of twelve old men, but greatly conducive to the good appearance of Hiram's charity. On passing through this portal, never closed to anyone from six a.m. till ten p.m., and never open afterwards, except on application to a huge, intricately hung, medieval bell, the handle of which no uninitiated intruder can possibly find, the six doors of the old men's abodes are seen, and beyond them is a slight iron screen, through which the more happy portion of the Barchester elite pass into the Elysium of Mr. Harding's dwelling.

Everything in this passage, with one exception, is devoted to the business of localisation, a rough test of which is whether one can draw a map or make a picture from the data. Here the facts are more than adequate for this purpose. The exception is the word "Elysium." Like the adjective "blessed" in the description of Mr. Elton's house, it is a means of connecting utilitarian description with the immediate situation of the characters. It points the contrast between the situation of the bedesmen, kept strictly to the letter of Hiram's will, and the happier lot of the Warden. The two areas are separated by a screen; a slight screen, it is true, but one of iron nevertheless, a barrier which shuts these poor Adams out of Paradise. And further, there is an irony in "Elysium," because the peace for which it stands is about to be rudely invaded by the forces of reform.

If this example is a regression, the next is so subtle and complicated that it can almost stand as a summary of the various uses to which description can be put:

> On a grey but dry November morning Dorothea drove to Lowick in company with her uncle and Celia. Mr. Casaubon's home was the manor-house. Close by, visible from some parts of the garden, was the little church, with the old parsonage opposite. In the beginning of his career, Mr. Casaubon had only held the living, but the death of his brother had put him in possession of the manor also. It had a small park, with a fine old oak here and there, and an avenue of limes towards the south-west front, with a sunk fence between park and pleasure-ground, so that from the drawing-room windows the glance swept uninterruptedly along a slope of greensward till the limes ended in a level of corn and pastures, which often seemed to melt into a lake under the setting sun. This was the happy side of the house, for the south and east looked rather melancholy even under the brightest morning. The grounds here were more confined, the flower-beds showed no careful tendance, and large clumps of trees, chiefly of sombre yews, had risen high, not ten yards from the windows. The building, of greenish stone. was in the old English style, not ugly, but small windowed and melancholy-looking; the sort of house that must have children, many flowers, open windows, and little vistas of bright things, to make it seem a joyous home. In this latter end of autumn, with a sparse remnant of yellow leaves falling slowly athwart the dark evergreens in a stillness without a sunshine, the house too had an air of autumnal decline, and Mr. Casaubon, when he presented himself, had no bloom that could be thrown into relief by that background (*Middlemarch*, Book I, Chap. IX).

Here, obviously, is localisation. We know where we are and could paint the scene. Here too are the remains of the man-made, man-centred landscape of the eighteenth century in the mention of the avenue of limes and the sunk fence, and the (probably unconscious) glance back to the paintings of Claude: "a level of corn and pastures, which often seemed to melt into a lake under the setting sun." Added to this is a selection of detail and colour which helps to present character and situation. Casaubon is at one with the autumnal decline; like the November morning, he too is grey and dry. The choice of season is deliberate, and provides an emphasis which is parallel to the concordance of mood and scene which we have noted in the novel of terror, but raised here by George Eliot to the level of symbol. The happy side of the house stands for the sort of life that Dorothea will renounce in her marriage; there will be no children, no vistas of bright things on her side of the house of marriage.

All this, however, is still in the future, and we need to be reminded of the situation again when Dorothea and Casaubon are actually married. George Eliot does this in describing their arrival at Lowick after the honeymoon, and the bright contrasts in the final sentence leave us in doubt that Dorothea has reached the winter of her discontent:

> Mr. and Mrs. Casaubon, returning from their wedding journey, arrived at Lowick Manor in the middle of January. A light snow was falling as they descended at the door, and in the morning, when Dorothea passed from her dressing-room into the blue-green boudoir that we know of, she saw the long avenue of limes lifting their trunks from a white earth, and spreading white branches against the dun and motionless sky. The distant flat shrank in uniform whiteness and low-hanging uniformity of cloud. The very furniture in the room seemed to have shrunk since she saw it before; the stag in the tapestry looked more like a ghost in his ghostly blue-green world; the volumes of polite literature in the bookcase looked more like immovable imitations of books. The bright fire of dry oak-boughs burning on the dogs seemed an incongruous renewal of life and glow—like the figure of Dorothea herself as she entered carrying the red-leather cases containing the cameos for Celia (Book III, Chap. XVIII).

The same contrast of light and shade can be seen in the next example, from *The Mayor of Casterbridge*. But where the passages from *Middlemarch* look back to the restrained landscapes of Claude, Hardy's description continues many features of the Salvator Rosa landscape, and the cult of the picturesque which it inspired:

> These precincts embodied the mournful phases of Casterbridge life, as the south avenues embodied its cheerful moods. The whole way along here was sunless, even in summer time;

in spring, white frosts lingered here when other places were steaming with warmth; while in winter it was the seed-field of all the aches, rheumatisms, and torturing cramps of the year. The Casterbridge doctors must have pined away for want of sufficient nourishment, but for the configuration of the landscape on the north-eastern side.

The river—slow, noiseless, and dark,—the Schwarzwasser of Casterbridge—ran beneath a low cliff, the two together forming a defence which had rendered walls and artificial earthworks on this side unnecessary. Here were ruins of a Franciscan priory, and a mill attached to the same, the water of which roared down a back-hatch like the voice of desolation. Above the cliff, and behind the river, rose a pile of buildings, and in the front of the pile a square mass cut into the sky. It was like a pedestal lacking its statue. This missing feature, without which the design remained incomplete, was, in truth, the corpse of a man; for the square mass formed the base of the gallows, the extensive buildings at the back being the county gaol. In the meadow where Henchard now walked the mob were wont to gather whenever an execution took place, and there to the tune of the roaring weir they stood and watched the spectacle.

The exaggeration which darkness imparted to the glooms of this region impressed Henchard more than he had expected. The lugubrious harmony of the spot with his domestic situation was too perfect for him, impatient of effects, scenes and adumbrations. It reduced his heartburning to melancholy, and he exclaimed, "Why the deuce did I come here!" He went on past the cottage in which the old local hangman had lived and died, in times before that calling was monopolized all over England by a single gentleman; and climbed up by a steep back lane into the town (Chap. XIX).

Good as it is, this passage is a retrogressive step. Like Mrs. Radcliffe, Hardy gives the game away and admits to manipulation when he tells us how much the scene harmonised with Henchard's mood. All the same, the thing is better done than it is by Disraeli or Wilkie Collins, partly because, as with Scott, the locality is actual and not imagined.

But the time has come to sum up. The nature of the novel, in its beginnings, was such that a greater degree of localisation of the characters was required than in the older literary forms, because these characters were less universal, more closely related to their own day and age. This localisation was achieved by setting them in a solidly constructed environment. But it is not long before description is being used more widely, to reveal, first, general characteristics, and then particular moods. There is not much point in telling the reader that So-and-so felt melancholy and leaving it at that. In drama participation in the moods of the characters is achieved through the direct contact between actor and audience, and is embodied in action, in pauses and tones of voice, and so forth. But participation in the novel is much less direct (we read it all in our own internal tone of voice, for example) and one way to make the connection is through the evocative power of descriptive passages. Here, as we have seen, the novelist was able to learn something from the development of landscape painting at this time.[9]

Next, description can rise to the level of symbol, and so stand for more than the writer expresses directly, or else express in succinct form what otherwise might have been more laborious. And there is also that aspect of the question which has only been implicit in my discussion, an aspect put at its plainest by L. P. Hartley in *A Perfect Woman*, a novel published in 1955: "There was surely no sympathetic fallacy in the idea that the earth reflected one's own moods and that one could project oneself into it; not to have felt akin to it would have argued insensitiveness, lack of imagination" (Chap. XVIII). But everywhere the primary requirement is that of relevance, and next to relevance, refusal to rig the description. When these essentials have been observed, the descriptive passages take their place in the texture of the novel, and cannot be detached and enjoyed for their own sake, nor wished away from the novel without damaging its fabric.

[9] It is worth noting that painting is still having an influence on the descriptive powers of the novelist in our own day. The following passage is taken from Virginia Woolf's *Between The Acts*: "The roof was weathered red-orange; and inside it was a hollow hall, sunshafted, brown, smelling of corn, dark when the doors were shut, but splendidly illuminated when the doors at the end stood open, as they did, to let the wagons in—the long, low wagons, like ships of the sea, breasting the corn, not the sea, returning in the evening, shagged with hay." If we compare this with Jane Austen's passage describing Mr. Elton's house we can see a decisive change from utility to evocation; and evocation, I would suggest, is a dominant characteristic of contemporary fictional description, and can be found at its best in the work of women novelists like Elizabeth Bowen, Rosamund Lehmann and Iris Murdoch. It is not too much to say that, in Virginia Woolf's case, she would not have written quite as she did without the example of the Impressionists before her, and without the modification of visual awareness which their work brought about. We remember in this connection that her sister, Vanessa Bell, is a sensitive painter, that her brother-in-law is the critic Clive Bell, and that she was the close friend and biographer of Roger Fry.

Compared with plot, theme, language, or character, place as an aspect of fiction has always been relegated to a secondary position. But it is precisely place, "the named, identified, concrete, exact and exacting . . . gathering-spot of all that has been felt," argues Eudora Welty, that constitutes the real essence of a story. It makes an aesthetic experience concrte, lends it a local habitation and a name, and thus enables the reader to keep his feet firmly planted on the ground. A novel, observes the author, is essentially bound up in the local, the real, the present, and the day-to-day experience of life. A novelist with a distinct sense of place will, therefore, find it easier to sift the essential in a character, incident, or setting from the random, irrelevant, and meaningless elements of life. Place, she concludes, is an all-inclusive framework; it conditions a novelist's mode of characterization, his sense of direction—in brief, his entire point of view.

place in fiction

EUDORA WELTY

Place is one of the lesser angels that watch over the racing hand of fiction, perhaps the one that gazes benignly enough from off to one side, while others, like character, plot, symbolic meaning, and so on, are doing a good deal of wing-beating about her chair, and feeling, who in my eyes carries the crown, soars highest of them all and rightly relegates place into the shade. Nevertheless, it is this lowlier angel that concerns us here. There have been signs that she has been rather neglected of late; maybe she could do with a little petitioning.

What place has place in fiction? It might be thought so modest a one that it can be taken for granted: the location of a novel; to use a term of the day, it may make the novel "regional." The term, like most terms used to pin down a novel, means little; and Henry James said there isn't any difference even between "the English novel" and "the American novel," since there are only two kinds of novels at all, the good and the bad. Of course Henry James didn't stop there, and we all hate generalities, and so does place. Yet as soon as we step down from the general view to the close and particular, as writers must and readers may and teachers well know how to, and consider what good writing may be, place can be seen, in her own way, to have a great deal to do with that goodness, if not to be responsible for it. How so?

First, with the goodness—validity—in the raw material of writing. Second, with the goodness in the writing itself—the achieved world of appearance, through which the novelist has his whole say and puts his whole case. There will still be the lady, always, who dismissed *The Ancient Mariner* on grounds of implausibility. Third, with the goodness—the worth —in the writer himself: place is where he has his roots, place is where he stands; in his experience out of which he writes it provides the base of reference, in his work the point of view. Let us consider place in fiction in these three wide aspects.

Wide, but of course connected—vitally so. And if in some present-day novels the connection has apparently slipped, that makes a fresh reason for us to ponder the subject of place. For novels, besides being the pleasantest things imaginable, are powerful forces on the side. Mutual understanding in the world being nearly always, as now, at low ebb, it is comforting to remember that it is through art that one country can nearly always speak reliably to another, if the other can hear at all. Art, though, is never the voice of a country; it is an even more precious thing, the voice of the individual, doing its best to speak, not comfort of any sort, indeed, but truth. And the art that speaks it most unmistakably, most directly, most variously, most fully, is fiction; in particular, the novel.

Why? Because the novel from the start has been bound up in the local, the "real," the present, the ordinary day-to-day of human experience. Where the imagination comes in is in directing the use of all this. That use is endless, and there are only four words, of all the millions we've hatched, that a novel rules out: "Once upon a time." They make a story a fairy tale by the simple sweep of the remove—by abolishing the present and the place where we are instead of conveying them to us. Of course we shall have some sort of fairy tale with us always—just now it is the historical novel. Fiction is properly at work on the here and now, or the past made here and now; for in novels *we* have to be there. Fiction provides the ideal texture through which the feeling and meaning that permeate our own personal, present lives will best show through. For in his theme—the most vital and important part of the work at hand—the novelist has the blessing of the inexhaustible subject: you and me. You and

232

me, here. Inside that generous scope and circumference—who could ask for anything more?—the novel can accommodate practically anything on earth; and has of course done so. The novel so long as it be *alive* gives pleasure, and must always give pleasure, enough to stave off the departure of the Wedding Guest forever, except for that one lady.

It is by the nature of itself that fiction is all bound up in the local. The internal reason for that is surely that *feelings* are bound up in place. The human mind is a mass of associations—associations more poetic even than actual. I say, "The Yorkshire Moors," and you will say, "*Wuthering Heights*," and I have only to murmur, "If Father were only alive—" for you to come back with "We could go to Moscow," which certainly is not even so. The truth is, fiction depends for its life on place. Location is the cross-roads of circumstance, the proving ground of "What happened? Who's here? Who's coming?"—and that is the heart's field.

Unpredictable as the future of any art must be, one condition we may hazard about writing: of all the arts, it is the one least likely to cut the cord that binds it to its source. Music and dancing, while originating out of place—groves!—and perhaps invoking it still to minds pure or childlike, are no longer bound to dwell there. Sculpture exists out in empty space: that is what it commands and replies to. Toward painting, place, to be so highly visible, has had a curious and changing relationship. Indeed, wasn't it when landscape invaded painting, and painting was given, with the pro-fane content, a narrative content, that this worked to bring on a revolution to the art? Impressionism brought not the likeness-to-life, but the mystery of place onto canvas; it was the method, not the subject, that told this. Painting and writing, always the closest two of the sister arts (and in ancient Chinese days only the blink of an eye seems to have separated them), have each still closer connection with place than they have with each other; but a difference lies in their respective requirements of it, and even further in the way they use it—the written word being ultimately as different from the pigment as the note of the scale is from the chisel.

One element, which has just been mentioned, is surely the underlying bond that connects all the arts with place. All of them celebrate its mys-tery. Where does this mystery lie? Is it in the fact that place has a more lasting identity than we have, and we unswervingly tend to attach our-selves to identity? Might the magic lie partly too in the *name* of the place —since that is what *we* gave it? Surely, once we have it named, we have put a kind of poetic claim on its existence; the claim works even out of sight—may work forever sight unseen. The Seven Wonders of the World still give us this poetic kind of gratification. And notice we do not say simply "The Hanging Gardens"—that would leave them dangling out of reach and dubious in nature; we say "The Hanging Gardens of Babylon," and there they are, before our eyes, shimmering and garlanded and exactly elevated, to the Babylonian measurement.

Edward Lear tapped his unerring finger on the magic of place in the limerick. There's something unutterably convincing about that Old Person of Sparta who had twenty-five sons and one darta, and it is surely beyond question that he fed them on snails and weighed them in scales, because we know where that Old Person is *from*—Sparta! We certainly do not need further to be told his *name*. "Consider the source." Experience has ever advised us to base validity on point of origin.

Being shown how to locate, to place, any account is what does most toward *making* us believe it, not merely allowing us to, may the account be the facts or a lie; and that is where place in fiction comes in. Fiction is a lie. Never in its inside thoughts, always in its outside dress.

Some of us grew up with the china night-light, the little lamp whose lighting showed its secret and with that spread enchantment. The outside is painted with a scene, which is one thing; then, when the lamp is lighted, through the porcelain sides a new picture comes out through the old, and they are seen as one. A lamp I knew of was a view of London till it was lit; but then it was the Great Fire of London, and you could go beautifully to sleep by it. The lamp alight is the combination of internal and external, glowing at the imagination as one; and so is the good novel. Seeing that these inner and outer surfaces do lie so close together and so implicit in each other, the wonder is that human life so often separates them, or appears to, and it takes a good novel to put them back together.

The good novel should be steadily alight, revealing. Before it can hope to be that, it must of course be steadily visible from its outside, presenting a continuous, shapely, pleasing, and finished surface to the eye.

The sense of a story when the visibility is only partial or intermittent is as endangered as Eliza crossing the ice. Forty hounds of confusion are after it, the black waters of disbelief open up between its steps, and no matter which way it jumps it is bound to slip. Even if it has a little baby moral in its arms, it is more than likely a goner.

The novel must get Eliza across the ice; what it means—the way it proceeds—is always in jeopardy. It must be given a surface that is continuous and unbroken, never too thin to trust, always in touch with the senses. Its world of experience must be at every step, through every moment, within reach as the world of appearance.

234

This makes it the business of writing, and the responsibility of the writer, to disentangle the significant—in character, incident, setting, mood, everything—from the random and meaningless and irrelevant that in real life surround and beset it. It is a matter of his selecting and, by all that implies, of changing, "real" life as he goes. With each word he writes, he acts—as literally and methodically as if he hacked his way through a forest and blazed it for the word that follows. He makes choices at the explicit demand of this one present story; each choice implies, explains, limits the next, and illuminates the one before. No two stories ever go the same way, though in different hands one story might possibly go any one of a thousand ways; and though the woods may look the same from outside, it is a new and different labyrinth every time. What tells the author his way? Nothing at all but what he knows inside himself: the same thing that hints to him afterward how far he has missed it, how near he may have come to the heart of it. In a working sense, the novel and its place have become one: work has made them, for the time being, the same thing, like the explorer's tentative map of the known world.

The reason why every word you write in a good novel is a lie, then, is that it is written expressly to serve the purpose; if it does not apply, it is fancy and frivolous, however specially dear to the writer's heart. Actuality, it is true, is an even bigger risk to the novel than fancy writing is, being frequently even more confusing, irrelevant, diluted, and generally far-fetched than ill-chosen words can make it. Yet somehow, the world of appearance in the novel has got to *seem* actuality. Is there a reliable solution to the problem? Place being brought to life in the round before the reader's eye is the readiest and gentlest and most honest and natural way this can be brought about, I think; every instinct advises it. The moment the place in which the novel happens is accepted as true, through it will begin to glow, in a kind of recognizable glory, the feeling and thought that inhabited the novel in the author's head and animated the whole of his work.

Besides furnishing a plausible abode for the novel's world of feeling, place has a good deal to do with making the characters real, that is, themselves, and keeping them so. The reason is simply that, as Tristram Shandy observed, "We are not made of glass, as characters on Mercury might be." Place *can* be transparent, or translucent: not people. In real life, we have to express the things plainest and closest to our minds by the clumsy word and the half-finished gesture; the chances are our most usual behavior makes sense only in a kind of daily way, because it has become familiar to our nearest and dearest, and still demands their con-

235

stant indulgence and understanding. It is our describable outside that defines us, willy nilly, to others, that may save us, or destroy us, in the world; it may be our shield against chaos, our mask against exposure; but whatever it is, the move we make in the place we live has to signify our intent and meaning.

Then think how unprotected the poor character in a novel is, into whose mind the author is inviting us to look—unprotected and hence surely unbelievable! But no, the author has expressly seen to believability. Though he must know all, again he works with illusion. Just as the world of a novel is more highly selective than that of real life, so character in a novel is much more definite, less shadowy than our own, in order that we may believe in it. This is not to say that the character's scope must be limited; it is our vision of it that is guided. It is a kind of phenomenon of writing that the likeliest character has first to be enclosed inside the bounds of even greater likelihood, or he will fly to pieces. Paradoxically, the more narrowly we can examine a fictional character, the greater he is likely to loom up. We must see him set to scale in his proper world to know his size. Place, then, has the most delicate control over character too: by confining character, it defines it.

Place in fiction is the named, identified, concrete, exact and exacting, and therefore credible, gathering-spot of all that has been felt, is about to be experienced, in the novel's progress. Location pertains to feeling; feeling profoundly pertains to place; place in history partakes of feeling, as feeling about history partakes of place. Every story would be another story, and unrecognizable as art, if it took up its characters and plot and happened somewhere else. Imagine *Swann's Way* laid in London, or *The Magic Mountain* in Spain, or *Green Mansions* in the Black Forest. The very notion of moving a novel brings ruder havoc to the mind and affections than would a century's alteration in its time. It is only too easy to conceive that a bomb that could destroy all trace of places as we know them, in life and through books, could also destroy all feelings as we know them, so irretrievably and so happily are recognition, memory, history, valor, love, all the instincts of poetry and praise, worship and endeavor, bound up in place. From the dawn of man's imagination, place has enshrined the spirit; as soon as man stopped wandering and stood still and looked about him, he found a god in that place; and from then on that was where the god abided and spoke from if ever he spoke.

Feelings are bound up in place, and in art, from time to time, place undoubtedly works upon genius. Can anyone well explain otherwise what makes a given dot on the map come passionately alive, for good and all, in a novel—like one of those Novae that suddenly blaze with inexplicable fire in the heavens? What brought a *Wuthering Heights* out of Yorkshire, or a *Sound and the Fury* out of Mississippi?

If place does work upon genius, how does it? It may be that place can focus the gigantic, voracious eye of genius and bring its gaze to point. Focus then means awareness, discernment, order, clarity, insight— they are like the attributes of love. The act of focusing itself has beauty and meaning; it is the act that, continued in, turns into meditation, into poetry. Indeed, as soon as the least of us stands still, that is the moment something extraordinary is seen to be going on in the world. The drama, old beyond count as it is, is no older than the first stage. Without the amphitheater around it to persuade the ear and bend the eye upon a point, how could poetry ever have been spoken, how have been heard? Man is articulate and intelligible only when he begins to communicate inside the strict terms of poetry and reason. Symbols in the end, both are permanent forms of the act of focusing.

Surely place induces poetry, and when the poet is extremely attentive to what is there, a meaning may even attach to his poem out of the spot on earth where it is spoken, and the poem signify the more because it does spring so wholly out of its place, and the sap has run up into it as into a tree.

But we had better confine ourselves here to prose. And then, to take the most absolutely unfanciful novelist of them all, it is to hear him saying, "*Madame Bovary—c'est moi.*" And we see focusing become so intent and aware and conscious in this most "realistic" novel of them all as to amount to fusion. Flaubert's work is indeed of the kind that is embedded immovably as rock in the country of its birth. If, with the slicers of any old (or new) criticism at all, you were to cut down through *Madame Bovary*, its cross-section would still be the same as the cross-section of that living earth, in texture, color, composition, all; which would be no surprise to Flaubert. For such fusion always means accomplishment no less conscious than it is gigantic—effort that must exist entirely as its own reward. We all know the letter Flaubert wrote when he had just found, in the morning paper, in an account of a minister's visit to Rouen, a phrase in the Mayor's speech of welcome

which I had written the day before, textually, in my *Bovary*. . . . Not only were the idea and the words the same, but even

237

the rhythm of the style. It's things like this that give me pleasure. . . . Everything one invents is true, you may be perfectly sure of that! Poetry is as precise as geometry. . . . And besides, after reaching a certain point, one no longer makes any mistakes about the things of the soul. My poor Bovary, without a doubt, is suffering and weeping this very instant in twenty villages of France.

And now that we have come to the writer himself, the question of place resolves itself into the point of view. In this change-over from the objective to the subjective, wonderful and unexpected variations may occur.

Place, to the writer at work, is seen in a frame. Not an empty frame, a brimming one. Point of view is a sort of burning-glass, a product of personal experience and time; it is burnished with feelings and sensibilities, charged from moment to moment with the sun-points of imagination. It is an instrument—one of intensification; it acts, it behaves, it is temperamental. We have seen that the writer must accurately choose, combine, superimpose upon, blot out, shake up, alter the outside world for one absolute purpose, the good of his story. To do this, he is always seeing double, two pictures at once in his frame, his and the world's, a fact that he constantly comprehends; and he works best in a state of constant and subtle and unfooled reference between the two. It is his clear intention—his passion, I should say—to make the reader see only one of the pictures —the author's—under the pleasing illusion that it is the world's; this enormity is the accomplishment of a good story. I think it likely that at the moment of the writer's highest awareness of, and responsiveness to, the "real" world, his imagination's choice (and miles away it may be from actuality) comes closest to being infallible for his purpose. For the spirit of things is what is sought. No blur of inexactness, no cloud of vagueness, is allowable in good writing; from the first seeing to the last putting down, there must be steady lucidity and uncompromise of purpose. I speak, of course, of the ideal.

One of the most important things the young writer comes to see for himself is that point of view *is* an instrument, not an end in itself, that it is useful as a glass, and not as a mirror to reflect a dear and pensive face. Conscientiously used, point of view will discover, explore, see through—it may sometimes divine and prophesy. Misused, it turns opaque almost at once and gets in the way of the book. And when the good novel is finished, its cooled outside shape, what Sean O'Faolàin has called "the veil of reality," has all the burden of communicating that initial, spontaneous, overwhelming, driving charge of personal inner feeling that was the novel's reason for being. The measure of this representation of life corresponds most tellingly with the novel's life expectancy: whenever its world of outside appearance grows dim or false to the eye, the novel has expired.

Establishing a chink-proof world of appearance is not only the first responsibility of the writer; it is the primary step in the technique of every sort of fiction: lyric and romantic, of course; the "realistic," it goes without saying; and other sorts as well. Fantasy itself must touch ground with at least one toe, and ghost stories must have one foot, so to speak, in the grave. The black, squat, hairy ghosts of M. R. James come right out of Cambridge. Only fantasy's stepchild, poor science-fiction, does not touch earth anywhere; and it is doubtful already if happenings entirely confined to outer space are ever going to move us, or even divert us for long. Satire, engaged in its most intellectual of exercises, must first of all establish an impeccable *locus operandi*; its premise is the kingdom where certain rules apply. The countries Gulliver visits are the systems of thought and learning he satirizes made visible one after the other and set in operation. But while place in satire is a purely artificial construction, set up to be knocked down, in humor place becomes its most revealing and at the same time is itself the most revealed. This is because humor, it seems to me, of all forms of fiction, entirely accepts place for what it is.

"Spotted Horses," by William Faulkner, is a good case in point. At the same time that this is just about Mr. Faulkner's funniest story, it is the most thorough and faithful picture of a Mississippi crossroads hamlet that you could ever hope to see. True in spirit, it is also true to everyday fact. Faulkner's art, which often lets him shoot the moon, tells him when to be literal too. In all its specification of detail, both mundane and poetic, in its complete adherence to social fact (which nobody knows better than Faulkner, surely, in writing today), by its unerring aim of observation as true as the sights of a gun would give, but Faulkner has no malice, only compassion; and even and also in the joy of those elements of harlequinade-fantasy that the spotted horses of the title bring in—in all that shining fidelity to place lies the heart and secret of this tale's comic glory.

Faulkner is, of course, the triumphant example in America today of the mastery of place in fiction. Yoknapatawpha County, so supremely and exclusively and majestically and totally itself, is an everywhere, but only because Faulkner's first concern is for what comes first—Yoknapatawpha, his own created world. I am not sure, as a Mississippian myself, how widely it is realized and appreciated that these works of such marvelous imaginative power can also stand as works of the carefullest and purest representation. Heightened, of course: their specialty is they are twice as true as life, and that is why it takes a genius to write them. "Spotted Horses" may not have happened yet; if it had, some others might have tried to make a story of it; but "Spotted Horses" could happen tomorrow —that is one of its glories. It could happen today or tomorrow at any little crossroads hamlet in Mississippi; the whole combination of irresistibility is there. We have the Snopses ready, the Mrs. Littlejohns ready, nice Ratliff and the Judge ready and sighing, the clowns, sober and merry, settled for the evening retrospection of it in the cool dusk of the porch; and the Henry Armstids armed with their obsessions, the little periwinkle-eyed boys armed with their indestructibility; the beautiful, overweening spring, too, the moonlight on the pear trees from which the mockingbird's song keeps returning; and the little store and the fat boy to steal and steal away at its candy. There are undoubtedly spotted horses too, in the offing—somewhere in Texas this minute, straining toward the day. After Faulkner has told it, it is easy for one and all to look back and see it.

Faulkner, simply, knew it already; it is a different kind of knowledge from Flaubert's, and proof could not add much to it. He was born knowing, or rather learning, or rather prophesying, all that and more; and having it all together at one time available while he writes is one of the marks of his mind. If there *is* any more in Mississippi than is engaged and dilated upon and made twice as real as it used to be and applies now to the world, in one story "Spotted Horses," then we would almost rather not know it—but I don't bet a piece of store candy that there is. In Faulkner's humor, even more measurably than in his tragedy, it is all there.

It may be going too far to say that the exactness and concreteness and solidity of the real world achieved in a story correspond to the intensity of feeling in the author's mind and to the very turn of his heart; but there lies the secret of our confidence in him.

Making reality real is art's responsibility. It is a practical assignment, then, a self-assignment: to achieve, by a cultivated sensitivity for observing life, a capacity for receiving its impressions, a lonely, unremitting, unaided, unaidable vision, and transferring this vision without distortion to it onto the pages of a novel, where, if the reader is so persuaded, it will turn into the reader's illusion. How bent on this peculiar joy we are, reader and writer, willingly to practice, willingly to undergo, this alchemy for it!

240

What is there, then, about place that is transferable to the pages of a novel? The best things—the explicit things: physical texture. And as place has functioned between the writer and his material, so it functions between the writer and reader. Location is the ground-conductor of all the currents of emotion and belief and moral conviction that charge out from the story in its course. These charges need the warm hard earth underfoot, the light and lift of air, the stir and play of mood, the softening bath of atmosphere that give the likeness-to-life that life needs. Through the story's translation and ordering of life, the unconvincing raw material becomes the very heart's familiar. Life *is* strange. Stories hardly make it more so; with all they are able to tell and surmise, they make it more believably, more inevitably so.

I think the sense of place is as essential to good and honest writing as a logical mind; surely they are somewhere related. It is by knowing where you stand that you grow able to judge where you are. Place absorbs our earliest notice and attention, it bestows on us our original awareness; and our critical powers spring up from the study of it and the growth of experience inside it. It perseveres in bringing us back to earth when we fly too high. It never really stops informing us, for it is forever astir, alive, changing, reflecting, like the mind of man itself. One place comprehended can make us understand other places better. Sense of place gives equilibrium; extended, it is sense of direction too. Carried off we might be in spirit, and should be, when we are reading or writing something good; but it is the sense of place going with us still that is the ball of golden thread to carry us there and back in every sense of the word to bring us home.

What can place *not* give? Theme. It can present theme, show it to the last detail—but place is forever illustrative: it is a picture of what man has done and imagined, it is his visible past, result. Human life is fiction's only theme.

Novels that are written about place for its own sake are a little the fashion now. They are not very good, and are mentioned here because they represent the opposite use of place from that I have tried to describe. Place applied to for the sake of its surface excitement gives a sort of second-hand glamour to what we might call the Isle of Capri novel, but it gives no authority to it. If these novels are showy and vulgar underneath, it is because they have been vulgarly felt. Drifters write them, and while some drifters may be talented with words, drifting is not an emotion, and can scarcely provide a theme not statable in two words ("I'm drifting"). Restlessness is a different matter, a serious one; but even so it is only an intimation of feeling, or perhaps the first step toward or away from it; it is not the thing itself. Being on the move is no substitute for feeling. Nothing is. And no love or insight can be at work in a shifting and never-defined position, where eye, mind, and heart have never willingly focused on a steadying point.

Surely books suffer as people do from the ailment of lack of base of reference. It comes out in a novel as uncertainty about what the characters really think or mean, ambiguity about what they do or fail to do, or as a queer haphazardness in the novel's shape or form. The trouble is, of course, that if a character has no established world to operate in, no known set of standards to struggle within or against, then whatever disaster may befall, there is no crisis; and although the problem is a moral one, the crisis is an artistic one. The artistic failure is the more certainly fatal, and when sensation rushes in to try to fill the vacuum, the novel takes on the strange consistency of gas, lurid, tell-tale, and soporific. This is allowed to happen, usually, without the author's taking any responsibility for it. "How can *I* say what this is all about?" he seems to be remarking as he passes through. "*I* just *write* here."

When we write a novel out of the saturation of place, we have more to draw on than we know, but when we write with no roots struck down, we will have to be exploiters snatching the first things that glitter on top, and trying to be the first one there, too, or these will be gone. In the end we will have only ourselves—unfixed, unconnected, and not so much sensitive to the world as vulnerable to it. We have flown straight out of detachment by denying attachment. Did we not know these things are too inextricably connected—and to the heart, too—to try to tamper with, as closely perhaps as love and hate?

The bad novel of today is unhappily like the tale told to the analyst. It is not communication, it is confession—often of nothing more than some mild weakness. It is self-absorbed, self-indulgent, too often self-pitying. And it's dull.

Surely what is indicated is for us not to confess ourselves, but to commit ourselves. Only when the best writer on earth is ready and willing, and of course able, to commit himself to his subject can he truly know it —that is, absorb it, embrace it in his mind, take it to his heart, speak it in plain words. This has to be done. As in the experience of our deepest hearts we make no surrender, so in good literature we give and expect no quarter, no compromise. That very sternness is the source of joy.

Should the writer, then, write about home? It is both natural and sensible that the place where we have our roots should become the setting, the first and primary proving ground, of our fiction. Location, however, is not simply to be used by the writer—it is to be discovered, as each novel itself, in the act of writing, is discovery. Discovery does not imply that the place is new, only that we are. Place is as old as the hills. Kilroy at least has been there, and left his name. Discovery, not being a matter of writing our name on a wall, but of seeing what that wall is, and what is over it, is a matter of vision.

One can no more say, "To write stay home," than one can say, "To write leave home." It is the writing that makes its own rules and conditions for each person. And though place is home, it is for the writer writing simply *locus*. It is where the particular story he writes can be pinned down, the circle it can spin through and keep the state of grace, so that for the story's duration the rest of the world suspends its claim upon it and lies low as the story in peaceful extension, the *locus* fading off into the blue.

Naturally, it is the very breath of life, whether one writes a word of fiction or not, to go out and see what is to be seen of the world. For the artist to be unwilling to move, mentally or spiritually or physically, out of the familiar is a sign that spiritual timidity or poverty or decay has come upon him; for what is familiar will then have turned into all that is tyrannical.

One can only say: writers must always write best of what they know, and sometimes they do it by staying where they know it. But not for safety's sake. Although it is in the words of a witch—or all the more because of that—a comment of Hecate's in *Macbeth* is worth our heed: "Security/ Is mortal's chiefest enemy." In fact, when we think in terms of the spirit, which are the terms of writing, is there a conception more stupefying than that of security? Yet writing of what you know has nothing to do with security: what is more dangerous? How can you go out on a limb if you do not know your own tree? No art ever came out of not risking your neck. And risk—experiment—is a considerable part of the joy of doing, which is the lone, simple reason all writers of serious fiction are willing to work as hard as they do.

The open mind and the receptive heart—which are at last and with fortune's smile the informed mind and the experienced heart—are to be gained anywhere, any time, without necessarily moving an inch from any present address. There must surely be as many ways of seeing a place as there are pairs of eyes to see it. The impact happens in so many different ways.

It may be the stranger within the gates whose eye is smitten by the crucial thing, the essence of life, the moment or act in our long-familiar midst that will forever define it. The inhabitant who has taken his fill of a place and gone away may look back and see it for good, from afar, still there in his mind's eye like a city over the hill. It was in the New Zealand stories, written eleven thousand miles from home and out of homesickness, that Katherine Mansfield came into her own. Joyce transplanted not his subject but himself while writing about it, and it was as though he had never left it at all: there it was, still in his eye, exactly the way he had last seen it. From the Continent he wrote the life of Dublin as it was then into a book of the future, for he went translating his own language of it on and on into a country of its own, where it set up a kingdom as renowned as Prester John's. Sometimes two places, two countries, are brought to bear on each other, as in E. M. Forster's work, and the heart of the novel is heard beating most plainly, most passionately, most personally, when two places are at meeting point.

There may come to be new places in our lives that are second spiritual homes—closer to us in some ways, perhaps, than our original homes. But the home tie is the blood tie. And had it meant nothing to us, any other place thereafter would have meant less, and we would carry no compass inside ourselves to find home ever, anywhere at all. We would not even guess what we had missed.

It is noticeable that those writers who for their own good reasons push out against their backgrounds nearly always passionately adopt the new one in their work. Revolt itself is a reference and tribute to the potency of what is left behind. The substitute place, the adopted country, is sometimes a very much stricter, bolder, or harsher one than the original, seldom more lax or undemanding—showing that what was wanted was structure, definition, rigidity—perhaps these were wanted, and understanding was not.

Hemingway in our time has sought out the formal and ruthless territories of the world, archaic ones often, where there are bull fight arenas, theaters of hunting and war, places with a primitive, or formidable, stripped-down character, with implacable codes, with inscrutable justices, and inevitable retributions. But whatever the scene of his work, it is the *places* that never are hostile. People give pain, are callous and insensitive, empty and cruel, carrying with them no pasts as they promise no futures. But place heals the hurt, soothes the outrage, fills the terrible vacuum that these human beings make. It heals actively, and the response is given consciously, with the ardent care and explicitness, respect and delight, of a

244

lover, when fishing streams or naming over streets becomes almost something of the lover's secret language—as the careful conversations between characters in Hemingway bear hints of the secret language of hate. The response to place has the added intensity that comes with the place's not being native or taken for granted, but found, chosen; thereby is the rest more heavily repudiated. It is the response of the *aficionado*; the response, too, is adopted. The title "A Clean Well Lighted Place" is just what the human being is not, for Hemingway, and perhaps it is the epitome of what man would like to find in his fellow man but never has yet, says the author, and never is going to.

We see that point of view is hardly a single, unalterable vision, but a profound and developing one of great complexity. The vision itself may move in and out of its material, shuttle-fashion, instead of being simply turned on it, like a telescope on the moon. Writing is an expression of the writer's own peculiar personality, could not help being so. Yet in reading great works one feels that the finished piece transcends the personal. All writers great and small must sometimes have felt that they have become part of what they wrote even more than it still remains a part of them.

When I speak of writing from where you have put down roots, it may be said that what I urge is "regional" writing. "Regional," I think, is a careless term, as well as a condescending one, because what it does is fail to differentiate between the localized raw material of life and its outcome as art. "Regional" is an outsider's term; it has no meaning for the insider who is doing the writing, because as far as he knows he is simply writing about life. Jane Austen, Emily Brontë, Thomas Hardy, Cervantes, Turgenev, the authors of the books of the Old Testament, all confined themselves to regions, great or small, but are they regional? Then who from the start of time has not been so?

It may well be said that all work springing out of such vital impulse from its native soil has certain things in common. But what signifies is that these are not the little things that it takes a fine-tooth critic to search out, but the great things, that could not be missed or mistaken, for they are the beacon lights of literature.

It seems plain that the art that speaks most clearly, explicitly, directly, and passionately from its place of origin will remain the longest understood. It is through place that we put out roots, wherever birth, chance, fate, or our traveling selves set us down; but where those roots reach toward—whether in America, England, or Timbuktu—is the deep and running vein, eternal and consistent and everywhere purely itself—that feeds

245

and is fed by the human understanding. The challenge to writers today, I think, is not to disown any part of our heritage. Whatever our theme in writing, it is old and tried. Whatever our place, it has been visited by the stranger, it will never be new again. It is only the vision that can be new; but that is enough.

PART SEVEN
modes of presentation

The artificial separation of form and content in the criticism
of fiction, says Mark Schorer, is most unfortunate because
technique and subject matter in art are one and indivisible.
A writer's technique is actually the means by which he
discovers, objectifies, explores, and evaluates his subject, and
his technical dexterity determines his success. Defoe in *Moll
Flanders*, for example, so lacks technical skill that he has
written something closer to a social history of the mercantile
mind than great fiction. Lawrence in *Sons and Lovers* simply
has not the power to separate himself sufficiently from the
subject in order to fully understand it. In Joyce's *Ulysses*,
however, we see an artist with the technical strength to mold
the subject matter into a superbly coherent whole. In fact,
Schorer concludes, the triumph of our finest modern fiction
is that the authors have the technical mastery to uncover the
full complexity of the modern spirit, the real difficulty
of personal morality, and the ugly fact of evil.

technique as discovery

MARK SCHORER

Modern criticism, through its exacting scrutiny of literary texts, has
demonstrated with finality that in art beauty and truth are indivisible and
one. The Keatsian overtones of these terms are mitigated and an old
dilemma solved if for beauty we substitute form, and for truth, content.
We may, without risk of loss, narrow them even more, and speak of technique and subject matter. Modern criticism has shown us that to speak
of content as such is not to speak of art at all, but of experience; and that
it is only when we speak of the *achieved* content, the form, the work of art
as a work of art, that we speak as critics. The difference between content,
or experience, and achieved content, or art, is technique.

When we speak of technique, then, we speak of nearly everything.
For technique is the means by which the writer's experience, which is his
subject matter, compels him to attend to it; technique is the only means

he has of discovering, exploring, developing his subject, of conveying its meaning, and, finally, of evaluating it. And surely it follows that certain techniques are sharper tools than others, and will discover more; that the writer capable of the most exacting technical scrutiny of his subject matter, will produce works with the most satisfying content, works with thickness and resonance, works which reverberate, works with maximum meaning.

We are no longer able to regard as seriously intenaed criticism of poetry which does not assume these generalizations; but the case for fiction has not yet been established. The novel is still read as though its content has some value in itself, as though the subject matter of fiction has greater or lesser value in itself, and as though technique were not a primary but a supplementary element, capable perhaps of not unattractive embellishments upon the surface of the subject, but hardly of its essence. Or technique is thought of in blunter terms from those which one associates with poetry, as such relatively obvious matters as the arrangement of events to create plot; or, within plot, of suspense and climax; or as the means of revealing character motivation, relationship, and development; or as the use of point of view, but point of view as some nearly arbitrary device for the heightening of dramatic interest through the narrowing or broadening of perspective upon the material, rather than as a means toward the positive definition of theme. As for the resources of language, these, somehow, we almost never think of as a part of the technique of fiction—language as used to create a certain texture and tone which in themselves state and define themes and meanings; or language, the counters of our ordinary speech, as forced, through conscious manipulation, into all those larger meanings which our ordinary speech almost never intends. Technique in fiction, all this is a way of saying, we somehow continue to regard as merely a means to organizing material which is "given" rather than as the means of exploring and defining the values in an area of experience which, for the first time *then*, are being given.

Is fiction still regarded in this odd, divided way because it is really less tractable before the critical suppositions which now seem inevitable to poetry? Let us look at some examples: two well-known novels of the past, both by writers who may be described as "primitive," although their relative innocence of technique is of a different sort—Defoe's *Moll Flanders* and Emily Bronte's *Wuthering Heights*; and three well-known novels of this century—*Tono Bungay*, by a writer who claimed to eschew technique; *Sons and Lovers,* by a novelist who, because his ideal of subject matter ("the poetry of the immediate present") led him at last into the fallacy of spontaneous and unchangeable composition, in effect eschewed technique; and *A Portrait of the Artist as a Young Man,* by a novelist whose practice made claims for the supremacy of technique beyond those made by anyone in the past or by anyone else in this century.

Technique in fiction is, of course, all those obvious forms of it which are usually taken to be the whole of it, and many others; but for the present purposes, let it be thought of in two respects particularly: the uses to which language, as language, is put to express the quality of the experience in question; and the uses of point of view not only as a mode of dramatic delimitation, but more particularly, of thematic definition. Technique is really what T. S. Eliot means by "convention"—any selection, structure, or distortion, any form or rhythm imposed upon the world of action; by means of which—it should be added—our apprehension of the world of action is enriched or renewed. In this sense, everything is technique which is not the lump of experience itself, and one cannot properly say that a writer has no technique or that he eschews technique, for, being a writer, he cannot do so. We can speak of good and bad technique, of adequate and inadequate, of technique which serves the novel's purpose, or disserves.

In the prefatory remarks to *Moll Flanders,* Defoe tells us that he is not writing fiction at all, but editing the journals of a woman of notorious charter, and rather to instruct us in the necessities and the joys of virtue than to please us. We do not, of course, take these professions seriously, since nothing in the conduct of the narrative indicates that virtue is either more necessary or more enjoyable than vice. On the contrary, we discover that Moll turns virtuous only after a life of vice has enabled her to do so with security; yet it is precisely for this reason that Defoe's profession of didactic purpose has interest. For the actual morality which the novel enforces is the morality of any commercial culture, the belief that virtue pays—in worldly goods. It is a morality somewhat less than skin deep, having no relation to motives arising from a sense of good and evil, least of all, of evil-*in*-good, but exclusively from the presence or absence of food, drink, linen, damask, silver, and time-pieces. It is the morality of measurement, and without in the least intending it, *Moll Flanders* is our classic revelation of the mercantile mind: the morality of measurement, which Defoe has completely neglected to measure. He fails not only to evaluate this material in his announced way, but to evaluate it at all. His announced purpose is, we admit, a pious humbug, and he meant us to read the book as a series of scandalous events; and thanks to his inexhaustible pleasure in excess and exaggeration, this element in the book continues to amuse us. Long before the book has been finished, however, this element has also become an absurdity; but not half the absurdity as that which Defoe did not intend at all—the notion that Moll could live a rich and full life of crime, and yet, repenting, emerge spotless in the end. The point is, of course, that she has no moral being, nor has the book any moral life. Everything is external. Everything can be weighed, measured, handled, paid for in gold, or expiated by a prison term. To this, the whole texture of the novel testifies: the bolts of goods, the inventories, the itemized accounts, the landlady's bills, the lists, the ledgers: all this, which taken together comprises what we call Defoe's method of circumstantial realism.

He did not come upon that method by any deliberation: it represents precisely his own world of value, the importance of external circumstance to Defoe. The point of view of Moll is indistinguishable from the point of view of her creator. We discover the meaning of the novel (at unnecessary length, without economy, without emphasis, with almost none of the distortions or the advantages of art) in spite of Defoe, not because of him. Thus the book is not the true chronicle of a disreputable female, but the true allegory of an impoverished soul—the author's; not an anatomy of the criminal class, but of the middle class. And we read it as an unintended comic revelation of self and of a social mode. Because he had no adequate resources of technique to separate himself from his material, thereby to discover and to define the meanings of his material, his contribution is not to fiction but to the history of fiction, and to social history.

The situation in *Wuthering Heights* is at once somewhat the same and yet very different. Here, too, the whole novel turns upon itself, but this time to its estimable advantage; here, too, is a revelation of what is perhaps the author's secret world of value, but this time, through what may be an accident of technique, the revelation is meaningfully accomplished. Emily Bronte may merely have stumbled upon the perspectives which define the form and the theme of her book. Whether she knew from the outset, or even at the end, what she was doing, we may doubt; but what she did and did superbly we can see.

We can assume, without at all becoming involved in the author's life but merely from the tone of somnambulistic excess which is generated by the writing itself, that this world of monstrous passion, of dark and gigantic emotional and nervous energy, is for the author, or was in the first place, a world of ideal value; and that the book sets out to persuade us of the moral magnificence of such unmoral passion. We are, I think, expected, in the first place, to take at their own valuation these demonic beings, Heathcliff and Cathy: as special creatures, set apart from the cloddish world about them by their heightened capacity for feeling, set apart, even, from the ordinary objects of human passion as, in their transcendental, sexless relationship, they identfy themselves with an uncompromising landscape and cosmic force. Yet this is absurd, as much of the detail that surrounds it ("Other dogs lurked in other recesses") is absurd. The novelist Emily Bronte had to discover these absurdities to the girl Emily; her technique had to evaluate them for what they were, so that we are persuaded that it is not Emily who is mistaken in her estimate of her characters, but they who are mistaken in their estimate of themselves. The theme of the moral magnificence of unmoral passion is an impossible theme to sustain, and what interests us is that it was device—and this time, mere, mechanical device—which taught Emily Bronte that, the needs of her temperament to the contrary, all personal longing and reverie to the contrary, perhaps—that this was indeed not at all what her material must mean as art. Technique objectifies.

To lay before us the full character of this passion, to show us how it first comes into being and then comes to dominate the world about it and the life that follows upon it, Emily Bronte gives her material a broad scope in time, lets it, in fact, cut across three generations. And to manage material which is so extensive, she must find a means of narration, points of view, which can encompass that material, and, in her somewhat crude concept of motive, justify its telling. So she chooses a foppish traveller who stumbles into this world of passionate violence, a traveller representing the thin and conventional emotional life of the far world of fashion, who wishes to hear the tale: and for her teller she chooses, almost inevitably, the old family retainer who knows everything, a character as conventional as the other, but this one representing not the conventions of fashion, but the conventions of the humblest moralism. What has happened is, first, that she has chosen as her narrative perspective those very elements, conventional emotion and conventional morality, which her hero and heroine are meant to transcend with such spectacular magnificence; and second, that she has permitted this perspective to operate through-

253

out a long period of time. And these two elements compel the novelist to see what her unmoral passions come to. Moral magnificence? Not at all; rather, a devastating spectacle of human waste; ashes. For the time of the novel is carried on long enough to show Heathcliff at last an emptied man, burned out by his fever ragings, exhausted and will-less, his passion meaningless at last. And it goes even a little further, to Lockwood, the fop, in the graveyard, sententiously contemplating headstones. Thus in the end the triumph is all on the side of the cloddish world, which survives.

Perhaps not all on that side. For, like Densher at the end of *The Wings of the Dove,* we say, and surely Hareton and the second Cathy say, "We shall never be again as we were!" But there is more point in observing that a certain body of materials, a girl's romantic daydreams, have, through the most conventional devices of fiction, been pushed beyond their inception in fancy to their meanings, their conception as a written book—that they, that is, are not at all as they were.

Technique alone objectifies the materials of art; hence technique alone evaluates those materials. This is the axiom which demonstrates itself so devastatingly whenever a writer declares, under the urgent sense of the importance of his materials (whether these are autobiography, or social ideas, or personal passions)—whenever such a writer declares that he cannot linger with technical refinements. That art will not tolerate such a writer H. G. Wells handsomely proves. His enormous literary energy included no respect for the techniques of his medium, and his medium takes its revenge upon his bumptiousness. "I have never taken any very great pains about writing. I am outside the hierarchy of conscious and deliberate writers altogether. I am the absolute antithesis of Mr. James Joyce. . . . Long ago, living in close conversational proximity to Henry James, Joseph Conrad, and Mr. Ford Madox Ford, I escaped from under their immense artistic preoccupations by calling myself a journalist." Precisely. And he escaped—he disappeared—from literature into the annals of an era.

Yet what confidence! "Literature," Wells said, "is not jewelry, it has quite other aims than perfection, and the more one thinks of 'how it is done' the less one gets it done. These critical indulgences lead along a fatal path, away from every natural interest towards a preposterous emptiness of technical effort, a monstrous egotism of artistry, of which the later work of Henry James is the monumental warning. 'It,' the subject, the thing or the thought, has long since disappeared in these amazing works;

nothing remains but the way it has been 'manipulated.' " Seldom has a literary theorist been so totally wrong; for what we learn as James grows for us and Wells disappears, is that without what he calls "manipulation," there is no "it," no "subject" in art. There is again only social history.

The virtue of the modern novelist—from James and Conrad down—is not only that he pays so much attention to his medium, but that, when he pays most, he discovers through it a new subject matter, and a greater one. Under the "immense artistic preoccupations" of James and Conrad and Joyce, the form of the novel changed, and with the technical change, analogous changes took place in substance, in point of view, in the whole conception of fiction. And the final lesson of the modern novel is that technique is not the secondary thing that it seemed to Wells, some external machination, a mechanical affair, but a deep and primary operation; not only that technique *contains* intellectual and moral implications, but that it *discovers* them. For a writer like Wells, who wished to give us the intellectual and the moral history of our times, the lesson is a hard one: it tells us that the order of intellect and the order of morality do not exist at all, in art, except as they are organized in the order of art.

Wells's ambitions were very large. "Before we have done, we will have all life within the scope of the novel." But that is where life already is, within the scope of the novel; where it needs to be brought is into novels. In Wells we have all the important topics in life, but no good novels. He was not asking too much of art, or asking that it include more than it happily can; he was not asking anything of it—as art, which is all that it can give, and that is everything.

A novel like *Tono Bungay*, generally thought to be Wells's best, is therefore instructive. "I want to tell—*myself*," says George, the hero, "and my impressions of the thing as a whole"—the thing as a whole being the collapse of traditional British institutions in the twentieth century. George "tells himself" in terms of three stages in his life which have rough equivalents in modern British social history, and this is, to be sure, a plan, a framework; but it is the framework of Wells's abstract thinking, not of his craftsmanship, and the primary demand which one makes of such a book as this, that means be discovered whereby the dimensions of the hero contain the experiences he recounts, is never met. The novelist flounders through a series of literary imitations—from an early Dickensian episode, through a kind of Shavian interlude, through a Conradian episode, to a Jules Verne vision at the end. The significant failure is in that end, and in the way that it defeats not only the entire social analysis of the bulk of the novel, but Wells's own ends as a thinker. For at last George finds a purpose in science. "I decided that in power and knowledge lay the salvation of my life, the secret that would fill my need; that to these things I would give myself."

But science, power and knowledge, are summed up at last in a destroyer. As far as one can tell Wells intends no irony, although he may here have come upon the essence of the major irony in modern history. The novel ends in a kind of meditative rhapsody which denies every value that the book had been aiming toward. For of all the kinds of social waste which Wells has been describing, this is the most inclusive, the final waste. Thus he gives us in the end not a novel, but a hypothesis; not an individual destiny, but a theory of the future; and not his theory of the future, but a nihilistic vision quite opposite from everything that he meant to represent. With a minimum of attention to the virtues of technique, Wells might still not have written a good novel; but he would at any rate have established a point of view and a tone which would have told us what he meant.

To say what one means in art is never easy, and the more intimately one is implicated in one's material, the more difficult it is. If, besides, one commits fiction to a therapeutic function which is to be operative not on the audience but on the author, declaring, as D. H. Lawrence did, that "One sheds one's sicknesses in books, repeats and presents again one's emotions to be master of them," the difficulty is vast. It is an acceptable theory only with the qualification that technique, which objectifies, is under no other circumstances so imperative. For merely to repeat one's emotions, merely to look into one's heart and write, is also merely to repeat the round of emotional bondage. If our books are to be exercises in self-analysis, then technique must—and alone can—take the place of the absent analyst.

Lawrence, in the relatively late Introduction to his *Collected Poems,* made that distinction of the amateur between his "real" poems and his "composed" poems, between the poems which expressed his demon directly and created their own form "willy-nilly," and the poems which, through the hocus pocus of technique, he spuriously put together and could, if necessary, revise. His belief in a "poetry of the immediate present," poetry in which nothing is fixed, static, or final, where all is shimmeriness and impermanence and vitalistic essence, arose from this mistaken notion of technique. And from this notion, an unsympathetic critic like D. S. Savage can construct a case which shows Lawrence driven "concurrently to the dissolution of personality and the dissolution of art." The argument suggests that Lawrence's early, crucial novel, *Sons and Lovers*, is another example of meanings confused by an impatience with technical resources.

The novel has two themes: the crippling effects of a mother's love on the emotional development of her son; and the "split" between kinds of love, physical and spiritual, which the son develops, the kinds represented by two young women, Clara and Miriam. The two themes should, of course, work together, the second being, actually, the result of the first: this "split" is the "crippling." So one would expect to see the novel developed, and so Lawrence, in his famous letter to Edward Garnett, where he says that Paul is left at the end with the "drift towards death," apparently thought he had developed it. Yet in the last few sentences of the novel, Paul rejects his desire for extinction and turns towards "the faintly humming, glowing town," to life—as nothing in his previous history persuades us that he could unfalteringly do.

The discrepancy suggests that the book may reveal certain confusions between intention and performance.

The first of these is the contradiction between Lawrence's explicit characterizations of the mother and father and his tonal evaluations of them. It is a problem not only of style (of the contradiction between expressed moral epithets and the more general texture of the prose which applies to them) but of point of view. Morel and Lawrence are never separated, which is a way of saying that Lawrence maintains for himself in this book the confused attitude of his character. The mother is a "proud, *honorable* soul," but the father has a "small, *mean* head." This is the sustained contrast; the epithets are characteristic of the whole; and they represent half of Lawrence's feelings. But what is the other half? Which of these characters is given his real sympathy—the hard, self-righteous, aggressive, demanding mother who comes through to us, or the simple, direct, gentle, downright, fumbling, ruined father? There are two attitudes here. Lawrence (and Morel) loves his mother, but he also hates her for compelling his love; and he hates his father with the true Freudian jealousy, but he also loves him for what he is in himself, and he sympathizes more deeply with him because his wholeness has been destroyed by the mother's domination, just as his, Lawrence-Morel's, has been.

This is a psychological tension which disrupts the form of the novel and obscures its meaning, because neither the contradiction in style nor the confusion in point of view is made to right itself. Lawrence is merely

257

repeating his emotions, and he avoids an austerer technical scrutiny of his material because it would compel him to master them. He would not let the artist be stronger than the man.

The result is that, at the same time that the book condemns the mother, it justifies her; at the same time that it shows Paul's failure, it offers rationalizations which place the failure elsewhere. The handling of the girl, Miriam, if viewed closely, is pathetic in what it signifies for Lawrence, both as man and artist. For Miriam is made the mother's scape-goat, and in a different way from the way that she was in life. The central section of the novel is shot through with alternate statements as to the source of the difficulty: Paul is unable to love Miriam wholly, and Miriam can love only his spirit. The contradictions appear sometimes within single paragraphs, and the point of view is never adequately objectified and sustained to tell us which is true. The material is never seen as material; the writer is caught in it exactly as firmly as he was caught in his experience of it. "That's how women are with me," said Paul. "They want me like mad, but they don't want to belong to me." So he might have said, and believed it; but at the end of the novel, Lawrence is still saying that, and himself believing it.

For the full history of this technical failure, one must read *Sons and Lovers* carefully and then learn the history of the manuscript from the book called *D. H. Lawrence: A Personal Record*, by one E. T., who was Miriam in life. The basic situation is clear enough. The first theme—the crippling effects of the mother's love—is developed right through to the end; and then suddenly in the last few sentences, turns on itself, and Paul gives himself to life, not death. But all the way through, the insidious rationalizations of the second theme have crept in to destroy the artistic coherence of the work. A "split" would occur in Paul; but as the split is treated, it is superimposed upon rather than developed in support of the first theme. It is a rationalization made from it. If Miriam is made to insist on spiritual love, the meaning and the power of theme one are reduced; yet Paul's weakness is disguised. Lawrence could not separate the investigating analyst, who must be objective, from Lawrence, the subject of the book; and the sickness was not healed, the emotion not mastered, the novel not perfected. All this, and the character of a whole career, would have been altered if Lawrence had allowed his technique to discover the fullest meaning of his subject.

A Portrait of the Artist as a Young Man, like *Tono Bungay* and *Sons and Lovers*, is autobiographical, but unlike these it analyzes its material rigorously, and it defines the value and the quality of its experience not by appended comment or moral epithet, but by the texture of the style. The theme of *A Portrait*, a young artist's alienation from his environment, is explored and evaluated through three different styles and methods as Stephen Dedalus moves from childhood through boyhood into maturity. The opening pages are written in something like the stream of consciousness of *Ulysses*, as the environment impinges directly on the consciousness of the infant and the child, a strange, opening world which the mind does not yet subject to questioning, selection, or judgment. But this style changes very soon, as the boy begins to explore his surroundings, and as his sensuous experience of the world is enlarged, it takes on heavier and heavier rhythms and a fuller and fuller body of sensuous detail, until it reaches a crescendo of romantic opulence in the emotional climaxes which mark Stephen's rejection of domestic and religious values. Then gradually the style subsides into the austerer intellectuality of the final sections, as he defines to himself the outlines of the artistic task which is to usurp his maturity.

A highly self-conscious use of style and method defines the quality of experience in each of these sections, and, it is worth pointing out in connection with the third and concluding section, the style and method evaluate the experience. What has happened to Stephen is, of course, a progressive alienation from the life around him as he progressed in his initiation into it, and by the end of the novel, the alienation is complete. The final portion of the novel, fascinating as it may be for the developing aesthetic creed of Stephen-Joyce, is peculiarly bare. The life experience was not bare, as we know from *Stephen Hero*; but Joyce is forcing technique to comment. In essence, Stephen's alienation is a denial of the human environment; it is a loss; and the austere discourse of the final section, abstract and almost wholly without sensuous detail or strong rhythm, tells us of that loss. It is a loss so great that the texture of the notation-like prose here suggests that the end is really all an illusion, that when Stephen tells us and himself that he is going forth to forge in the smithy of his soul the uncreated conscience of his race, we are to infer from the very quality of the icy, abstract void he now inhabits, the implausibility of his aim. For *Ulysses* does not create the conscience of the race; it creates our consciousness.

In the very last two or three paragraphs of the novel the style changes once more, reverts from the bare, notative kind to the romantic prose of Stephen's adolescence. "Away! Away! The spell of arms and voices: the white arms of roads, their promise of close embraces and the black arms of tall ships that stand against the moon, their tale of distant nations. They are held out to say: We are alone—come." Might one not say that the austere ambition is founded on adolescent longing? That the excessive intellectual severity of one style is the counterpart of the excessive lyric relaxation of the other? And that the final passage of A *Portrait* punctuates the illusory nature of the whole ambition?

For *Ulysses* does not create a conscience. Stephen, in *Ulysses,* is a little older, and gripped now by guilt, but he is still the cold young man divorced from the human no less than the institutional environment. The environment of urban life finds a separate embodiment in the character of Bloom, and Bloom is as lost as Stephen, though touchingly groping for moorings. Each of the two is weakened by his inability to reach out, or to do more than reach out to the other. Here, then, is the theme again, more fully stated, as it were in counterpart.

But if Stephen is not much older, Joyce is. He is older as an artist not only because he can create and lavish his Godlike pity on a Leopold Bloom, but also because he knows now what both Stephen and Bloom mean, and *how much,* through the most brilliant technical operation ever made in fiction, they can be made to mean. Thus *Ulysses,* through the imaginative force which its techniques direct, is like a pattern of concentric circles, with the immediate human situation at its center, this passing on and out to the whole dilemma of modern life, this passing on and out beyond that to a vision of the cosmos, and this to the mythical limits of our experience. If we read *Ulysses* with more satisfaction than any other novel of this century, it is because its author held an attitude toward technique and the technical scrutiny of subject matter which enabled him to order, within a single work and with superb coherence, the greatest amount of our experience.

In the United States during the last twenty-five years, we have had many big novels but few good ones. A writer like James T. Farrell apparently assumes that by endless redundancy in the description of the surface of American Life, he will somehow write a book with the scope of *Ulysses.* Thomas Wolfe apparently assumed that by the mere disgorging of the raw material of his experience he would give us at last our epic. But except in a physical sense, these man have hardly written novels at all.

The books of Thomas Wolfe were, of course, journals, and the primary role of his publisher in transforming these journals into the semiblance of novels is notorious. For the crucial act of the artist, the unique act which is composition, a sympathetic editorial blue pencil and scissors were substituted. The result has excited many people, especially the young, and the ostensibly critical have observed the prodigal talent with the wish that it might have been controlled. Talent there was, if one means by talent inexhaustible verbal energy, excessive response to personal experience, and a great capacity for auditory imitativeness, yet all of this has nothing to do with the novelistic quality of the written result; until the talent is controlled, the material organized, the content achieved, there is simply the man and his life. It remains to be demonstrated that Wolfe's conversations were any less interesting as novels than his books, which is to say that his books are without interest as novels. As with Lawrence, our response to the books is determined, not by their qualities as novels, but by our response to him and his qualities as a temperament.

This is another way of saying that Thomas Wolfe never really knew what he was writing *about*. Of Time and the River is merely a euphemism for Of Man and his Ego. It is possible that had his conception of himself and of art included an adequate respect for technique and the capacity to pursue it, Wolfe would have written a great novel on his true subject— the dilemma of romantic genius; it was his true subject, but it remains his undiscovered subject, it is the subject which *we* must dig out for him, because he himself had neither the lamp nor the pick to find it in and mine it out of the labyrinths of his experience. Like Emily Bronte, Wolfe needed a point of view beyond his own which would separate his material and its effect.

With Farrell, the situation is opposite. He knows quite well what his subject is and what he wishes to tell us about it, but he hardly needs the novel to do so. It is significant that in sheer clumsiness of style, no living writer exceeds him, for his prose is asked to perform no service beyond communication of the most rudimentary kind of fact. For his ambitions, the style of the newspaper and the lens of the documentary camera would be quite adequate, yet consider the diminution which Leopold Bloom, for example, would suffer, if he were to be viewed from these, the technical perspectives of James Farrell. Under the eye of this technique, the material does not yield up enough; indeed, it shrinks.

More and more writers in this century have felt that naturalism as a method imposes on them strictures which prevent them from exploring through all the resources of technique the full amplifications of their subjects, and that thus it seriously limits the possible breadth of aesthetic meaning and response. James Farrell is almost unique in the complacency with which he submits to the blunt techniques of naturalism; and his fiction is correspondingly repetitive and flat.

That naturalism had a sociological and disciplinary value in the nineteenth century is obvious; it enabled the novel to grasp materials and make analyses which had eluded it in the past, and to grasp them boldly; but even then it did not tell us enough of what, in Virginia Woolf's phrase, is "really real," nor did it provide the means to the maximum of reality coherently contained. Even the Flaubertian ideal of objectivity seems, today, an unnecessarily limited view of objectivity, for as almost every good writer of this century shows us, it is quite as possible to be objective about subjective states as it is to be objective about the circumstantial surfaces of life. Dublin, in *Ulysses*, is a moral setting: not only a city portrayed in the naturalistic fashion of Dickens' London, but also a map of the modern psyche with its oblique and baffled purposes. The second level of reality in no way invalidates the first, and a writer like Joyce shows us that, if the artist truly respects his medium, he can be objective about both at once. What we need in fiction is a devoted fidelity to every technique which will help us to discover and to evaluate our subject matter, and more than that, to discover the amplifications of meaning of which our subject matter is capable.

Most modern novelists have felt this demand upon them. André Gide allowed one of his artist-heroes to make an observation which considerably resembles an observation we have quoted from Wells. "My novel hasn't got a subject. . . . Let's say, if you prefer it, it hasn't got *one* subject. . . . 'A slice of life,' the naturalist school said. The great defect of that school is that it always cuts its slice in the same direction; in time, lengthwise. Why not in breadth? Or in depth? As for me I should like not to cut at all. Please understand; I should like to put everything into my novel." Wells, with his equally large blob of potential material, did not know how to cut it to the novel's taste; Gide cut, of course—in every possible direction. Gide and others. And those "cuts" are all the new techniques which modern fiction has given us. None, perhaps, is more important than that inheritance from French symbolism which Huxley, in the glittering wake of Gide, called "the musicalization of fiction." Conrad anticipated both when he wrote that the novel "must strenuously aspire to the plasticity of sculpture, to the colour of painting, and to the magic suggestiveness of music—which is the art of arts," and when he said of that early but wonderful piece of symbolist fiction, *Heart of Dark-*

262

ness, "It was like another art altogether. That sombre theme had to be given a sinister resonance, a tonality of its own, a continued vibration that, I hoped, would hang in the air and dwell on the ear after the last note had been struck." The analogy with music, except as a metaphor, is inexact, and except as it points to techniques which fiction can employ as fiction, not very useful to our sense of craftsmanship. It has had an approximate exactness in only one work, Joyce's final effort, and an effort unique in literary history, *Finnegans Wake,* and here, of course, those readers willing to approach the "ideal" effort Joyce demands, discovering an inexhaustible wealth and scope, are most forcibly reminded of the primary importance of technique to subject, and of their indivisibility.

The techniques of naturalism inevitably curtail subject and often leave it in its original area, that of undefined social experience. Those of our writers who, stemming from this tradition, yet, at their best, achieve a novelistic definition of social experience—writers like the occasional Sherwood Anderson, William Carlos Williams, the occasional Erskine Caldwell, Nathaniel West, and Ira Wolfert in *Tucker's People,* have done so by pressing naturalism far beyond itself, into positively gothic distortions. The structural machinations of Dos Passos and the lyrical interruptions of Steinbeck are the desperate maneuvers of men committed to a method of whose limitations they despair. They are our symbolists *manqué,* who end as allegorists.

Our most accomplished novels leave no such impression of desperate and intentional struggle, yet their precise technique and their determination to make their prose work in the service of their subjects have been the measure of their accomplishment. Hemingway's *The Sun Also Rises* and Wescott's *The Pilgrim Hawk* are works of art not because they may be measured by some external, neo-classic notion of form, but because their forms are so exactly equivalent with their subjects, and because the evaluation of their subjects exists in their styles.

Hemingway has recently said that his contribution to younger writers lay in a certain necessary purification of the language; but the claim has doubtful value. The contribution of his prose was to his subject, and the terseness of style for which his early work is justly celebrated is no more valuable, as an end in itself, than the baroque involutedness of Faulkner's prose, or the cold elegance of Wescott's. Hemingway's early subject, the exhaustion of value, was perfectly investigated and invested by his bare style, and in story after story, no meaning at all is to be inferred from the fiction except as the style itself suggests that there is no meaning in life.

This style, more than that, was the perfect technical substitute for the convenional commentator; it expresses and it measures that peculiar morality of the stiff lip which Hemingway borrowed from athletes. It is an instructive lesson, furthermore, to observe how the style breaks down when Hemingway moves into the less congenial subject matter of social affirmation: how the style breaks down, the effect of verbal economy as mute suffering is lost, the personality of the writer, no longer protected by the objectification of an adequate technique, begins its offensive intrusion, and the entire structural integrity slackens. Inversely, in the stories and the early novels, the technique was the perfect embodiment of the subject and it gave that subject its astonishing largeness of effect and of meaning.

One should correct Buffon and say that style is the subject. In Wescott's *Pilgrim Hawk,* a novel which bewildered its many friendly critics by the apparent absence of subject, the subject, the story, is again in the style itself. This novel, which is a triumph of the sustained point of view, is only bewildering if we try to make a story out of the narrator's observations upon others; but if we read his observations as oblique and unrecognized observations upon himself the story emerges with perfect coherence, and it reverberates with meaning, is as suited to continuing reflection as the greatest lyrics.

The rewards of such respect for the medium as the early Hemingway and the occasional Wescott have shown may be observed in every good writer we have. The involutions of Faulkner's style are the perfect equivalent of his involved structures, and the two together are the perfect representation of the moral labyrinths he explores, and of the ruined world which his novels repeatedly invoke and in which these labyrinths exist. The cultivated sensuosity of Katherine Anne Porter's style has charm in itself, of course, but no more than with these others does it have aesthetic value in itself; its values lie in the subtle means by which sensuous details become symbols, and in the way that the symbols provide a network which is the story, and which at the same time provides the writer and us with a refined moral insight by means of which to test it. When we put such writers against a writer like William Saroyan, whose respect is reserved for his own temperament, we are appalled by the stylistic irresponsibility we find in him, and by the almost total absence of theme, or defined subject matter, and the abundance of unwarranted feeling. Such a writer inevitably becomes a sentimentalist because he has no means by which to measure his emotion. Technique, at last, is measure.

These writers, from Defoe to Porter, are of unequal and very different talent, and technique and talent are, of course, after a point, two different

264

things. What Joyce gives us in one direction, Lawrence, for all his imperfections as a technician, gives us in another, even though it is not usually the direction of art. Only in some of his stories and in a few of his poems, where the demands of technique are less sustained and the subject matter is not autobiographical, Lawrence, in a different way from Joyce, comes to the same aesthetic fulfilment. Emily Bronte, with what was perhaps her intuitive grasp of the need to establish a tension between her subject matter and her perspective upon it, achieves a similar fulfilment; and, curiously, in the same way and certainly by intuition alone, Hemingway's early work makes a moving splendor from nothingness.

And yet, whatever one must allow to talent and forgive in technique, one risks no generalization in saying that modern fiction at its best has been peculiarly conscious of itself and of its tools. The technique of modern fiction, at once greedy and fastidious, achieves as its subject matter not some singleness, some topic or thesis, but the whole of the modern consciousness. It discovers the complexity of the modern spirit, the difficulty of personal morality, and the fact of evil—all the untractable elements under the surface which a technique of the surface alone can not approach. It shows us—in Conrad's words, from *Victory*—that we all live in an "age in which we are camped like bewildered travellers in a garish, unrestful hotel," and while it puts its hard light on our environment, it penetrates, with its sharp weapons, the depths of our bewilderment. These are not two things, but only an adequate technique can show them as one. In a realist like Farrell, we have the environment only, which we know from the newspapers; in a subjectivist like Wolfe, we have the bewilderment only, which we record in our own diaries and letters. But the true novelist gives them to us together, and thereby increases the effect of each, and reveals each in its full significance.

Elizabeth Bowen, writing of Lawrence, said of modern fiction, "We want the naturalistic surface, but with a kind of internal burning. In Lawrence every bush burns." But the bush burns brighter in some places than in others, and it burns brightest when a passionate private vision finds its objectification in exacting technical search. If the vision finds no such objectification, as in Wolfe and Saroyan, there is a burning without a bush. In our committed realists, who deny the resources of art for the sake of life, whose technique forgives both innocence and slovenliness—in Defoe and Wells and Farrell, there is a bush but it does not burn. There, at first glance, the bush is only a bush; and then, when we look again, we see that, really, the thing is dead.

We do not have procedures for dealing with prose fiction,
Philip Rahv argues, that are as exact or as subtle as those
we have for the criticism of poetry. This is curious because our
fiction writers have been as successful in their art as our poets
have been; yet their criticism of fiction is far behind that of
the poets. Indeed, our very success in the criticism of poetry
has led us into a fundamental and serious error in our evaluation
of fiction—the overemphasis on technique. For example, our
critics mistakenly and excessively stress symbols, allegories,
and mythic patterns. Or in their zeal they take style to be
a most important mark of fine, imaginative prose. In short,
we now see an unfortunate formalist tendency to reduce the
worth of a novel or short story to the sum of its technique.
What this approach overlooks is the fact that there are many
aspects of creativity other than the mastery of technique.
We may have brilliant literary technicians who
are in no profound sense real artists.

fiction and the
criticism of fiction

PHILIP RAHV

The novel is at the present time universally recognized as one of
the greater historic forms of literary art. Its resources and capacities
appear to be commensurate with the realities and consciousness of the
modern epoch, and its practitioners, having inherited a good many of
the functions once exercised by poetry and the drama, no longer feel the
slightest need to engage in the kind of apologetics that were quite
common even as late as a hundred years ago, when in respectable
quarters novel-writing and novel-reading were still looked upon as activities falling below the level of true cultural aspiration. But if the novel was
then still widely regarded as a thing somewhat effeminate and moon-
shiny, fit mainly for the consumption of young ladies, it was at the same
time quickly impressing itself upon the mind of the age as a newfangled

form full of rude plebeian energy, unruly, unpredictable and ungovernable in its appropriation of materials from unprocessed reality—"the conscience of a blackened street impatient to assume the world." Much of the life the novel contains is defined by these contrary reactions, one pointing to its origin in romance and the other to its revitalization through the new principle of realism.

Among the last apologies for the novel—an apology in which we fully sense, however, the surge of confidence and power generated by the phenomenal rise of this relatively new genre—is the preface that the Goncourt brothers wrote for their novel *Germinie Lacerteux* (1864). "Now that the novel," they observed, "is broadening, growing, beginning to be a great, serious, impassioned living form of literary study and social research, now that by means of analysis and psychological inquiry it is turning into contemporary moral history, now that the novel has imposed upon itself the investigations and duties of science, one may again make a stand for its liberties and privileges." This memorable formulation is in the main still acceptable to us. The one dated element in it is of course the reference to science, a reference all too patently of its period and linked to the development of the naturalistic school in French fiction. At the time not a few writers were so impressed by the triumphs of scientific method as to want to borrow some of its magic for themselves, yet at bottom it was not so much a matter of faith in science (though doubtless that played its part too) as of an intention to gain prestige for the novel by means of an honorific association. But apart from that the formulation I have cited has scarcely lost its cogency. The one question arising in connection with it is whether it is still necessary at this late date again to make a stand for the novel's liberties and privileges. So far as the intelligent reader at large is concerned such a stand may well be redundant. But it is not in the least redundant, I think, so far as some present-day critics of fiction are concerned and the reading-practices to which they have been habituating us.

My argument rests on a premise that most of us will surely accept, and that is that 20th Century criticism has as yet failed to evolve a theory and a set of practical procedures dealing with the prose-medium that are as satisfactory in their exactness, subtlety and variety as the theory and procedures worked out in the past few decades by the critics of poetry. It may well be, as is so frequently said, that in art there is no such thing as progress. But, then, criticism is only partially an art, so little of an art perhaps as to admit in some periods not only change, as all the arts do, but also gradual development toward a more accurate knowledge. One is certainly disposed to think so when comparing the present state of poetry-criticism with its state, say, forty or fifty years ago. The criticism of poetry has of late acquired a rich consciousness which may be defined objectively as the self-consciousness of the medium—an historic acquisition that, acting as a force in its own right, has already considerably affected the writing of poetry and may be expected to affect it even more in the near future.[1]

In fiction the prevailing situation is quite different. Is it not a curious fact that while we have had in this century novelists as fully accomplished in their métier as the poets we all esteem are in theirs, none of these novelists have made a contribution to the theory of fiction that comes anywhere near what the poets have attained in their critical forays? You can go through all the essays of Thomas Mann, for instance, without finding anything of really clinching interest for students of the novel as a form; and Mann is surely an exceptionally intellectual and self-conscious artist. Nor will you find, in this respect, any truly close insights in Joyce or Proust. Both *The Portrait of the Artist* and *Ulysses* contain some discussions of aesthetic structure on a fairly abstract level, and these are of no help to us if we are on the lookout for the differentia distinguishing the prose-narrative from the other verbal arts. In Proust you encounter a metaphysical theory of the aesthetic meaning of time that generalizes the author's creative experience, but it scarcely yields the kind of concrete illumination of the novelistic form that we gain in poetic theory from the discursive writings of poet-critics like Valéry, Eliot, Pound, Empson, Ransom and Tate. As for American novelists of our time such as Fitzgerald, Wolfe, Faulkner and Hemingway, they have influenced fictional modes solely through their practice, steering clear of theoretical divagations. Henry James differs of course from the novelists I have mentioned by virtue of his unusual effort to formulate in critical terms his fascination with method and technique. But James, like Flaubert, is not a novelist of our age. Chiefly he belongs to that heroic period

[1] Let us keep in mind, though, that the sway of consciousness is by no means an unmixed blessing. At the heart of consciousness there is always equivocation. One can do no more than hope that this heightened and elaborated awareness of the poetic medium, which is after all a kind of wisdom or self-knowledge, will not soon provide us with another melancholy illustration of Hegel's famous dictum that the owl of Minerva begins its flight only when the shades of night are gathering. Not that I in the least associate myself with Edmund Wilson's thesis that verse is a "dying technique." Still, we know that in this world nothing comes free, and one wonders what the price of so intense a consciousness will turn out to be in this instance.

of the past century when the novel fought and won its fight for recognition as an autonomous literary genre making good its claims to the status of high art. At present, however, the practitioners of fiction appear to lack sufficient motive to engage in the analytic study of problems specific to their medium. Such studies are mostly left to professional critics and scholars.

The authority of fact often proves irresistible. I am inclined to think that it is precisely the fact of signal progress that we have witnessed in the criticism of poetry that accounts in some ways for the observable lag in the criticism of fiction. We must beware of taking a simplistic view of progress. In criticism, as in any other sphere, it is never a unilinear, harmonious forward movement in which every critical concern is equally well served. On the contrary, progress is necessarily an uneven and ir-regular process: the advantage gained at one point is ordinarily paid for by regress or loss at another point. And to entertain some such notion of what progress comes to in reality is to understand why the very success of the poetry critics has of late begun to exert an influence on the criticism of prose which is far from salutary. For the commanding posi-tion assumed by poetic analysis has led to the indiscriminate importation of its characteristic assumptions and approaches into a field which re-quires generic critical terms and criteria of value that are unmistakably its own. Just as Zola, the Goncourt brothers and other pioneers of the naturalist school associated the novel with science for the sake of the prestige that this conjunction seemed to confer upon their literary ambi-tions, so now critics of fiction are attempting to assimilate it to the poem, thus impeding an adequate inspection of the qualities and effects of the prose-medium. This effort to deduce a prosaics from a poetics is *au fond* doomed to fail, for it is simply not the case that what goes for a micro-scopic unit such as the lyric poem goes equally well for the macroscopic compositions of the writer of narrative prose.

In this paper I wish to isolate three biases that can be traced directly or indirectly to this recent infection of the prose-sense by poetics. The first bias is manifested in the current obsession with the search for symbols, allegories and mythic patterns in the novel—a search conducted on the unanalysed assumption that to locate such symbols in a fictional work is somehow tantamount to a demonstration of its excellence. The fact that the same symbols and patterns are just as easily discoverable in the worst as in the best novels counts for nothing among the pursuers of this type of research. The second bias, even more plainly deriving from

270

the sensibility of poetry, is the one identifying style as the "essential activity" of imaginative prose, an identification that confuses the intensive speech proper to poetry with the more openly communicative, functional and extensive language proper to prose. The third bias is that of technicism, which may be defined as the attempt to reduce the complex structure and content of the novel to its sum of techniques, among which language is again accorded a paramount place. This third bias, which includes the second and exceeds it, is epitomized in Mark Schorer's well-known essay "Technique as Discovery," presenting in summary form an extreme version of the formalist tendency that has played a leading role in the poetics of our time. Mr. Schorer makes no bones about his indebtedness to the theorists of poetry. In the course of his argument he states this to be the fact, not once but repeatedly, evidently unaware that so large an indebtedness in itself poses a problem and points to a predicament.

In examining this bias toward symbolism, allegory and mythic patterning in the reading of fiction, one is first of all struck by its debilitating effect on the critical mind. There was a time not so long ago when it was clearly understood among us that allegory is an inferior mode scarcely to be compared to symbolism in imaginative efficacy; it was also understood that myth and symbol are by no means synonymous terms. But by now all such elementary though essential distinctions have gone by the board. The younger critics have taken to using all three terms almost interchangeably and always with an air of offering an irrefutable proof of sensibility, with the result that they have been nearly emptied of specific meaning and turned into little more than pretentious counters of approbation.[2] But the more these terms lose their reference to anything concrete beyond themselves, the easier becomes their conversion into verbal symbols in their own right, symbols of admission and belonging to a school at present academically and critically dominant. And if you add to this sacred triad the famed pair of paradox and irony your initiation is well nigh complete.

[2] The word "myth" in particular is being put to such multiple and varied use these days—as when people speak of the myth of racial superiority, or of the myth of the proletariat, or of the mythology of Americanism—that if any sense at all is to be made of the mythic concern in literature, then the least a critic can do is to discriminate sharply between the broad, popular, loosely analogical employment of the term and what Robert Graves rightly, I think, calls the "true myth," which he defines as "the reduction to narrative shorthand of ritual mime."

An example is wanted. There is Mr. Robert W. Stallman, for instance, who rather unnerves one with his literal passion for up-to-date notions in criticism. In an essay on Stephen Crane, he writes that

> like Conrad, Crane puts language to poetic uses, which, to define it, is to use language reflexively and to use language symbolically. It is the works which employ this reflexive and symbolic use of language that constitute what is permanent of Crane. It is the language of symbol and paradox; the wafer-like sun [the reference is to Crane's memorable sentence in *The Red Badge of Courage:* "The red sun was pasted in the sky like a wafer"]; or in "The Open Boat" the paradox of "cold, comfortable sea-water," an image which calls to mind the poetry of W. B. Yeats with its fusion of contradictory emotions. This single image evokes the sensation of the whole experience of the men in the boat. . . . What is readily recognizable in this paradox of "cold, comfortable sea-water" is that irony of opposites which constituted the personality of the man who wrote it.[3]

And preceding this paragraph with its wholesale disgorgement of shibboleths lifted from contemporary poetry-criticism, there is a passage in which Mr. Stallman bares his fixation on the sentence previously quoted ("The red sun was pasted in the sky like a wafer"), in which he professes to see the "key to the symbolism of the whole novel." Why? Because the initials, J. C., of Jim Conklin, the tall, spectral soldier who dies in so grotesque a fashion, ineluctably suggests to Mr. Stallman that he represents Jesus Christ. Thus *The Red Badge of Courage,* which is something of a *tour de force* as a novel and which is chiefly noted for the advance it marks in the onset of realism on the American literary scene, is transmogrified into a religious allegory. All that is lacking in this analysis to give it the final certification of the *Zeitgeist* is the word "myth." Observe, too, that the evidence for this thesis is drawn, not from a study of the narrative progression of Crane's novel as a whole, but from a single image and the amalgam of the initials of the tall soldier's name with the name of Jesus Christ. It is entirely characteristic of Mr. Stallman's approach (and of the critical school to which he is attached) that it never even occurs to him that to speak of "the symbolism of the whole novel" is

---

[3] Cf. "Stephen Crane," p. 269, in *Critiques and Essays in Modern Fiction,* edited by John W. Aldridge (New York, 1952).

perhaps in this case a piece of sheer gratuity, that the novel is actually "about" what it seems to be, war and its impact on human beings moved by pride, bravado, fear, anxiety and sudden panic. If it is symbolic, it is in the patent sense in which all good art, in so far as it opens out to the world at large by transcending its immediate occasions and fixed, exclusive meanings, can be said to be symbolic. But to attribute a symbolic character to Crane's novel in this universal sense has nothing whatever to do with Mr. Stallman's idea of symbolism, an idea indistinguishable from the "fallacy of misplaced concreteness," systematically applied to works of literature.

The absurdity of Mr. Stallman's reading of Crane becomes all too apparent when you look up the text to check on his quotations. He professes to see a poetic paradox in the phrase "cold, comfortable sea-water," but in point of fact within the context of the story the juxtaposition of "cold" and "comfortable" cannot strike us as paradoxical but rather as wholly natural. The situation is that the four shipwrecked men in the tiny boat—the captain, the correspondent, the oiler, and the cook—are dog-tired, not having slept for two days. It is night, and three of them are sleeping in the water-drenched bottom of the boat while the correspondent is rowing:

> The wind became stronger, and sometimes a wave raged out like a mountain cat, and there was to be seen the sheen and sparkle of a broken crest.
>
> The captain, in the bow, moved on his water-jar and sat erect. "Pretty long night," he observed to the correspondent. . . .
>
> "Did you see that shark playing around?"
>
> "Yes, I saw him. He was a big fellow all right."
>
> . . . Later the correspondent spoke into the bottom of the boat. "Billie!" There was a slow and gradual disentanglement. "Billie, will you spell me?"
>
> "Sure," said the oiler.
>
> As soon as the correspondent touched the cold, comfortable sea-water in the bottom of the boat and had huddled close to the cook's life-belt he was deep in sleep.

Now obviously the water *in* the boat feels "comfortable" as against the waves beating *at* the boat, pictured throughout the story as black, menacing, sinister. In contrast the water at the bottom of the boat, in which the men have been sleeping, seems positively domesticated. Hence the adjective "comfortable." Only by carefully sequestering the phrase "cold, comfortable sea-water" from its context can you make it out to be paradoxical.

As for the sentence ending Chapter IX of *The Red Badge of Courage* —"The sun was pasted in the sky like a wafer"—it would seem to me that the verb "pasted" is quite as important to its effect as the substantive "wafer." Moreover, in the first edition of the novel "wafer" was preceded by "fierce," a modifier hardly suggestive of the Christian communion. Crane liked to speak of himself as an impressionist, and as a stylist he was above all concerned with getting away from the morbidly genteel narrative language of his time; the daring colloquialism "pasted in the sky" must have appealed to him on the well-known avante-garde principle of "make it new." More particularly, this concluding sentence of Chapter IX illustrates perfectly what Conrad described as "Crane's unique and exquisite faculty . . . of disclosing an individual scene by an odd simile." Conrad's remark has the aptitude of close critical observation, whereas Mr. Stallman's far-fetched religious exegesis is mere *Zeitgeist* palaver.

No wonder that this critic is quite as partial to allegory as he is to symbolism. Thus in a study of Conrad he claims that "The Secret Sharer" is a double allegory—"an allegory of man's moral conscience and . . . of man's aesthetic conscience. The form of 'The Secret Sharer,' to diagram it, is the form of the capital letter L—the very form of the captain's room. (It is hinted at again in the initial letter of Leggatt's name.) One part of the letter L diagrams the allegory of the captain's divided soul, man in moral isolation and spiritual disunity. The other part of the letter represents the allegory of the artist's split soul. . . . The captain stands at the angle of the two isolations and the two searches for selfhood."[4] It is the inescapable logic of this obsession with symbols and allegories that it is bound to decline into a sort of mechanistic Kabbala that scrutinizes each sign and letter of the printed page for esoteric or supernal meanings. The plain absurdity of Mr. Stallman's reading of "The Secret Sharer" should not, however, deter us from recognizing that this mode, which he carries to an extreme, is a fairly representative one nowadays and that it is greatly favored by abler critics who at times still manage to retain some sense of proportion. My concern is not with Mr. Stallman's

[4] Cf. "Life, Art, and 'The Secret Sharer,'" p. 241, in *Forms of Modern Fiction*, edited by William Van O'Connor (Minneapolis, 1948).

absurdities as such. I cite him only because his very excess brings to light the fantastication inherent in the approach he shares with a good many other people.[5]

What, at bottom, is the animating idea behind this exaltation of symbolism in current critical practice? As I see it, its source is not directly literary but is to be traced to an attitude of distaste toward the actuality of experience—an attitude of radical devaluation of the actual if not downright hostility to it; and the symbol is of course readily available as a means of flight from the actual into a realm where the spirit abideth forever. If the typical critical error of the 'thirties was the failure to distinguish between literature and life, in the present period that error has been inverted into the failure to perceive their close and necessary relationship. Hence the effort we are now witnessing to overcome the felt reality of art by converting it into some kind of schematism of spirit; and since what is wanted is spiritualization at all costs, critics are disposed to purge the novel of its characteristically detailed imagination working through experiential particulars—the particulars of scene, figures and action: to purge them, that is to say, of their gross immediacy and direct empirical expressiveness.[6] It is as if critics were saying that the representation of experience, which is the primary asset of the novel, is a mere appearance; the really and truly real is to be discovered somewhere else, at some higher level beyond appearance. The novel, however, is the most empirical of all literary genres; existence is its original and inalienable datum; its ontology, if we may employ such a term in relation to it is "naïve," commonsensical, positing no split between appearance and reality. "The supreme virtue of a novel," as Henry James insisted, "the merit on which all its other merits . . . helplessly and submissively depend," is its truth of detail, its air of reality or "solidity of specification."

---

[5] The payoff of the rage for symbolism is surely Mr. Charles Feidelson's recent book, *Symbolism and American Literature,* the fundamental assumption of which is that "to consider the literary work as a piece of language is to regard it as a symbol, autonomous in the sense that it is quite distinct both from the personality of the author and the world of pure objects, and creative in the sense that it brings into existence its own meaning." In this curious work the interest in symbolism has quite literally consumed the interest in literature.

[6] An amusing confirmation of this mood has been provided by Lionel Trilling in a recent essay. Mr. Trilling reports that students have now "acquired a trick of speaking of money in Dostoevsky's novels as 'symbolic,' as if no one ever needed, or spent, or gambled, or squandered the stuff—and as if to think of it as an actuality were subliterary." But this is a "trick" which young people, in a society as powerfully dominated by the cash-nexus as ours is, would hardly be capable of inventing for themselves. They must have learned it from their readings in contemporary criticism.

"If it be not there, all other merits are as nothing, and if these be there, they owe their effect to the success with which the author has produced the illusion of life." It is an illusion in the sense that what is recounted has not really happened but has been imagined by the author; but this cannot mean that it is an illusion in relation to itself too, that the novel dreams itself as it were. There is not some other novel, composed of spiritual and moral integers, hovering somewhere behind the illusion of life with which the novelist has sought to infuse his fictive world. We are of course free to interpret that world and to approach it from different angles and on different levels. But to interpret a fiction is one thing; to dissolve it is something else again, and we do dissolve it when treating it as a mere appearance, of the senses only, of interest only to the extent that it provides a domicile for symbols, supersensible forms comparable to Plato's Ideas. Such a notion has little in common with the literary theory of symbolism, though on the surface it may look like a logical extension of it. It belongs rather to metaphysics. The obsession with symbolism is at bottom expressive of the reactionary idealism that now afflicts our literary life and that passes itself off as a strict concern with aesthetic form.

This is not to say, to be sure, that fiction excludes symbolization. On the contrary, works of fiction abound in symbolic devices and the more significant among them have symbolic import. But when we speak of the symbolic import of a novel what we have in mind is nothing more mysterious than its overplus of meaning, its suggestiveness over and above its tissue of particulars, the actual representation of which it is comprised: and that is scarcely the same thing as treating these particulars as "clues" which it is the ingenious critic's task to follow up for hidden or buried meanings that are assumed to be the "real point" of the text under examination. In the long run this procedure cannot but make the text itself dispensable; it ceases to be of use once you have extracted the symbols it contains. The text, however, is not a container, like a bottle; it is all there is; and the symbol-hunting critics are unwittingly reasserting the dichotomy of form and content which they ostensibly reject. *Moby Dick*, for instance, is a work of which certain basic elements, such as the whale, the sea and the quest, have both symbolic and direct representational value. There is no consensus of opinion among commentators as to what the symbolic value of those elements comes to in specific, exact terms; and it is a proof of the merit of this work that no such consensus is in fact possible. The narrative, not being an allegory, has no meanings that can be mentally tabulated and neatly accounted for. Its symbols are integrally a part of its fictive reality, and it is precisely their organic character that renders them immune to purely intellectual specification.

One should also be on the lookout against mistaking the creative intent of the conscious symbolic device employed by many modern writers. A novella like *Death in Venice,* in which the symbolic device is used again and again and always with exemplary control, will serve as a splendid example. One device in it is the introduction of a series of figures playing the part of "messengers" to Aschenbach (e.g., the "stranger with the pilgrim air" who appears at the very opening of the narrative and the gondolier who ferries him like Charon over to the Lido) whose function is at once to warn the hero and to foretell his doom. This function, however, has no independent "meaning"; it falls rather within the sphere of the technique devised to vivify our sense of the basic theme, which is the relationship between Aschenbach and Tadzio. This as well as the other symbolic devices to which Mann has recourse belong more to the compositional than to the thematic element of the novella. Mann succeeds in it to the degree in which he convinces us that the relationship between Aschenbach and Tadzio with its tragic consummation is actual and that it *is* what it appears to be. Hence it can be said that whatever symbolic value we may discover in the story is incremental, so to speak, to its actuality. It is a value, in other words, gained in the process of the story's actualization; it has no prior claim to existence and least of all can it lay claim to being its rationale. Nor is it its "essence," but rather a gift freely offered as the story comes to life, and in this sense it is more gratuitous than necessary. This would explain why it is so tractable, that is, why it is open to varying and contradictory interpretations. For anything a fiction might conceivably be a symbol of is inevitably far less compelling than what it immediately is in its felt unity of reality and appearance. To convert the experience it embodies into a symbol pure and simple is to empty it of its palpable substance. Thus what the objection to the excessive critical emphasis on symbolism comes down to is that, in making for a split between spirit and sense, it goes so far in conceptualizing the literary object as to drain it of its existential qualities.

The second bias in the contemporary idea of the prose-medium is that of language, a bias which Mr. Ransom not so long ago brought out into the open in committing himself to the view that "fiction, in being literature, will have style as its essential activity." In dealing with this view we know exactly where we stand, for Mr. Ransom's candor leaves us in no doubt as to its origin. In his essay, "The Understanding of Fiction," he is quite explicit on that point, declaring that "following that criticism of poetry which has made such a flourish in our time," he brings to fiction "a set of procedural biases gained elsewhere. . . ." And he goes on to say that since "the criticism of poetry has been an intensive one, concentrating for the most part upon the linguistic detail of the lyric passage," he would like to begin by citing "a few passages . . . from reputable fictions, as an indication of the sort of fixed images or exempla, which I carry around with me, and from which I must start; they will not be poetry but they will be like fictional analogues of lyrical moments." He then proceeds to quote a paragraph from Jane Austen, several paragraphs from *Daisy Miller*, and a paragraph consisting of just sixteen lines from *War and Peace*, taken from the chapter portraying Napoleon coming upon Prince Andrey as he lies wounded on the battlefield. The conclusion Mr. Ransom implicitly comes to is that Tolstoy is not so good a writer as Jane Austen and Henry James. The author of *War and Peace*, he remarks, "does not possess fully the technical advantages of a style. For concentration he substitutes repetition. . . ."

Now quite apart from the fact that the passages from Jane Austen and James are quoted as they wrote them while the passage from Tolstoy is given in translation, the procedure adopted by Mr. Ransom, that of citing sixteen lines from a novel of nearly twelve-hundred pages, does not seem to justify itself from the standpoint of critical method. A passage so brief might be cited to illustrate some special usage but scarcely the overall effects of a narrative style, for such effects are secured not locally, in the short run, but in the long run, by accumulation and progression. Moreover, for the purpose of my argument here, it is not in the least necessary for me to dispute Mr. Ransom's judgment of the comparative value of the three prose-styles he has examined. Let me grant him his judgment—that Tolstoy is inferior as a stylist. What is not acceptable, however, is the implicit estimate of the three novelists involved in this judgment. We cannot but suspect the relevance of a standard the application of which elevates the author of *Mansfield Park* above the author of *War and Peace*. To my mind, *War and Peace* and *Anna Karenina* are both greater works of literature than any of Jane Austen's or James's novels; and if I am right in this respect (I imagine that most qualified readers of fiction would probably agree with me), then perhaps it is the test chosen by Mr. Ransom, the criterion of language or style in the poetry sense of the term, which is at fault. In applying other criteria—character-creation, for instance, or the depth of life out of which a novelist's moral feeling springs, or the capacity in constructing a plot (plot, that is, the Aristotelian sense as the soul of an action) to invest the contingencies of experience with the power of the inevitable—we shall be persuaded soon enough that Tolstoy far outranks Jane Austen. Plainly the difficulty is with the linguistic criterion, which when applied unilaterally is likely to expose us to false valuations, such as that of ranking Turgenev above both Tolstoy and Dostoevsky (for Turgenev is generally admitted to be a better stylist than either of his coevals), or a storyteller like Ivan Bunin above his contemporary Chekhov. In the same way, if we turn to American fiction for examples, few would deny that Dos Passos is a better writer of prose than Dreiser; but is he on that account also the superior novelist? I think not. Dreiser's fictive world, for all his sloppiness as a stylist, is far more solid and meaningful than that of Dos Passos.

Mr. Leavis is another critic who, coming to prose with habits of mind acquired in the study of poetry, adopts a view similar to that of Mr. Ransom. He, too, is a great believer in "exemplifying," as he calls it; and he has noted that while it is easier to cite examples from poetry, prose demands the same approach even if it does not admit it quite so readily. "With the novel it is so much harder to apply in a critical method the realization that everything the novelist does is done with words, here, here, and here, and that he is to be judged as an artist (if he is one) for the same kind of reason as a poet is. Poetry works by concentration; for the most part, success or failure is obvious locally. . . . But prose depends ordinarily on cumulative effect, in such a way that a page of a novel that is on the whole significant may appear undistinguished or even bad. . . ." But though Mr. Leavis is fully aware of the hazard involved in transferring the poetry-critic's method of local exemplification to the study of narrative prose, he nevertheless comes out in its favor because he sees no alternative. The trouble lies, I think, in his reluctance to draw a sharp enough distinction in principle between prosaic and poetic speech. Is it really the case that language plays the same role in both media? In looking to narrative prose for "fictional analogues of lyrical moments," as Mr. Ransom does, are we not in effect ignoring the crucial differences between the use to which language is put in poetry as against its use in prose and hence denying the latter the status of a separate genre?

The approach to the prose-medium I am disputing is not an isolated one. It is deeply imbedded in the history of modern literary criticism and scholarship. More or less the same approach was advocated by the extreme wing of the Russian formalists, who were also inclined to overreact to the undeniable fact that fiction is made up of words, just like poetry. In the controversy that developed around this issue, it was the more moderate formalist Victor Zhirmunsky who was in the right, I believe, when he protested against the superstition of the word by which his colleagues appeared to have been overcome. According to Zhirmunsky's theory, a novel and a lyric poem are not to be equated as works of verbal art because the relation in them between theme and composition is quite different. Words in a novel, say, by Tolstoy, or Stendhal, are closer to everyday speech and openly communicative in function, whereas in a poem the verbalization is wholly determined by the aesthetic design and is in that sense an end in itself. There is such a thing, to be sure, as a purely formal prose, in which the elements of style and composition dominate (as in the work of Leskov, Remizov and Biely), but it is precisely the "ornamentalism" of such prose that basically differentiates it from the narrative language of novelists like Stendhal, Tolstoy, or Dostoevsky, who achieve expressiveness chiefly through extensive rather than intensive verbal means.

I might add tnat "ornamental prose" is a technical term in Russian criticism which does not at all mean the same thing as "ornate prose." As D. S. Mirsky explains in his *History of Russian Literature*, "ornamental" prose fiction "is not necessarily marked by conventionally uplifted diction." It may be crudely realistic or even blatantly coarse. It is mainly distinguished by the fact that it keeps the reader's attention fixed on the small detail: the words, their sounds, their rhythm. "It is the opposite of Tolstoy's or Stendhal's analytical prose. It is the declaration of independence by the smaller unit. . . . Ornamental prose has a decided tendency to escape the control of the larger unit, to destroy the wholeness of the work." I suppose that in English the work of Virginia Woolf would to some extent correspond to what the Russians mean by "ornamental" prose fiction, as would a novel like *Nightwood;* and among the younger American novelists there are not a few "ornamental" writers of prose to whom the test of local exemplification would apply, for the effects they seek depend almost entirely on stylization, on the perceptibility, to borrow a phrase much favored by the formalists, of the mode of expression. But the norms of the novel are scarcely those of ornamentalism, or of art-prose, a related term employed by the German critic Ernst Robert Curtius in a fine critical passage comparing Balzac and Flaubert:

Balzac's creative power equals that of the greatest writers. Is he their equal also as an artist? It is evident that Balzac cannot be weighed in the scale of Flaubert's art-ideal. This ideal is that of art for art's sake. To Flaubert the value of a work hinges upon the quality of style, the faultless purity of language, the rhythms of the paragraphs and the music of the prose. His ideal was to transmute reality into imperishable verbal substance. He called it: *faire du réel écrit*. Flaubert's language is art-prose in the sense in which one speaks of the art-prose of the Greeks and Romans. That was for Flaubert an inner necessity, which had its psychological grounds. An author like Balzac, in whom a world of living figures strains toward the light, cannot possibly write that way and has no need to do so. The artificial linking of artistry and the novel, for which Flaubert is responsible and which degenerates into a mannerism in the Goncourt brothers, leads to a blind alley.

The norms of the novel cannot accommodate a declaration of independence by the smaller unit, the word, the phrase, the sentence or the paragraph. Normatively the language of the novel does not possess the autonomous value that it has in poetry. It only intermittently lends itself to that verbal play characteristic of poetic speech, a play which uncovers the phonic texture of the word while at the same time releasing its semantic potential. In prose the relation between the word or sign and its referent is more firmly fixed and necessarily conventionalized than in poetry, where this relation is continually maneuvered so as to exploit the discord no less than the concord of sign and referent. Why is it, asks Suzanne Langer in her book *Feeling and Form,* that the lyric poem is of all literary genres the one most directly dependent on verbal means—the sound and evocative power of words, meter, alliteration, rhyme, and other rhythmic devices, such as repetition, archaisms, and grammatical distortion? Her answer is that "the motif . . . of a lyric is usually nothing more than a thought. a vision, a mood, or a poignant emotion, which does not offer a very robust framework for the creation of a piece of virtual history. . . . The lyric poet uses every quality of language because he has neither plot nor fictitious characters, nor, usually any intellectual argument to give his poem continuity. The lure of verbal preparation and fulfillment has to do nearly everything. . . ." Admitting that Miss Langer somewhat overstates her case, what she is saying on the whole is so self-evident as to be hardly more than a truism. It is a truism, however, which poetry critics, carried away by the simultaneous turn toward dramatic speech and intellectual elaboration in modern verse, are inclined to forget, with the result that they almost never stress the radical difference between the illusion of life or air of reality created in a poem and that created in a story or a novel or a play. Actually, the dramatic as well as the narrative (epic) resources of the modern poetic medium are extremely limited and the imagery it employs, however dramatic its impact on its own chosen ground, is no substitute for the bodying forth of character in action.

The late Christopher Caudwell is the critic who has made the most of the difference between poetic and prosaic language. In his book, *Illusion and Reality,* he wrote that the "poetic word is the logos, the word-made-flesh, the active will ideally ordering, whereas the novel's word is the sign, the reference, the conversationally pointing gesture." And again: "Painting, poetry and melody all have this in common—the timeless universal quality of the human genus rather than the interesting complications and sub-complications of a group of human individuals." It seems to me that he gets to the bottom of the distinction we are seeking to define when he says that "poetry concentrates on the immediate affective associations of the word," whereas the story goes first to "the object or entity symbolized by the word" in order to draw its associations from that. "The poem and the story both use sounds which awake images of outer reality and affective reverberations; but in poetry the affective associations are organized by the structure of the language, while in the novel they are organized by the structure of the outer reality portrayed. . . . Hence the hero of the novel is not like the 'hero' of poetry, a universal common 'I,' but a real concrete individual." The reader of the poem lives in the words of the poem and identifies with the poet, while the reader of the novel does not identify with the novelist but immerses himself instead in his fictive world, in which he finds "a more or less consistent mock-reality that has sufficient stuff in it" to stand between him and external reality. This means that the emotional associations in the novel are attached not to its words but to the mock-reality which they bring into being. "That is why rhythm, 'preciousness' and style are alien to the novel; why the novel translates so well; why novels are not composed of words. They are composed of scenes, actions, *stuff,* and people, just as plays are. A 'jewelled' style is a disadvantage to the novel because it distracts the eye from the things and people to the words—not as words, as black outlines, but as symbols to which a variety of feeling-tone is directly attached. . . ." There are of course poetic passages in novels (as in Melville and Lawrence) as there are novelistic passages in poetry, but that in no way changes the characteristics of the two genres.

It seems to me that in Caudwell's formulation, which I have summed up all too briefly, we get at last to the root of the matter. It is the only theory which brings to bear a fundamental principle of explanation telling us why poetry is the form most indissoluble from its language while fiction is translatable with but minor loss to the integrity of the text. It explains why we are able to recognize Dostoevsky's greatness as a novelist at the same time that we are not in the least impressed by his stylistic powers. He is in fact a most indifferent stylist, but that hardly bothers us in reading him, for once we are caught up by the moving current of mock-reality in his narratives we cease noticing the words as such: the language becomes a kind of transparent envelope or medium through which we watch the action. Stendhal is another novelist of the first order whose stylistic gifts are unimpressive. Valéry goes so far as to speak of his "negligence, the wilful negligence, the contempt for all the formal qualities of style." But if so many of us have been drawn into Stendhal's fictive world and utterly won by it, it must be that the word *stylist*, or even the word *writer,* and the word *novelist* are not really synonymous. Sartre once observed that the poet is a writer who refuses to "utilize" language. An admirable formula, and the obverse of it would be that the novelist is a writer who is more often than not perfectly willing to utilize language. And if he is also a fine stylist, that is something thrown into the bargain. This bargain may inspire us with gratitude, but that is hardly a sufficient basis for an aesthetic of prose.

For the poet the major problem is always style, which it seldom is for the novelist. If you look into the working notebooks of two novelists so vastly different as James and Dostoevsky you are struck by the fact that verbal stylization is never among the difficulties they wrestle with. In these private notebooks both writers are talking to themselves, as it were, talking in an effort to define their subject, that above all, and further to see their way through the plot, the complications of the intrigue, the arrangement of scenes, the temporal sequence, the narrative perspective or point of view, etc., etc. The language in which all these things are to be embodied they take more or less for granted. In the notebook outlining the scenario of *Crime and Punishment* Dostoevsky is greatly worried by such problems as to whether to tell the story in the first or third person, i.e., whether to let Raskolnikov tell the story in the form of a diary or whether to adopt the stance of the omniscient author; he has not as yet made up his mind whether Raskolnikov is to commit suicide or repent and go to Siberia to expiate his crime; and his entire conception of the novel changes upon deciding to introduce the Marmeladov family into the plot. These are clearly problems of theme and structure, exclusively, never of stylization. When he repeatedly complained that because of his poverty, the material pressure he was under to write rapidly in order to meet the monthly schedule of the periodicals in which his work was serialized, he could never turn in a performance as finished as that of Turgenev's for example, he did not mean that given more time he would apply himself to improving his diction and sentence-structure. What he had in mind, rather, is that with less pressure on him he would have been able to organize his plots and design his scenes more carefully. He would have been able, in other words, to construct a more powerful and convincing illusion of life, a fictive world of superior consistency drawn more accurately to scale.

All that we can legitimately ask of a novelist in the matter of language is that it be appropriate to the matter in hand. What is said must not stand in a contradictory relation to the way it is said, for that would dispel the illusion of life and with it the credibility of the fiction. A Dostoevskyean story cannot be appropriately told in the style, say, of Dreiser, as that style is too cumbersome and the pace too slow. Dostoevsky's style has a kind of headlong, run-on quality which suits perfectly the speed of narration and the dramatic impetuosity of the action. But in itself, if we set out to examine it in small units, it is not rewarding. The principle of Dostoevsky's language is velocity; once it has yielded him that it has yielded nearly everything that his dramatic structure requires of it. The exact opposite of Dostoevsky is a novelist like Proust, whose themes and structures are undramatic and who must therefore secure his effects primarily through stylization. Proust's themes are essentially poetic-ironic rather than dramatic—memory, the intermittences of the heart, nostalgia for childhood, the vocation of the artist, illusion and disillusion with the great social world. There is of course action in Proust, but this action is rendered undramatically, in a mode shifting from analytic meditation to rhapsody and back again; and meditation and rhapsody are closely allied to the poetic medium. The intrinsic nature of Proust's themes and his conception of them as "enchanted realms," as he put it, in which "the dust of reality is mixed with magic sand," are such that they demand a master of language for their realization. It is pointless, however, to ask of a novelist whose themes do not require such an intensive stylistic effort that he captivate us through language when he is quite capable of captivating us through other means.

So far as Mr. Mark Schorer's essay "Technique as Discovery" is concerned, I think I have already dealt with it to the extent that it uniquely puts emphasis on style as an element of novelistic technique. For the rest, what is mainly to be objected to in Mr. Schorer's approach is his exclusive and almost vindictive emphasis on technique which leads him to say that "when we speak of technique in the novel we speak of nearly everything." His notion is that because technique objectifies the materials of art it also *ipso facto* evaluates them in a moral and intellectual sense. To me this formulation represents a monistic scheme, a violent simplification that leaves out of account any number of problems, such as that of creative personality, of the conditioned historical outlook prompting writers to settle upon some techniques while rejecting others, and the problem of the personal and unforeseen which, as Malraux has noted, is always present in our experience of a masterpiece. If by some chance the text of *Hamlet* had been lost to us, we would plainly be unable to imagine it despite all our accumulated knowledge of Shakespeare's techniques. And how are we to reconcile Mr. Schorer's point of view with Proust's precept that style is essentially a matter not of technique but of vision? The implication of that precept is that the technique of a true artist is dictated by an inner need and can be imitated only superficially. Vision is inimitable.

In a way everything Mr. Schorer says about the importance of technique is true, but true only in the trite sense that the novelist cannot render a single scene without some kind of technique, adequate or inadequate. But does Mr. Schorer really intend us to understand him in this altogether obvious manner? He remarks that if Thomas Wolfe had had the right sort of respect for technique and the ability to pursue it he would have written "a great novel on his true subject—the dilemma of romantic genius." Plausible as this sounds, does it actually mean anything more than if Wolfe had been a different kind of man he would have written different books? Tautologies are not insights. There is something anterior to technique and that is sensibility. Wolfe's sensibility was such that he was unable to conceive of the subject of romantic genius in a genuinely novelistic spirit; all he could do is spill the subject rather than express it; and the sensibility of Wolfe is not something he could alter. Sensibility can be cultivated under the appropriate conditions but it can scarcely be learned

285

as a technique is learned. Let us beware of regarding technique as some sort of gimmick which it takes a certain amount of intelligence to master, after which the writer is at liberty to "create" to the top of his bent. One detects in such ideas an unconscious predisposition toward scientism, toward purely manipulative notions of the creative process and a tendency to subject it to rationalization. Let us recall T. S. Eliot's statement about Massinger—that he was a brilliant master of technique without being in any profound sense an artist. This can only mean that even though without technique we can do nothing in art, technique is not nearly enough.

POINT OF VIEW

John E. Tilford, Jr., defines *point of view* in a novel as a method of narration. For instance, the author may choose one of the two basic ways of telling a story. He may narrate his story from the inside—that is, he may make one of his characters do it. Or he may manipulate his story from the outside, as a more-or-less omniscient author. But the ultimate objective in both these methods of narration is to achieve verisimilitude. Although first-person narration is the more direct method, it may not be the simpler, since such a story must inevitably remain limited to the point of view of the narrator (as in *Robinson Crusoe* and *Wuthering Heights*). In the second method of narration (third-person narration), the author is omniscient, and this allows him sufficient freedom to maneuver his materials into any form he chooses (for example, Fielding, Thackeray, or George Eliot). Tilford proceeds to show how a novelist may combine these two methods of narration to achieve certain special effects, exemplified by Lawrence Durrell's four-volume *Alexandria Quartet.*

point of view
in the novel

JOHN E. TILFORD, JR.

To many serious readers of novels, the term *technique* is likely to be somewhat forbidding, perhaps to suggest the kind of esoteric matters which mousy little professors talk to each other about in footnote-laden monographs. There is, I confess, some justification for this suspicion.

If readers say, however, that they are concerned not with the technique of a novel, but with its story, its meaning, its subject matter, perhaps its author's interpretation of life, they overlook one thing. There could be no story, no meaning, no subject matter, no interpretation of life without technique. As Mark Schorer says, "When we speak of technique, . . . we speak of nearly everything. For technique is the means by which the writer's experience, which is his subject matter, compels him to attend to it; technique is the only means he has of discovering, exploring, developing his subject, of conveying its meaning, and, finally, of evaluating it." The novel, in short, exists only by means of technique. Thus "everything is technique," Schorer observes, "which is not the lump of experience itself." Hence, like it or not, all readers are ineluctably concerned with the technique of the novels they read.

There are many aspects of novelistic technique, of course, dealing with plot, characterization, setting, dialogue, symbolism, and style—all to the end of the novelists' achieving their purposes. The aspect fundamental to all the others, however, is the method of narration employed—or, as it is commonly expressed, the point of view from which novelists tell their stories. Now point of view has received much critical attention in recent years—beginning, probably, with Henry James' obsession with it in his last novels and his discussion of it in the Prefaces to the New York edition of his works, a little over half a century ago. But novelists have of course been concerned with it from the beginning of this form of literary art.

Here I should like briefly to explore a few of the main points of view novelists have chosen, to suggest not only the nature of point of view but something of its significance in the novelists' achievement of their purposes.

All art is communication. Hence one of the first things the reader of a novel is likely to be curious about is, Who is communicating? The obvious answer is, of course, the novelist. True. Samuel Richardson tells *Clarissa*, Charles Dickens tells *Great Expectations*, Emily Brontë tells *Wuthering Heights*, Leo Tolstoy tells *War and Peace*, Joseph Conrad tells *Lord Jim*, James Joyce tells *A Portrait of the Artist as a Young Man*, William Faulkner tells *The Sound and the Fury*, John P. Marquand tells *The Late George Apley*, Lawrence Durrell tells *The Alexandria Quartet*. Yet in each of these novels the author uses a different method to communicate his story: letters written by the characters in *Clarissa*; the hero's memoirs in *Great Expectations*; a minor character's recollections in *Wuthering Heights*; the omniscient, roving author himself in *War and Peace*; a nosy mariner who tries to figure out the protagonist's character in *Lord Jim*; and so on. But all of these methods—and many more—are merely variations on the two basic ways of storytelling. The novelist can tell his story from the inside—that is, he can make one of the characters do it. Or he can tell it from the outside, as a more-or-less omniscient author.

But it is not merely a simple, arbitrary choice between these two methods. The novelist must consider the focus of his story, the number and relations of his characters, the complexity of his plot and structure, the meaning of his story in all its parts as a whole. All are directly related to the point—or points—of view from which he narrates. Consider this opening sentence from a recent novel:

> If you really want to hear about it, the first thing you'll probably want to know is where I was born, and what my lousy childhood was like, and how my parents were occupied and all before they had me, and all that David Copperfield kind of crap, but I don't feel like going into it, if you want to know the truth.

The point of view here, in J. D. Salinger's *Catcher in The Rye*, is unmistakably established. Let anyone who thinks point of view a minor matter try to retell a few pages of this story in the third person, substituting "Holden Caulfield" for the narrator's "I." He might have the same plot, but he would find it impossible to retain much of the original focus, tone, conviction, and meaning—not to mention the flavor of the style. On the other hand, anyone would find it impossible to recast *War and Peace* in the first person: the action is too complex, the important characters are too many, the scene is too vast for the story to be told by a single character.

One of the basic functions of fiction, paradoxically, is to sound true. The point of view from which the story is told has much to do with verisimilitude. How, we ask, does the narrator know what he tells us? For we want to believe our fiction, at least while we're reading it.

The quickest way to achieve verisimilitude, as the quotation from Salinger suggests, is to let a witness tell the story. Chaucer well knew this over five hundred years ago when he made himself a character in his own *Canterbury Tales*; and novelists early and late have known it too— Defoe, Dickens, Thackeray, and Melville among the early ones; Conrad, Fitzgerald, Hemingway, and Warren among the late. In good first-person narrative, there is no apparent difference between a fictional autobiography like Robinson Crusoe's and a real one like Benjamin Franklin's. Even when the events narrated are impossible or fantastic, this method makes them seem credible, for the time being, as in *Gulliver's Travels* or *Wuthering Heights*. "Call me Ishmael," says Melville's narrator in *Moby Dick*, and we are ready to believe anything he tells us about Captain Ahab and his grumpy whale.

If first-person narration is the most direct method, however, it is not necessarily the simplest. To begin with, the narrator can fairly report only what he says and does and what he hears and sees others saying and doing, as in Crusoe's ingenuous chronicle. But in longer and more complex novels, like Dickens' *David Copperfield,* authors have to use all manner of devices so that the narrator can report, as necessary, other characters' thoughts and events he does not see: intercepted letters, overheard conversations, other characters' accounts, and often the manifestation of considerable naïveté on the part of the narrator. Copperfield, for example, must make it plain to the reader that Agnes is in love with him and that Steerforth is a cad, while he remains unaware—unaware without seeming lamentably stupid.

Despite such difficulties, however, countless novelists have restricted the point of view to that of their protagonist-narrators, in full-length autobiographies like Copperfield's as well as in limited accounts of crucial periods in their lives, like those of Frederic Henry in Ernest Hemingway's *A Farewell to Arms* and of Gene Forrester in John Knowles' *A Separate Peace.* But the infinite possibilities of telling stories from the inside have inspired novelists to continual experiment.

One variation is the multiple first-person method with its point of view shifting from character to character, used extensively in eighteenth-century epistolary novels like Richardson's *Clarissa* and Smollett's *Humphrey Clinker.* These stories are told wholly through letters written by the various characters. Rampant as this device once was—over five hundred epistolary novels were published in the last sixty years of the eighteenth century—its artificiality and the demands on the reader's credulity have made it almost extinct.

Another version of multiple first-person narration is for authors to let several characters tell the story, in one way or another. *The Moonstone,* a delightful Victorian mystery novel by Wilkie Collins, consists of eight "narratives," written by six characters, each recounting the same events from his point of view, with gradually intensifying suspense. Again, in Faulkner's *As I Lay Dying,* the action is related, more or less chronologically, through the minds of nineteen different characters, in fifty-nine short sections. Here there is no pretense that the characters are writing—Faulkner simply renders the thoughts of each, as he participates in the action. Learning how all of these people feel about the events and about each other helps sharpen the reader's interest in what would otherwise be a dreary and tasteless account of a burial journey.

Sometimes, to note another and important variation, novelists choose as narrators relatively minor characters, who are often more observers of the action than participants in it. Laurence Sterne probably inaugurated this procedure in the 1760's with *The Life and Opinions of Tristram Shandy,* in which Tristram tells little of himself and much of his father and of his wonderful Uncle Toby. (Tristram, in fact, does not manage to get born until almost a third of the novel is done.) Thackeray uses this method in *The Newcomes,* narrated by Arthur Pendennis, who a few years earlier served as the hero of the novel *Pendennis,* related by Thackeray in his own familiar third-person role of genial omniscience. Similarly, in *The Way of All Flesh,* Samuel Butler gives the account of Ernest Pontifex's career through the recollections of his godfather, Mr. Overton.

One of the most skillfully made fictional memoirs of this kind is *The Late George Apley,* which John P. Marquand candidly subtitles "A Novel in the Form of a Memoir." The novel appears to be a collection of letters, notebooks, and miscellaneous papers, with brief comments by Mr. Willing, Apley's old friend, who arranges the materials and occasionally interpolates his own reminiscences. Its piquantly ironic tone is achieved through Willing's innocent reflections of the attitudes and prejudices of the proper Bostonian—a tone scarcely possible had Marquand told it from any other point of view. Because of its unusual possibilities, a number of other recent authors have found this variation of first-person narrative appealing —among them F. Scott Fitzgerald in *The Great Gatsby,* in which Nick Carraway comes to understand the inner struggles of Jay Gatsby, whom he knew only slightly; and Robert Penn Warren in *All the King's Men,* in which the life of Jack Burden, the narrator, becomes highly enmeshed with that of Willie Stark, the protagonist, and deeply affected by it. No ordinary first-person or third-person narrations could have served so well.

One of the most audacious novels told from the point of view of a minor character, however, is Emily Brontë's *Wuthering Heights,* which has inspired Lord David Cecil to find in it matters of cosmic significance and to label it "the one perfect work of art amid all the vast varied canvases of Victorian fiction" (*Early Victorian Novelists,* 1934). It is scarcely that, I think; but is certainly one which it is fashionable to make ecstatic noises about, these days.

Emily Brontë must have realized that, told in the third person, her story would appear little more than an outlandish Gothic yarn. Yet neither of the principals, Cathy and Heathcliff, can narrate it because, if for no other reason, both are slated to die before the story is over. So Miss Brontë chose to have most of it told by Nelly Dean, a simple country woman who sees much of the action, participates in some of it, and manages to find out about the rest of it by one means or another. As we can believe in Nelly, we tend to believe what she says. That Cathy and Heathcliff should confess their inmost secrets to her and that she should witness some of their most passionate encounters may seem egregiously contrived; still, we find ourselves accepting it, more or less. But Nelly is not only a witness; in her commentary she embodies the reactions of a sensible, normal person to the preposterous gnashings of Heathcliff and the perfervid wailings of Cathy.

And that is not all: Miss Brontë's cleverest trick was to provide two witnesses to these wild activities. Nelly Dean tells her story not directly to the reader, but to a Mr. Lockwood, who dutifully writes it all down in his journal, complete with Yorkshire dialect. Moreover, at the beginning and end of the novel, he witnesses some of the action himself. This double point of view, from people of vastly different social and intellectual levels, achieves both an impelling credibility and an unusually curious tone. Most readers overlook the clumsiness of the narrative method and would probably be startled to realize that they know Cathy and Heathcliff from the outside only—and mostly third hand, at that.

Hence, using a character other than the protagonist affords the novelist several advantages. The story is told by somebody inside it, with resultant verisimilitude. Moreover, the narrator-participant-witness provides a consistent, compelling focus for the action, and his commentary and evaluation, from his point of view, allow him to serve as a kind of guide to the reader. Finally, this method may add to the complexity of the story and increase its possibilities for richness.

Despite its long and honorable history, first-person narration is still a less common way of telling a story, probably, than is third-person narration. In the latter, the author is omniscient—he knows everything about his characters, inside and out, and about their actions, though, of course, he is quite particular about what he chooses to reveal. This method hence affords the author great freedom, but it does have one inescapable disadvantage: in varying degrees the author always stands between the story and the reader, sometimes quite obviously, as in the case of a Fielding or a Thackeray or a George Eliot, who are always talking with the reader about their characters; sometimes unobtrusively, as in the case of a Hemingway or a Joyce, who *qua* authors practically disappear.

We might note two broad classes of third-person narration. In the first, the story is told sequentially, from the shifting points of view of many characters, usually according to who is the center of attention at a given time in the action. In one scene the author may report the private thoughts of any of the characters participating and, if he chooses, comment on those thoughts. This method is the only feasible one, of course, for panoramic novels with many characters, like Thackeray's *Vanity Fair*.

Sometimes, by restraining his omniscience, the author limits the point of view to only a few of the main characters. This is the most usual kind of narration in the novels of the later nineteenth and the twentieth centuries—as suggested by Tolstoy's *Anna Karenina*, Thomas Hardy's *Return of the Native*, and William Golding's *Lord of the Flies*. The author may still be present as commentator, as guide, and even as judge of his characters and their doings, as in earlier novels; or he may present the action and dialog with little or no authorial intrusion—and hence with apparent objectivity—as in most recent ones.

The second kind of third-person narration is that in which the author restricts the point of view exclusively, or almost so, to that of one character, giving his thoughts only—and depicting only the action he participates in and as it appears to him—as in the case of Elizabeth Bennett in Jane Austen's *Pride and Prejudice*, of Lambert Strether in Henry James' *The Ambassadors*, and of Stephen Dedalus in James Joyce's *A Portrait of the Artist as a Young Man*. In *A Portrait of the Artist*, for instance, one of the best-known novels of this kind, everything is seen as it appears to Stephen Dedalus; only his thoughts and reactions do we know, except through dialog. Everything, including description and narration of action, is presented with detachment and without comment—dramatically, as it were. The result is unity of focus, intensity, strong identification of the reader with one character, and a certain esthetic distance not possible in first-person narration.

As both first-person and third-person narration have particular advantages in story-telling, we should not be surprised to find an author sometimes combining the two, as does Joseph Conrad, in *Lord Jim*. Instead of disguising his novel as a memoir, Conrad provides a third-person framework and then introduces a narrator, Captain Marlow, who tells the rest of the story. After four chapters of omniscient authorization about Jim's early life, Marlow himself enters the action, becomes Jim's friend, and plays a significant part in his life thereafter. The point of view then becomes Marlow's, as he tries to piece together Jim's life and character both from his own knowledge and from the testimony of many people who have come in contact with him. All Marlow has found he relates to some men on a hotel verandah. The novel ends with a long letter from Marlow to one of the auditors, telling of Jim's last days.

One of Conrad's innovations is that the story does not proceed chronologically; rather it moves back and forth in time in a kind of "chronological looping method," as Joseph Warren Beach calls it. Conrad's intention is to let his reader, like Marlow, come to know Jim much as he would come to know a person in real life, a little bit here, a little bit there, over a long period of time. The main interest lies not in plot or in suspense in the usual sense ("What will happen next?"), though there is enough of that; it lies in Marlow's and the reader's rediscovery of the elusiveness of the human soul. As the primary point of view is Marlow's, the reader cannot help seeing and feeling about Jim as he does; and as the reader is also, in effect, listening to Marlow's account, he is like one of the men on the verandah and almost becomes a part of the novel himself. The result is a singular tension and poignancy.

In *The Sound and the Fury*, for another instance, Faulkner employs an even more intricate procedure. The first three parts of the novel he tells from the points of view, successively, of three characters, whose streams of consciousness he reports. The first is an idiot; the second, his brother, dead eighteen years; the third, another brother. The fourth section Faulkner tells as omniscient author with the point of view moving among three other characters. From all this the reader, if he perseveres, may get some notion of what happened in three generations of a rather untidy family. But the depth and breadth afforded by the first three points of view, supplemented by the fourth, more detached section, give him an opportunity for insight a single point of view could not have offered.

A final and very recent example of this combination is Lawrence Durrell's four-volume *Alexandria Quartet*, for which the author claims a new method of narration. The first two volumes of the tetralogy, *Justine and Balthazar*, are narrated by a character named Darley, who associates with the other and more important people in the story, the second volume being in good part Balthazar's comment on and supplement to what Darley has written in *Justine*, with, hence, a shifting point of view. The third volume, *Mountolive*, is, rather oddly, told by the omniscient author, with the point of view moving freely from character to character in a quite old-fashioned way, though, as is the custom these days, without authorial comment. All three, however, deal with action occurring during the same period of time. Durrell calls these first three volumes "siblings," saying that he is "trying to complete a four-decker novel whose form is based on the relativity proposition," as these parts "are to be deployed spatially," not serially. "They interlap, interweave, in a purely spatial relation," he goes on; "Time is stayed." It is almost as if, ideally, the first three volumes should be read simultaneously. In any event, the fourth volume, *Clea,* is a true sequel to the preceding three, again with Darley as narrator.

What Durrell's technique allows is both an intimate picture of the goings-on Darley participated in and a broader, supplementary statement of actions beyond Darley's ken—all put together, in time, by the reader's imagination into a complete and intricate whole.

This necessarily brief exploration of a few of the basic points of view from which novelists have chosen to tell their stories may suggest how important their choice is to the achievement of their purposes. My readers will think of a hundred other novels which I could have cited—perhaps Joyce's *Ulysses,* or Virginia Woolf's *To the Lighthouse,* or John Dos Passos' *U.S.A.* Such works as these raise problems beyond the scope of this study; but, despite their unusual qualities, in one way or another the points of view these authors employ are only variations on or refinements of the ones I have noted. Besides, though their techniques have sometimes been spectacular and their influence noteworthy, novelists continue, by and large, to tell their stories from points of view pretty well developed by the end of the nineteenth century.

Point of view in fiction, observes Wayne C. Booth, is, in fact, a technical problem. Whether technique is the novelist's mode of discovering his artistic meaning or a manner of working his will upon the audience, it should be assessed only in the light of the larger meanings or effects it is designed to serve. After discarding conventional terminology (e.g., tragedy, comedy, tragicomedy, epic, satire, etc.), Booth works out in this essay a fresh "tabulation" of the forms the author's voice can take in a story. He points out how a narrator may be dramatized or undramatized, in accordance with the depth and intensity of his involvement with the story. Furthermore, a narrator may be conscious of himself as a writer (as in *Tom Jones, The Catcher in the Rye*), or he may seem to be unaware of his role as an author (Camus's *The Stranger*, Saul Bellow's *The Victim*). In the course of elaborating other possibilities of point of view, Booth defines *distance* as the degree to which the reader is asked to forget the artificiality of the work and lose himself in it.

distance and
point-of-view:
an essay in classification

WAYNE C. BOOTH

> But he [the narrator] little knows what surprises lie in wait for him, if someone were to set about analysing the mass of truths and falsehoods which he has collected here.
>
> "Dr. S." in *Confessions of Zeno*

Like other notions used in talking about fiction, point-of-view has proved less useful than was expected by the critics who first brought it to our attention. When Percy Lubbock hailed the triumph of Henry James's dramatic use of the "central intelligence," and told us that "the whole intricate question of method, in the craft of fiction," is governed by "the relation in which the narrator stands to the story," he might have predicted that many critics would, like E. M. Forster, disagree with him. But he could hardly have predicted that his converts would produce, in forty years of elaborate investigations of point-of-view, so little help to the author or critic who must decide whether this or that technique in a particular work is appropriate to this or that effect. On the one hand we have been given classifications and descriptions which leave us wondering why we have bothered to classify and describe; the author who counted the number of times the word "I" appears in each of Jane Austen's novels may be more obviously absurd than the innumerable scholars who traced in endless detail the *"Ich-Erzählung,"* or *"erlebte Rede,"* or *"monologue intérieur"* from Dickens to Joyce or from James to Robbes-Grillet. But he is no more irrelevant to literary judgment. To describe particulars may be interesting but it is only the preliminary to the kind of knowledge that might help us explain the success or failure of individual works.

On the other hand, our efforts at formulating useful principles have been of little more use because they have been overtly prescriptive. If to count the number of times "I" occurs tells us nothing about how many times "I" should occur, to formulate abstract appeals for more "showing" and less "telling," for less authorial commentary and more drama, for more realistic consistency and fewer arbitrary shifts which remind the reader that he is reading a book, gives us the illusion of having discovered criteria when we really have not. While it is certainly true that some effects are best achieved by avoiding some kinds of telling, too often our prescriptions have been for "the novel" entire, ignoring what James himself knew well: there are "5,000,000 ways to tell a story," depending on one's overall purposes. Too many Jamesians have tried to establish in advance the precise degree of realistic intensity or irony or objectivity or "aesthetic distance" his work should display.

It is true that dissenting voices are now heard more and more frequently, perhaps the most important being Kathleen Tillotson's recent inaugural lecture at The University of London, *The Tale and the Teller.* But the clichés about the superiority of dramatic showing over mere telling are still to be found everywhere: in scholarly journals, in the literary quarterlies, in the weekly reviews, in the latest book on how to read a novel, and in dust-jacket blurbs. "The author does not tell you directly but you find out for yourself from their [the characters] every word, gesture, and act," a Modern Library jacket tells us about Salinger's *Nine Stories.* That this is praise, that Salinger would be in error if he were found telling us anything directly, is taken for granted.

Since the novelist's choices are in fact practically unlimited, in judging their effectiveness we can only fall back on the kind of reasoning used by Aristotle in the *Poetics*: *if* such-and-such an effect is desired, *then* such-and-such points-of-view will be good or bad. We all agree that point-of-view is in some sense a technical matter, a means to larger ends; whether we say that technique is the artist's way of discovering his artistic meaning or that it is his way of working his will upon his audience, we still can judge it only in the light of the larger meanings or effects which it is designed to serve. Though we all at times violate our own convictions, most of us are convinced that we have no right to impose on the artist abstract criteria derived from other kinds of work.

But even when we have decided to put our judgments in the hypothetical "if-then" form, we are still faced with an overwhelming variety of choices. One of the most striking features of our criticism is the casual way in which we allow ourselves to reduce this variety, thoughtlessly, carelessly, to simple categories, the impoverishment of which is evident whenever we look at any existing novel. On the side of effect critics at one time had a fairly large number of terms to play with—terms like tragedy, comedy, tragi-comedy, epic, farce, satire, elegy, and the like. Though the neo-classical kinds were often employed in inflexible form, they did provide a frame of discourse which allowed the critic and artist to communicate with each other: 'if the effect you want is what we have traditionally expected under the concept "tragedy," then your technique here is inadequate.' If what we are working for is a first-rate comedy, Dryden tells us in "An Essay of Dramatic Poesy," then here are some rules we can count on; they may be difficult to apply, they may require painstaking discussion, and they will certainly require genius if they are to be made to work, but they can still be of help to artist and critic because they are based on an agreement about a recognised literary effect.

In place of the earlier kinds, we have generally substituted a criticism based on qualities that are supposed to be sought in all works. All novels are said to be aiming for a common degree of realistic intensity; ambiguity and irony are discussed as if they were always beauties, never blemishes. Point-of-view should always be used "consistently," because otherwise the realistic illusion will be destroyed.

When technical means are related to such simplified ends, it is hardly surprising that they are themselves simplified. Yet we all know that our

experience of particular works is more complex than the simple terminology suggests. The prescriptions against "telling" cannot satisfy any
reader who has experienced *Tom Jones, The Egotist, Light in August,* or
Ulysses (the claim that the author does not address us directly in the last
of these is one of the most astonishingly persistent myths in modern
criticism). They explicitly contradict our experience of dozens of good
novels of the past fifteen years which, like Joyce Cary's posthumous *The
Captive and the Free,* have rediscovered for us how lively "telling" can be.
We all know, of course, that "too much" of the author's voice is, as Aristotle said, unpoetic. But how much is too much? Is there an abstract rule
applicable to "the novel," quite aside from the needs of particular works
or kinds?

Our experience with the great novels tells us that there is not. Most
novels, like most plays, cannot be purely dramatic, entirely shown as taking place in the moment. There are always what Dryden called "relations,"
narrative summaries of action that takes place "off-stage." And try as we
will to ignore the troublesome fact, "some parts of the action are more
fit to be represented, some to be related." But related by whom? When?
At what length? The dramatist must decide, and his decision will be based
in large part on the particular needs of the work in hand. The novelist's
case is different mainly in that he has more devices to choose from; he
may speak with all of the voices available to the dramatist, and he may
also choose—some would say he is also tempted by—some forms of telling not easily adapted to the stage.

Unfortunately our terminology for the author's many voices has been
inadequate. If we name over three or four of the great narrators—say Cervantes' Cid Hamete Benengeli, Tristram Shandy, the "author" of *Middlemarch* and Strether in *The Ambassadors* (with his nearly effaced "author"
using his mind as a reflector of events)—we find again that to describe any
of them with conventional terms like "first-person" and "omniscient" tells
us little about why they succeed while others, described in the same terms,
fail. Some critics do, indeed, talk about the problem of "authority," showing that first-person tales produce difficulties in stories which do not allow
any one person to know all that goes on; having made this point, which
seems so obvious, they are often then driven to find fault with stories like
Moby Dick, in which the author allows his narrator to know of events that
happen outside his designated sphere of authority.

We can never be sure that enriching our terms will improve our criticism. But we can be quite sure that the terms with which we have long

been forced to work cannot help us in discriminating among effects too subtle—as are all actual literary effects—to be caught in such loose-meshed nets. Even at the risk of pedantry, then, it should be worth our while to attempt a richer tabulation of the forms the author's voice can take.

(1) Perhaps the most overworked distinction is that of "person." To say that a story is told in the first or the third person, and to group novels into one or the other kind, will tell us nothing of importance unless we become more precise and describe how the particular qualities of the narrators relate to specific desired effects. It is true that choice of the first person is sometimes unduly limiting; if the "I" has inadequate access to necessary information, the author may be led into improbabilities. But we can hardly expect to find useful criteria in a distinction that would throw all fiction into two, or at most three, heaps. In *this* pile we see *Henry Esmond*, "A Cask of Amontillado," *Gulliver's Travels* and *Tristram Shandy*. In *that* we have *Vanity Fair, Tom Jones, The Ambassadors*, and *Brave New World*. But the commentary in *Vanity Fair* and *Tom Jones* is in the first person, often resembling more the intimate effect of *Tristram Shandy* than that of many third person works. And again, the effect of *The Ambassadors* is much closer to that of the great first-person novels, since Strether in large parts 'narrates" his own story, even though he is always referred to in the third person.

Further evidence that this distinction is ordinarily overemphasized is seen in the fact that all of the following functional distinctions apply to both first and third-person narration alike.

(2) There are *dramatised* narrators and *undramatised* narrators. The former are always and the latter are usually distinct from the implied author who is responsible for their creation.

(a) THE IMPLIED AUTHOR (THE AUTHOR'S 'SECOND SELF')

Even the novel in which no narrator is dramatised creates an implicit picture of an author who stands behind the scenes, whether as stage-manager, as puppeteer, or as an indifferent God, silently paring his finger-nails. This implied author is always distinct from the "real man"—whatever we may take him to be—who creates a superior version of himself as he creates his work; any successful novel makes us believe in an "author" who amounts to a kind of "second self." This second self is usually a highly refined and selected version, wiser, more sensitive, more perceptive than any real man could be.

In so far as a novel does not refer directly to this author, there will be no distinction between him and the implied, undramatized narrator; for example, in Hemingway's *The Killers* there is no narrator other than the implicit second self that Hemingway creates as he writes.

(b) UNDRAMATISED NARRATORS

Stories are usually not as rigorously scenic as *The Killers*; most tales are presented as passing through the consciousness of a teller, whether an "I" or a "he." Even in drama much of what we are given is narrated by someone, and we are often as much interested in the effect on the narrator's own mind and heart as we are in learning what *else* the author has to tell us. When Horatio tells of his first encounter with the ghost in *Hamlet*, his own character, though never mentioned explicitly as part of the narrative event, is important to us as we listen. In fiction, as soon as we encounter an "I" we are conscious of an experiencing mind whose views of the experience will come between us and the event. When there is no such "I," as in *The Killers*, the inexperienced reader may make the mistake of thinking that the story comes to him unmediated. But even the most naïve reader must recognise that something mediating and transforming has come into a story from the moment that the author explicitly places a narrator into the tale. even if he is given no personal characteristics whatever.

One of the most frequent reading faults comes from a naïve identification of such narrators with the authors who create them. But in fact there is always a distinction, even though the author himself may not have been aware of it as he wrote. The created author, the "second self," is built up in our minds from our experience with all of the elements of the presented story. When one of those elements is an explicit reference to an experiencing narrator, our view of the author is derived in part from our notion of how the presented "I" relates to what he claims to present. Even when the "I" or "he" thus created is ostensibly the author himself—Fielding, Jane Austen, Dickens, Meredith—we can always distinguish between the narrator and the created author who presents him. But though the distinction is always present, it is usually important to criticism only when the narrator is explicitly dramatised.

(c) DRAMATISED NARRATORS

In a sense even the most reticent narrator has been "dramatised" as soon as he refers to himself as "I," or, like Flaubert, tells us that "we" were in the classroom when Charles Bovary entered. But many novels dramatise their narrators with great fullness. In some works the narrator becomes a major person of great physical, mental and moral vividness (*Tristram Shandy, Remembrance of Things Past,* and *Dr. Faustus*); in such works the narrator is often radically different from the implied author who creates him, and whose own character is built up in our minds partly by the way in which the narrator is made to differ from him. The range of human types that have been dramatised as narrators is almost as great as the range of other fictional characters—one must say "almost" because there are some characters who are unqualified to narrate or reflect a story.

We should remind ourselves that many dramatised narrators are never explicitly labelled as narrators at all. In a sense, every speech, every gesture, narrates; most works contain disguised narrators who, like Molière's *raissonneurs,* are used to tell the audience what it needs to know, while seeming merely to act out their roles. The most important unacknowledged narrators are however, the third-person "centres of consciousness" through whom authors filter their narrative. Whether such "reflectors," as James sometimes called them, are highly-polished, lucid mirrors reflecting complex mental experience, or the rather turbid, sense-bound "camera eyes" of much fiction since James, they fill precisely the function of avowed narrators.

> Gabriel had not gone to the door with the others. He was in a dark part of the hall gazing up the staircase. A woman was standing near the top of the first flight, in the shadow also. He could not see her face but he could see the terra-cotta and salmon-pink panels of her skirt which the shadow made appear black and white. It was his wife. She was leaning on the banisters, listening to something. Gabriel was surprised at her stillness and strained his ear to listen also. But he could hear little save the noise of laughter and dispute on the front steps, a few chords struck on the piano and a few notes of a man's voice singing . . . He asked himself what is a woman standing on the stairs in the shadow, listening to distant music, a symbol of.

The very real advantages of this method, for some purposes, have been a dominant note in modern criticism. Indeed, so long as our attention is on such qualities as naturalness and vividness, the advantages seem overwhelming. It is only as we break out of the fashionable assumption that all good fiction seeks these qualities in the same degree that we are

303

forced to recognise disadvantages. The third-person reflector is only one mode among many, suitable for some effects but cumbersome and even harmful when other effects are desired.

(3) Among dramatised narrators, whether first-person or third-person reflectors, there are mere *observers* (the "I" of *Tom Jones, The Egoist, Troilus and Criseyde*), and there are *narrator-agents* who produce some measurable effect on the course of events (ranging from the minor involvement of Nick in *The Great Gatsby* to the central role of Tristram Shandy, Moll Flanders, Huckleberry Finn, and—in the third-person—Paul Morel in *Sons and Lovers*). Clearly any rules we might discover about observers may or may not apply to narrator-agents, yet the distinction is seldom made in talk about point-of-view.

(4) All narrators and observers, whether first or third-person, can relay their tales to us primarily as *scene* ("The Killers," *The Awkward Age*), primarily as *summary* or what Lubbock called "picture" (Addison's almost completely non-scenic tales in *The Spectator*) or, most commonly, as a combination of the two.

Like Aristotle's distinction between dramatic and narrative manners, the somewhat different modern distinction between telling and showing does cover the ground. But the trouble is that it pays for broad coverage with gross imprecision. Narrators of all shapes and shades must either report dialogue alone or support it with "stage directions" and description of setting. But when we think of the radically different effect of a scene reported by Huck Finn and a scene reported by Poe's Montresor, we see that the quality of being "scenic" suggests very little about literary effect. And compare the delightful summary of twelve years given in two pages of *Tom Jones* (III, i), with the tedious showing of even ten minutes of uncurtailed conversation in the hands of a Sartre when he allows his passion for "durational realism" to dictate a scene when summary is called for. We can only conclude that the contrast between scene and summary, between showing and telling—indeed, between any two dialectical terms that try to cover so much ground—is not prescriptive or normative but loosely descriptive only. And as description, it is likely to tell us very little until we specify the kind of narrator who is providing the scene or the summary.

(5) Narrators who allow themselves to tell as well as show vary greatly depending on the amount and kind of *commentary* allowed in addi-

tion to a direct relating of events in scene and summary. Such commentary can, of course, range over any aspect of human experience, and it can be related to the main business in innumerable ways and degrees. To treat of it as if it were somehow a single device is to ignore important differences between commentary that is merely ornamental, commentary that serves a rhetorical purpose but is not part of the dramatic structure, and commentary that is integral to the dramatic structure, as in *Tristram Shandy*.

(6) Cutting across the distinction between observers and narrator-agents of all these kinds is the distinction between *self-conscious narrators*, aware of themselves as writers (*Tom Jones, Tristram Shandy, Barchester Towers, The Catcher in the Rye, Remembrance of Things Past, Dr. Faustus*), and narrators or observers who rarely if ever discuss their writing chores (*Huckleberry Finn*) or who seem unaware that they are writing, thinking, speaking, or "reflecting" a literary work (Camus' *The Stranger*, Lardner's *Haircut*, Bellow's *The Victim*).

(7) Whether or not they are involved in the action as agents, narrators and third-person reflectors differ markedly according to the degree and kind of *distance* that separates them from the author, the reader, and the other characters of the story they relate or reflect. Such distance is often discussed under terms like "irony," or "tone," but our experience is in fact much more diverse than such terms are likely to suggest. "Aesthetic distance" has been especially popular in recent years as a catch-all term for any lack of identification between the reader and the various norms in the work. But surely this useful term should be reserved to describe the degree to which the reader or spectator is asked to forget the artificiality of the work and "lose himself" in it; whatever makes him aware that he is dealing with an aesthetic object and not real life increases "aesthetic distance," in this sense. What I am dealing with is more complex and more difficult to describe, and it includes "aesthetic distance" as one of its elements.

In any reading experience there is an implied dialogue among author, narrator, the other characters, and the reader. Each of the four can range, in relation to each of the others, from identification to complete opposition, on any axis of value or judgment; moral, intellectual, aesthetic, and even physical (does the reader who stammers react to the stammering of H. C. Earwicker as I do? Surely not). The elements usually discussed under "aesthetic distance" enter in of course; distance in time and space, dif-

ferences of social class or conventions of speech or dress—these **and**
many others serve to control our sense that we are dealing with an aesthetic object, just as the paper moons and other unrealistic stage effects
of some modern drama have had an "alienation" effect. But we must not
confuse these effects with the equally important effects of personal beliefs
and qualities, in author, narrator, reader, and all others in the cast of
characters. Though we cannot hope to deal with all of the varieties of control over distance that narrative technique can achieve, we can at least
remind ourselves that we deal here with something more than the question of whether the author attempts to maintain or destroy the illusion of
reality.

(a) The *narrator* may be more or less distant from the *implied author.*
The distance may be moral (Jason vs. Faulkner; the barber vs. Lardner,
the narrator vs. Fielding in *Jonathan Wild*). It may be intellectual (Twain
and Huck Finn, Sterne and *Tristram Shandy* in the matter of bigotry about
the influence of noses, Richardson and *Clarissa*). It may be physical or
temporal: most authors are distant from even the most knowing narrator
in that they presumably know how "everything turns out in the end"; and
so on.

(b) The *narrator* also may be more or less distant from the *characters*
in the story he tells. He may differ, for example, morally, intellectually and
temporally (the mature narrator and his younger self in *Great Expectations*
or *Redburn*), morally and intellectually (Fowler the narrator and Pyle the
American in Greene's *The Quiet American*, both departing radically from
the author's norms but in different directions), morally and emotionally
(Maupassant's "The Necklace," and Huxley's "Nuns at Luncheon," in
which the narrators affect less emotional involvement than Maupassant
and Huxley clearly expect from the reader).

(c) The *narrator* may be more or less distant from the *reader's* own
norms, e.g., physically and emotionally (Kafka's *The Metamorphosis*);
morally and emotionally (Pinkie in *Brighton Rock*, the miser in Mauriac's
Knot of Vipers; the many moral degenerates that modern fiction has managed to make into convincing human beings).

One of the standard sources of plot in modern fiction—often advanced
in the name of repudiating plot—is the portrayal of narrators whose characteristics change in the course of the works they narrate. Ever since
Shakespeare taught the modern world what the Greeks had overlooked

in neglecting character change (compare *Macbeth* and *Lear* with *Oedipus*), stories of character development or degeneration have become more and more popular. But it was not until we had discovered the full uses of the third-person reflector that we found how to show a narrator changing *as he narrates*. The mature Pip, in *Great Expectations*, is presented as a generous man whose heart is where the reader's is supposed to be; he watches his young self move away from the reader, as it were, and then back again. But the third-person reflector can be shown, technically in the past tense but in effect present before our eyes, moving toward or away from values that the reader holds dear. The twentieth-century has proceeded almost as if determined to work out all of the permutations and combinations on this effect: start far and end near; start near and end far; start far, move close, but lose the prize and end far; start near, like Pip, move away but see the light and return close; start far and move farther (many modern "tragedies" are so little tragic because the hero is too distant from us at the beginning for us to care that he is, like Macbeth, even further at the end); start near and end nearer . . . I can think of no theoretical possibilities that haven't been tried; anyone who has read widely in modern fiction can fill in examples.

(*d*) The *implied author* may be more or less distant from the *reader*. The distance may be intellectual (the implied author of *Tristram Shandy*, not of course to be identified with Tristram, is more interested in and knows more about recondite classical lore than any of his readers), moral (the works of Sade), and so on. From the author's viewpoint, a successful reading of his book will reduce to zero the distance between the essential norms of his implied author and the norms of the postulated reader. Often enough there is very little distance to begin with; Jane Austen does not have to convince us that pride and prejudice are undesirable. A bad book, on the other hand, is often a book whose implied author clearly asks that we judge according to norms we cannot accept.

(*e*) The *implied author* (and reader) may be more or less distant from *other characters*, ranging from Jane Austen's complete approval of Jane Fairfax in *Emma* to her contempt for Wickham in *Pride and Prejudice*. The complexity that marks our pleasure in all significant literature can be seen by contrasting the kinds of distance in these two situations, though there is no sign of disapproval. The *author* can be inferred as approving of her almost completely. But the chief *reflector*, Emma, who has the largest share of the job of narration, is definitely disapproving of Jane Fairfax for most

307

of the way. In *Pride and Prejudice,* on the other hand, the narrator is non-committal toward Wickham for as long as possible, hoping to mystify us; the author is secretly disapproving; and the chief reflector, Elizabeth, is definitely approving for the first half of the book.

It is obvious that on each of these scales my examples do not begin to cover the possibilities. What we call "involvement" or "sympathy" or "identification," is usually made up of many reactions to author, narrators, observers, and other characters. And narrators may differ from their authors or readers in various kinds of involvement or detachment, ranging from deep personal concern (Nick in *The Great Gatsby,* MacKellar in *The Master of Ballantrae,* Zeitblom in *Dr. Faustus*) to a bland or mildly amused or merely curious detachment (Waugh's *Decline and Fall*).

In talk about point-of-view in fiction, the most seriously neglected of these kinds of distance is that between the fallible or unreliable narrator and the implied author who carries the reader with him as against the narrator. If the reason for discussing point-of-view is to find how it relates to literary effects, then surely the moral and intellectual qualities of the narrator are more important to our judgment than whether he is referred to as "I" or "he," or whether he is privileged or limited, and so on. If he is discovered to be untrustworthy, then the total effect of the work he relays to us is transformed.

Our terminology for this kind of distance in narrators is almost hopelessly inadequate. For lack of better terms, I shall call a narrator *reliable* when he speaks for or acts in accordance with the norms of the work (which is to say, the implied author's norms), *unreliable* when he does not. It is true that most of the great reliable narrators indulge in large amounts of incidental irony, and they are thus "unreliable" in the sense of being potentially deceptive. But difficult irony is not sufficient to make a narrator unreliable. We should reserve the term unreliable for those narrators who are presented as if they spoke *throughout* for the norms of the book and who do not in fact do so. Unreliability is not ordinarily a matter of lying, although deliberately deceptive narrators have been a major resource of some modern novelists (Camus' *The Fall,* Calder Willingham's *Natural Child,* etc.). It is most often a matter of what James calls *inconscience;* the narrator is mistaken, or he pretends to qualities which the author denies him. Or, as in *Huckleberry Finn,* the narrator claims to be naturally wicked while the author silently praises his virtues, as it were, behind his back.

Unreliable narrators thus differ markedly depending on how far and in what direction they depart from their author's norms; the older term "tone," like the currently fashionable "distance," covers many effects that we should distinguish. Some narrators, like Barry Lyndon, are placed as far "away" from author and reader as possible, in respect to every virtue except a kind of interesting vitality. Some, like Fleda Vetch, the reflector in James's *The Spoils of Poynton*, come close to representing the author's ideal of taste, judgment, and moral sense. All of them make stronger demands on the reader's powers of inference than does reliable narration.

(8) Both reliable and unreliable narrators can be *isolated*, unsupported or uncorrected by other narrators (Gully Jimson in *The Horse's Mouth*, Henderson in Bellow's *Henderson the Rain King*) or supported or corrected (*The Sound and the Fury*). Sometimes it is almost impossible to infer whether or to what degree a narrator is fallible; sometimes explicit corroborating or conflicting testimony makes the inference easy. Support or correction differs radically, it should be noted, depending on whether it is provided from within the action, so that the narrator-agent might benefit (Faulkner's *Intruder in the Dust*) or is simply provided externally, to help the reader correct or reinforce his own views *as against the narrator's* (Graham Green's *The Power and the Glory*). Obviously the effects of isolation will be radically different in the two cases.

(9) Observers and narrator-agents, whether self-conscious or not, reliable or not, commenting or silent, isolated or supported, can be either *privileged* to know what could not be learned by strictly natural means or *limited* to realistic vision and inference. Complete privilege is what we usually call omniscience. But there are many kinds of privilege and very few "omniscient" narrators are allowed to know or show as much as their authors know.

We need a good study of the varieties of limitation and their function. Some limitations are only temporary, or even playful, like the ignorance Fielding sometimes imposes on his "I" (as when he doubts his own powers of narration and invokes the Muses for aid, e.g. *Tom Jones* XIII, i). Some are more nearly permanent but subject to momentary relaxation, like the generally limited, humanly realistic Ishmael in *Moby Dick*, who can yet break through his human limitations when the story requires ("'He waves brave, but nevertheless obeys; most careful bravery that!' murmured Ahab"—with no one present to report to the narrator). And some are confined to what their literal condition would allow them to know (first person, Huck Finn; third person, Miranda and Laura in Katherine Anne Porter's stories).

The most important single privilege is that of obtaining an inside view, because of the rhetorical power that such a privilege conveys upon a narrator. A curious ambiguity in our notions of "omniscience" is ordinarily hidden by our terminology. Many modern works that we usually classify as narrated dramatically, with everything relayed to us through the limited views of the characters, postulate fully as much omniscience in the silent author as Fielding claims for himself. Our roving visitation into the minds of sixteen characters in Faulkner's *As I Lay Dying*, seeing nothing but what those minds contain, may seem in one sense not to depend on an omniscient narrator. But this method is omniscience with teeth in it: the implied author demands our absolute faith in his powers of divination. We must never for a moment doubt that he knows everything about each of these sixteen minds, or that he has chosen correctly how much to show of each. In short the choice of the most rigorously limited point-of-view is really no escape from omniscience—the true narrator is as "unnaturally" all-knowing as he ever was. If evident artificiality were a fault—which it is not—modern narration would be as faulty as Trollope's.

Another way of suggesting the same ambiguity is to look closely at the concept of "dramatic" story-telling. The author can present his characters in a dramatic situation without in the least presenting them in what we normally think of as a dramatic manner. When Joseph Andrews, who has been stripped and beaten by thieves, is overtaken by a stage-coach, Fielding presents the scene in what by some modern standards must seem an inconsistent and undramatic mode. "The poor wretch, who lay motionless a long time, just began to recover his senses as a stage-coach came by. The postilion hearing a man's groans, stopped his horses, and told the coachman, he was certain there was a dead man lying in the ditch . . . A lady, who heard what the postilion said, and likewise heard the groan, called eagerly to the coachman to stop and see what was the matter. Upon which he bid the postilion alight, and look into the ditch. He did so, and returned, 'That there was a man sitting upright, as naked as ever he was born.' " There follows a splendid description, hardly meriting the name of *scene*, in which the selfish reactions of each passenger are recorded. A young lawyer points out that they might be legally liable if they refuse to take Joseph up. "These words had a sensible effect on the coachman, who was well acquainted with the person who spoke them; and the old gentleman above mentioned, thinking the naked man would afford him frequent opportunities of showing his wit to the lady, offered to join with the company in giving a mug of beer for his fare; till partly alarmed by the threats of the one, and partly by the promises of the other, and being perhaps a little moved with compassion at the poor creature's condition, who stood bleeding and shivering with the cold, he at length agreed."' Once Joseph is in the coach, the same kind of indirect reporting of the "scene" continues, with frequent excursions, however superficial, into the minds and hearts of the assembly of fools and knaves, and occasional guesses when complete knowledge seems inadvisable. If to be dramatic is to show characters dramatically engaged with each other, motive clashing with motive, the outcome depending upon the resolution of motives, then this scene is dramatic. But if it is to give the impression that the story is taking place by itself, with the characters existing in a dramatic relationship vis-à-vis the spectator, unmediated by a narrator and decipherable only through inferential matching of word to word and word to deed, then this is a relatively undramatic scene.

On the other hand, an author can present a character in this latter kind of dramatic relationship with the reader without involving that character in any internal drama at all. Many lyric poems are dramatic in this sense and totally undramatic in any other. "That is no country for old men—" Who says? Yeats, or his "mask," says. To whom? To us. How do we know that it is Yeats and not some character as remote from him as Caliban is remote from Browning in "Caliban upon Setebos"? We infer it as the dramatised statement unfolds; the need for the inference is what makes the lyric *dramatic* in this sense. Caliban, in short, is dramatic in two senses; he is in a dramatic situation with other characters and he is in a dramatic situation over-against us. Yeats, or if we prefer "Yeats' mask," is dramatic in only one sense.

The ambiguities of the word dramatic are even more complicated in fiction that attempts to dramatise states of consciousness directly. Is *A Portrait of the Artist as a Young Man* dramatic? In some respects, yes. We are not told about Stephen. He is placed on the stage before us, acting out his destiny with only disguised helps or comments from his author. But it is not his actions that are dramatised directly, not his speech that we hear unmediated. What is dramatised is his mental record of everything that happens. We see his consciousness at work on the world. Sometimes what it records is itself dramatic, as when Stephen observes himself in a scene with other characters. But the report itself, the internal record,

311

is dramatic in the second sense only. The report we are given of what goes on in Stephen's mind is a monologue uninvolved in any modifying dramatic context. And it is an *infallible* report, even less subject to critical doubts than the typical Elizabethan soliloquy. We accept, by convention, the claim that what is reported as going on in Stephen's mind really goes on there, or in other words, that Joyce knows how Stephen's mind works. "The equation of the page of his scribbler began to spread out a widening tail, eyed and starred like a peacock's; and, when the eyes and stars of its indices had been eliminated, began slowly to fold itself together again. The indices appearing and disappearing were eyes opening and closing; the eyes opening and closing were stars . . ." Who says so? Not Stephen, but the omniscient, infallible author. The report is direct, and it is clearly unmodified by any "dramatic" context—that is, unlike a speech in a dramatic scene, we do not suspect that the report has here been in any way aimed at an effect on anyone but the reader. We are thus in a dramatic relation with Stephen only in a limited sense—the sense in which a lyrical poem is dramatic.

Indeed if we compare the act of reporting in *Tom Jones* with the act of reporting in *Portrait*, the former is in one sense considerably more dramatic; Fielding dramatises himself and his telling, and even though he is essentially reliable we must be constantly on our toes in comparing word to word and word to deed. "It is an observation sometimes made, that to indicate our idea of a simple fellow, we say, he is easily to be seen through: nor do I believe it a more improper denotation of simple book. Instead of applying this to any particular performance, we choose rather to remark the contrary in this history, where the scene opens itself by small degrees; and he is a sagacious reader who can see two chapters before him." Our running battle to keep up with these incidental ironies in Fielding's narration is matched, in *Portrait*, with an act of absolute, unquestioning credulity.

We should note finally that the author who eschews both forms of artificiality, both the traditional omniscience and the modern manipulation of inside views, confining himself to "objective" surfaces only, is not necessarily identical with the "undramatised author" under (2) above. In *The Awkward Age*, for example, James allows himself to comment frequently, but only to conjecture about the meaning of surfaces; the author is dramatised, but dramatised as partially ignorant of what is happening.

(10) Finally, narrators who provide inside views differ in the depth

312

and the axis of their plunge. Boccaccio can give inside views, but they are extremely shallow. Jane Austen goes relatively deep morally, but scarcely skims the surface psychologically. All authors of stream-of-consciousness narration attempt to go deep psychologically, but some of them deliberately remain shallow in the moral dimension. We should remind ourselves that any sustained inside view, of whatever depth, temporarily turns the character whose mind is shown into a narrator; inside views are thus subject to variations in all of the qualities we have described above, and most importantly in the degree of unreliability. Generally speaking, the deeper our plunge, the more unreliability we will accept without loss of sympathy. The whole question of how inside views and moral sympathy interrelate has been seriously neglected.

Narration is an art, not a science, but this does not mean that we are necessarily doomed to fail when we attempt to formulate principles about it. There are systematic elements in every art, and criticism of fiction can never avoid the responsibility of trying to explain technical successes and failures by reference to general principles. But the question is that of where the general principles are to be found. Fiction, the novel, point-of-view—these terms are not in fact subject to the kind of definition that alone makes critical generalisations and rules meaningful. A given technique cannot be judged according to its service to "the novel," or "fiction," but only according to its success in particular works or kinds of works.

It is not surprising to hear practising novelists report that they have never had help from critics about point-of-view. In dealing with point-of-view the novelist must always deal with the individual work: which particular character shall tell this particular story, or part of a story, with what precise degree of reliability, privilege, freedom to comment, and so on. Shall he be given dramatic vividness? Even if the novelist has decided on a narrator who will fit one of the critic's classifications—"omniscient," "first-person," "limited omniscient," "objective," "roving," "effaced," and so on—his troubles have just begun. He simply cannot find answers to his immediate, precise, practical problems by referring to statements that the "omniscient is the most flexible method," or "the objective the most rapid or vivid," or whatever. Even the soundest of generalisations at this level will be of little use to him in his page-by-page progress through his novel. As Henry James's detailed records show, the novelist discovers his narrative technique as he tries to achieve for his readers the potentialities of his developing idea. The majority of his choices are consequently choices

313

of degree, not kind. To decide that your narrator shall not be omniscient decides practically nothing. The hard question is, just how *inconscient* shall he be? To decide that you will use first-person narration decides again almost nothing. What kind of first-person? How fully characterised? How much aware of himself as a narrator? How reliable? How much confined to realistic inference, how far privileged to go beyond realism? At what points shall he speak truth and at what points utter no judgment or even utter falsehood?

There are no doubt *kinds* of effect to which the author can refer— e.g., if he wants to make a scene more amusing, poignant, vivid, or ambiguous, or if he wants to make a character more sympathetic or more convincing, such-and-such practices may be indicated. But it is not surprising that in his search for help in his decisions, he should find the practice of his peers more helpful than the abstract rules of the textbooks: the sensitive author who reads the great novels finds in them a storehouse of precise examples, examples of how *this* effect, as distinct from all other possible effects, was heightened by the proper narrative choice. In dealing with the types of narration, the critic must always limp behind, referring constantly to the varied practice which alone can correct his temptations to over-generalise.

Although some writers do try for a scientific detachment from
their subjects, says George P. Elliott, very few artists can
maintain the position with any consistency; and, furthermore,
they are unwise to try. In fact, in Elliott's opinion, an author's
deep interest and involvement in his material is more congenial
to real achievement than in aloofness. There remains, however,
the question of how much a writer should openly interfere.
Does he ever jeopardize his art by "meddling"? Elliott agrees
that author meddling may become a fault if the writer
interferes at significant moments of a character's speaking,
thinking, or acting. But ordinarily an author's intrusion is
either harmless or a boon to the work. When Tolstoy, for
instance, turns aside to quarrel with a French historian, this
does not mar the dramatic action; or when Dickens evaluates
his characters, either by implication or by direct comment, he
actually adds to the moral and aesthetic significance of the work.

the novelist
as meddler

GEORGE P. ELLIOTT

The word "novel" has been used to describe almost every sort of
long fiction. The "Odyssey," an epic poem, is sometimes called the first
novel. "Tristram Shandy," a satiric autobiography with no plot whatever,
is called a novel, and so is "Alice in Wonderland." But "novel" has also
been used more strictly a good deal of the time, to describe the sort of
long prose fiction which has been dominant in Western literature for over
two centuries. In this essay, "novel" means this one species and not the
larger genus.

Not many novels are formally pure in this restricted use of the term
"novel." None of the three books listed above is properly a novel, though
"Tristram Shandy" is partly one; neither are "Don Quixote," "The Castle,"
and "Moby Dick." T. S. Eliot and André Gide have said that as pure, as

"novelistic" a novelist as ever wrote is Georges Simenon. Perhaps they are right; if so, the lack of strength in his pure novels only suggests the necessity to adulterate fiction, as gold or silver must be adulterated, with some baser alloys, to make them strong. Flaubert and James are commonly referred to as formal masters of the novel; an inspection of "Madame Bovary" and "Portrait of a Lady" would disclose the extent to which these books are strengthened with alloys of romance and satire. "War and Peace," "Bleak House," "The Red and the Black," "Huckleberry Finn," "The Brothers Karamazov," "Remembrance of Things Past," "Tom Jones": all these celebrated books are commonly called novels, and all are by any formal criterion manifestly imperfect. In other words, the novel is odd in this: great representatives of the form are impure and imperfect.

The novel, the realistic species of long prose fiction, is differentiated from realistic drama by far more than the form in which it is printed. James's advice to the novelist to disappear into his material, which he must *render, present, dramatize,* pushes the novel towards drama and away from essay; yet a true novel is not just a realistic play with stage directions spelled out and speakers described rather more fully than is conventional with printed plays. A novel presents the characters' hidden life with an extensiveness, intimacy, and analytic subtlety which drama forbids, and it is a story controlled by a narrative voice.

Here is a formal definition of the (realistic) novel.

In the novel, (1) objects, behavior, and social customs resemble those existing in some actual society at some actual time, and motivation is probable, which is to say that the characters are mostly in the middle range of experience without being altogether consistent and if their behavior is extremely irrational it is presented in the light of convention as criminal or mad; (2) the principle for selecting and arranging the parts derives primarily from concern to reveal and to explore the pattern of relations, both hidden and open, of characters with one another, with social institutions, with ideas, with the natural world, or each with himself and his own beliefs; and (3) the reader's relation to the imagined characters is appreciably modified by the attitude of the narrator (who may or may not also be the author) towards the reader, towards the moral and social values of the world he is describing, and towards the characters as imagined persons, including the narrator's earlier self if that self is one of the characters.

The content of the novel, as here defined, is intercourse among a few credible characters and between them and the reader, who knows them by their public actions, their intimate words, and their unrecognized impulses. But this is also the area of moral concern. Both in fiction and in life, an attitude towards the behavior and motive of individuals related in and to a natural and social world almost necessarily becomes moral as it becomes engaged. The scientific attitude towards behavior and motive is that of detached observation; Balzac, Flaubert, and Zola all announced their intention of assuming this disengaged stance, but in fact neither they nor any other novelist worth reading ever did so consistently. The esthetic attitude of pure interest is much more congenial to a writer than the scientific one, the novel being, after all, a form of art. "Let us become epicures of experience, valuing it according to its refinement and intensity." Gide is the practicing apologist of this attitude. It is possible to read his "Strait Is the Gate" and "Lafcadio's Adventures" in such a way as to value Alissa's spiritual agony above Lafcadio's zeal for gratuitous malice only because imagining her agony is a more refined and intense pleasure than imagining his malice. Pleasure of this kind is of course a part of the enjoyment afforded by even as non-esthetic, propagandistic a novel as "Uncle Tom's Cabin." But Gide's theoretical amorality is in fact extremely rare in fiction; it is also possible to read his finest novel, "Strait Is the Gate," as a work of moral commitment. The very process of writing a novel and imagining characters engages the spirit, and this engagement almost necessarily assumes a moral quality. Even Gide the esthete trembles on the verge of *ought*; his position can be imagined as this: "To purify experience to its finest and then to explore it, either actually or imaginatively, is my (the?) highest good." In sum, it is possible for a novelist to take the position of purely esthetic engagement with matters which are the heart of moral concern, but it is rare for him to do so and the results at best are lacking in strength.

Meanwhile, perfect or imperfect, great or small, whatever the moral stance, novels and part-novels all face certain problems in common. Formally, the most important of these is point of view. The ideal held up by James the theorist and by his critical descendants is of an invisible, inaudible author; preferably there should be no narrator; if he is there he must meddle with the characters and their world only ironically, that is, in such a way as to reveal his own character; to author and reader, a narrator should be only another personage in the story. But since almost all substantial novelists do in fact meddle (including James the novelist) and since such meddling is apt to be not just formal but also moral in nature, this essay will concern itself both with ways in which author-meddling

317

does not damage a novel but instead leaves it pretty much unscathed and also with ways by which such meddling can be turned to a novel's advantage, and then at the end with the one sort of meddling for which there is no forgiveness.

A harmless sort of intrusion is for the author to turn from the story to expound his theories on some subject or other directly to the reader. His justification for doing this is that you should understand the true nature of old maids, the gods, social upheaval, story-telling, whatever, in order to appreciate the significance of his characters' acts and thoughts. But what ordinarily happens is that you listen for a while to what the author as a private person has to say, and then you go back into the world of the novel with your own opinions on the subject intact and with your connection with the characters untouched; for as a man of opinions a novelist is no better than his neighbor.

> In devotion woman is sublimely superior to man. It is the only superiority she cares to have acknowledged, the only quality which she pardons man for letting her excel him in.

I doubt it; but this disagreement does not interfere with my understanding of Eugénie Grandet, of whom it is said, or with my affection for Balzac, who said it. Tolstoy's long quarrel with the French historians, in "War and Peace," and his elaborate theory of history have so little to do with what is valuable in the novel that a disagreeing reader takes to skipping those sections. The most to be learned from those chapters is the hardly surprising knowledge that a novelist, who is primarily concerned with individuals, finds the way of an historian, who is primarily concerned with social movements, exasperating and uncongenial. Meanwhile, however, the long asides do not damage the novel proper, because they are presented only and separately and because an understanding of the characters' behavior does not depend upon them. One can find Tolstoy's notions about how to write a history of the Napoleonic invasion of Russia silly and yet find, while reading the novel proper, that every action and thought of every important character during his account of that invasion rings absolutely true. For the worth of the novel, the truth of this ring is what matters.

So long as an author is saying *This is what I think*, all goes well enough; when he begins to say *This is what you ought to think*, the reader is likely to resist. Even so, if this preaching is open and is separable from the novel proper, it will do no essential harm.

> That is the whole history of the search for happiness, whether it be your own or somebody else's that you want to win. It ends, and it always ends, in the ghastly sense of the bottomless nothingness into which you will inevitably fall if you strain any further.

I feel Lawrence pushing me with his rhetoric to accept this as true not only for the character who is dimly supposed to be thinking it, but for the world at large. I not only doubt the truth of this opinion, I also balk at being pushed. Even so, my pleasure in "The Fox" remains unimpaired, and my regard for Lawrence continues only slightly impaired.

When a novelist's comments on experiences strike you as true and good, your pleasure is increased.

> There are in the music of the violin—if one does not see the instrument itself, and so cannot relate what one hears to its form, which modifies the fullness of the sound—accents which are so closely akin to those of certain contralto voices, that one has the illusion that a singer has taken her place amid the orchestra. One raises one's eyes; one sees only the wooden case, magical as a Chinese box; but, at moments, one is still tricked by the deceiving appeal of the Siren; at times, too, one believes that one is listening to a captive spirit, struggling in the darkness of its masterful box, a box quivering with enchantment, like a devil immersed in a stoup of holy water; sometimes, again, it is in the air, at large, like a pure and supernatural creature that reveals to the ear, as it passes, its invisible message.

This passage has little or nothing to do with any of the characters in Proust's novel, except as it is one of the opinions of Marcel the narrator, who in such respects is Proust himself. But it and a thousand others of its kind constitute much of the excellence of the book. It has a legitimate if slight tonal function in the section in which it occurs, "Swann in Love"; but its main virtue is to give elegant expression to something true, something with which one cannot disagree and for which one could not possibly have found better words.

To a novelist with the urge to tell the reader what something of the world is like, the best, hopeless advice is: Be subtle, be wise.

A description of surroundings is likely to be closer to the heart of a novel than is a general comment on life, because the circumstances in which a character acts modify what he does and our understanding of him. The operative principle here is plain enough: the amount and intensity of the description of anything should be proportionate to the importance of that thing in revealing character but should not be determined by the author's personal interest in the thing described.

Descriptions of nature are notoriously long-winded and are commonly skipped—for example, those in the romances of Scott and Cooper. Descriptions of hunting and fishing sometimes go on longer than necessary, even the famous set-pieces of Tolstoy in "War and Peace" and of Hemingway in many of his fictions. Readers who like hunting and fishing for their own sake find the passages delightful, but those who are indifferent to those sports find the descriptions excessive for presenting character— though they are not very damaging to the novel since they are abridgeable by the impatient reader. Surely the authors dwelt upon these scenes at such length mostly because they themselves loved those sports. But here is a description of nature, from Mary Webb's "Precious Bane," which is wholly justified.

> When I look out of my window and see the plain and the big
> sky with clouds standing up on the mountains, I call to mind
> the thick, blotting woods of Sarn, and the crying of the mere
> when the ice was on it, and the way the water would come into
> the cupboard under the stairs when it rose at the time of the
> snow melting. There was but little sky to see there, saving
> that which was reflected in the mere; but the sky that is in the
> mere is not the proper heavens. You see it in a glass darkly,
> and the long shadows of rushes go thin and sharp across the
> sliding stars, and even the sun and moon might be put out
> down there, for, times, the moon would get lost in lily leaves,
> and times, a heron might stand before the sun.

It is a novel of country people who see the world alive with mysterious connections, as the narrator in this description does; and none of the novel's descriptions go on too long.

Closer yet to the heart of fiction are descriptions of man-made things, for the artifacts a character has made or has chosen to exist among affect him, reveal him. Here, the usual advice is to let concrete things speak for

320

themselves, and Flaubert is the model. Emma goes with Léon to the house of the wet-nurse who is taking care of her baby.

> The ground-floor bedroom—the only bedroom in the house—had a wide uncurtained bed standing against its rear wall; the window wall (one pane was mended with a bit of wrapping paper) was taken up by the kneading-trough. In the corner behind the door was a raised slab for washing, and under it stood a row of heavy boots with shiny hobnails and a bottle of oil with a feather in its mouth. A Mathieu Laensberg almanac lay on the dusty mantelpiece among gun flints, candle ends, and bits of tinder. And as a final bit of clutter there was a figure of Fame blowing her trumpets—a picture probably cut out of a perfume advertisement and now fastened to the wall with six shoe tacks.

The author imposes on the reader no attitude towards this room and the items in it he has chosen to describe; "a final bit of clutter" does not exceed the bounds of reasonable observation. Two sentences later, Léon's attitude is given: "it seemed to him a strange sight, this elegant lady in her nankeen gown here among all this squalor." Indeed, this is about as meticulously hands-off as a novelist can be. But here is a passage from "Our Mutual Friend" which operates on another principle entirely.

> Mr. and Mrs. Veneering were bran-new people in a bran-new house in a bran-new quarter of London. Everything about the Veneerings was spick and span new. All their furniture was new, all their friends were new, all their servants were new, their plate was new, their carriage was new, their harness was new, their horses were new, their pictures were new, they themselves were new, they were as newly-married as was lawfully compatible with their having a bran-new baby, and if they had set up a great-grandfather, he would have come home in matting from the Pantechnicon, without a scratch upon him, French-polished to the crown of his head.
>
> For, in the Veneering establishment, from the hall-chairs with the new coat of arms, to the grand pianoforte with the new action, and upstairs again to the new fire-escape, all things were in a state of high varnish and polish. And what was observable in the furniture, was observable in the Ve-

neerings—the surface smelt a little too much of the workshop and was a trifle sticky.

This description is not so concrete as Flaubert's, but surely it is fictionally valuable to learn a little about this house in such a way as to learn far more about what its owners are like; and Dickens' openly satiric view of the Veneerings is surely no less legitimate than Flaubert's professedly objective but, in the whole novel, covertly satiric view of the world of "Madame Bovary." And here is a passage from "The Ambassadors." Strether is visiting Miss Gostrey's place in Paris.

> Her compact and crowded little chambers, almost dusky, as they at first struck him, with accumulations, represented a supreme general adjustment to opportunities and conditions. Wherever he looked he saw an old ivory or an old brocade, and he scarce knew where to sit for fear of a misappliance. The life of the occupant struck him, of a sudden, as more charged with possession even than Chad's or than Miss Barrace's; wide as his glimpse had lately become of the empire of "things," what was before him still enlarged it; the lust of the eyes and the pride of life had indeed thus their temple. It was the innermost nook of the shrine—as brown as a pirate's cave. In the brownness were glints of gold; patches of purple were in the gloom; objects, all, that caught, through the muslin, with their high rarity, the light of the low windows. Nothing was clear about them but that they were precious, and they brushed his ignorance with their contempt as a flower, in a liberty taken with him, might have been whisked under his nose.

This is literary impressionism: there is not a concrete image in the passage; yet, by suggesting the effect the room makes on Strether, James succeeds in creating in the reader's mind a sense of the room, its owner, and its viewer. And though James's own attitude toward the room is as scrupulously absent as was Flaubert's towards the wet-nurse's room, one is in no doubt of James's esthetic love of it.

In "Laocoön," Lessing suggests that, in a competition between a visual and a verbal representation of a thing, the visual must win. If he is right, as he probably is even for people with strong image-making faculties, the usual advice about the best way to describe things in a novel needs qualifying. It is no more valuable to let the things in the room speak for themselves as Flaubert does than it is to give the impression of a room as James does or to give both that and also the narrator's opinion of the room and its inhabitants as Dickens does. Words can carry a thing-in-itself not at all and an image of the thing vividly but imperfectly; but they can, marvelously if less vividly, carry someone's impression of it and relation to it.

Because a point of view is, literally, geographically fixed, there is a kind of assumption that the metaphorical "point of view" of fiction should be fixed too. To a writer who feels bound to maintain one consistent point of view and to keep the same distance from events and people, all sorts of special benefits come from his restricting himself to one clearly defined consciousness, which ordinarily means using *I*. The most obvious benefit of *I* is the increase of credibility: "I was there, I saw it." That the body of "Wuthering Heights" is narrated by Nelly Dean, the respectable house-keeper, to Lockwood, the respectable lawyer, gives the book a credibility and solidity it could not possibly have had if told in the free manner of a Gothic horror story. Another benefit of *I* is that certain of the actual author's narrative or stylistic peculiarities can be put to use by being so disposed as to reflect upon and reveal the character of *I*. Conrad's fond-ness for generalizing was never put to better use than when it became part of Marlow's character as he tells "Heart of Darkness," nor James's famous ambiguity than as it opened depths in the story within a story of "The Turn of the Screw."

But it is only theoretically that lack of consistency in point of view matters very much. Critical prescriptions are to be reached inductively: if many good novels violate a formal prescription, then that prescription must be modified or discarded; and many do violate the one about con-sistent point of view. "The Possessed" is told by an *I* most of the time, but when it is inconvenient for the *I* to be present at a scene, he simply disappears from the book and the scene is told by Dostoievsky from the unspecified point of view conventional in narratives of all sorts; nor does the book suffer from it. And in "Crime and Punishment"—which is surely one of the greatest novels—Dostoievsky begins one chapter:

> It would be difficult to describe the exact reasons which gave
> Mrs. Marmeladov the idea of the absurd funeral meal.

For the rest of the paragraph, Dostoievsky speculates on her possible motives. But during the course of the chapter he gets more and more involved with her—presenting her, to be sure, by external description and by objective reporting of what she says—until early in the next chapter he is close enough to say:

Mrs. Marmeladov remained standing in the same place, as though thunderstruck. She could not understand how Mr. Luzhin could have disavowed her father's hospitality, for by now she believed in it blindly.

Only a narrow theory would object to such a shift in how much the novelist should allow himself to reveal of what is going on in a character's mind. Fielding is sometimes reproved for his intrusions and shifts, even though "Tom Jones" is as much satire as realistic novel.

[Jones] returned the fellow his empty pistol, advised him to think of honester means of relieving his distress, and gave him a couple of guineas for the immediate support of his wife and his family; adding, 'he wished he had more for his sake, for the hundred pound that had been mentioned was not his own.'

Our readers will probably be divided in their opinions concerning this action; some may applaud it perhaps as an act of extraordinary humanity, while those of a more saturnine temper will consider it as a want of regard to that justice which every man owes his country. Partridge certainly saw it in that light; for he testified much dissatisfaction on the occasion, quoted an old proverb, and said, he should not wonder if the rogue attacked them again before they reached London.

The highwayman was full of expressions of thankfulness and gratitude. He actually dropped tears, or pretended so to do.

Here Fielding moves from a rather distant reporting of action to an author-comment which would break any illusion, back to an even cooler reporting. But the shift is open, the author's voice is clear, and the story and characters have vigor enough to survive the comments of writer and reader alike. *Here is the way to look at my characters*: this is bad only if the author's way of looking is stupid and the characters but half-alive.

The theory that the Dostoievsky-Fielding-Balzac method is so inferior to the Conrad-Joyce-Flaubert method as to render their novels inferior as works of art makes one huge assumption: that the reader of a novel should not feel himself in the hands of an artificer or story-teller and that the novelist's true art is to create an illusory actuality, appearing to have no art. But this assumption goes too far. It is the equivalent of that theatrical assumption that the audience can be looking through a fourth wall

324

into an actual room. Just as a spectator never really forgets that he is in a theater watching actors, so the reader of a novel does not really forget he is being told a story. When the narrator is open about his rôle as story-teller, as most have been in every sort of fiction, the reader happily allows him all sorts of liberties of point of view: everyone recognizes the artifice and enjoys it. Only when consistency is promised must inconsistency disturb.

As for fixity of remove—the steady distance which "point of view" metaphorically promises—it is made nothing by the example of the best, Tolstoy. He moves at will from the most panoramic aloofness above a battlefield to an account of the inmost feelings of a man at the moment before his death, and he moves anywhere between when and as it pleases him; and it is hard to imagine this lordly freedom troubling a reader for any reason but a narrow literary theory or his own private and uninteresting pathology. There is a great peace in delivering oneself into the hands of a writer who *knows*: "Tell us what you know, any way you will."

In fiction the point of view that matters most, and is least like the geographical one, is the author's set of values, what he considers important, especially morally; for this gets at the heart of the novel, the character's being and doing. The subject is so important, and so tricky, that I am looking at it under two aspects: first, the relation of the author's values to the reader, and then the author's relation to the characters he is creating.

Before going on, I must spell out an assumption: that everyone concerned with a novel, reader, writer, and character, has a set of attitudes, preferences, judgments, or values about human conduct, and that, whether these values are conscious or unconscious, articulated with logical coherence or only manifest in sometimes contradictory acts, they must finally be considered, if the world moral is to mean anything, moral values. This is no more than an *ad hoc* definition, much too loose to satisfy any ethical philosopher. Its justification in this essay is to insist that everyone says, or at least implies, "good" or "bad" when he looks at human conduct or when he himself acts: the hyperconscious esthete for whom the high good is savoring refined experience; the self-indulgent reader who seems to ask no more than that a novel remove him from moral concern but who is also asking for the author and the story to assure him, at least temporarily, that self-indulgence and sloth are all right; even Faulkner's feeble-minded Ike Snopes, whose great good is to love, though he knows that the world

325

thinks he should not love, a cow. These are extreme cases. Typically, people accept the code of conduct of their society, class, religion, province, whatever, without much distinguishing between convention and morality. It is a considerable part of the novelist's art both to let the reader understand the code of the imagined world and also to define the characters as they conform to, modify, rebel against, ignore, affirm, use this code.

The novelist's understanding of the imagined society's code of manners and values is essential to the reader's understanding of the characters, but the novelist's own code need not be and seldom is identical with the imagined code. Even where there is a substantial agreement, as with Jane Austen, the excellent novelist yet has a moral vision which much of the time perceives in the characters, including the narrator if there is one, a disparity between official reason and private motive, between society's requirements and the heart's need, that delights the reader and rings true to what he knows. One may say that a novelist will be interested in manners and convention, if only because he needs them to portray his people, and that his code of moral values may greatly differ from that code of manners but cannot utterly deny it. Any sort of writer who, like a mystic, says that social mores are of no importance or who, like a nihilist, says that all actual societies deserve destruction will have little interest in writing novels. Tolstoy the radical prophet necessarily rejected the works of Tolstoy the novelist. To this extent a true novelist is conservative: he says that the society he is writing about is worth at least our attention, for within it and of it are people worth noticing, worthy of our concern. The coherence of a novel depends in part upon the coherence of its characters and of their society. No doubt the society which every novel presents could or should be improved; meanwhile, something has been presented worthy of improvement. Nobody who can be considered an adequate reader of fiction requires that the code of conduct in the novel's world be the "right" code, if only because a part of what a novel can do is to bring news of strange parts, news of people with unfamiliar customs or with different attitudes towards familiar customs. Similarly, no reader asks that the novelist's own moral code be the "right" one; for those who think they know exactly what the right code is and how to apply it to a given occasion are happier with sermons than with a form so relative, so much a network of relationships and opinions, as the novel.

Nevertheless, since the narrator, whether the novelist himself or a character, is in fact going to have his own personal and moral opinions about the characters, his expression of them openly need not interfere with the reader but may very well please and help him. Both Dickens the novelist and David Copperfield the narrator dislike and disapprove of Uriah Heep, and any reasonable reader so fully shares this attitude that the expression of it adds to his pleasure. But in "Bleak House" Esther Summerson's view of herself is not likely to be identical with a reader's view of her; her humility is too conscious and she is too keen to report the praise of others for her to be accepted at her own evaluation, or, for that matter, at that of the other characters; and in this very disparity Dickens' own estimation of her reveals itself—to the reader's pleasure—as being not identical with any of those in the book. When the expressed view of a character is neither acceptable in itself nor dramatically acceptable as being a character's but is eccentrically the author's own, trouble may enter in but it need not be very serious. Fielding's excessive affection for and approval of Sophia in "Tom Jones" need interfere only slightly with a reader's somewhat reserved fondness for her; and Richardson's almost commercial equating of virtue and virginity in "Pamela" impairs the book but does not prevent one from seeing Pamela's holding out for marriage as a matter of some moral interest and complexity. In both these cases, the authors have created characters and situations of sufficient vitality to flourish apart from their creators' opinions of them. Bad trouble comes when the characters lack this vitality—in which case the author's opinion of them will not help or hurt much anyway. Worst of all is for the characters and actions to exist chiefly to demonstrate the author's views— whether Dostoievsky's anemic saints or Genet's evil-be-thou-my-good satanists or Katherine Mansfield's only-to-be-pitied victims. For in such cases the author's opinions come to be what matters, not the characters, and the reader has experience of polemic in the guise of fiction.

The relation of reader to writer is like that of two acquaintances talking about a mutual friend (in this case a character in a novel). The writer may express his opinions and the reader wants to make up his own mind on the evidence of the character's actions and thoughts. The trouble is, he can't. The analogy to the friends and their mutual acquaintance breaks down, because all the reader can know of the character is what the writer tells, shows, arranges, and comments on. The reader may think he is free to make his own connection with a character but in fact he is controlled.

Flaubert's ambition in "Madame Bovary" was to do nothing but present the evidence. However, what reader is (or should be) allowed to admire Homais? Every novelist, even if he does not overtly develop his personal and moral opinions as such, has those opinions and they will manifest themselves whether he intends them to or not. "In a corner of every notary's heart lie the moldy remains of a poet," Flaubert opines like any Balzac and then ducks back into the story out of sight. But whether it shows itself overtly, the author's moral judgment will—must—inform the very structure of action and delineation of character. That Emma Bovary should kill herself at the end of the book is right and inevitable in every way, including that of reflecting the author's moral views; but that the details of her dying are reported so extensively and with such vividness mainly reflects Flaubert's punishing cruelty, just as the hideous blind man's improbable appearance outside Emma's window at the moment of her death singing a love-ditty reflects very little more than Flaubert's weakness for romantic irony.

If a novelist is wise enough, he need manifest his moral views only in the actions and contours of his characters and in little cues along the way; if he is not wise enough for that, at least he will do no harm by telling the reader his opinions openly so the reader can estimate how much the novelist's opinions are affecting the presentation of characters and his response to them.

The reader prefers not to trouble himself over the writer's attitude to the character, though he will keep an eye on the narrator when the story is told in the first person. When he agrees with the writer, as he agrees with Dickens about Uriah Heep, or when the writer is so powerful and wise as to give the ultimate illusion "life is really like that," as Tolstoy often does, then the reader happily pays attention only to the characters and actions. But the novelist can never afford to neglect the reader. He must never forget that his connection with a character does not exist for its own sake only but exists partly to create the reader's connection with the character.

In this the most intimate and crucial of novelistic relationships—the writer creating character—there is, finally, the necessity on the novelist not to meddle. He may like the character as a person, and say so; he may disapprove and say so; he may develop all sorts of general theories about the type of person the character is or the social institutions he belongs to; he may be close to the character sometimes and far off at others; he may do all he can to control and direct the reader's response to the character when the character's acts or thoughts are not the instant focus of attention. But at the moment of action, of speaking, of thinking, of choice, he must not interfere; for if at that moment anything whatever gets between the character and the reader, nothing good will be created. Dickens notoriously could not let a dying child alone. Here is the death of Jo in "Bleak House." The trouble is not with Dickens' comment at the end but with what Jo is represented as saying.

> "Jo, my poor fellow!"
> "I hear you, sir, in the dark, but I'm a-gropin—a-gropin—
> let me catch hold of your hand."
> "Jo, can you say what I say?"
> "I'll say anything as you say, sir, for I knows it's good."
> "Our Father."
> " 'Our Father!'—yes, that's wery good, sir."
> "Which art in Heaven."
> " 'Art in Heaven'—is the light a-comin, sir?"
> "It is close at hand. Hallowed be thy name!"
> " 'Hallowed be—thy—' "
> The light is come upon the dark benighted way. Dead!
> Dead, your Majesty. Dead, my lords and gentlemen.
> Dead, Right Reverends and Wrong Reverends of every order.
> Dead, men and women, born with Heavenly compassion in
> your hearts. And dying thus around us every day.

Plato loved Socrates, Boswell loved Dr. Johnson, in "Heart of Darkness" Marlow had strong and complicated feelings about Kurtz; yet the deaths of those three subjects affect us far more than Jo's does because their telling is clean. Tolstoy himself sometimes falters even in his greatest fictions. At the moment of the death of Ivan Ilych, Tolstoy does not just report what was going on in the character's mind but makes his wish Ivan's.

> "And the pain?" he asked himself. "What has become of
> it? Where are you, pain?"
> He turned his attention to it.
> "Yes, here it is. Well, what of it? Let the pain be."
> "And death . . . where is it?"
> He sought his former accustomed fear of death and did
> not find it. "Where is it? What death?" There was no fear
> because there was no death.
> In place of death there was light.
> "So that's what it is!" he suddenly exclaimed aloud.
> "What joy!"

The reader knows he is no longer seeing Ivan's experience plain and responding to that, as he feels he has been doing up to this passage of the story; he also sees this as Tolstoy's wish and must shove Tolstoy aside in order to get cleanly to Ivan.

Here, ultimately, technical advice to a novelist becomes moral advice to any man. Grant others their otherness. "Justice," says Socrates in "The Republic," "means minding one's own business and not meddling with other men's concerns"—which concern, for a novelist, is the intercourse of reader and character. At the moment of greatest intimacy, of creation, do not judge, or you will be judged for having judged. Like a god, grant your creatures their free will. Like a father, give your children their independence. Like a friend, love them and leave them alone.

According to Lawrence Edward Bowling there is general
confusion about the stream of consciousness because critics
have not recognized the variations in the technique nor have
they distinguished this method from a similar one. In order
to clarify the misunderstanding, Bowling defines the *stream of
consciousness* as that method which gives us a direct quotation
from the mind, without the author's comment or analysis.
A writer may present, therefore, either (1) the whole stream
of consciousness, including the nonverbal elements, or he may
(2) limit his quotation to what Bowling calls *interior
monologue*—those thoughts and feelings which the mind
translates into language. If the author himself intervenes to
interpret, analyze, or comment, however, he employs a
fundamentally different method which should
be labeled *internal analysis*.

what is the
stream of consciousness
technique?

LAWRENCE EDWARD BOWLING

Despite the fact that the stream of consciousness technique occupies
an important position in twentieth-century fiction, there is no general
agreement as to where the method originated or what it really is. As
Frederick J. Hoffman observes, "Writers and critics are both confused by
the idea of 'interior monologue,' or the 'stream of consciousness,' as it
is more familiarly known." [1] Elizabeth Drew says that the stream of consciousness technique was "invented by Dorothy Richardson." [2] Katharine F. Gerould remarks that Henry James "introduced the method into
English fiction." [3] In an editorial note appended to the English edition

[1] *Freudianism and the Literary Mind* (1945), p. 125.
[2] *The Modern Novel* (1926), p. 256.
[3] "The Stream of Consciousness," *Sat. Rev. of Lit.*, IV (Oct. 22, 1927), 233.

of Edouard Dujardin's *Les Lauriers sont coupés*, James Laughlin holds that Dujardin invented interior monologue.[4] In making this statement, he is following the position taken by Dujardin in *Le Monologue intérieur*, in which he attempts to describe and define the method first used by him, he says, in *Les Lauriers*.

This state of general confusion is due chiefly to two main factors. The critics have failed to recognize different variations within the stream of consciousness technique, and they have failed also to distinguish this technique from another similar method with which it is often confused. Consequently, when they use a particular technical term, they are not always talking about the same thing, and the definitions which they formulate do not really fit the type of writing which they have in mind.

The best way to begin to clarify the situation is to examine some of these definitions and check them against specific examples of the type of writing which they are intended to define. Since Dujardin is held by some critics, including himself, to have invented the narrative method which is sometimes referred to as *the stream of consciousness technique* and which Dujardin has defined as *interior monologue*, a good starting point is his definition:

> De cet ensemble d'observations nous conclurons que le monologue intérieur, comme tout monologue, est un discours du personnage mis en scène et a pour objet de nous introduire directement dans la vie intérieure de ce personnage, sans que l'auteur intervienne par des explications ou des commentaires, et, comme tout monologue, est un discours sans auditeur et un discours non prononcé;
>
> mais il se différencie du monologue traditionnel en ce que:
>
> quant à sa matière, il est une expression de la pensée la plus intime, la plus proche de l'inconscient,
>
> quant à son esprit, il est un discours antérieur à toute organisation logique, reproduisant cette pensée en son état naissant et d'aspect tout venant,
>
> quant à sa forme, il se réalise en phrases directes réduites au minimum syntaxial. . . .
>
> —*Le Monologue intérieur* (1931), pp. 58–59.[5]

---

[4] *We'll to the Woods No More* (1938).

[5] From this collection of observations we shall conclude that the interior monologue, like every monologue, is a speech of the stage character and intends to

Most of this definition indicates that Dujardin intends to include the whole of the consciousness, particularly that "nearest the unconscious"; yet the facts that he calls his method *monologue intérieur*, uses such terms as *discours* and *pensée*, and describes interior monologue as being identical with spoken monologue except for the vocalization imply either that he is speaking of only one level of consciousness (the level nearest ordinary speech) or that he assumes all consciousness to come under the heading of interior monologue. If interior monologue is what Dujardin really means, his definition should be revised to apply to only that part of a character's interior life *farthest from* the unconscious; on the other hand, if he intends to include *all* conscious mental processes, then his definition should be made sufficiently comprehensive to include such non-language phenomena as images and sensations, and the technique which he is defining should be called not *interior monologue* but *the stream of consciousness technique*.

In order to determine which of the two Dujardin means (or should mean) in his definition, we may consider representative excerpts from *Les Lauriers sont coupés* (1887), which Dujardin says demonstrates the technique that he is defining. *Les Lauriers* is not a great or a particularly exciting novel. Its general theme might be stated as the duping of a naive young man, Daniel Prince, by a very clever actress, Lea d'Arsay, who is less interested in his heart than in his wallet. This theme had already been sufficiently taken care of, at far greater length and for much higher stakes, by both Zola and Balzac. Beside their detailed and thorough handling, Dujardin's slender efforts look tame. However, there is an important difference between his work and theirs. Dujardin disregards the moral and social aspects of the theme and focuses attention upon the psychological reactions of the main character. The whole of the book is taken from the mind of Daniel Prince. Even external scenery and the speeches of other characters come to us through his consciousness.

The most realistic and most flexible instance of interior monologue in *Les Lauriers sont coupés* is the following excerpt from a reverie in which

---

introduce us directly to the inner life of this character, without the author's intervention by explanations or commentaries; and, like every monologue it is a speech unheard and not pronounced;

but it differs from the traditional monologue in that:

with respect to its subject, it is an expression of the most intimate thought closest to the subconscious,

with respect to its spirit, it is a discourse anterior to all logical organization, reproducing this average thought at the moment of its birth,

with respect to its form, it is accomplished in direct sentences reduced to a syntactical minimum.

Prince imagines himself at the apartment of Lea d'Arsay, trying to persuade her to elope with him:

> . . . certainement, elle me priera de rester un peu; je verrai
> son fin sourire de frais démon; lente elle fera sa toilette du
> soir.—Asseyez-vous dans le fauteuil, et soyez sage! Elle me
> parlera, dans un beau geste cérémonieux; je répondrai, sem-
> blablement:—Oui, mademoiselle! Je m'assoirai dans le fau-
> teuil; le bas fauteuil en velours bleu, à la bande large brodée;
> là elle s'est posée sur mes genoux, il y a quinze jours; et je
> m'assoirai dans le bas fauteuil, auprès d'elle, en face de l'ar-
> moire à glace; elle sera debout et mettra son chapeau sur la
> table de peluche; ajustant ses cheveux par de petits coups,
> à gauche, avec des pauses, se considérant, devant, derrière,
> par de petits coups, me regardant, riant, faisant des grimaces,
> gamine . . . [1924 ed., p. 38] [6]

Although this reverie may be a bit more complex and concrete than many
soliloquies commonly found in fiction and drama, it may still be classified
as interior monologue, without unduly forcing that term. Both the narrated
action and the reverie speeches are formulated in Prince's mind on the
thought level of consciousness and in the form of language. His mental
processes here are the same as if he were talking. It should be observed,
however, that this passage (although it is actually the best example of
interior monologue to be found in Les Lauriers) does not fit Dujardin's
definition. There is nothing illogical or disorganized about it; it is drawn
from the area of consciousness farthest from the unconscious; and the
sentences are in no way reduced to a syntactic minimum.

    With the exception of the above reverie and a very few other brief
passages, the technique in Les Lauriers is far less flexible and realistic
than Dujardin's remarks in Le Monologue intérieur would lead us to expect. Let us consider, for example, the stiff formality of the second paragraph of the novel:

[6] . . . certainly, she will beg me to stay a little; I shall see the sly, cooly demonic
smile; she will dress slowly. "Sit in the chair and be good!" She will speak to
me in a lovely ceremonial gesture; I will answer in the same way: "Yes, mad-
moiselle!" I shall sit in the chair; the low, blue velvet chair with the wide em-
broidered stripes; she sat on my knees there fifteen days ago; and I shall sit in
the low chair, near her, opposite the bureau; she will be standing and will put
her hat on the plush table; adjusting her hair with short strokes, to the left,
with pauses, gazing at herself, in front, in back, with short strokes, looking at
one, laughing, putting on airs, a hoyden.

Car sous le chaos des apparences, parmi les durées et les
sites, dans l'illusion des choses qui s'engendrent et qui s'en-
fantent, un parmi les autres, un comme les autres, distinct des
autres, semblable aux autres, un le même et un de plus, de
l'infini des possibles existences, je surgis; et voici que le
temps et le lieu se précisent; c'est l'aujourd'hui; c'est l'ici;
l'heure, le lieu, un soir d'avril, Paris, un soir clair de soleil
couchant, les monotones bruits, les maisons blanches, les
feuillages d'ombres; les soir plus doux, et une joie d'être
quelqu'un, d'aller; les rues et les multitudes, et, dans l'air
très lointainement étendu, le ciel; Paris à l'entour chante, et,
dans la brume des formes aperçues, mollement il encadre
l'idée.[7]

Although we are supposed to be inside the character's mind, sharing his
most spontaneous, unpolished thoughts, just as they are born, we find
that this paragraph is a highly-polished, "literary" sentence. The many
parenthetical phrases and the inverted word-order, resulting in a periodic
construction, indicate that the character had the whole paragraph carefully worked out all the way to the end before he began soliloquizing
the first of it. To be convincing, interior monologue must be no more
logical and formal than ordinary speech, but this sentence is more formal
and "literary" than most writing. In interior monologue, the mind moves
along in a loose manner, tacking on one idea after another, as they come
—not in the periodic manner implied by this sentence.

Let us now consider the one passage in *Les Lauriers sont coupés*—the
only passage of its kind in the book—which most nearly conforms to
Dujardin's definition. As Daniel Prince sits in Lea d'Arsay's apartment
before their evening walk, his mind is at first concerned with the April
evening and the anticipated stroll. After briefly recalling a girl whom he
had met on the street earlier in the day, Prince falls asleep and dreams of
his parents at home and of his first love, Antonia, until Lea wakes him

[7] For under the chaos of appearances, among the durations and the sites, in the
illusion of things which are engendered and which are born, one among others,
one like others, distinct from others, similar to others, the same one and another, one out of the infinity of possible existences, I came into view; and then
time and place are clarified; it is today, it is here; the time, the place, and
April evening, Paris, a clear evening at sunset, the monotonous noises, the
white houses, the shadowy foliage; the mildest evening, and a joy of being
someone, of going; the streets and the crowds, and, in the far extended atmosphere, the sky; Paris sings round the town, and in the mist of perceived forms,
indolently it frames the idea.

with her laughter. Presumably the pushing-dragging sensation in the dream is Lea's shaking him.

> . . . la belle nuit d'avril . . . tout à l'heure nous nous promene-
> rons . . . l'air frais . . . nous allons partir . . . tout à l'heure
> . . . les deux bougies . . . là . . . au cours des boulevards . . .
> "j't'aim'mieux qu'mes moutons" . . . j't'aim'mieux . . . cette
> fille, yeux éhontés, frêle, aux lèvres rouges . . . la chambre,
> la cheminée haute . . . la salle . . . mon père . . . tous trois
> assis, mon père, ma mère . . . moi-même . . . pourquoi ma
> mère est-elle pâle? . . . elle me regarde . . . nous allons diner,
> oui, sous le bosquet . . . la bonne . . . apportez la table . . .
> Léa . . . elle dresse la table . . . mon père . . . le concierge
> . . . une lettre . . .une lettre d'elle? . . . merci . . . un ondoie-
> ment, une rumeur, un lever de cieux . . . et vous, à jamais
> l'unique, la primitive aimée, Antonia . . . tout scintille . . . vous
> riez-vous? . . . les becs de gaz s'alignant infiniment . . . oh!
> . . . la nuit . . . froide et glacée, la nuit . . . Ah!!! mille épou-
> vantements!!! quoi? . . . on me pousse, on m'arrache, on me
> tue . . . Rien . . . un rire . . . la chambre . . . Léa . . . Sapristi
> . . . m'etais-je endormi? . . . [pp. 90–91].[8]

As prescribed in the definition, this passage does a fair job of "introducing us directly into the interior life of the character, without the author's intervention by means of explanations or comments." At least some of it is "nearest the unconscious, . . . anterior to all logical organization," and it is "effected through direct sentences reduced to the syntactic minimum." The question remains, however: should this type of writing be defined by so limited a term as *interior monologue*? Although certain fragments of the passage can be definitely placed in this classification, much

---

[8] . . . the lovely April night . . . soon we shall take a walk . . . the cool air . . . we are going to leave . . . soon . . . the two candles . . . there . . . along the boulevards . . . "I love you more than all else." . . . I love you more . . . this girl, eyes unblushing, frail, with red lips . . . the room, the high chimney . . . the room . . . my father . . . all three seated, my father, my mother . . . myself . . . why is my mother pale? . . . she looks at me . . . we are going to have dinner, yes, below the grove . . . the maid, bring the table . . . Lea . . . she is setting the table . . . my father . . . the porter . . . a letter . . . a letter from her? . . . thank you . . . an undulation, a distant murmur, a rising up of heavens . . . and you, forever the sole, the primeval loved one, Antonia . . . everything sparkles . . . you're laughing? the lamp-posts lined up infinitely . . . Oh! . . . the night . . . cold and icy, the night . . . Oh!!! A thousand terrors!!! What? . . . I am being pushed, carried off, slain . . . Nothing . . . a laugh . . . the room . . . Lea . . . Sapristi . . . had I been asleep? . . .

of the excerpt deals with pure sensations and images which the mind does not translate into language. It may be stretching the term unduly to say that *interior monologue* may include all linguistic mental activity, but it is certainly going too far to assume, as Dujardin does, that *interior monologue* can cover the whole of the consciousness. The narrative method employed in this dream-passage should, therefore, be designated as *the stream of consciousness technique.*

Although it is not easy to determine the exact point at which the mind drops below the level of language usage and functions by means of pure images and sensations, we do know that there is always in the consciousness a vast amount of mental activity which our minds never translate into language, and any attempt on the part of a writer to make a character *think* this non-language material into language form (that is, into interior monologue) sounds awkward and unreal. One of the fundamental errors made by Dujardin, both in the application and in the definition of his method, is the assumption that the whole of the consciousness can be presented in the form of interior monologue. This mistake is responsible for much of the self-conscious awkwardness of *Les Lauriers* and also for the superficial distinction which Dujardin attempts to draw between his technique and the method—which he calls *traditional monologue*—used by such writers as Balzac and Dostoevsky.

The self-conscious awkwardness due to forcing non-language material into interior monologue may be illustrated by two brief examples. In the third paragraph of *Les Lauriers*, Prince is made to soliloquize as follows about his friend Chavainne: "Je lui ai confié, à ce brave ami, mon histoire amoureuse." [9] Later, as they walk along together, Prince sandwiches in bits of his soliloquy between their conversation (p. 19):

> —Eh bien, et votre passion? [asks Chavainne]
> Me demande-t-il; je vais lui dire.
> —Toujours à peu près de même.
> Nous marchons, côte à côte.[10]

In the first of these examples, it would not occur to Prince that he need remind himself that Chavainne is his friend or that he has already told Chavainne about his love-affair. In the second example, it is likewise unnatural for Prince to think, "He asks me; I shall tell him," and "We

---

[9] "To him, to this brave friend, I confided my love story."
[10] "Now then, and your passion?" he asks me; I am going to tell him.
"Always just about the same."
We walk, side by side.

walk along, side by side." Prince would normally be *aware* of these facts, but his mind would not formulate these ideas into soliloquy. As we walk down the street and pass a house, we are aware that we are walking and we are aware that we see the house, but we do not bother to say silently to ourselves, "I am walking down the street; there is a house; I am passing the house." This type of awareness we do not normally express to ourselves in language form, and any attempt on the part of a writer to make a character lift such phenomena to the same level of consciousness as ordinary interior monologue seems cumbersome and formal. A large part of *Les Lauriers* is of this type of writing.

In attempting to draw a distinction between his technique in *Les Lauriers* and the method used by his predecessors, Dujardin cites a monologue from Dostoevsky's "An Unpleasant Predicament." The following excerpt from this monologue, along with Dostoevsky's prefatory comment, will help us to evaluate the grounds on which Dujardin makes his distinction:

> It is well known that whole trains of thought sometimes pass through our brains instantaneously as though they were sensations without being translated into human speech, still less into literary language. But we will try to translate these sensations of our hero's, and present to the reader at least the kernel of them, so to say, what was most essential and nearest to reality in them. For many of our sensations when translated into ordinary language seem absolutely unreal. That is why they never find expression, though every one has them. Of course Ivan Ilyitch's sensations and thoughts were a little incoherent. But you know the reason.
>
> "Why," flashed through his mind, "here we all talk and talk, but when it comes to action—it all ends in nothing. Here, for instance, take this Pseldonimov: he has just come from his wedding full of hope and excitement, looking forward to his wedding feast. . . . This is one of the most blissful days of his life. . . . Now he is busy with his guests, is giving a banquet, a modest one, poor, but gay and full of genuine gladness. . . . What if he knew that at this very moment I, I, his superior, his chief, am standing by his house listening to the music? Yes, really how would he feel? No, what would he feel if I suddenly walked in? . . .

". . . I shall jest a little again with the bride; h'm! . . . I may even hint that I shall come again in just nine months to stand godfather, he-he! And she will be sure to be brought to bed by then. They multiply, you know, like rabbits. And they will all roar with laughter and the bride will blush; I shall kiss her feelingly on the forehead, even give her my blessing . . . ." [11]

The unbiased critic will see no essential difference between this passage and the best examples of interior monologue, in *Les Lauriers*. In fact, Ivan Ilyitch's reverie in the last paragraph is quite similar to Daniel Prince's reverie quoted above as the best of Dujardin's efforts in this direction. Dujardin attempts to disqualify the Ilyitch passage, however, on the ground that it is a *translation* on the part of the author and not a *direct copy* of the character's exact thoughts. In support of his argument, Dujardin cites Dostoevsky's prefatory paragraph, particularly the sentence in which Dostoevsky says, "We will try to *translate* these sensations of our hero's." In conclusion, Dujardin remarks: "Dostoïewsky, on le voit, après s'être excusé de ce manque de logique, announce qu'il 'essaie d'interpréter,' ce qui est, à proprement parler, *le contraire du monologue intérieur.*" [12] Dujardin makes a serious blunder here, for he has completely misunderstood Dostoevsky's meaning in the first paragraph. What Dostoevsky is really saying is this: a vast amount of what normally passes through our minds and which we ordinarily refer to as *thoughts* is really a series of sensations (and images) which our minds never translate into language; if we try to translate these sensations and images into the language of ordinary *speech,* our translations sound stiff and strange; if we try to translate them into *literary* language, the result sounds even less convincing; since we cannot make a character think *all* his consciousness into language, let us present only that part of Ivan Ilyitch's mental activity which is nearest to the reality of human speech, that part which may be reasonably and convincingly rendered in the form of interior monologue. In this apology for the limitations of an author, Dostoevsky reveals that he is aware of an important fact which Dujardin seems to overlook, both in his definition in *Le Monologue intérieur* and in his practice in *Les Lauriers sont coupés*: that the whole of the consciousness cannot be presented as interior monologue.

[11] *An Honest Thief and Other Stories,* tr. Constance Garnett.
[12] One sees Dostoevsky, after having excused himself from lack of logic, announce that he is "trying to interpret," what is, so to speak, *the opposite of the interior monologue. Le Monologue intérieur,* p. 71.

Analyzing the soliloquy itself, we find that it is a translation only in the sense that all fiction is a "translation" on the part of the author. It is possible to find other interior monologues which are more flexible and realistic than Ivan Ilyitch's. Likewise, we can find conversations in some novels which are more flexible and realistic than those in other novels. To say that Ivan Ilyitch's soliloquy is not interior monologue, because it is not ultra-realistic, would be like saying that the speeches in some novels are not speeches, because they do not conform to the literary standards of a later or an earlier period. The fact is that the Dostoevsky soliloquy is less formal and more convincing than most of the soliloquies in *Les Lauriers*, and it will stand comparison with those in such recent works as Hemingway's *For Whom the Bell Tolls*, in which interior monologue is used intermittently; Faulkner's *The Sound and the Fury*, in which it is employed extensively; [13] and Virginia Woolf's *The Waves*, a novel rendered exclusively in the form of interior monologues. Here, for example, is a typical excerpt from the mind of one of the six characters in *The Waves* (1931):

> "Now Miss Hudson," said Rhoda, "has shut the book. Now the terror is beginning. Now taking her lump of chalk she draws figures, six, seven, eight, and then a cross and then a line on the blackboard. What is the answer? The others look; they look with understanding. Louise writes; Susan writes; Jinny writes; even Bernard has now begun to write. But I cannot write." [p. 20]

Everything about this passage is the same as if it were a vocalized speech: the quotation marks, the narrative tag *said Rhoda*, and the logical arrangement and punctuation of the sentences. At first, the reader mistakes these monologues for speeches, but a complete reading of *The Waves* reveals that not one word is spoken throughout the entire book. The characters merely soliloquize to themselves in the presence of each other. By way of introducing her book, the author might well have made some such prefatory remarks as those in which Dostoevsky prepares his readers for Ivan Ilyitch's interior monologue.

It is difficult to understand or to agree with the line of reasoning by which Dujardin attempts to disqualify the interior monologues of his predecessors, just as it is difficult also to make his definition square with his

---

[13] For an analysis of the stream of consciousness technique as employed in this novel, see my article, "The Technique of *The Sound and the Fury*," *Kenyon Review* (Autumn, 1948).

practice. His main thesis in *Le Monologue intérieur* is the contention that he invented this technique, in *Les Lauriers,* and Joyce perfected and popularized it, in Molly Bloom's forty-five-page, unpunctuated monologue at the end of *Ulysses.* The fact is that Dujardin's definition is a far more exact statement of the method of the Molly Bloom monologue than of *Les Lauriers.* He seems to have formulated it more upon the basis of Joyce's work than upon his own. The best way to get a clear impression of the Joyce monologue is to read several pages of it consecutively, but a brief excerpt will give a fair idea of the technique employed throughout this section of the book:

> nothing like a kiss long and hot down to your soul almost paralyses you then I hate that confession when I used to go to Father Corrigan he touched me father and what harm if he did where and I said on the canal bank like a fool but whereabouts on your person my child on the leg behind high up was it yes rather high up was it where you sit down yes O Lord couldn't he say bottom right out and have done with it what has that got to do with it and did you whatever way he put it I forget no father and I always think of the real father what did he want to know for when I already confessed it to God he had a nice fat hand the palm moist always I wouldn't mind feeling it neither would he Id say by the bullneck in his horsecollar I wonder did he know me in the box I could see his face he couldnt see mine of course hed never turn or let on. [14]

There is nothing in this passage or in the whole section which may not reasonably be classed as legitimate interior monologue. That is to say, the section contains no mental activity other than that which appears as silent soliloquy and the character is not forced by the author to soliloquize into language any phenomena which seem awkward or out of place on the language level of consciousness. As stated in Dujardin's definition, syntax is at a minimum; the content is the character's most intimate thoughts, nearest the unconscious (at least, as near as monologue approaches the unconscious); and there is no intervention or explanation on the part of the author. This passage is the most realistic example of interior monologue we have considered, but the difference between it and the Dostoevsky monologue is a matter of degree and not of kind. It will be observed,

[14] *Ulysses,* Modern Library edition, pp. 725–726.

for example, that even Joyce does not attempt to present the whole of the consciousness as interior monologue but restricts himself, as Dostoevsky does, to what is most essential and nearest to the reality of ordinary human speech.

In one respect, however, Dujardin is nearer than Dostoevsky to Joyce's use of interior monologue. Dostoevsky, like most of his predecessors and many modern writers, presents only intermittent excerpts from a character's mind. Dujardin, like Joyce and certain other twentieth-century novelists, focuses primary attention upon the meanderings of the mind, not as a means to an end, but as an important end in itself.

The twentieth-century novelist most frequently referred to as the typical writer of stream of consciousness fiction—and held by some to have invented this method—is Dorothy Richardson. In the introduction to *Pointed Roofs* (1919), May Sinclair comments as follows upon Miss Richardson's technique: "Obviously, she [the author] must not interfere; she must not analyze or comment or explain. . . . And there are some things she must not be. She must not be the wise, all-knowing author. She must be Miriam Henderson. She must not know or divine anything that Miriam does not know or divine." Speaking of Miss Richardson's *Honeycomb*, Joseph Warren Beach quotes Miss Sinclair's comment and agrees with it: "It is not as if the author were there to interpret for us. The fundamental assumption of Miss Richardson's method is that the author should not be there. . . . The narrative is simply the stream of consciousness of the heroine." [15]

With these comments, let us compare a few examples of Miss Richardson's writing. In the following passage, a man with whom Miriam is talking makes a remark which excites her mind into a soliloquy:

"The vagaries of the Fair, dear girl," he said presently, in a soft blurred tone.

That's one of his phrases, thought Miriam—that's old-fashioned politeness; courtliness. Behind it he's got some sort of mannish thought . . . "the unaccountability of women" . . . who can understand a woman—she doesn't even understand herself—thought he'd given up trying to make out. He's gone through life and got his own impression; all utterly wrong . . . talking about them with an air of wisdom to young men like Gerald . . . my dear boy, a woman never knows her own mind. How utterly detestable mannishness is; so mighty

---

[15] *The Twentieth Century Novel: Studies in Technique* (1932), pp. 388, 392.

and strong and comforting when you have been mewed up with women all your life, and then suddenly, in a second, far away, utterly imbecile and aggravating with a superior self-satisfied smile because a woman says one thing one minute and another the next. Men ought to be horsewhipped, all the grown men, all, all, horsewhipped until they apologize on their knees.

—*Honeycomb* (1917), p. 137.

This is good interior monologue and agrees perfectly with the above quoted remarks. The following excerpt, although it is not monologue, also conforms to Miss Sinclair's and Professor Beach's comments. As Miriam goes out West End Street, these are the sights and sounds which impress themselves upon her consciousness.

grey buildings rising on either side, feeling away into the approaching distance—angles sharp against the sky . . . softened angles of buildings against other buildings . . . high moulded angles soft as crumb, with deep undershadows . . . creepers fraying from balconies . . . strips of window blossoms across the buildings, scarlet, yellow, high up; a confusion of lavender and white pouching out along a dipping sill . . . a wash of green creeper up a white painted house front . . . patches of shadow and bright light. . . . Sounds of visible near things streaked and scored with broken light as they moved, led off into untraced distant sounds . . . chiming together. [*Ibid.*, p. 125]

This type of writing, to be distinguished from interior monologue, may be designated as *sensory impression*. In interior monologue, the mind is active; from concrete sensory impressions, it works toward abstract thoughts and ideas. In sensory impression, the mind is more or less passive; it is concerned merely with perceiving concrete sense impressions. In reveries and dreams, the mind seems to be in this same state, and the same technique may be used in presenting these imaginary sensory impressions. To present this area of consciousness, many authors use brief phrases separated by three elliptical dots, as Miss Richardson does in this passage (Compare Daniel Prince's dream in *Les Lauriers*.) A noun is commonly used to designate an object not in motion, and a participle is attached if movement is indicated. *Sensory impression* is the writer's nearest approach

343

to putting pure sensations and images on paper. This is the area of consciousness which Dostoevsky and most other writers either omit or present indirectly in the form of *internal analysis*. The distinguishing characteristic of certain twentieth-century psychological novelists is that they attempt to present directly and dramatically the *whole* of the consciousness.

In each of the above two passages, it may be said, without qualification, that the author does "not interfere, . . . analyze or comment or explain," and that the passages are "simply the stream of consciousness of the heroine." The question remains, however: does Miss Richardson employ this same objective, dramatic technique throughout the whole of the novel or in only a few intermittent instances? If it is not correct to say, "The narrative is simply the stream of consciousness of the heroine," then how does her usual method differ from this technique and what should it be called?

To discover that Miss Richardson does intervene in order to analyze and interpret, we need look no farther than the first paragraph of *Honeycomb*:

> When Miriam got out of the train into the darkness she knew that there were woods all about her. The moist air was rich with the smell of trees—wet bark and branches—moss and lichen, damp dead leaves. She stood on the dark platform snuffing the rich air. It was the end of her journey. Anything that might follow would be unreal compared to that moment. Little bulbs of yellow light further up the platform told her where she must turn to find the things she must go to meet. "How lovely the air is here." The phrase repeated itself again and again, going with her up the platform towards the group of lights.

Nothing about this paragraph impresses one as being unusual. It is certainly not the stream of consciousness of the heroine. "How lovely the air is here" is the only part of the passage which is an exact copy of any part of the character's mind, and this fragment is inclosed in quotation marks to indicate that it is different from the remainder of the passage. The sentence beginning "The phrase repeated itself again and again . . ." cannot by any standard be defended as a direct report of the character's actual thought; this is an abstract commentary on the part of the author, intervening between us and the character's mind to give us a *summary* of the

344

character's thought. If we were really inside Miriam's stream of consciousness, we could not find any such summary statement; we would simply *hear* the phrase repeating itself. The statement that "it is not as if the author were there to interpret for us" is not correct, for the author is definitely present in this passage. Instead of introducing us directly into the interior life of the character, the author stands as an interpreter between us and the character's mind and gives us her *interpretation* of what the character feels and thinks. This method of writing should be called, not the stream of consciousness technique but *internal analysis*, since it is the author's *analysis* of what is taking place inside the character. Internal analysis and the stream of consciousness technique are fundamentally different: the one *summarizes*, the other *dramatizes*; the one is *abstract*, the other is *concrete*.

In stating that Dorothy Richardson is not "the wise, all-knowing author," that she does "not know or divine anything that Miriam does not know or divine," Miss Sinclair is thinking of the author's tendency to follow closely the experiences of the heroine and to present things in the order in which they reveal themselves to that character; but Miss Richardson does not always adhere to this practice, as is illustrated by her comment in the following sentence from *Honeycomb* (p. 138): "Responding to her companion's elaborate apologetic petition for permission to smoke it did not occur to Miriam to confess that she herself occasionally smoked." In this sentence, the author reveals herself as being aware of something which "did not occur to Miriam." Although Miss Richardson usually identifies herself with her main character—and this is one of this author's distinguishing characteristics—she does not restrict herself completely to this point of view.

Commenting upon the stream of consciousness technique, Elizabeth Drew defines it as "the method of creating character and interpreting life invented by Dorothy Richardson, that method by which we never pass out of the realm of one person's immediate experience, and one person's consciousness is the standard of reference for the whole existence." As pointed out in the preceding paragraph, this type of statement applies fairly well to Miss Richardson's method; but it does not correctly describe the stream of consciousness technique. Elsewhere, Miss Drew remarks of Miss Richardson's method: "she is entirely occupied with the reporting of the impressions made upon her conscious and unconscious mind by the experiences of life." This time, Miss Drew quotes a representative passage from *Interim* to illustrate the method of which she is speaking:

The hushed happiness that had begun in the dining room half
an hour ago seized her again suddenly, sending her forward
almost on tiptoe. It was securely there; the vista it opened
growing in beauty as she walked . . . bearing within her in
secret unfathomable abundance the gift of old-English rose
and white gracious adorable womanhood . . .

"The recording of all these phenomena is," says Miss Drew, "a new ex-
periment in literature." [16] The question is, does the passage quoted from
Interim bear out or refute Miss Drew's remarks? She says the passage is
a "reporting of the impressions," "the recording of all these phenomena."
But is it correct to say of this passage that it is a *report* or a *recording*?
These terms imply an exact copy. What the author gives us in this passage
is not an exact copy, not a direct quotation, but an indirect statement.
Miss Richardson's customary method may be called the stream of consciousness technique only in the sense that she leads us along the *bank
of the stream* and describes for us in her own words what she sees; only
occasionally does she bring us to a vantage point from which we can
behold the stream itself. In making this distinction, we are not questioning
in any way the literary quality of either type of writing but merely insisting
that between the technique employed in the last three passages considered from Miss Richardson's work and that exemplified in the first two
passages there is a fundamental difference and that, if confusion is to be
avoided, the two methods must not be called by the same name.

On the basis of the foregoing discussion, the stream of consciousness technique may be defined as that narrative method by which the
author attempts to give *a direct quotation of the mind*—not merely of the
language area but of the whole consciousness. Like the kind of direct
quotation which is applied to the spoken word, the stream of consciousness technique may be applied exclusively throughout a whole book or
section of a book, or intermittently in short fragments. The only criterion
is that it introduce us directly into the interior life of the character, without any intervention by way of comment or explanation on the part of the
author. If the author limits his direct quotation to that area of consciousness in which the mind formulates its thoughts and feelings into language,
the method may still be called by the comprehensive term *the stream of
consciousness technique,* but in this case it would be more exact to apply
the more restricted term *interior monologue.* If, however, the author inter-

[16] *The Modern Novel,* pp. 256, 84, 88.

venes in any way between the reader and the character's consciousness in order to analyze, comment, or interpret, then he is employing not the stream of consciousness technique but a fundamentally different method which may correctly be designated *internal analysis*. The latter is an indirect statement in the words of the author; the former is a direct quotation of the character's consciousness.

Since symbol hunting has become such a popular sport and since symbols in prose fiction have become such a sure sign of literary worth, Ursula Brumm thinks that it is time to examine the true nature of symbols and their real function in the novel. She acknowledges, at the outset, that realistic fiction may contain symbols which reinforce the meaning, but symbolism in the full sense provides us with a transcendent embodiment of the meaning. In James's *The Golden Bowl*, the bowl itself is analogous to the action, but, more than that, it is a mystical symbol of faith amid the increasing secularization of the world. At their best, symbolic novels can be a rich source of values, but at their worst, they may so disregard the actual and the typical that they are an unconscious parody of symbolic fiction. The critics themselves, Miss Brumm concludes, may be responsible for these failures because their enthusiasm for symbols may have influenced young writers to try too hard for symbolic meaning.

symbolism
and the novel
URSULA BRUMM

We live in the age of symbolism in literature. But we accept the fact calmly, if with no particular enthusiasm. For symbolism makes no burdensome demands on us; it exacts neither tragic participation nor the effort of precise reflection, above all it entails no decision for or against anything. Indeed we are scarcely conscious of its ascendency. Symbolism has pervaded poetry long enough for us to be perfectly accustomed to it. Its conquest of the novel and the drama has been gradual and unobtrusive. And in both these fields its ascendency has for the most part been discreetly camouflaged under a deliberate show of realism. The triumph of symbolism as a habit of thought is most strikingly evidenced by the considerable number of critics who, in their enthusiasm for symbols, more and more unqualifiedly equate literature with symbolism. The symbol has come to be the major criterion of literary value. "Since symbolism is the necessary condition of literature, all novels are symbolic," says William York Tindall in his *The Literary Symbol* (1955). So far as I am aware, this flat statement and others similarly dogmatic have not so far aroused objections except from Philip Rahv in his essay "Fiction and the Criticism of Fiction" (*Kenyon Review*, Spring 1956). To support his thesis Tindall adduces a number of modern novels (by Henry Green, Virginia Woolf, and James Joyce), the symbolic elements in which he merely assembles and presents without critical evaluation. To go symbol hunting in the novel is a highly popular sport these days. If a novel contains symbols that you can pick out like raisins from a bun, it can claim to be literature.

The purpose of this essay is to examine the nature and function of symbols in the novel. Lyric poetry, which is governed by wholly different laws, lies outside the scope of the discussion. Our aim is to define, as exactly as possible, the role played by symbols in prose literature. This is no simple task, for both symbol and novel are essentially collective concepts, which respectively lump together the most diverse varieties of symbolism and narrative fiction. Precision, perhaps even extreme simplification in statement, can alone shed light on the very complex relations between novel and symbol, and I am well aware of the dangers inherent in this approach. I am also aware that finding even one critical flaw in the armor of symbolism is a sure way of making oneself unpopular these days.

Although the historical approach to any critical problem is now considered hopelessly outmoded, we do heed the perspective of history, if only as a check against our private prejudices and currently accepted views. And in fact the historical test shows that the prevailing opinion cannot be right: Symbolism, in the specific sense developed by modern writers, is not the necessary condition of literature, nor are all novels symbolic. (For neither we nor the proponents of the dogma take it to mean every work of art is vaguely symbolic for the simple reason that it represents life.) The great nineteenth-century novel is not the product of an imagination working in symbolic forms. It is a representation of life, but not a symbolic representation. Stendhal, Balzac, Tolstoy, to mention only the greatest, did without symbols in the specific sense; for many good reasons, there is no room for the symbol in their works. This most significant tradition of the novel is non-symbolic, or at least neutral in regard to the symbol.

In its origins the European novel, in contrast to the early American novel, is a child of the Age of Enlightenment and of historicism. The so-called realistic novel of the late eighteenth and early nineteenth centuries is empirical in both its attitudes and its technical procedures. It is realistic, not because it set out to produce an absolutely faithful re-creation of reality, but because it holds that only what actually is can furnish trustworthy data concerning our destiny as human beings. In this sense it is agnostic, sceptical, empirical, and secular. In his *The Rise of the Novel* (1957) Ian Watt has shown that the novels of Defoe, Fielding, and Richardson were born of the same *Zeitgeist* as the philosophies of Locke and Descartes. They are critical and unprejudiced studies of life as represented by memorable personages whose destiny is determined by their individual character, by their particular place in society, and by the times they lived in and the ideas prevalent in those times. (That our contemporary critics should choose to regard these characters simply as the product of their social status is another prejudice that will not stand the historical test.) The same is true of the novels of Stendhal, Balzac, and Tolstoy. The particular classical form of the novel which they created and which has received the rather dubious designation of "realistic" (for simplicity's sake we shall use the term too) is in a certain sense antisymbolic, for it is opposed to the entire class of elements to which the symbol belongs. The realistic novel owes its origin to rejecting the paradigms that had for centuries determined literary forms: fable, legend, myth, and the traditional, typical stories and characters from the storehouse of world literature that were constantly being reworked (i.e., the "archetypes" that have become so popular again today.) The realistic novel is against types, against the changeless decked out in varying guises, against the authority of the eternal and the accepted. It is concerned with the individual and idiosyncratic, that is, the particular in its particular circumstances, with reality as experienced by the individual as constituting the only genuine version of reality. The realistic novel is the purest embodiment in literature of the modern scientific sceptical approach (but how quickly the "modern" becomes old and passé! for which only an observed and measured reality was valid as the raw material for cognition and creation. Only this kind of reality seemed reliable enough to serve the novelist as the basis for a portrayal of life. This attitude has little use for symbols, since a symbol always represents something that remains to be demonstrated, unless it has already been accepted on faith.

In its empiricism the classical novel was at one with historiography, which, just at this time, and setting out from similar intellectual principles, was tremendously enlarging its field of operations and its horizon.

Like historiography, the novel proposed to investigate and depict the concrete and specific form of reality at a particular time in a particular place.
Hence the historical element, and especially the element of contemporary history, has an important and indeed indispensable place in these
novels. There is scarcely one of them that does not establish the historical
period of the events within the first few pages."*Le 15 mai 1796, le général
Bonaparte fit son entrée dans Milan*—so Stendhal begins *La Chartreuse de
Parme,* and this event is the fulcrum in the life and destiny of Fabrizio del
Dongo. But it is never the mythopoeic aspect of history which these writers
seek out and emphasize; history is always referred to the individual. Even
situations that invite mythopoeic treatment are passed over, and indeed,
whatever illusion naturally attaches to such situations is consciously destroyed. Stendhal "disenchants" Napoleon's battles; Tolstoy "demythifies"
the great fire of Moscow. He states emphatically that it was not set by the
inhabitants to demonstrate their and Russia's spirit of resistance. It was
no patriotic beacon and no symbol; the city was built of wood, and therefore was bound to go up in flames when the citizens left and enemy soldiers moved in. The exact empirical truth means more to Tolstoy than
even the most apt symbolic interpretation. A symbolist would say that
here the artist in Tolstoy was defeated by the historian. But the truth is
that we here have a manifestation of the principle of the historical novel,
which derives the meaning of events solely from experienced and duly
established reality.

What are the principles of artistic creation in this kind of novel? The
most important principle has to do with subject matter. Almost all of
these novels were written for the sake of the great discovery of the age,
the personality of the individual; it is this that shapes the novel. Julien
Sorel, Fabrizio del Dongo, Balzac's many heroes, Pierre Bezukhov, Prince
Andrey, and Anna Karenina are personalities of fascinating interest, and
as such they justify the work of art. They are characteristic, but they are
not typical. On the contrary, they are unique and incomparable, but they
are so constructed that in them the problems of the human situation
stand out with particular force. If it is the task of the novel to show how
character, milieu, historical period, and the individual's relations to others
shape his destiny, there can be no further question as to what principle
governs the selection of subject matter. It must be the principle of a
causality, not precisely demonstrable but accepted because factually
present, between the external world and human actions, the same causality that in a wider context is also the concern of the historian. Certain

352

elements in the specific circumstances shape the actions and destiny of the hero. Hence certain details of the circumstances are important; and so the novelist depicts them for the reader. Stendhal begins his *Le rouge et le noir* with a quite full description of the small and not especially interesting village of Verrières. Verrières is significant only with respect to Julien Sorel. It constitutes the particular reality into which he was born and which he tries to leave behind; in addition it is characteristic for petit-bourgeois life in provincial France at that particular time. Or take Ippolito Nievo's great novel of 1867, *Confessions of an Octogenarian*,[1] recently rediscovered in Italy, with its description of the picturesque but shabby castle of Fratta, north of Venice, where the hero, a penniless relative of the castellan, spent his youth toward the end of the eighteenth century. Nievo depicts the dilapidated towers, the archaic cavern of a kitchen, the incompetent administrative hierarchy, the inhabitants of the castle and their diversions.

Are these symbols? In the specific sense, they are not. They are genuine components of empirical reality, taken into the novel as such components and not because they have the capacity to be images. But they are components in which the forces that shape this empirical reality concentrate and become visible. From this point of view they are seen to concretize the meaning sought in reality. The castle of Fratta, though not the village of Verrières, comes close to being a symbol. It is in a certain sense "a visible sign of something invisible," insofar as it is taken to express forces that remain partially invisible because they can only be conceived in the abstract. The old castle, still managed in accordance with feudal custom, is among other things also a symbol of the superannuated and chaotic conditions prevailing in Italy at the time. Or better, it is the concrete and particular expression of the ideas and forces that shape the reality; and as such it can assume the functions of a symbol. The outstanding difference between such "realistic" symbols and the symbols of modern literature is that, unlike the latter, the former are not compact images that make a single strong sensual impression, but are often extensive and not easily delimitable segments of reality. In addition they are always genuine components of reality, actually to be found in it (the true realist does not manipulate reality to produce them); they are not indications added by the author simply to make his meaning clear. This difference already shows the difference between the realistic and the symbolic

[1] The original title of the posthumously published book was *Confessions of an Italian*.

353

novel. The former seeks meaning in actual experience and is content to be taught by it; the latter imposes a particular meaning on reality. Correspondingly, the symbol in the realistic novel is always causally related to its meaning—the symbol represents the hidden cause; whereas in the symbolic novel it is a transcendent embodiment of the intended meaning: for example, a lamb can stand for an innocent victim or a bird with a broken wing for a frustrated longing.

Because the structure of the Italian states had degenerated in the eighteenth century, life in Fratta had precisely these characteristics, and hence the castle can also be seen as a symbol of conditions in Italy. In this case the symbolic function is a secondary, subordinate quality of the phenomena, their primary role remaining in their import as reality. This of course does not mean that the realistic novel excludes phenomena and images which the characters in the novel interpret metaphorically in relation to their own lives, as for example when the defeated hero sees the gallows by the roadside as a symbol of his unsuccessful life. These and similar symbols are always subjective interpretations by the characters in the novel, not by the author. The realistic author wants to see the phenomena of this world in their objectivity, and he sees them in all their characteristic configuration and multiplicity, for their particular configuration is precisely what holds at least a partial meaning for him. In contrast, the symbolist boldly undertakes to reduce the multiplicity of phenomena to the level of signs. He dematerializes the world, and in so doing deindividualizes it, deprives it of specific characteristics. It is not an accident that modern symbolic novels grow shorter and shorter.

Since the realistic symbol is a direct reflection of the intended meaning, it has "expressionistic" potentialities, which, boldly conceived, lead directly to the Expressionist technique of the twentieth century. The symbolic novel, on the other hand, descends not from the realistic but from the romantic novel. To voice whatever meaning is intended, Expressionism renounces the empirical probability of events. Symbolism achieves the same end by renouncing the causal connection between meaning and image; it gives the image a transcendent meaning. The difference between the realistic and the transcendent symbol can be illustrated by a comparison. In *The Literary Symbol*, W. Y. Tindall cites only one example from the realm of the realistic novel. Referring to Tolstoy's *Anna Karenina*, he writes: "When Vronsky . . . rides his mare to death at the races, breaking her back by his awkwardness or zeal, his action, unnecessary to the plot and far from realistic, embodies his relationship with Anna." Here we have a situation, of rare occurrence in Tolstoy, where the author manipulates events in the interest of a symbolic foreshadowing. Yet the symbol remains realistic, for horse-racing, as every reader of the novel knows, is a natural element in the life of the Russian aristocracy. The animal that Vronsky kills clearly belongs in his world. Its death is brought about by his impetuosity and thoughtlessness. And in so far as these contribute to Anna's ruin, the episode can assume the functions of a symbol for the relationship between Anna and Vronsky. If we compare this to Henry James's golden bowl with its mysterious crack, which similarly serves as symbol for the relationship between two lovers, the difference is at once apparent. The bowl exists in the novel solely for the sake of its symbolic character, and by possessing this character it controls the structure of the plot. Tolstoy's symbol is a possible interpretation of a subordinate event which the reader can also take at its face value. But a reader who misses the meaning of James's golden bowl will miss the entire novel. Only in *The Golden Bowl* do we have symbolism in the full sense of the term—the symbol as image, expressing the meaning it is meant to convey in image and not in a causal nexus. For the strange way in which the bowl is found and bought at the no less strange art dealer's establishment after all bears merely a semblance of causal relation to the plot, a semblance that will not stand up under the slightest scrutiny. And between symbol and meaning, between the bowl and the relationship of the two lovers, there is no causal nexus at all but only a mysterious parallel. In addition, the bowl was not cracked by any of the characters in the novel. It is a motif outside the realm of reality, with magic powers. Its breaking releases magic effects, which bring the two lovers together again.

I have called this kind of symbol "transcendent" because here an image embodies a meaning with which it has no direct connection. The golden bowl with its crack stands for little Maggie Verver's imperiled relationship to her princely husband. This kind of transcendent symbol is a belated manifestation of faith, a last faint reflection of religious convictions, a surviving vestige of magic amid the secularization of our world. For the transfer of meaning to the image does not arise, as in the case of the less pretentious metaphor, from a daring comparison. It stems from the world of faith, myth, legend, fairy tale, magic. It is a parallel, with magic as connecting link. In *The Golden Bowl* the fairy tale elements are clearly visible through the modern disguise. The beautiful daughter of the (dollar-King) father who is looking for a son-in-law; the motif of the wedding gift with the secret flaw or curse, which is rendered harmless by cleverness and persistence—these are age-old fairy tale situations, familiar in a thousand variations. There is even an interesting variation of the wicked stepmother motif. It is this world of fairy tale and myth to which the symbol traces its origin, and it has maintained the closest relationship with it down to this day. It is no coincidence that mythological and legendary motifs, which the early realistic novel would have rejected, appear today in the novel together with the symbol. How strong is the connection between modern symbolism and its mythological origins is apparent from Eliot's "Notes on The Waste Land." "Not only the title," Eliot writes, "but the plan and a good deal of the incidental symbolism of the poem were suggested by Miss Jessie L. Weston's book on the Grail legend, *From Ritual to Romance.*" As a further source Eliot mentions Frazer's *Golden Bough.* After all, meaning and image are not comparable in rational terms; the connection between them is metasensory.   .

Even when the symbolic novel does not make use of more or less disguised mythological material, it tends to draw its images from the realms of religion and myth. And this is not so simply because the most striking images are to be found in religion and myth but rather because it is only these realms that provide an authoritative interpretation of the symbol through the belief, or at least a memory of the belief, that genuinely links meaning and image. Symbols without such a mythological past are private inventions, and as such they cannot be counted on to affect our imagination. Virginia Woolf's lighthouse and Eliot's cocktails are feeble results of private symbol-making, as are the railway terminals and gas stations which have recently been so popular as symbols of man's homelessness. On the other hand, when Henry James uses not any random precious object with a crack in it as his symbol, but a golden bowl, he establishes a connection with our memories of the sacred symbol of the Grail, which—and James alludes to this—traditionally expresses the sublime and supernatural meaning of human relations.

Symbolism, which has been considered "one of the most sophisticated movements in literary history,"[2] still actually draws its basic sustenance from the faith of a magic-mythical past. The presuppositions for a symbolic literature in our time are two, an imagination hungry for images, and a vague idea that our lives are somehow determined by indefinable principles which operate outside the domain of cause and effect but which have a hidden meaning that manifests itself in external phenomena. This is more or less the credo at which modern man has

[2] Charles Feidelson, *Symbolism and American Literature,* 1953, p. 4.

arrived, and to it the symbolic novel addresses itself. Here lies the secret of its origin and its success. In our souls we are still, or once again, romantics, whether we like it or not. The basic tendency of symbolic literature is its orientation toward the intuited, intangible, indeterminate. To be a Christian is as out of fashion as to be an atheist; one is simply a symbolist, for that leaves all roads open and involves no commitment. "Indirection," "suggestion," and "allusion" are key words of symbolistic criticism and are used as positive criteria in literary appraisal. W. Y. Tindall defines the symbolic novel thus: "As tight and reflexive poems, symbolist novels *insinuate* their meanings by a concert of elements. Images, *allusions, hints,* changes of rhythm, and tone—in short *all the devices of suggestion*—support and sometimes carry the principal burden" (italics mine). Here vagueness of content has become a criterion of value. It demands the counterbalancing effect of cosmic form, which hence has assumed such great importance today.

We have tried to reduce the innumerable variations of the symbol in the novel to its two major types: the cause-linked "realistic" symbol, and the transcendent or magic symbol of the poetic novel. Both are creatures of man's imagination in its quest for meaning, and in some of their variants they approach each other quite closely. Thus, for example, we find the realistic symbol for the sake of which reality has to be decidedly tampered with, and the transcendent symbol which is convincingly anchored in reality. Nevertheless, these two types of symbol are of different origin, and it would be false to assume that one has evolved from the other. That they have not is proved by the basically different mentalities expressed in their opposing attitudes toward reality.

How did the magic symbol enter the novel, the literary form which by its very nature is tied to reality? It is tempting to find the answer in the great influence and great prestige of symbolist poetry, especially that of the French symbolists. And in fact this is essentially true so far as the modern novel is concerned. But it is interesting to note that the lyrical symbolists in their turn found an influential model in the novel. I refer to Novalis's fragmentary poetic novels, especially his *Heinrich von Ofterdingen,* which centers around the "blue flower," the most famous symbol of German Romanticism. In the author's conception, *Heinrich von Ofterdingen* is a "poetic" and "romantic" novel, that is, a radically unrealistic novel which loftily and deliberately disregards all the conditions of real life. The medieval poet Heinrich von Ofterdingen roams the world searching for the meaning of nature and its laws, the meaning of love and of

357

poetry. The revelation of their meaning occurs, in typically romantic fashion, in the form of legend and fairy tale. Here we have a world completely dominated by the miraculous and the symbolic, with the "blue flower" functioning as a sort of symbol of symbols, representing the most secret meaning of the poet's art. This novel shuns the realities of human life to a degree that has scarcely been attempted since. Henry James's *Golden Bowl*, in which the symbol also has a dominant role, at least maintains the appearances of nineteenth-century reality, even if on closer scrutiny the timeless fairy tale elements show through.

The important role of the symbol in the American novel cannot, however, be adequately explained by models in European romanticism or by the influence of the French symbolists. Symbolism is a native American growth, which flourished in this country earlier and more vigorously than elsewhere. It draws its sustenance from the soil of Calvinism, a fact that again corroborates, in a different way, our observation concerning the ancestry of the symbol in the world of faith. American symbolism is a form of secularized and aestheticized Calvinism. Hawthorne's allegories, Emerson's principle that "every natural fact is a symbol of a spiritual fact," and Melville's scarcely maintained faith in the meaningfulness of the world—"some certain significance lurks in all things, else all things are of little worth and the round world itself but an empty cipher"—are steps in the progressive secularization of the Calvinist interpretation of the world, which in its turn is indebted to medieval typology and exegesis of the Scriptures. The Calvinist is a realist who accepts the facts of his world and does not try to alter them. He considers it his task to interpret them in the light of Biblical precedents, and to this end he contrives a structure of parallels between Biblical and secular events. Thus he distinguishes himself from other realists by his technique of interpretation, which is not secular and causal but transcendental, which is based on faith, and which establishes suprasensory points of reference for all things earthly. From this it is only a step to the transcendent symbol, which also operates according to the system of an inner parallelism between meaning and phenomenon, but which has freed itself both from rigid dependence on reality and from the dogmatic bonds of the Calvinist faith. This emancipation was accomplished by the American Transcendentalists, abetted by the European romanticists and romantic philosophers with their faith in fairy tale and myth.

The religious basis of American symbolism was already noted by F. O. Matthiessen in his *American Renaissance*, and observed even more clearly by Yvor Winters. Winters recognized that the Calvinist tradition gave its particular stamp to American literature far into the nineteenth century. Winters's well known essay is an attack on romanticism, and this includes symbolism, though he does not specifically condemn it. Charles Feidelson, in his *Symbolism and American Literature*, has an interesting essay in which he too demonstrates the Calvinist ancestry of this American symbolism. He discusses the same authors as Winters, but his sympathies are decidedly symbolist. His claims for the services rendered by symbolism are of the broadest: "In the central work of Hawthorne, Whitman, Melville and Poe, symbolism is at once technique and theme. It is a governing principle: not a stylistic device, but a point of view." This is no longer literary criticism; as the tone of the passage shows, it is a literary manifesto. The particular *hybris* of the symbolist faith is apparent in the assumption that the symbol is to determine the perspective of the work of art, the "point of view," as Feidelson puts it. Yet Feidelson does see some of the problems inherent in symbolism: arbitrariness of interpretation, anti-rationalism, and, as the final consequence of the speculative nature of the image-symbol, "the possibility of the meaninglessness of meaning." He tries to meet these problems by improvising a philosophy of symbolism. Starting out from Cassirer, for whom poetry is still a world of illusion and fantasy, distinct from that of logical truth, Feidelson argues: "It is quite possible to take poetry as the norm and to regard logical statements as the fantasy; this indeed seems the more natural outcome of a philosophy which begins in a contrast between logical sign and creative symbol. . . . The symbolist . . . redefines the whole process of knowing and the status of reality in the light of poetic method. He tries to take both poles of perception into account at once, to view the subjective and objective worlds as functions of the forms of speech in which they are rendered." Such a definition is no more than philosophical sleight-of-hand. It is a dialectically dressed up version of a faith whose principal dogma is obviously redemption by "poetic method," by "forms of speech," by style. The dyed-in-the-wool symbolists accepted this faith early; they are even now sacrificing at its altar.

For Melville's Moby Dick, which has both a real existence and a symbolic function, the Biblical-typological interpretation is still partly determinative. For Henry James and his generation the images of the Calvinistic typology have grown pale, and a purely aesthetic motivation replaces the religious one. In Stephen Crane's colorful imagery we see a last reflection of religious symbolism—"the red sun was pasted in the sky like a wafer"—but here, as Philip Rahv has pointed out, it assumes a purely decorative function. Here we have the beginning of the aesthetic playing with symbols as images and embodiments of meaning, a typical trap for overzealous critics who try to ascribe a profoundly symbolic value to every image used. It is interesting to note that in other literatures, too, symbolism begins to flourish just at the moment when the religious symbols that had earlier dominated imagination lose their dogmatic hold. James Joyce's A Portrait of the Artist as a Young Man derives its dense symbolic structure from the aesthetic use of religious symbols, a technique which in this case is justified and even necessitated by the subject matter, for the hero's road leads from the Church to art. His constant practice of reinterpreting the religious symbols of his childhood in secular terms gives the reader convincing insight into his state of mind.

Symbolism becomes questionable when themes concerning modern man and his dilemma in a world full of facts and problems are represented in novels composed in the technique of all-dominating symbolism. The result is a discrepancy between theme and technique, for the symbolist has neither sympathy nor patience with the nature of facts and their consequences for man. Writers like Truman Capote, Frederick Buechner, or Jean Stafford escape the dangers of this discrepancy by sublimating contemporary history into a personal essence, depriving it of almost any import. At best they can show contemporary problems as reflected in a mentality which takes refuge in symbols. The case is different with symbolists like Paul Bowles and Malcolm Lowry. In such novels as The Sheltering Sky or Under the Volcano these writers attempt to use the technique of symbolism in portraying the destiny of politically conscious characters thoroughly aware of contemporary events. Their theme is the failure and final disintegration of the highly civilized mentality of Europeans or Americans; but they do not attempt to evolve their symbols from the reality that is inseparable from the theme; instead, they prefer to take them from some colorful exotic setting. Or rather, they make the entire exotic setting a symbol for the mental state of their heroes. In consequence, they have to transport their heroes to the exotic setting where image-symbols adequate to their problems flourish, to North Africa or to Mexico. But this procedure results not only in negating the causal connection between symbol and meaning, it actually inverts their relationship. Since the image-symbols of disintegration are to be found only in exotic countries, these unfortunate occidentals have to go where they can perish both in reality and symbolically, but under circumstances that bring about their downfall only in the transcendent meaning of the symbol and exclude the realm of causality. The true causes remain unrepresented, just as the world that formed these characters is pushed aside with the symbolist's typical disregard for the factual and characteristic.

Contrary to the widely held opinion, this marks not the high point but the dead end of symbolic fiction. For the sober medium of prose remains bound to the solidity of the world of realities. Its most significant subject matter is man as a spiritual being conditioned by material reality. Dismissing this objective in favor of pure subjectivity is something that only lyric poetry can risk with impunity. Conrad's colonials who perish in the tropics follow their profession—making money—and their greed, and suffer the fate they themselves have thereby challenged. But Bowles's and Lowry's heroes drift without will or desire, like lost children, in exotic places that have every appearance of being under the spell of a wicked witch, so deceitful, malicious, and inexplicable is everything that happens there. These novels are fairy tales of evil. Here excessive speculation over meanings has not only robbed the world of reality, but emptied it of meaning.

Much more to the point, even if less spectacular than the oppressive symbolism of these novels, is for example Saul Bellow's comparable story, "Seize the Day." Its literary technique holds to the theme and evolves its images from the theme.

It may be suggested that many young writers today are influenced more than is good for either them or their work by critics who have swallowed symbolism whole and who nourish their enthusiasm by providing symbolic interpretations of all past and present literature without any sense of differences in style. This results in a vicious circle of criticism and creative literature. The natural relationship between the two is reversed and writers are made to go to school to critics. In this way criticism acquires a concealed power to lay down laws and determine the future. No such power rightfully belongs to it. Let us maintain the separation of powers in literature too. Let the critics be content with their judicial functions and let them keep their hands off legislation.

(*Translated from the German by Willard R. Trask*)

Andrew H. Wright looks broadly at irony, particularly irony
in fiction, in order to show how the concept can throw light on
the art. What marks the ironic point of view, he says, is that
it dwells on the contradictions in human experience with
considerable interest yet with objectivity. An ironic writer's
work, moreover, may range all the way from the delightfully
comic to the profoundly tragic, for all reveal the disparity
between the ideal and the actual. He may move us to laughter,
to compassion, or to disgust, but in any case the important
thing which results from his ironic point of view is the
complexity of contradiction in both his characters and their
actions. For instance, his characters may tend to contradict
themselves: clever Emma, in *Emma*, is, nonetheless,
self-deceived; and Billy, in *Billy Budd,* is at the same
time both gentle and violent. In short, the ironist singles
out and highlights those paradoxes and absurdities in
the human situation which catch his eye.

irony and fiction

ANDREW H. WRIGHT

Although discourse is not yet sufficiently universal to permit the use
of the term "irony" without some explanation, the word does have clear
meanings of a limited sort: dramatic irony, verbal irony, romantic irony,
the irony of fate—all are used with some precision by nearly every one
who speaks or writes. And in recent years irony has come to be used as a
critical term for "indicating that recognition of incongruities which . . .
pervades all poetry to a degree far beyond what our conventional criticism has heretofore been willing to allow." [1] Indeed, the difficulties about
the word stem not from the fact that it has no definitions but from the fact
that it has too many: current usages have thinned down the term, reduced
its scope. It has therefore seemed to me desirable to examine irony afresh:

[1] Cleanth Brooks, *The Well Wrought Urn: Studies in the Structure of Poetry*
(New York, 1947), pp. 191–192.

to survey and justify its application to a world view, to discuss its relationship to other modes, and to demonstrate its application objectively to works of art, fiction in particular. The lines do cross, but not so far, perhaps, as to prevent clarity of exposition. My plea is to look at irony broadly; my application, in the latter part of this paper, is chiefly to the novel.

Irony no more begins than ends with Socrates. Its origins are, like so many other interesting beginnings, lost in pre-history. The term "Socratic irony" is in fact of very recent coinage. But, retrospectively at least, it is around Plato's great teacher that the subjective significance of the word now attaches itself when we think of Greece in the great age. Socratic irony, according to the *New English Dictionary*, is "dissimulation, pretence; esp. in reference to the dissimulation of ignorance practised by Socrates as a means of confuting an adversary." And, as J. A. K. Thomson points out (or as a reading of Theophrastus will show us), irony had a pejorative connotation in Plato's day.[2] It is therefore no compliment when Thrasymachus makes his famous accusation of Socrates in the first book of the *Republic* (336ff.). But whether or not Socratic irony is more than a dialectical tool is a disputed point.

Certainly Socratic irony, so-called, can be used as a weapon. Bishop Thirlwall describes it thus: "The writer effects his purpose by placing the opinion of his adversary in the foreground, and saluting it with every demonstration of respect, while he is busied in withdrawing one by one all the supports on which it rests: and he never ceases to approach it with an air of deference, until he has completely undermined it, when he leaves it to sink by the weight of its own absurdity." [3] As examples Thirlwall adduces Plato and Pascal; but it seems to me that there is a vast difference between the two men in this respect. Pascal, in the *Provincial Letters*, is espousing the Jansenist cause and opposing that of the Jesuits. His irony consists in a pretended humility only—designed to trip the Jesuits into disclosing their own inconsistencies. Pascal is a satirist, using irony as an instrument of attack; Socrates (in Plato's version), though he does destroy the view of his adversaries through a shrewd affectation of humility, still insists that although "we are most willing and anxious" to get at the truth, "the fact is that we cannot." (*Republic*, I, 336). This suggests that a wider interpretation of Socratic irony is possible. Irving Babbitt,

[2] *Irony, an Historical Introduction* (Cambridge, Mass., 1927), p. 3.
[3] Connop Thirlwall, "On the Irony of Sophocles," *Philological Museum*, II (1833), 484.

among others, denies that "Socrates is insincere in his profession of ignorance; for though his knowledge may be as light in comparison with that of the ordinary Athenian, he sees that in comparison with true and perfect knowledge it is only darkness." [4] In short, there is, in Socratic irony, pretended humility, but also (at least arguably) real humility, and at bottom a recognition of the contradictions in human experience. Socratic irony is, in this interpretation, a pervasive aspect of character—or, in Kierkegaard's phrase, an "existential determination."

So is Romantic irony—irony as regarded by the German theorists of the late eighteenth century. Professor Sedgewick defines it as "the attitude of mind held by a philosophic observer when he abstracts himself from the contradictions of life and views them all impartially, himself perhaps included in the ironic vision." [5] Sedgewick remarks the close connection between the detachment of the Romantic ironists and that of Socrates, and reminds us that in fact Friedrich Schlegel equates the two. But there is another aspect of Romantic irony, at least in its later development in German literature: this is the divided world view of the Romantic whose ideals have given way to a different *Weltansicht*, but who with some ardor and affection clutches at what he now believes to be illusory. An example is provided by Eichendorff's *Aus dem Leben Eines Taugenichts*, in which there is a real contradiction between the commitment of the *Taugenichts* to a glowing Romantic ideal, and the utter ridiculousness of his behavior: Eichendorff is so detached from the situation that pity and laughter, sympathy and derision—all can be expressed at once. So Romantic irony really goes further than that of Socrates; Jankélévitch, with admirable clarity, suggests that "l'ironie socratique contestait seulement l'utilité et la certitude d'une science de la nature; l'ironie romantique contestera . . . l'existence même de la nature." [6]

To regard fate ironically is also to possess an attitude toward the world:

> It must have occurred to most men . . . now and then to
> reflect how little the good and ill of their lot has corresponded
> with their hopes and fears. All who have lived long enough in
> the world must be able to remember objects coveted with im-
> patient eagerness, and pursued with long and unremitting toil,

[4] *Rousseau and Romanticism* (Boston and New York, 1919), p. 244.
[5] G. G. Sedgewick, *Of Irony, Especially in Drama,* University of Toronto Studies, Philology and Literature Series no. 10 (1935), pp. 15–16.
[6] Vladamir Jankélévitch, *L'Ironie* (Paris, 1936), p. 8.

which in possession have proved tasteless and worthless: hours embittered with anxiety and dread by the prospect of changes which brought with them the fulfilment of the most ardent wishes: events anticipated with trembling expectation which arrived, past, and left no sensible trace behind them: while things of which they scarcely heeded the existence, persons whom they met with indifference, exerted the most important influence on their character and fortunes. When, at a sufficient interval and with altered mood, we review such instances of the mockery of fate, we can scarcely refrain from a melancholy smile.[7]

The irony of fate involves contradiction between what can reasonably be expected, and what unreasonably—but actually—takes place. "Fortune," Chaucer tells us in the *Troilus*, "semeth trewest whan she wol bygyle." But here fate is regularly perverse; it may sometimes be capricious, as in *Lord Jim*, in which it is supremely ironic that the *Patna*, from which Jim jumps in the certainty that it will sink, does in fact remain afloat and is towed to shore by a French vessel—a circumstance which underlines the cowardice of the hero of the novel.

Ample justification exists, therefore, for considering irony a world view. "Irony is an existential determination," says Kierkegaard, "and nothing is more ridiculous than to suppose that it consists in the use of a certain phraseology, or when an author congratulates himself upon succeeding in expressing himself ironically. Whoever has essential irony has it all day long, not bound to any specific form, because it is the infinite within him."[8]

Of the contradictions in human experience the ironic man has a perception which yields a marvelous detachment, and a detachment which grants a perception. There is, in the disengagement of the ironist, an objectivity which is not scientific, because not disinterested or dispassionate. In fact the ironist is deeply concerned with both aspects of the contradictions he perceives; and this concern leads to an ambivalence of attitude to one side and to the other—to both at once. Searching the orchards of human experience he finds the bittersweet apple of confusing appearance and ambiguous essence—and he becomes a man of the divided, the ironic, vision.

---

[7] Thirlwall, p. 487.
[8] Soren Kierkegaard, *Kierkegaard's Concluding Unscientific Postscript,* trans, by David F. Swenson and Walter Lowrie (Princeton, 1941), p. 449.

This has led some to feel that "the basic feature of every irony is a contrast between a reality and an appearance." [9] But the matter is not so simple: the ironist is not sure which is and which merely seems. Who, for instance, would dare say that Don Quixote's tragic and lovable "illusions" are only appearance and that the real world is that of Sancho Panza? How, then, are we to judge the issues involved? Professor Chevalier's answer is that irony is "a mode of escape from the fundamental problems and responsibilities of life" (p. 12). More specifically, he says, "irony characterizes the attitude of one who, when confronted with the choice of two things that are mutually exclusive, chooses both. He cannot bring himself to give up one for the other, and he gives up both. But he reserves the right to derive from each the greatest possible passive enjoyment. And this enjoyment is Irony" (p. 79). Dr. Mudrick, writing on Jane Austen, calls irony a "neutral discoverer and explorer of incongruities" and says that "of itself it draws no conclusions." [10] That this is an oversimplification can be seen by further reference to *Don Quixote*. Here are two world views presented and contrasted: the chivalric, as epitomized in the hero; and the common-sense, as represented by Sancho Panza. In the course of the book it becomes clear that Cervantes, though he sharply satirizes the noble philosophy of *Jerusalem Delivered*, much prefers it to the necessary, ordinary, matter-of-fact approach of Sancho Panza. This is not to say that the author abandons one for the other; there is a duality profoundly ironic. But neither is he uncommitting. Take, for instance, the famous chapter (I, xxii) in which Don Quixote (wearing a basin on his head and riding the ridiculous Rocinante) frees the galley slaves and is rewarded for his pains by both insults and a severe stoning. It seems to me that the reader of this chapter must applaud the nobility of sentiment which prompts Don Quixote's act, and at the same time censure the hero's arrant foolishness, his inadequacy of judgment, in performing the deed. The whole relationship of Cervantes to the world view which he presents is extremely complex; but it is perfectly apparent that he does not remove himself irresponsibly from the matters which concern him so deeply; nor does he fail to make clear that Don Quixote (*because* of his noble predilections) does sometimes perform acts worthy of reprehension. In short, Cervantes judges, he commits himself.

[9] Haakon M. Chevalier, *The Ironic Temper: Anatole France and His Time* (New York, 1932), p. 42.
[10] Marvin Mudrick, *Jane Austen: Irony as Defense and Discovery* (Princeton, 1952), p. 3.

On the other hand, no ironist can be doctrinaire—as the examples just adduced must show. None of them sees a clear and present answer. There is vigor, there is humility, there is sympathy, in the ironist's search, there is judgment finally—but never serene certainty. Irony comes as the result of the quest for meaning in the universe, as the result of human experience; it is not a piece of equipment, like an entrenching tool, with which a man starts out. And this result is the true divided vision—that of Chaucer, Cervantes, Swift, and Jane Austen.

The ironic man may look at the contradictions in human experience tragically or comically. Whether he does the one or the other (or perhaps both) depends upon facts and dispositions separate from, though perhaps not easily separable from, his inclination to irony. Nevertheless, there is a tendency to think that irony and humor must coexist: Saintsbury, for example, remarks that "an ironist without humor is almost inconceivable." [11] But Meredith has already taught us that the humorous perception is one of incongruity in man, between what he is and what he thinks he is, between expectation and fulfilment, pretence and actuality. The touchstone of the comic apprehension is a belief in common sense, a confidence that corrigibility is no dream.[12] The ironic perception, on the other hand, is, as we have seen, one of contradictions in human experience—not merely of closable gaps. This suggests that such a work as *Emma* can be read on more than one level. There is much amusement to be derived from Miss Woodhouse's almost wilful self-deception in believing, for instance, that Frank Churchill is in love with her. This is comedy—for there is an incongruity between conceit and essence which is plainly temporary and reparable. But there is a real contradiction between the warm kindness which she consistently and genuinely displays to her father, and the callous bare-civility with which she regards Miss Fairfax. This is irony.

And indeed there may be irony without humor. Oedipus diligently searches for the slayer of King Laius, when he himself has unknowingly done the deed: the central irony of the play consists in the contrast between human justice and divine justice: it is no mere incongruity, but a flat contradiction. Axel Heyst, in *Victory*, risks personal involvement by helping a desperate Morrison, who is so grateful that he journeys to England to promote a coaling scheme in order to repay Heyst. There Morri-

[11] George Saintsbury, *A Saintsbury Miscellany: Selections from His Essays and Scrap Books* (New York, 1947), p. 136.
[12] See George Meredith, *Essay on the Idea of Comedy and the Uses of the Comic Spirit* (London, 1877), pp. 46, 47, 78.

son dies: and it is an irony (which Conrad does not omit to indicate) that the impulse lying behind this chain of circumstances should be generous and, in a sense, selfless; ironic that Heyst should have sent Morrison to destruction when the very opposite was intended. But no one laughs.

High tragedy and deep irony are often (perhaps always) closely related. The essence of the tragic vision comes in the painful realization of the distance between divine possibility and human aspiration. Tragedy thus moves on two—or at least two—levels, the divine and the human; one of the signs of tragedy is the concern for the supra-human, whether it be the mythological system of the Greeks, or the Christian scheme, or another. For tragedy is concerned not only with morality (in its broadest sense) but with the well-springs of human action. Kafka's *The Castle* turns upon the exploration of the contrast, indeed the contradiction, between the human and the divine. K.'s quest is to understand, to set up lines of communication, to mediate—but he is unsuccessful. Here are tragedy and irony together.

So much, then, for irony in its subjective aspect. There is not only historical sanction for considering irony as a world view, there is historical evidence to suggest that the ironist is characterized by his recognition of the antitheses in human experience: his is an interested objectivity; he is detached but not indifferent, withdrawn but not removed. He may, as an observer of the human scene, be moved to compassion, disgust, laughter, disdain, sympathy, or horror—the whole range of reaction is evidently his: what distinguishes him uniquely is a rare and artistically fruitful combination of complexity, distance, implication.

But the artist is not the work of art: between the artistic impulse and the created object lie two transfiguring facts—the fact of the unconscious and the fact of materials. Given the artist's skill, there is not, nor can there be, a point-to-point correspondence between his conscious ratiocinations and what he creates. "And when the process is over," one artist tells us, "when the picture or symphony or lyric or novel (or whatever it is) is complete, the artist, looking back on it, will wonder how on earth he did it. And indeed he did not do it on earth." [13] This is said here by way of shifting focus to the work of art. How does the ironic artist express his vision? The question must be answered formally: we must look—in the case of the novel—to subject, structure, characterization, and style—those inseparables which must for the purposes of analysis be separated.

---

[13] Edward Morgan Forster, "The *Raison d'Être* of Criticism in the Arts," in *Two Cheers for Democracy* (London, 1951), p. 123.

The ironic theme, or subject, is one of contradiction, and to discover the theme requires a whole and disinterested judgment of the novel. "What is it about?" is at once the most important critical question and the most difficult to answer, for both totality and firmness of impression must be experienced from the work· of art. So far as irony is concerned there is an additional difficulty, owing to the litotes and antiphrasis commonly called ironic, but which may in fact not underlie a thematic irony. A good example of the unironic is provided by *Jonathan Wild the Great*, the subject of which is human villainy. Here Fielding draws a contrast between the dynamic, unscrupulous, "great" hero and the generous, naive, "silly" Heartfree. But this is not an ironic work, despite the author's free use of rhetorical irony (about which more will be said later). For there is contrast merely, not contradiction: Fielding's commitment is wholly to the values of Heartfree; they are exposed, and strengthened, in the conflict with Jonathan Wild.

But in *Billy Budd* there is genuine irony. Billy is "a sort of upright barbarian, much such perhaps as Adam might presumably have been ere the urbane Serpent wriggled himself into his company." [14] He is simple, honest, direct, candid; and it is a combination of his noble qualities (together with the stutter that makes him momentarily dumb) that causes him to strike the complicated and disingenuous Master-at-arms, John Claggart. " 'Struck dead by an angel of God. Yet the angel must hang!' " (p. 229)— so exclaims Captain Vere, thus expressing the central irony of the story. For Billy strikes Claggart in righteous anger, "a generous young heart's virgin experience of the diabolical incarnate and effective in some men . . ." (p. 259). It is cruel, but just and necessary in worldly terms, that Billy should hang. But the story displays, with painful clarity, the unresolvable conflicts between justice and mercy, experience and innocence, noble anger and devilish calculation.

What is required in many instances is a fresh look at novels whose themes have been too shallowly interpreted. The theme, for example, of *Sense and Sensibility* is stated in the title, and throughout much of the book sensibility seems to be the straw-man which sense is to, and does in fact, overthrow.

> Marianne Dashwood was born to an extraordinary fate.
> She was born to discover the falsehood of her own opinions,
> and to counteract, by her conduct, her most favourite max-

---

[14] Herman Melville, *Billy Budd*, ed. F. Barron Freeman (London, 1948), p. 147.

ims. She was born to overcome an affection formed so late in life as at seventeen, and with no sentiment superior to strong esteem and lively friendship, voluntarily to give her hand to another!—and *that* other, a man who had suffered no less than herself under the event of a former attachment, whom, two years before, she had considered too old to be married,—and who still sought the constitutional safeguard of a flannel waistcoat!

But so it was.[15]

And so Marianne makes a prudent marriage. Yet sense is not the only victor: for by a parallel irony Elinor marries, for love, a man whose early history discloses him to be energetic, passionate, *sensible*. Here, then, in one of Jane Austen's simplest novels is found the genuinely ironic theme.

But we are already at the point of analyzing structure. How does the novelist tell his story? For our purposes the question can be answered by reference to the techniques of point of view. In the drama the very nature of the medium permits an exterior viewpoint whence irony can proceed, or rather through which it exists: "dramatic irony" is always, and rightly, defined in terms of viewpoint.[16] But in narratives meant to be read, several methods, including that of dramatic irony, are employed. Robert Elliott has recently shown that *A Tale of a Tub* achieves its unity through a very subtle and complex point of view: the purported writer of the work is not Swift but "his favorite ingénu, an 'I' who egregiously identifies himself with the very abuses that Swift is attacking."[17] Nor have many critics failed to notice that Conrad's management of point of view yields up complex ironies: in *Lord Jim,* for instance, the hero never once speaks directly; the writer is ostensibly relating a story told by Marlow who has pieced the tale together from accounts not only by Jim but by several others.

There is, however, much still to be done in the way of structural analysis of this sort. Jane Austen's novels, for instance, have often been too shallowly comprehended, because her readers do not attend to point of view. One example must suffice.

A few years before, Anne Elliot had been a very pretty girl, but her bloom had vanished early; and even in its height,

---

[15] *Sense and Sensibility,* ed. R. W. Chapman (Oxford, 1926), p. 378.
[16] Professor Sedgewick's study, cited above, is invaluable on this subject.
[17] Robert C. Elliott, "Swift's *Tale of a Tub:* an Essay in Problems of Structure," *PMLA,* LXVI (1952), 443.

her father had found little to admire in her, (so totally different were her delicate features and mild dark eyes from his
own); there could be nothing in them now that she was faded
and thin, to excite his esteem. He had never indulged much
hope, he had now none, of ever reading her name in any
other page of his favourite work [the Baronetage]. All equality
of alliance must rest with Elizabeth; for Mary had merely connected herself with an old country family of respectability and
large fortune, and had therefore *given* all the honour, and received none: Elizabeth would, one day or other, marry suit-
ably.[18]

The first sentence, up to the semi-colon, seems to be an account by a
detached chronicler; then, in a subordinate clause, Jane Austen insinu-
ates the viewpoint of Sir Walter, while continuing to write as though she
were the mere historian. The last sentence is very clearly the expression
of Sir Walter's opinion, except that the eye is arrested by the word
"merely," which changes the tenor of the entire statement, and in fact
takes it away from Anne's father. At bottom, then, questions of style are
raised, and to these we must turn our attention, after briefly considering
characterization.

To present people in all their complexity is, for the ironic artist, to
present them as self-contradictory. Tom Jones is a fine fellow whose
faults must be winked at, covertly approved; Jeanie Deans's integrity and
drive are quite dauntless; Becky Sharp is plainly and simply wicked. But
a difference in emphasis amounts to a difference in kind: Emma, though
marvelously clever, is constantly self-deceived; Billy Budd is both gentle
and violent; Lambert Strether, at once New World and Old. This difference
in emphasis, in the direction of irony, is achieved through the formal
means which have thus far been suggested, and also through style, to
which we shall now turn.

Rhetorical irony is as old as the traceable history of the word. Antiphrasis, the irony of rhetorical reversal, refers to speech "in which the
intended meaning is the opposite of that expressed in the words used"
(*NED*); and, as Professor Sedgewick points out, "the truth [is] to be
understood from tone, gesture, or known circumstance." [19] Thus Swift
does not for a moment really believe that "a young healthy child well

[18] *Persuasion,* ed. R. W. Chapman (Oxford, 1926), p. 6.
[19] Sedgewick, p. 9.

372

nursed is at a year old a most delicious, nourishing, and wholesome food, whether stewed, roasted, baked, or boiled;"[20] he is, and we know it from the extravagance and horror and specificity of his proposal, clearly urging reform of the English system of dealing with the Irish poor. Litotes, as Aristotle told us long ago, is the irony of understatement; it is achieved usually, though not always, through the use of multiple negatives. But what must be made clear is that rhetorical irony is not necessarily the sign of an ironic view: in "A Modest Proposal," the whole sense must be completely reversed; no ambiguities lurk in the background: this is a piece of satire, one of the weapons of which is rhetorical irony.

These verbal techniques are, however, often used to implement the ironic vision. The first sentence of *Pride and Prejudice* is an example: "It is a truth universally acknowledged, that a single man in possession of a good fortune, must be in want of a wife." Here the key words are "a truth universally acknowledged," giving an air of false grandeur to a trifle, and rendered deliciously anticlimactic in the next sentence, when it is made clear that the author is concerned not with a universe but with a "neighbourhood." The word "truth" also has a double edge. Still, the statement cannot be reversed, nor is it meant to be.

Language as the raw material of literature imposes upon the artist certain rules which cannot be safely transgressed: the writer, dependent upon a tradition, cannot wholly disregard it. Even Gertrude Stein's automatic writing is deeply founded upon a linguistic history; her failure is not in departing altogether, but in veering too far, from the requirements of diction and syntax. Language and its principles are in a sense the shadow which falls between the creative impulse and the work of art. On the other hand, language, having a logic of its own, can disclose that of which the artist may be only vaguely aware, or of which he may be quite unconscious: "Et l'ayant dite," writes Claudel, "je sais ce que j'ai dit."[21] So language—like clay or paint—is a transfiguring material, not a lens through which the artist projects his vision. But, unlike clay or paint, language is a human instrument, a human achievement with a human structure—and is therefore both intrinsically and potentially expressive of the contradictions of man's heart and mind. It is for this reason that literature is more adequate than any other of the arts to ironic expression. On one

[20] "A Modest Proposal for Preventing the Children of Poor People from Being a Burthen to Their Parents or Country and for Making Them Beneficial to the Publick," in Temple Scott, ed., *The Prose Works of Jonathan Swift, D.D.*, VII (London, 1905), 209.
[21] "La Ville," quoted by E. M. Forster in the essay cited above, p. 124.

level, irony exhibits the contradictions between hope and fulfilment, judgment and actuality, the apparent and the palpable. But on another—and higher—level, it displays the confusion to which the data of sense and instinct give rise: simple reversals no longer yield a "truer" view of the situation, and, far from comforting the reader with a sense of divine superiority, dislocate the narrow catchwords and easy dogmas which bind our existence to a superficial apprehension of the world's possibilities.